BUSINESS ISSUES, COMPETITION AND ENTREPRENEURSHIP

DEVELOPMENTS ON COURTS' INVOLVEMENT IN ARBITRATION

VOLUME 1

THE RULE OF LAW

BUSINESS ISSUES, COMPETITION AND ENTREPRENEURSHIP

Additional books and e-books in this series can be found on Nova's website under the Series tab.

BUSINESS ISSUES, COMPETITION AND ENTREPRENEURSHIP

DEVELOPMENTS ON COURTS' INVOLVEMENT IN ARBITRATION

VOLUME 1

THE RULE OF LAW

GEORGIOS I. ZEKOS

nova science publishers
New York

Library of Congress Cataloging-in-Publication Data

ISBN: 978-1-53614-730-8

Published by Nova Science Publishers, Inc. † New York

To my Mother/ Στη Μητέρα μου

Κλειώ Αντωνίου Κρυστάλη

CONTENTS

performing an escalating number of tasks that were once accomplished by the government, privatization has become so prevalent and involves "delegation" of state authority to private parties. This can be seen as a legal basis for the independence of arbitration under National Authority Management Arbitration (NAMA).

INTRODUCTION

In the current globalization, the law entangled in economic and political developments, which moves into a new dimension of de-politicization, de-centralization and de-individualization., Thus, due to globalization the advent of global markets destabilizes the control prospective of national policy, and so also the probabilities of legal regulation and the utilization of the rule of law. To that extent, globalization generates a set of problems intrinsic to law itself, consisting in a modification to the dominant lawmaking developments. In globalization the law institutionalizes the global move in power from governmental actors to economic actors which means that in globalization the law contributes to a dual constitution of autonomous sectors of world society. Therefore it could be argued that globalization can impose the generation of the establishment of courts and arbitration as co-equal dispute systems as well.

The default form of dispute resolution is litigation. Parties resolve their disputes in court if not they agree otherwise[1]. By agreeing to arbitrate, parties supersede the litigation default rule[2]. Arbitration is a function of contract and therefore of voluntary agreement.[3] International arbitration law is "contractarian" in character as well[4]. It is worth mentioning that parties jointly decide whether to go to ad hoc arbitration or to choose

---

[1] G Zekos, *The Independence Of Arbitration*, 2016 Nova Science Publications New York USA. www.novapublishers.com.

[2] Christopher R. Drahozal, *Why Arbitrate? Substantive Versus Procedural Theories of Private Judging*, 22 Am. Rev. Int'l Arb. 163, 165 (2011). Stephen J. Ware, *Principles of Alternative Dispute Resolution § 1.5(b)*, at 6 (2d ed. 2007).

[3] *Rent-A-Center, West, Inc. v. Jackson*, 130 S. Ct. 2772 (2010) ("The FAA reflects the fundamental principle that arbitration is a matter of contract."); *First Options of Chicago, Inc. v. Kaplan*, 514 U.S. 938 (1995), p. 943 ("Arbitration is simply a matter of contract between the parties; it is a way to resolve those disputes — but only those disputes — that the parties have agreed to submit to arbitration.").

[4] G Zekos, *International Commercial and Marine Arbitration*, 2008 Routledge-Cavendish Publishers London www.routledge.com. G Zekos, Arbitrability and Regulation (EU) No 1215/2012, *Dispute Resolution Journal* Vol. 70 No. 4 JurisNet, LLC 2015 www.arbitrationlaw.com See Chapter 28 G Zekos, An investigation of WTO Arbitration Mechanism, *ICDR Handbook on Arbitration & ADR*, 3rd Edition, JurisNet LLC 2017 www.arbitrationlaw.com.

institutional arbitration[5]. Law merely reflects a determinate resolution of the controversy as contemplated fitting by those who have the power and authority to resolve the issue within a specific society[6]. Common law and civil law systems are all, to some degree, amalgams in which case law works alongside codes and statutes[7].

At present, at first sight there are the advantages of speed, simplicity and economy associated with arbitration and so judicial involvement should be kept to the minimum or even to zero in order to avoid undermining those goals. Arbitration agreements are to be construed according to general rules governing the interpretation of contracts, taking into account the intention of the parties and the strong public policy in favor of arbitration. There is federal policy in favor of arbitral dispute resolution giving rise to the widespread use of arbitration clauses in commercial contracts[8]. The Court's decisions interpreting the FAA formed a body of law enforcing arbitration agreements firmly along with their terms and elevating the arbitration clause to a "super-contract.[9]"

Is arbitration a legal system or not? Has arbitration emerged prior to the courts? Is there a need all legal systems such as arbitration and courts to be identical formally or they have to award justice rather than their formality? Is arbitration alternative to courts or merely a semi-independent based on the authority of courts? Is arbitration complementary to courts? Is arbitration a co-equal and independent to courts dispute mechanism in a single jurisdiction? Is there a courts' involvement in arbitration? Does law allow and regulate arbitration in a jurisdiction? What constitutes a legal system? Does the constitution legalize arbitration as an alternative dispute system in a single jurisdiction? Does the constitution aid the independence of arbitration? Are courts a legal system by law and the constitution attributes the authority? Can arbitration be an alternative dispute system since it is not entirely autonomous? Can arbitration guarantee legal certainty, predictability, and settlement? Do courts or arbitration generate justice by resolving disputes on the merits?

Arbitration[10] is one form of alternative dispute resolution (ADR)[11]. ADR is often lauded for its potential to produce "better" quality outcomes including fairness leading to

---

[5] Pilar Perales Viscasillas, The Role of Arbitral Institutions Under the 2010 UNCITRAL Arbitration Rules, 6 *Lima Arb*. 26, 31 (2014). Rémy Gerbay, The Functions of Arbitral Institutions 45 (2016); *Practitioner's Handbook on International Commercial Arbitration* (Frank-Bernd Weigand ed., 2009).

[6] Neil MacCormick, *Institutions of Law: An Essay in Legal Theory* (Oxford: Oxford University Press, 2007) 255-61.

[7] G Zekos, *The United States of Europe in place of the European Union,* 2017 Nova Science Publications New York USA. www.novapublishers.com.

[8] *Marmet Health Care Ctr., Inc. v. Brown*, 132 S. Ct. 1201, 1203 (2012) (quoting KPMG LLP v. Cocchi, 132 S.Ct. 23, 25 (2011) (*per curiam*) (quoting *Mitsubishi Motors Corp. v. Soler Chrysler-Plymouth, Inc*., 473 U.S. 614, 631 (1985) (internal quotation marks omitted); see also *Southland Corp. v. Keating*, 465 U.S. 1, 10 (1984) (declaring the FAA reflects a "national policy favoring arbitration").

[9] Jill I. Gross, Justice Scalia's Hat Trick and the Supreme Court's Flawed Understanding of Twenty-First Century Arbitration, 81 *Brooklyn L. Rev*. 160, 2015.

[10] G Zekos, Arbitration's status under EU law, *The Journal of World Investment & Trade* 13 (2012) 390–419, www.brill.nl/jwit, G Zekos, *Constitution, Arbitration and Courts* www.novapublishers.com, G. Zekos, The European Union's New Competition Approach and Arbitration, 4 *Hertfordshire L .J.* 36 (2006). G. Zekos, Antitrust/Competition Arbitration in EU versus U.S. Law, (2008) *Journal of International Arbitration* 1–29,

the same justice outcome than courts[12]. Moreover, ADR boom is motivated by concerns about efficiency, access and justice[13]. It must be taken into account that ADR were envisioned as an alternative to litigation, with its own manifest substantive and procedural characteristics[14]. In other words the aim was to create a less formal forum than litigation. Maritime/Commercial arbitration is commended as an economical and speedy alternative to judicial recourse[15]. Maritime arbitration[16] arises from disputes involving contracts for the carriage of goods, insurance, or shipping[17]. In addition arbitration "is a matter of consent, not coercion, and parties are generally free to structure their arbitration agreements as they see fit.[18]" To that extent, arbitration enhances access to justice by permitting claimants to bring claims they could not afford to bring in court[19]. Furthermore, arbitration is defined in the Halsbury's Laws of England[20] as "the reference of a dispute or difference between not less than two parties for determination, after

---

Berkovitz v. Arbib & Houlberg, Inc., 130 N.E. 288, 290 (1921) (Cardozo, J.) ("Arbitration is a form of procedure whereby differences may be settled.").

[11] Other forms of ADR include mediation, mini-trial, and summary jury trial. Hans Smit, The Future Of International Commercial Arbitration: A Single Transnational Institution? 25 *Colum. J. Transnat'l L.* 8, 9 (1983) ("Rather than permit international disputes to be settled in national courts, many parties often prefer to submit them to a tribunal that is not part of the governmental structure of a particular state. Nationalistic favoritism can be avoided by selecting a forum in a neutral state.").

[12] Harry T. Edwards, Alternative Dispute Resolution: Panacea or Anathema? 99 *Harv. L. Rev.* 668, 669 (1986) at 677, 679 (noting the two concerns that ADR will replace rule of law with non-legal values and diminish the development of legal rights for the disadvantaged).

[13] Carrie Menkel-Meadow, Pursuing Settlement in an Adversary Culture: A Tale of Innovation Co-opted or "the Law of ADR," 19 *Fla. St. U. L. Rev.* 1, 6 (1991) ("In what has become a commonly recognized division in the literature and advocacy about ADR, we see two basically different justifications for processes that resolve cases short of trial—what I call quantitative- efficiency claims versus qualitative-justice claims.").

[14] Carrie Menkel-Meadow, The Trouble with the Adversary System in a Postmodern, Multicultural World, 38 *Wm. & Mary L. Rev.* 5, 12 (1996); (The intention was to create a less formal forum than litigation.) Alexander J.S. Colvin, An Empirical Study of Employment Arbitration: Case Outcomes and Processes, 8 *J. Empirical Legal Stud.* 1, 2 (2011).

[15] *Plymouth-Carver Reg'l Sch. Dist. v. J. Farmer & Co.*, 553 N.E.2d 1284, 1285 (Mass. 1990) (citing *Marino v. Tagaris*, 480 N.E.2d 286, 288 (Mass. 1985)) (claiming "predictability, certainty, and effectiveness" intertwined with voluntary arbitration).

[16] Georgios I. Zekos, Maritime Arbitration and the Rule of Law, 39 *J. Mar. L. & Com.* 523, 524 (2008) ("[Maritime arbitration has become popular as an alternative to litigation, because of the costs, delay and procedural complications of court proceedings."). at 541"in recent years the private sector has begun to use binding arbitration as the favored method of dispute resolution and the payback appears to be that arbitration is a 'quicker, less expensive and more private alternative to litigation.'"

[17] Society of Maritime Arbitrators, Inc., *Maritime Arbitration in New York*, http://www.smany.org/sma/about2.html ("[T]he origins of maritime arbitration can be traced as far back as the voyages of ships owned by ancient Phoenicians carrying the cargoes of Greek traders."). *Stolt-Nielsen v. AnimalFeeds Int'l Corp.*, 130 S. Ct. 1758 (2010) (No. 08-1198), 2009 WL 1144191, http://www.scotusblog.com/wp-content/uploads/2009/06/081198_certamicus maritime.pdf ("The international nature of shipping and the particular rules, standards and terminology that have emerged in the business of transporting cargoes across the oceans lend themselves to commercial arbitration where the contractual parties refer their disputes to be decided by a peer.").

[18] *Volt Info. Sciences, Inc. v. Bd. of Trs. of Leland Stanford Junior Univ.*, 489 U.S. 468, 479 (1989).

[19] Theodore Eisenberg & Elizabeth Hill, Arbitration and Litigation of Employment Claims: An Empirical Comparison, *Disp. Resol. J.*, Nov. 2003/Jan. 2004, at 44, 45. *Allied-Bruce Terminix Cos. v. Dobson*, 513 U.S. 265 (1995) "arbitration's advantages often would seem helpful to individuals, say, complaining about a product, who need a less expensive alternative to litigation." *Circuit City Stores, Inc. v. Adams*, 532 U.S. 105, 123 (2001) ("Arbitration agreements allow parties to avoid the costs of litigation, a benefit that may be of particular importance in employment litigation, which often involves smaller sums of money than disputes concerning commercial contracts.").

[20] *Halsbury's Laws of England*, 3rd Edition, Volume 2 at pg.2 para 2.

hearing both sides in a judicial manner, by a person or persons other than a court of competent jurisdiction." Maritime/Commercial arbitration is, in most jurisdictions, practiced in accordance with law made by the state[21]. It is argued that there is an arbitration war which is a battle over whether the United States will progressively have a privatized system of justice that forbids people from enforcing rights in court and, if so, what will be considered fair in that system[22].

It has to be taken into account that maritime arbitration often involves disputing parties coming from different countries and so coming from backgrounds of varying legal cultures giving rise to differences as to expectations, and the favored method and procedure used for the resolution of disputes. Arbitration proceedings cannot be instigated unless there is a valid arbitration clause which means that common model contracts covering a range of shipping activities usually encompass arbitration clauses such as the arbitration clause in the Lloyd's Standard Form.

States are more and more prepared to accept the transfer of adjudicative authority from courts to arbitrators[23] but regardless that a class of disputes is no longer resolved on the merits by judges but by private adjudicators who function in a legal market and whose decisions are insulated from court supervision on matters of law which in fact shows that there is no a real transfer of adjudicative authority from courts to arbitrators. It is argued that state courts are precisely those who, on behalf of the state, respecting the independence of the arbitration process, have simultaneously the obligation to support it. Is there the emergence of transnational legal orders in which private entities construct law without sovereign authorization[24]?

It has to be taken into account that the parties and the companies choose the arbitration as a consequence of the speed of the procedure, compared to the time of the courts. Nevertheless, there are doubts about the real effectiveness of the arbitration process. At the outset, the certainty of the judges does not mean legal certainty: even in case of an applicable law clause, in fact, any gap or profile that is not covered will attract the application of private international law or the *lex mercatoria*. Furthermore, speed is not assured: there are procedures that are complicated enough to take a long time, sometimes not less than two years; the cost of the procedures is very high; contesting the

[21] The Arbitration and Conciliation Act Cap 19, Laws of Nigeria 1990, Arbitration Act of England, 1996.

[22] Editorial, The Arbitration War, *N.Y. Times* (Nov. 26, 2010), https://perma.cc/3UCC-TZEW Daniel T. Deacon, Essay, Agencies and Arbitration, 117 *Colum. L. Rev.* 991, 1014-22 (2017); and David L. Noll, Regulating Arbitration, 105 *Calif. L.Rev.* 985, 1038-44 (2017).

[23] A Casella, On Market Integration and the Development of Institutions: The Case of International Commercial Arbitration (1996) 40 *Eur Econ Rev* 155, 1559; S Sassen, *Losing Control? Sovereignty in an Age of Globalization* (Columbia University Press, New York, 1996) 1416; W Mattli, Private Justice in a Global Economy: From Litigation to Arbitration (2001) 55 *Intl Org* 919.

[24] R Wai, Transnational Liftoff and Juridical Touchdown: The Regulatory Function of Private International Law in an Era of Globalization (2002) 40 *Col J Transnatl L* 207.

arbitration award or execution requires qualified professional competence which means that there is a need for a speedy and simple arbitration process independent from court[25].

Moreover, it is has to be taken into consideration that the finality of awards is principally vital in business transactions due to the cost of capital and the confusion that indecision generates to businesses and so the most focal consideration in a commercial dispute is that it be quickly and definitively decided which necessitate an autonomous dispute system not dependent on courts supervision[26].

International commercial arbitration is a legally binding dispute resolution process that substitutes for domestic courts. It could be said that, for instance, IJV partners do not have to rely on domestic courts in the host market for their enforcement mechanisms[27] and so International commercial arbitration permits foreign MNEs and host companies to state laws that apply to IJV contracts, and design their enforcement mechanisms to their needs[28].

The world of international arbitration has grown over recent decades, in socio-economic density and public visibility in addition to in terms of caseloads for arbitral institutions, ad hoc tribunals and courts[29]. On the one hand, in the field of international trade, arbitration is advantageous from judicial litigation for the reason that, among other things, it guarantees the neutrality of the forum. On the other hand, arbitration cannot be developed in the commercial environment of a state unless it is allowed from the domestic regulatory framework and the judicial system of that State. Should take place a degree to which the national legislation consent the judicial intervention in arbitration or arbitration has to become totally independent from national courts? Arbitration shall be "free" from the court, so as to respect the desire of the parties to establish an efficient procedure. Does arbitration need the support of national courts to make certain that the solution offered by arbitration will be effective? There is a need for International judicial effectiveness by not only realizing the legal and judicial dispute settlement objectives but also realizing the role of courts and arbitration in combination with their interrelation or the need for separate and independent roles in achieving justice.

Aim of this work, which is divided in two volumes, is to investigate the constitutionality[30] of arbitration and the establishment of arbitration as a co-equal & independent to courts dispute mechanism. In this volume of the whole work is investigated: Firstly, a historical reference will allow us to see the utility of arbitration in

---

[25] Luca G. Radicati di Brozolo, The Relation between Courts and Arbitration: Support or Hostility, Op. J., Vol. 1/2012, Paper n. 7, pp. 1 - 12, http://lider-lab.sssup.it/opinio.

[26] Edna Sussman, Why Arbitrate? The Benefits and Savings, *NYSBA J.*, Oct. 2009.

[27] Siegel, J. 2009. Is there a better commitment mechanism than cross-listing for emerging-economy firms: Evidence from Mexico. *Journal of International Business Studies*, 40(7): 1171–1191.

[28] Drahozal, C. R. 2009. Private ordering and international commercial arbitration. *Penn State Law Review*, 113: 1031–1050. Pinkham, B. C. 2010. Whose law is bigger: Arbitrating government-firm investment disputes in the EU. In M. W. Peng (Ed), *Global business*, 2nd ed: 267–268. Cincinnati, OH: Cengage Learning.

[29] Y. Dezalay and B.G. Garth, 'The role of lawyers in South and East Asia' in C. Antons (ed.), *Routledge Handbook of Asian Law* (London: Routledge, 2017), pp. 110-124.

[30] G Zekos, "*Constitution, Arbitration and Courts.*" www.novapublishers.com.

It is worth noting that private arbitration predates the public court system[37]. The ancient Sumerians, Persians, Egyptians, Greeks[38], and Romans all had a tradition of arbitration[39]. In Roman law, arbitration agreements were admissible as a reflection of the recognized principle of freedom of contract[40]. In arbitrations dating back to the Oxyrynchus Papyri from 427 A.D., merchants enthusiastically accepted as final the decisions of fellow merchants with knowledge and expertise in the related field[41]. Arbitration has, for that reason, historically functioned as an independent adjudicative dispute resolution mechanism. It is characteristic that arbitration was perceived as superior for resolving price or damages disputes[42]. Even in the 1800s arbitration was appreciated for its cost-saving advantages[43].

Arbitration's popularity has continued to flourish since Biblical times[44]. At the beginning the regulation of arbitration by national law was nonexistent and arbitration was crafted particularly to make possible the dispute resolution needs of a specific industry or a community avoiding to imitate the procedures of any judiciary. Arbitrators applied established custom as the legal rules and standards according to which rights and obligations of the parties were determined and this was an international commercial law applicable to these international transactions - the *lex mercatoria*- of those times. Maritime arbitration has ancient origins, and additionally, just as maritime law preceded "terrestrial" commercial law, maritime arbitration preceded international commercial arbitration, with its roots dating back to the times of the ancient *lex mercatoria*[45].

---

[37] William Holdsworth, xiv *A History of English law* 187 (A.L. Goodhart and H.G. Hanbury eds. 1964).

[38] Marcus Niebuhr Tod, International Arbitration Amongst the Greeks 170-74 (1913) (providing examples of international arbitrations in ancient times that led to the ancient Greeks' arbitration system). J Velissaropoulos-Karakostas, L'arbitrage dans la Grèce antique – Epoques archaïque et classique (2000) *Revue de l'arbitrage* 9-26.

[39] W. Durant, *The story of civilization: our common heritage* 127, 361 (1935).

[40] Schottelius, *Die Internationale Schiedsgerichtsbarkeit* (Cologne/Berlin 1957) p. 17 et seq.

[41] Margit Mantica, Arbitration in Ancient Egypt, 12 *Arb. J.* 155, 155-59, 160-61 (1957) Henry P. de Vries, International Commercial Arbitration: A Contractual Substitute for National Courts, 57 *Tulane L. Rev.* 42, 43 (1982) (explaining that arbitration thrived among commercial groups that preferred to keep their differences "in the family"). Lisa Bernstein, Private Commercial Law in the Cotton Industry: Creating Cooperation through Rules, Norms, and Institutions, 99 *Mich. L. Rev.* 1724, 1785 (2001) Lawrence M. Friedman, *A History of American Law* 45 (2d ed. 1985) (reporting Quakers' establishment of arbitration system to resolve citizen disputes in colonial Pennsylvania); Sabra A. Jones, Historical Development of Commercial Arbitration in the United States, 12 *Minn. L. Rev.* 240, 246-47 (1927) (noting New Amsterdam's 1647 ordinance establishing "The Board of Nine Men" to resolve disputes outside of courts in order to avoid "the great expense, loss of time and vexation" of litigation).

[42] *Delaware and H. Canal Co. v. Pennsylvania Coal Co.*, 50 N.Y. 250, 263 (N.Y. 1872), *Hamilton v. Insurance Co.*, 136 U.S. 242 (1890).

[43] In re *Grening*, 26 N.Y.S. 117 (*Ny.Sup.Gen.Term* 1893), referring to arbitration as among "simple and inexpensive methods of quieting disputes growing out of business transactions."

[44] Daniel E. Murray, Arbitration in the Anglo-Saxon and Early Norman Periods, 16 *Arb. J.* 193, 194-95 (1961) (discussing arbitration's use into the early twelfth century). *Derek Roebuck, Even Gods Needed Arbitration: Ancient Greek Arbitration* (2001).

[45] Robert Jarvis, An Annotated Bibliography of English-Language Materials on Maritime Arbitration, 14 *Tul. Mar. L.J.* 49 (1989), as well as Black, Maritime Arbitration in the Asian Century, 14 *Tul. Mar. L.J.* 261 (1990). Jonathan I. Charney, *Is International Law Threatened by Multiple International Tribunals?* 271 *Recueil Des Cours* 101, 118 (1999) (noting that several ad hoc and specialized international arbitration forums preceded the twentieth-century international courts) at 118 ("The Jay Treaty of 1794 marked the beginning of modern international arbitrations.").

Merchant law, *lex mercatoria*, had flourished during the medieval age and started to be nationalized afterwards. Modern *lex mercatoria* is an international law system applied by international merchants based on commercial rules and principles. General principles of law and common principles of law represent sources of the *lex mercatoria* and demonstrate an intention that the contract is not to be governed by national laws. Parties may refer to *lex mercatoria* plainly in the arbitration clause as the law to be applied to the arbitration which means that when the parties specify *lex mercatoria* as the law to be applied to the arbitration, the arbitrators are obliged to prove a real and creative effort to determine the principles of law and procedures to be applied. Moreover, determination of *lex mercatoria* as the law to be applied to the arbitration may either be done by an unequivocally referral or by a reference to general law principles, international commercial rules and principles and general terms and conditions of commerce. Besides, implied reference to *lex mercatoria* is present most usually when the parties grant the arbitrators the right to act as amiable compositeur. Arbitrators faced with such expressions must take care to precisely ascertain what the parties had in mind when they used a specific expression to describe the rules applicable to the dispute. It is characteristic that in the Turkish legal system arbitrators are not bound by the law to be applied to the arbitration and so they can rule based on generally applied commercial rules and principles which means that according to Article 533 of the Turkish Procedural Law, arbitral awards cannot be overruled as a result of the fact that they are against the substantive law[46]. Commercial rules and principles are interpreted as principles that have been applied for a long time and accepted as binding by merchants. Customs are to be construed as habits and not to be accepted as binding commercial rules and principles which means that they may only be used to clarify the parties' understandings. According to Article 28/4 of the UNCITRAL model law, an arbitral tribunal shall render its decision in line with the contract provisions and commercial rules and principles applicable to the commercial transaction. It has to be taken into account that arbitrators decide an arbitration case in line with bona fide principles and/or as a mediator or amiable compositeur only if the parties plainly authorize them to do so. It could be said that the *lex mercatoria* is a method for determining the appropriate rule or principle. In *Deutsche Schachtbau-und Tiefbohrgesellschaft v Ras Al Khaimah National Oil Co*[47] enforcement of a foreign award was resisted on the ground that the tribunal had chosen as the governing law a common denominator of principles underlying the laws of the different

[46] Harold J. Berman & Colin Kaufman, The Law of International Commercial Transactions (*Lex Mercatoria*), 19 *Harv. Int'l L.J.* 221 (1978). Özdemir, Didem, "Milletlerarası Ticari Tahkimde Esasa Uygulanacak Hukuk Olarak *Lex Mercatoria*," *Gazi Üniversitesi Hukuk Fakültesi Dergisi*, Jun-Dec 2003, Vol. VII, Issue 1-2, 130. Alangoya, *Yavuz, Medeni Usul Hukuku Esasları*, Istanbul, 2001, 585. Law No 4686 refers that "commercial rules and principles related to the applicable law shall be taken into account during the interpretation of the contract provisions," Klaus Berger, *The Creeping Codification of the Lex Mercatoria* (1999).

[47] [1987] 3 WLR 1027; rev'd on other grounds *Deutsche Schachtbau-und Tiefbohrgesellschaft mbH v. Shell International Petroleum Co Ltd* (No 1&2) [1990] 1 AC 295 David Rivkin, 'Enforceability of Arbitral Awards based on *Lex Mercatoria*' (1993) 9 *Arbitration International* 67, 68–70. *Eagle Star Insurance Co Ltd v. Yuval Insurance Co Ltd* [1978] 1 *Lloyd's* 357.

here that Lord Coke's opinion in Vynior's Case formed the basis for the common law doctrine that "1) either party to an arbitration might withdraw at any time before an actual award; and 2) that an agreement to arbitrate a future dispute was against public policy and not enforceable" and so the precedent established in Vynior's case illustrates the principle that the parties to a dispute cannot oust "the court of its jurisdiction" which means that courts cannot be deprived of their jurisdiction even by private agreement prevailing till FAA was passed in 1925.

Courts used as the basis for their refusal to enforce executory arbitration contracts on the theory that arbitrators are simply agents at the will of the parties who appoint them[60]. Arbitrators are summoned to settle on disputes objectively and are not subject to the parties' control. Many pre-industrial courts promoted common law rules in support of arbitration[61]. Moreover, some courts favoured arbitration as a result of its procedural simplicity and efficiency[62]. Other courts held that parties could not, by contract, oust the court of jurisdiction[63]. By contrast arbitration clauses do not "deprive the court of jurisdiction," rather, the court being the institution in control of a state's dispute system, in enforcing a liberally agreed upon contract containing an arbitration clause, is simply enforcing the desire of the parties, not admitting that it lacks jurisdiction over the proceedings.

On the one hand, in *Home Insurance Co. of New York v. Morse*[64] the court held that a person who consents to arbitration does not waive the right to a judicial forum. Moreover,

---

[60] Vynior's Case, 77 *Eng. Rep.* 597, 599 (K.B. 1609). 8 Co. Rep. 80a., Robert B. von Mehren, From Vynior's Case to Mitsubishi: The Future of Arbitration and Public Law, 477 *Prac. L. Inst./Com.* 177, 182 (1988). *Tobey v. County of Blistol*, 23 *Fed. Cas.* 1313, 1321-23 (C.C.D. Mass. 1845).

[61] *Campbell v. Western*, 3 Paige Ch. 124 (N.Y.Ch. 1832), at *8, n.1, at 128, n. 1"Awards are much favored, and the court will intend everything in their favor." *Tankersley v. Richardson*, 2 Stew. 130 (Ala. 1829) at 1829 WL 366, at * 1 "This Court must, in accordance with a rule repeatedly laid down, . . intend in favor of the award..."

[62] *Brush v. Fisher*, 70 *Mich.* 469, 448 (1888), at 447 "there is power in a court of equity to relieve against awards in some cases where there has been fraud and misconduct in the arbitrators, or they have acted under some manifest mistake. . ." at 448 "it is evident that there are greater objections to any general interference by courts with awards." *Campbell v. Western*, 3 Paige Ch. 124, 132 (N.Y.Ch. 1832): *Neely v. Buford*, 65 Mo. 448, at * 2 (1877)("courts are disposed to regard with favor these tribunals of the parties' own selection"). *Insurance Co. v. Morse*, 87 U.S. 445, 451 (1874), stating: "Agreements in advance to oust the courts of the jurisdiction conferred by law are illegal and void."

[63] *Kill v. Hollister*, 95 Eng. Rep. 532, 532 (K.B. 1746). The court gave judgment for the plaintiff because "the agreement of the parties [to arbitrate] cannot oust this court" of jurisdiction. 1 *Wils.* 129 (1746). Lord Kenyon's emphatic rejection of a motion to enforce a pre-dispute arbitration agreement: "It has been decided again and again that an agreement to refer all matters in difference to arbitration is not sufficient to oust the courts of law or equity of their jurisdiction." *E.g., Thompson v. Charnock*, 8 *Term R.*, 134, 139 (N. Y. ed. of 1834, 91).*Thompson v. Charnock*, (1799) 101 *Eng. Rep.* 1310 (K.B.) (Kenyon, C.J.) ("It is not necessary, now, to say how this point ought to be determined if it were res integra, it having been decided again and again that an agreement to refer matters in difference to arbitration, is not sufficient to oust courts of law and equity of their jurisdiction."); *Tobey v. County of Bristol*, 23 *F. Cas.* 1313, 1320-21 (C.C.D. Mass. 1845) (No. 14,065) (noting that courts are reluctant to compel parties to submit to arbitration precisely because award "shall be final" and shall "close against [the parties] the doors of the common courts of justice, provided by the government to protect rights and to redress wrongs").

[64] 87 U.S. 445 (1874). at 451-52. "There is no doubt of the general principle that parties cannot by contract oust the ordinary courts of their jurisdiction. That has been decided in many cases. Perhaps the first case I need refer to was a case decided about a century ago [referring to *Kill v. Hollester*]. That case was an action on a policy of insurance in which there was a clause that in case of any loss or dispute it should be referred to arbitration. It was decided there that an action would lie, although there had been no reference to arbitration."

the Supreme Court in this case[65] held that "[e]very citizen is entitled to resort to all the courts of the country, and to invoke the protection which all the laws or all those courts may afford him. A man may not barter away his life or his freedom, or his substantial rights" and so arbitration was not an alternative dispute mechanism co-equal to courts. On the other hand, in *Port Huron and N.W. Ry. Co. v. Callanan*[66] the court held "it is not expected that after resorting to such private tribunals either party may repudiate their action and fall back on the courts."

Michigan Supreme Court held that "There is power in a court of equity to relieve against awards in some cases where there has been fraud and misconduct in the arbitrators, or they have acted under manifest mistake. . . . But it is evident that there are greater objections to any general interference by courts with awards[67]" which shows a court's intervention but not complete conquest of the process which might cannot be avoided in some cases if the parties' want to use all the possibilities of courts' intervention in arbitration. Absent a unanimous agreement, the panel disbanded and the case had to go to the courts after the waste of time and cost of the arbitral proceeding[68]. Moreover, in *Pierce v. Kirby*[69] the court held that "a party who replies to a complaint at arbitration, but otherwise asserts that the arbitrators lack jurisdiction, does not forgo his right to a judicial forum" and so party's involvement in arbitration did not waive a right to sue showing arbitration as a non-binding procedure. The fear of prejudice practiced by one side of the trade against another is reported and so judicial independence was not likely, but the courts did not abandon the test that the expert trade association arbitrators were acting in a "quasi-judicial" capacity[70]. In *Adams' Adm'r v. Ringo*[71] specified that "the ancient niceties and technicalities applied to arbitrations have given way to a more liberal and rational construction. This mode of ending litigation is to be encouraged."

The ouster theory appeared to be a cause for judicial hostility to arbitration, mainly for the reason that courts continued to enforce proverbial "ousters," including settlement agreements, and arbitration awards[72]. Judge Cardozo explained the ouster principle in *Meacham v. Jamestown, Franklin and CClearfield R.R. Co*[73,] stating that "if jurisdiction is to be ousted by contract, we must submit to the failure of justice that may result from these and like causes. It is true that some judges have expressed the belief that parties ought to be free to contract about such matters as they please. In this state the law has

---

[65] *Home Insurance Co. of New York v. Morse* 87 U.S. 445 (1874) at 451.

[66] 34 N.W. 678, 679 (Mich. 1887).

[67] *Brush v. Fisher*, 38 N.W. 446, 476 (Mich. 1888).

[68] *Towne v. Jaquith*, 6 Mass. 46 (1809); *Green v. Miller*, 6 Johns 39 (N.Y. 1810).

[69] 21 *Wis.* 124 (Wis. 1866).

[70] *Cf. Graham v. Chamber of Com. of the City of Milwaukee*, 20 *Wis.* 63 (1865) (upholding the right of a member of Chamber to litigate a dispute with a fellow member, even though the rules required arbitration and court barred association from expelling member).

[71] 79 *Ky.* 211 (*Ky.App.* 1880).

[72] *Red Cross Line v. Atl. Fruit Co.*, 264 U.S. 109, 121 (1924). *Atl. Fruit Co. v. Red Cross Line*, 276 F. Supp. 319, 323-24 (S.D.N.Y. 1921) (refusing to compel arbitration notwithstanding a New York arbitration statute). *Kulukundis Shipping Co. v. Amtorg Trading Corp.*, 126 F.2d 978, 985 (2d Cir. 1942).

[73] 211 N.Y. 346, 105 N.E. 653 (1914): at 656.

long been settled to the contrary." Courts followed the lead of Lord Coke[74] and Blackstone[75] in holding that an executory agreement to arbitrate would not be enforced by the courts, because the removal of jurisdiction that it entailed was against sound public policy. Initially courts believed arbitration usurped their jurisdiction and viewed arbitration as a threat because "ordinary citizens . . . [made] their own law and disregard[ed] the judicial process[76]." Courts to a large extent granted themselves jurisdiction to invalidate arbitration awards[77]. Thus, courts have managed to get in the way of arbitration process and to gain a role in arbitration. Early courts protected their jurisdiction from competition with arbitrations and characteristically in *U.S. Asphalt Refining Co. v. Trinidad Lake Petroleum Co*[78] the court held that "The courts will scarcely permit any other body of men to even partially perform judicial work, and will never permit the absorption of all the business growing out of disputes over a contract by anybody of arbitrators, unless compelled to such action by statute." Some judges held that an agreement to arbitrate a dispute could not "oust" a court of its jurisdiction[79]. On the other hand, Joseph Story[80] thought that "courts will not specifically enforce arbitration agreements if the effect is to divest the ordinary jurisdiction of the common tribunals of justice." Additionally some courts held that public policy prohibits arbitration agreements from precluding litigation and private tribunals could not be held accountable under the law[81]. Thus, courts have taken the role of the guardian of public policy in a state and so arbitration considered not to be a safe, independent and fully alternative dispute mechanism. Regardless that arbitration predates litigation as a forum for dispute resolution arbitration has been historically disfavoured by Anglo-American courts. Entirely valid expressions of contractual assent were being methodically ignored and refused enforcement by the courts. The question to be answered is why there is a need to

---

[74] Vinior's Case, 77 *Eng. Rep.* 595 (K.B. 1609).

[75] Sarah E. Rudolph, Blackstone's Vision of Alternative Dispute Resolution, 22 *Memphis State L. Rev.* 279 (1992).

[76] Konstantinos Petrakis, The Role of Arbitration in the Field of Patent Law, 52 *Disp. Resol. J.* 24 (1997) (suggesting that such opposition to arbitration was a result of ancient courts resisting any procedures that would usurp their jurisdiction) (quoting United States Asphalt Refining Co. v. Trinidad Lake Petroleum Co., 222 F. 1006, 1012 (S.D.N.Y. 1915) (citing *Scott v. Avery*, 5 House of L. 811 [1856])).Thomas E. Carbonneau, Arbitral Justice: The Demise of Due Process in American Law, 70 *Tul. L. Rev.* 1945, 1947 (1996) Justice Story asked whether "tribunals possess adequate means of giving redress" or "close[d] . . . the doors of the common courts of justice, provided by the government to protect rights and to redress wrongs." Adam M. Smith, "Judicial Nationalism" in International Law: National Identity and Judicial Autonomy at the ICJ, 40 *Tex. Int'l L.J.* 197, 201 (2005) ("[J]udicial organs often bridled at . . . arbitration, [but] were not entirely averse to [it].").

[77] Linda R. Hirshman, The Second Arbitration Trilogy: The Federalization of Arbitration Law, 71 *Va. L. Rev.* 1305, 1310–11 (1985) ("[J]udicial doctrine rejecting enforcement of contracts to arbitrate became so entrenched that even critics felt powerless to defy precedent.").

[78] 222 F. 1006, 1007 at 1010-1011.

[79] *Allgre v. Maryland Ins. Co.*, 6 *Har. and Johns.* 408 (Md. 1825); *Randel v. Chesapeake, etc., Canal Co.*, 1 *Harring.* 233 (*Del.Super.* 1833); *Gray v. Wilson*, 4 *Watts* 39 (Pa. 1835); *Aspinwall v. Towsey*, 2 *Tyler* 328 (*Vt.* 1803); *Allen v. Watson*, 15 *Johns.* 205 (*N.Y. Sup.* 1819); and *Rowley v. Young*, 3 *Day* 118 (*Conn.* 1808).

[80] Joseph Story, 2 *Commentaries on Equity Jurisprudence*, at § 1457.

[81] *Hurst v. Litchfield*, 39 N.Y. 377, 379 (1868), stating that "stipulations [for arbitration] are regarded as against the policy of the common law, as having a tendency to exclude the jurisdiction of the courts." *Prince Steam-Shipping Co. v. Lehman*, 39 *Fed.* 704 (*D.C.* 1889): "Such agreements have repeatedly been held to be against public policy and void."

involve courts in arbitration agreements and why not arbitration itself to be able to deal with arbitration agreements legalising the whole process. Why not arbitration to be a self-contained method, co-equal and distinctive from litigation?

Moreover, there has been a long standing hostility between courts and arbitration[82]. In the 17th Century, English courts held arbitration was a non-binding process. English judges were paid fees based on the number of cases they decided and so arbitration infringed their livelihood[83]. The *Park Const. Co*[84] majority considered that English courts in the 1700s protected their jurisdiction against encroachments by arbitration – not for principles, but for self-interest. Consequently, private arbitration was seen as an economic threat to English judges, whose incomes often depended on fees from disputants[85]. The English courts became concerned that arbitration had the potential to displace or oust the courts' role in society. Through a series of court decisions limiting the effect of arbitration, the English courts began to view arbitration as a non-binding process based upon the principle of agency revocability. In US federal and state courts both followed ancient rules of English law[86] that "performance of a written agreement to arbitrate would not be enforced in equity, and... if an action at law were brought...such agreement could not be pleaded in bar of the action, nor would such an agreement be ground for a stay of proceedings until arbitration was had." Besides, Michael H. LeRoy and Peter Feuille[87] argue that "courts were not hostile to arbitration; they were not laissez-faire in sanctioning its use. Nor are they today in applying the pro-arbitration signal sent in *Gilmer* and *Circuit City...* courts today deny enforcement to a sizeable percentage of contested arbitration agreements is impressive evidence that the federal judiciary does not blindly toe the *Gilmer* and *Circuit City* line.*"* On the one hand, Jonathan R. Nelson[88] argues that judicial hostility to arbitration does not base on judicial

---

[82] The origins of the judicial antipathy to arbitration lie in "'ancient times' when the English courts fought for extension of jurisdiction--all of them being opposed to anything that would altogether deprive every one of them of jurisdiction." *Bernhardt v. Polygraphic Co. of Am.*, 350 U.S. 198, 210 n.5 (1956) (Frankfurter, J. concurring). The English hostility to arbitration was adopted by American courts because of the "antiquity of the rule" rather than "its excellence or reason."

[83] Preston D. Wigner, The United States Supreme Court's Expansive Approach to the Federal Arbitration Act: A Look at the Past, Present, and Future of Section 2, 29 *U. Rich. L. Rev.* 1499, 1502 (1995). C.H.S. Fifoot, *Lord Mansfield* 104-05 (1936): "The collaboration of judge and merchant, if it was to exercise its due influence upon the law, required adequate channels of communication. In the development of the special jury Lord Mansfield found the vital medium. . . . Lord Mansfield converted an occasional into a regular institution and trained a corps of jurors as a permanent liaison between law and commerce."

[84] *Park Const. Co. v. Independent School Dist. No. 32*, Carver County 209 *Minn.* 182 (1941).

[85] William M. Howard, The Evolution of Contractually Mandated Arbitration, *Arb. J.*, Sept. 1993, at 28. *Scott v. Avery*, 10 *Eng. Rep.* 1121 (H.L. 1856) (opinion of Lord Campbell).

[86] S. Rep. No. 5365, 68th Cong., 1st Sess, 2 (1924).

[87] Michael H. LeRoy and Peter Feuille, *Judicial Enforcement of Pre-Dispute Arbitration Agreements: Back to the Future*, www.ssrn.com p 103, p6-7 "American courts have never been hostile to arbitration, nor have they abdicated their role as public adjudicators. Courts have steered a more intermediate course by enforcing pre-dispute arbitration agreements, while reserving power to void or reform the most objectionable arrangements in these contracts." Michael H. Leroy, *Misguided Fairness? Regulating Arbitration By Statute: Empirical Evidence of Declining Award Finality*, www.ssrn.com.

[88] Jonathan R. Nelson, Judge Made Law and the Presumption of Arbitrability: David L. Threlkeld and *Co. v. Metallgesellschaft Ltd.*, 58 *Brook. L. Rev.* 279, 298, n.114 (1992), (Supreme Court's unsupported observation

jealousy. On the other hand, in the House Report No. 68-96 specified that judicial "jealousy" survived for long time[89]. Hailegabriel G. Feyissa[90] argues that "The main reason for the hostility between courts and arbitration was, *inter alia*, the belief that arbitration goes against public policy."

During the French Revolution arbitration believed to be the natural way of settling disputes and rendering justice and so that the national courts should simply be a subsidiary system. The French Revolution not only considered expansion of arbitration, but also the exclusion of professional judges altogether[91]. The law of 16-24 August 1790 prohibited any obstacle to arbitration in whatever manner or form. Even matters of personal status could be submitted to arbitration. Besides, the Supreme Court of France in its judgment of 10 July 1843[92] held that only courts of the state could guarantee the protection of sound justice and so arbitration clauses were null and void. In France,

---

that judicial hostility to arbitration rested upon judicial jealousy was considered and rejected in the well-reasoned opinion of the Second Circuit in *Kulukundis Shipping Co.*).

89 H.R. Rep. No. 68-96, at 1-2 (1924) ("The need for the law arises from an anachronism of our American law. Some centuries ago, because of the jealousy of the English courts for their own jurisdiction, they refused to enforce specific agreements to arbitrate upon the ground that the courts were thereby ousted from their jurisdiction. This jealousy survived for so long a period that the principle became firmly embedded in the English common law and was adopted with it by the American courts. The courts have felt that the precedent was too strongly fixed to be overturned without legislative enactment."). Lindsay R. Androski, A Contested Merger: The Intersection of Class Actions and Mandatory Arbitration Clauses, 2003 *U. Chi. Legal F.* 631, 635 ("Representative Mills of New York, who introduced the original bill in the House, explained that the FAA 'provides that where there are commercial contracts and there is disagreement under the contract, the court can enforce an arbitration agreement in the same way as other portions of the contract.' Similarly, the chairman of the New York Chamber of Commerce testified before the Senate that the Act would 'enable business men to settle their disputes expeditiously and economically, and (would) *reduce the congestion in the Federal and State courts.*' A Senate Judiciary Committee Report supporting the legislation explained that arbitration provides benefits to both consumers and businesses through speedier resolution and lower costs: 'The desire to avoid the delay and expense of litigation persists . . .'") at 634 ("Before congressional adoption of the FAA, contractual arbitration clauses were revocable at will. A party who had previously agreed to arbitration of disputes could opt unilaterally for litigation, severing the (now void) arbitration clause from the remainder of the agreement. Congress changed this option in 1924 with the adoption of the FAA.").

90 Hailegabriel G. Feyissa, The Role of Ethiopian Courts in Commercial Arbitration, *Mizan Law Review* Vol. 4 No.2, Autumn 2010, 298, p299.

91 Isser Woloch, *The New Regime: Transformations of The French Civic Order*, 1789-1820S, at 312-17 (1994). French Revolution not only considered all obligations, statutes and society as founded on the will of the people and the idea of contract (*contrat social*, Jean-Jacques Rousseau), but as a consequence also arbitration was considered a *droit naturel*. Moreover the Constitution of 1791 (Art. 86) and the Constitution of Year III (Art. 210) proclaimed the constitutional right of citizens to resort to arbitration. Huys and Keutgen, L'arbitrage en droit belge et international (Brussels 1981) p. 6. Clère, L'Arbitrage Revolutionnaire: Apogée et Déclin d'une Institution (1790-1806), *Revue de* l'arbitrage (1981) p. 3 et seq.

92 Cass Civ 10 July 1843 S 1843 p 561 and D 1843 p 343. The decision of the *Cour de cassation* of 1843 refused to recognize that a *clause compromissoire* agreeing on arbitration for future disputes was binding. It took until 1925 when, under pressure from institutions of commercial practice, a statute was enacted recognizing the validity of an arbitration agreement in commercial matters. A further indication of the gradually more favourable approach to arbitration is also that the courts interpreted the rule forbidding arbitration for State institutions to be only applicable for domestic contracts, but not for international contracts. A major reform and modernization of the French law of arbitration was, of course, enacted in 1980 and 1981. David, Arbitrage du XIXeet arbitrage du XXesiècle, Mélanges offerts à René Savatier (Paris 1965) p. 219 at p. 220 et seq. Böckstiegel, *Arbitration and State Enterprises – Survey on the National and International State of Law and Practice* (Deventer/Antwerp/Boston/Frankfurt/London 1984) p. 15; Rivero, Personnes Morales de Droit Public et Arbitrage, *Rev. arb.* (1973) p. 263 at p. 270 et seq. Derains, National Report France, Sanders And Van Den Berg, eds., ICCA International Handbook on Commercial Arbitration vol. II (Deventer/Boston) p. 1 et seq.; Böckstiegel, ed., *Schiedsgerichtsbarkeit in Frankreich* (Cologne/Berlin/Bonn/Munich 1983).

despite the enthusiasm during the French Revolution for arbitration, shortly thereafter arbitration was looked upon with mistrust and as a threat to the law.

Thus, a hostility of courts against arbitration developed in France as well. Merchants needed greater speed and flexibility for the settlement of their disputes than that provided by national courts and so courts have been forced to change their attitude towards arbitration[93] again in France. The current French Court of Appeal jurisprudence sees international arbitration as a self-standing, transnational legal order. As to Putrabali[94] the French *cour de cassation* recognized an arbitral award although it had been set aside in the country of its seat, that remains for the time being a position that the French legal system is free to take, for as long as the arbitration exception to the Brussels I Regulation remains.

Arbitration has existed since colonial times[95]. The English reversed their position on binding arbitration in 1889, but American courts continued down the old common law path[96]. The common law doctrine of revocability was followed by American courts until the enactment of the FAA in 1925[97]. Arbitration agreements were not enforced because of established precedent and so the old English rule was carried on long after courts

---

[93] J Delvolve, J Rouche, G Pointon, French Arbitration law and Practice, 2003 *Kluwer Law International* p3. In Germany, traditionally arbitration has been dominated by the principles, on the one hand, of pacta sunt servanda and, on the other hand, of good will and courtesy. The contractual nature of arbitration was stressed to the effect that the submission to arbitration was binding for the parties, but an action in court was at first indispensable for enforcement of an award. In 1930 a simplified procedure for the enforcement of arbitral awards was introduced. Kollmann, Die Schiedsgerichte in Industrie, Gewerbe und Handel (Munich/Berlin 1914) p. 282 et seq. *Gesetz über das Abkommen zur Vollstreckung ausländischer Schiedssprüche* vom 28. Juli 1930, Reichsgesetzblatt, Teil II, at p. 1067; and *Gesetz zur Änderung einiger Vorschriften der Zivilprozeßordnung über das schiedsrichterliche Verfahren* vom 25. Juli 1930, Reichsgesetzblatt, Teil I, at p. 361 et seq.

[94] http://conflictoflaws.net/2007/the-french-like-it-delocalized-lex-non-facit-arbitrum/), Professor Emmanuel Gaillard in his treatise, 'Les Aspects Philosophiques du Droit de l'Arbitrage International'. Hans Smit, Postscript: The Cour De Cassation's Decision in Putrabali, 18 *Am. Rev. Int'l Arb.* 309, 310 (2007) (describing Putrabali's reasoning that "an international arbitral award is not anchored in any national legal order and that [therefore] its validity must be determined by reference to the law of the country in which its recognition is sought" as "regrettable");

[95] Bruce L. Benson, An Exploration of the Impact of Modern Arbitration Statutes on the Development of Arbitration in the United States, 11 *J.L. Econ. and Org.* 479, 481-82 (1995) (discussing the use of arbitration in colonial America).

[96] *Meacham v. Jamestown, Franklin and Clearfield R.R. Co.,* 105 *N.E.* 653 (N.Y. 1914) (*Cardozo, J.*) ("If jurisdiction is to be ousted by contract, we must submit to the failure of justice that may result from these and like causes. It is true that some judges have expressed the belief that parties ought to be free to contract about such matters as they please. In this state the law has long been settled to the contrary."); *Hurst v. Litchfield*, 39 *N.Y.* 377, 379 (1868) ("Such stipulations [to arbitrate] are regarded as against the policy of the common law, as having a tendency to exclude the jurisdiction of the courts, provided by the government with ample means to entertain and decide all legal controversies.").

[97] *Tobey v. County of Bristol*, 23 *Fed. Cas.* 1313 (No. 14065) (*C.C.D. Mass.* 1845). A Massachusetts court refused to order specific performance of an arbitration agreement contained in a public works contract. Id. The Tobey court stated it was impractical to use equity to order arbitration and the plaintiff should exercise the legal remedies available. Id. In *Home Insurance Company of New York v. Morse*, 87 U.S. 445 (1874), the United States Supreme Court held pre-dispute agreements to arbitrate were invalid due to the common law revocability of such agreements. *Am. Sugar Ref. Co. v. Anaconda*, 138 F.2d 765, 766-67 (5th Cir. 1943) ("The act was passed not to oust the jurisdiction of the courts but to provide for maintaining their jurisdiction while at the same time recognizing arbitration agreements as affirmative defenses and providing a forum for their specific enforcement.").

themselves began to question whether it was founded in reason or justice; courts were hesitant to change established precedent[98]. The doctrine of revocability was grounded in the public law courts' fear that they might be displaced by a private process of dispute resolution and thereby be put out of work[99]. As the public court system arose and matured in England it displaced private arbitration in providing the main adjudicative function[100]. Arbitrators represented unwanted competition for common-law judges, whose compensation was tied in part to court fees. Judges as a result had strong incentives to increase their jurisdiction and stifle competing dispute resolution mechanisms[101]. Therefore, it could be argued that from the beginning the main concern was rather not the right application of law but purely the personal interests of a group of the society[102].

Even though common law courts were unenthusiastic to permit arbitrators to assert power over a controversy at the outset, they declared that courts should treat final awards as final in light of "every consideration of public policy[103]." Courts equate the finality of awards with preclusion of judicial re-determination of arbitrated disputes. In *Burchell v. Marsh*[104] held that substantive appeal of arbitration awards would consent to arbitration to become "the commencement, not the end, of litigation." Moreover, courts recognized that finality with the meaning of courts' review of awards was required to prevent arbitration from becoming a superfluous "commencement, and not the end, of litigation," and rejected substantive review of awards as a threat to the effectiveness, flexibility and

[98] S. Rep. No. 536 at 3 (1924). ("Established precedent has had its large part of course in perpetuating the old rules long after the courts themselves could no longer see that they were founded in reason or justice."). *Atlantic Fruit Co. v. Red Cross Line*, 5 F.2d 218, 220 (2d Cir. 1924) Holding that the federal court sitting in admiralty could not compel arbitration under an arbitration clause, Judge Hough declared: "[W]ithout legislation, and because the trend of modern opinion is toward the literal enforcement of the contracts of men of mature years and presumably sound mind, this court is asked to provide some method of overriding, or explaining away not only its own previous decisions but those of the Supreme Court, which for a generation or so have been regarded as declaring the law to be that any agreement contained in an executory contract, ousting in advance all courts of every whit of jurisdiction to decide contests arising out of that contract, will not be enforced by the courts so ousted."

[99] Katherine V.W. Stone, Private Justice, The Law of Alternative Dispute Resolution 305 (Foundation Press) (2003). Peter J. Smith IV, Investors win: *Howsam v. Dean Witter Reynolds, Inc.* makes entering Arbitration quicker, easier, and less expensive, 2003, 4 *Pepp. Disp. Resol. L.J.* 127.

[100] 14 William Holdsworth, *A History of English Law* 187 (A.L. Goodhart and H.G. Hanbury eds., 7th ed. 1956). English statute of 1697 authorized judicial enforcement of arbitration awards 9 and 10 William III c. 15 (1697). The introduction of the law stated: "for promoting trade and rendering the awards of arbitrators the more effectual in all cases, for the final determination of controversies referred to them by merchants and traders, or others, concerning matters of account or trade, or other matters. . . ." Henry Horwitz and James Oldham, John Locke, Lord Mansfield and Arbitration during the Eighteenth Century, 36 *The Historical J.* 137, 138-139 (1993). *U.S. Asphalt Ref. Co. v. Trinidad Lake Petroleum Co.*, 222 F. 1006, 1008–11 (S.D.N.Y. 1915) (discussing the policies that drove judicial refusal to specifically enforce contracts to resolve disputes in a private arbitral forum).

[101] *Bernhardt v. Polygraphic Co. of Am.*, 350 U.S. 198, 211 n.5 (1956) (Frankfurter, J., concurring) (noting that English courts fought "for extension of jurisdiction—all of them being opposed to anything that would altogether deprive every one of them of jurisdiction").

[102] Jonathan R. Macey, Judicial Preferences, Public Choice and the Rules of Procedure, 235 *J. Legal Stud.* 627 (1994) (arguing that judicial behavior is likely to conform to judges' rational self-interest rather than to the interest of economic efficiency).

[103] *Brazill v. Isham*, 12 *N.Y.* 9, 15 (1854). The court emphasized that awards, like court judgments, estop parties from pursuing further litigation.

[104] 58 U.S. (17 How.) 344, 349-50 (1854).

privacy of arbitration[105]. Courts limited review of awards to whether the arbitrators exceeded their authority or to whether the procedure was vitally unfair, essentially foreshadowing the limited review that survives in the FAA.

On the other hand, judicial distrust and doubt of arbitration tempered obvious enthusiasm for the finality of arbitration awards and so the meaning of the "finality" of arbitration was not clear. Thus, courts retained final control over awards and so courts "naturally tended to overstep their bounds, especially where they regard[ed] themselves as equally, or perhaps even better, qualified to settle the controversy"[106]. Furthermore, courts attempted to keep control over arbitration by declaring varied levels of authority to review awards for "mistake" of fact and law[107].

Arbitration has the capacity to enhance democratic governance in several important ways. First, it is possible for arbitration to achieve efficiency gains for the public justice system, as logic suggests that having formalized disputes resolved by arbitration will reduce the number left for resolution by public courts. Second, voluntary arbitration enhances personal autonomy by providing a means of governmentally enforceable dispute resolution to complement public adjudication. Democratic governance requires dispute resolution, and valuable democracy should recognize that it may be achieved through many different methods that allow disputants to "fit the forum to the fuss[108]."

Indeed, historical treatments of the pre-Revolutionary period suggest that what we now call "alternative dispute resolution," was the norm rather than the exception in the colonies[109] of England. Cohen[110] observed, after the passage of New York Arbitration Act's in 1920, that "this statute establishes legal machinery for protecting, safeguarding and supervising commercial arbitration.

Instead of narrowing the jurisdiction of the Supreme Court it broadens it ... Instead of being ousted of jurisdiction over arbitration, the courts are given jurisdiction over them, and ... the party aggrieved has his ready recourse to the courts." Julius Henry Cohen

---

[105] *White Star Mining Co. v. Hultberg*, 77 N.E. 327, 336 (Ill. 1906) (quoting *Burchell v. Marsh*, 58 U.S. 344, 349-50 (1854)).

[106] Frances T. Freeman Jalet, Judicial Review of Arbitration: The Judicial Attitude, 45 *Cornell. L.Q.* 519, 526 (1960) p 531. *Clark Millinery Co. v. Nat'l Union Fire Ins. Co.*, 75 S.E. 944, 949 (N.C. 1912) (acknowledging that "certainty is an essential of a good award," but finding it difficult to apply and therefore confining inquiry to whether award was sufficiently uncertain that it would be avoidable under contract law). *Berkovitz v. Arbib and Houlberg, Inc.*, 130 N.E. 288, 291 (N.Y. 1921) (warning courts that if arbitration does not end disputes, it is merely expensive and superfluous step in litigation).

[107] Arbitration of Interstate Commercial Disputes, Joint Hearings Before the Subcommittees of the Committees on the Judiciary, 68th Cong. 36 (Jan. 9, 1924) (brief submitted by Julius Henry Cohen) (emphasizing that there should be "delay only of a few days" between application and entry of judgment on arbitration award, and that defects warranting vacation, correction, or modification of award were those "so inherently vicious that, as a matter of common morality, [they] ought not to be enforced").

[108] Frank E.A. Sander and Stephen B. Goldberg, Fitting the Forum to the Fuss: A User-Friendly Guide to Selecting an ADR Procedure, 10 *Negot. J.* 49 (1994).

[109] Bruce H. Mann, The Formalization of Informal Law: Arbitration Before the American Revolution, 59 *N.Y.U. L. Rev.* 443, 468-81 (1984). Lawrence M. Friedman, History of American law 32-33, 94 (1973).

[110] Cohen, Julius H. (1921), 'The Law of Commercial Arbitration and the New York Statute', 31 *Yale Law Journal,* 147-160. p150.

thought of arbitration not to function as second-class adjudication[111] but not as independent and co-equal to courts. Moreover, with the number of cases being litigated on the rise, Congress passed the FAA in 1925 to make arbitration an equitable alternative to litigation that would reduce the number of cases in the court system[112]. Congress sought to encourage efficient and speedy dispute resolution but the question to be answered is if the current courts' involvement indicates an independent system or a supplement to courts. It is worth mentioning here[113] that before the subcommittee prior the enactment of FAA emphasized that court's only role should be to make certain that parties have agreed to arbitrate, in so doing waiving any right to trial by jury and ending the court's substantive involvement in arbitration process. This should be the principle nowadays as well. This subcommittee's proposal wanted the establishment of arbitration as a totally independent and alternative dispute system and so the only role left to courts was their declaration for no jurisdiction to deal with arbitration. In other words arbitration could be established as a self-contained method and co-equal to courts.

At the beginning of the twentieth century, arbitration was not extensively used outside of commercial disputes involving merchants[114]. In the 1920's, Julius Cohen and Charles Bernheimer[115] had a three step plan for promoting arbitration: "The first is to get a State statute, and then to get a Federal law to cover interstate and foreign commerce and admiralty, and third to get a treaty with foreign countries." Before the enactment, a party to an arbitration agreement could at any time prior to the award merely decline to

---

[111] Julius Henry Cohen and Kenneth Dayton, The New Federal Arbitration Law, 12 *Va. L. Rev.* 265, 281 (1926) 281 ([Arbitration] has a place also in the determination of the simpler questions of law—the questions of law which arise out of the[] daily relations between merchants as to the passage of title, the existence of warranties, or the questions of law which are complementary to the questions of fact which we have just mentioned. It is not the proper method for deciding points of law of major importance involving constitutional questions or policy in the application of statutes).

[112] *Southland Corp. v. Keating*, 465 U.S. 1, 13-16 (1984); see Richard C. Reuben, Public Justice: Toward a State Action Theory of Alternative Dispute Resolution, 85 *Cal. L. Rev.* 577, 601 (1997) (discussing the history of arbitration in the United States in the early twentieth century). *Bull NH Information Systems, Inc. v. Hutson*, 1998 WL 426047 (D. Mass. 1998), at *1: "the FAA is something of an anomaly in the field of federal-court jurisdiction because it creates a body of federal substantive law without simultaneously creating any independent federal question jurisdiction (internal quotes omitted). . . ."

[113] To Make Valid and Enforceable Certain Agreements for Arbitration, S. Rep. No. 68-536, at 17-18 (1st Sess.1924).

[114] Frances Kellor, *American Arbitration: Its History, Functions And Achievements* 6 (Kennikat Press 1972) (1948); Zeb-Michael Curtin, Note, Rethinking Prima Paint Separability in Today's Changed Arbitration Regime: The Case for Inseparability and Judicial Decision-making in the Context of Mental Incapacity Defenses, 90 *Iowa L. Rev.* 1905, 1910-13 (2005) (explaining that arbitration was limited to use among commercial actors at the time of the Federal Arbitration Act's (FAA) passage). Jeffrey W. Stempel, A Better Approach to Arbitrability, 65 *Tul. L. Rev.* 1377, 1380 (1991) ("The United States Arbitration Act . . . was written with the implicit assumption that it would be invoked by commercial actors having relatively equal bargaining power and emotive appeal to a jury.").

[115] Cohen testimony at Joint Hearings on S. 1005 and R. 646 before the Joint Committee of the Subcommittees on the Judiciary of the United States Senate and House of Representatives, 68th Cong. 1st Session 17, at 16 (1924). Julius Cohen, The New Federal Arbitration Law, 12 *Va. L. Rev.* 265 (1925-26).

arbitrate, and courts would not enforce the agreement[116]. Thus, even at that time courts managed to gain the first role in enforcing arbitration.

Many states institutionalized arbitration and arbitration was established by law to facilitate businesses to avoid messy lawsuits but the question to be answered is if the two methods are established as independent and co-equal dispute settlement mechanisms[117]. At the time of the FAA's enactment in 1925, Isaacs[118] proposed that there are two views of arbitration, as follows: the "legalistic view" that arbitration is purely a mode of trial and the "realistic view" that it is "a means of reaching results essentially different from those reached by a trial." Moreover, Isaacs[119] emphasized that judicial review of awards would foster legalistic, "trial-like" arbitration complete with formal procedure, records and opinions. In other words, courts considered as being the mechanism of attributing legitimacy to arbitration rather than a properly contacted arbitration itself being equally legitimate dispute system and so arbitration could be only a supplement to courts rather than a fully alternative, self-contained method, co-equal and being the second pole in co-existence with courts as dispute systems.

As arbitration gained thrust, courts began to distrust and envy arbitration, but even so they recognized that substantive review of arbitration awards would render arbitration a meaningless precursor to litigation[120]. Historically, the courts were reluctant to enforce agreements to arbitrate, on the theory that such agreements inappropriately ousted the courts of their right and obligation to apply the law of the sovereign to disputes arising within the jurisdiction of the sovereign. Therefore, courts consider themselves as the only institution having the privilege to safeguard the law of the sovereign by having jurisdiction to deal with contractual disputes between parties.

The concise analysis shows that arbitration has been emerged as an independent dispute mechanism but judges have managed to gain the first role in dispute settlement to the detriment of arbitration as a self-contained mechanism.

---

[116] W. Sturges, Commercial Arbitration and Awards, §76 at 237-39 (1930). Ian R. MacNeil, *American Arbitration Law*, pp.28, 34-37 (1992). Professor MacNeil regards "modern" arbitration statutes as those that make agreements to arbitrate future disputes irrevocable. *Id.* at 15.

[117] *Henderson v. Beaton*, 52 Tex. 29 (Tex. 1879), upholding the constitutionality of a Texas statute enacted in 1879 that provided for a board of referees or arbitrators to dispose of civil actions by the consent of parties. *Howard v. Sexton*, 1 Denio 440 (N.Y. Sup. 1845)(arbitration tribunal established under New York law is not defective even if arbitrators fail to take oath as established by law). *Wood v. Donaldson*, 17 Wend. 550 (N.Y.Sup.1837) (statute providing for arbitration in dispute involving contractor and creditors) Conger v. Dean, 3 Iowa 463 (Iowa 1856)(state statute did not provide common law right to submit controversies to arbitration, but prescribed procedures for judicial enforcement of arbitration awards).

[118] Nathan Isaacs, Two Views of Commercial Arbitration, 40 *Harv. L. Rev*. 929, 930-37 (1927). at 929.

[119] ibid at 934-35.

[120] Wesley Albor Sturges, *A Treatise on Commercial Arbitration and Awards* 792-97 (1930) (discussing judicial struggle to retain power to vacate awards for legal mistake without causing arbitration to become superfluous extra step in litigation). Wharton Poor, Arbitration Under the Federal Statute, 36 *Yale L.J.* 667, 676-78 (1927) (emphasizing finality as essential to protecting benefits of arbitration, but noting that arbitration "can by no means be relied upon as a solution of all litigious matters"); at 674-75 (explaining drafters' rejection of English model that allowed judicial review of arbitration awards for legal questions, and their insistence that "once the parties have agreed upon arbitration, they must accept the result the arbitrator reaches no matter how obviously and plainly wrong it appears").

2. Arbitration as a Legal System and Its Legal Basis

Both primary and secondary rules appear in the various national and international laws that relate to international commercial arbitration, although the primary rules relate almost entirely to procedural matters, while all of the rules that relate to the decision on the merits are secondary[121].

It could be said that International arbitration is a system in that it provides a distinct and definable mechanism for the resolution of disputes, but it is not a legal system. It is argued that International arbitration is a global, quasi-judicial system offering the legal infrastructure (norms, actors, and processes) for the consent-based settlement of disputes[122]. A useful example of a transaction-related definition of internationality is provided by Article 1492 of the French *Nouveau Code de Procédure Civile*. According to this provision, arbitration is "international" when it involves the interests of international trade entailing a transfer of goods, services or funds across national boundaries[123].

It is argued that international commercial arbitration does not constitute a legal system because it does not create results in itself, but only through the cooperation of national courts, which themselves act along with their own national laws, laws that are in turn validated by their own separate and independent national rules of recognition. These rules are often derived from, or are in line with, treaties and customary international law, especially the New York Convention. Nevertheless, the New York Convention does not validate national arbitration statutes; such statutes are valid by virtue of their being enacted compliant with the rule of recognition of the state that enacted them[124].

It is worth mentioning that most arbitral awards are voluntarily complied with, but this does not prove that international arbitration produces results by law independent of national legal systems. Nonetheless, losing parties do not comply with arbitral awards exclusively out of a sense of moral obligation, or just for the reason that members of their commercial society will mete out informal sanctions for noncompliance. Losing parties adhere to awards at least in part for the reason that they perceive those awards to be legally valid, and it is the fact that awards meet the standards of enforceability contained in state laws that makes them legal valid.

As Thomas Schultz argues that a legal system "must be sufficiently independent from other systems (otherwise it has no identity of its own but is merely a part of another

---

[121] Eyal Benvenisti, *The Conception of International Law as a Legal System*, 50 *German Y.B. Int'l L.* 393, 396-99 (2008).

[122] Stephan W. Schill, Developing a Framework for the Legitimacy of International Arbitration, in *Legitimacy: Myths, Realities, Challenges*, 789, 803-09 at 803 (Albert Jan van den Berg ed., 2015).

[123] Lowenfeld, *Lex Mercatoria*: An Arbitrator's View, 6 *Arb. Int'l* 133 (1990), at 146 (stating that "agreements without a choice of law clause are common in my experience").

[124] Thomas Schultz, *Transnational Legality: Stateless Law and International* Arbitration 122 (2014). Ernest A. Young, Supranational Rulings as Judgments and Precedents, 18 *Duke J. Comp. & Int'l L.* 477, 491-96 (2008) (suggesting that international arbitral awards are enforced more readily than judgments of international tribunals).

system).[125]" A legal system has to be adequately independent from other systems and so not being merely a part of another system or dependent by another system for it functionality. A legal system has to be adequately independent not requiring an "external" requirement for the existence of a legal system.

Legal systems have an "internal" requirement, which constitute the role of law in guiding normative conduct among members of a community related with a given legal system. International arbitration law does not even claim this kind of independence. Rather, it is both structurally dependent upon national legal systems (since it cannot enforce its own rules) and normatively dependent upon national legal systems (since it cannot autonomously determine which norms constitute it).

Is there a difference between private national and international arbitration? Even though international arbitration is illustrated as a challenge to the conventional conception of sovereign states as the only subjects of international law[126], states carry on to be the central actors and arbitration agreements and awards are dead letters without the support of state enforcement. On the other hand, there are many other tribunals contributing to the formation of international law.

Which is the legal basis upon which parties can decide that their dispute to be examined by arbitration? It has to be taken into account that international arbitration law is in actual fact "contractarian" in its make-up like judges, international commercial arbitrators have to resolve disputes on the basis of the appropriate legal rules, not on some other foundation, such as their own logic of fairness or of what the law should be.

It is worth mentioning that rendering a decision on the merits, as a rule but not inevitably in the form of a reasoned award identical to a judgment, is not the only function of international arbitral tribunals which means that there is a need to examine their principal function concerning their actual and perceived legitimacy[127].

It has to be taken into consideration that arbitrators have the legal power knowing as "arbitral authority" to bind the parties by issuing an award on the merits like judges[128] which means that there is a need for the recognition of a co-equality of arbitrators and judges.

The legal "arbitral authority" of arbitrators is attributed by the same law as to the one given to judges. The parties' authority to decide solving their dispute by arbitration is

---

[125] Thomas Schultz, *Some Critical Comments on the Juridicity of the Lex Mercatoria*, 10 Y.B. Private Int'l L. 667, 670 (2009) at 688.

[126] Zachary Douglas, *The Hybrid Foundations of Investment Treaty Arbitration*, 74 Brit. Y.B. Int'l L. 151, 162-64 (2003).

[127] Von Hoffmann (Bernd) v. Finanzamt Trier, Case No. C-145/96, Judgment of the Court, 17 (Sept. 16, 1997) ("The services of an arbitrator are principally and habitually those of settling a dispute between two or more parties.").

[128] Andrew D. Hurwitz, When Judges Err: Is Confession Good For The Soul? 56 *Ariz. L. Rev.* 343, 344 (2014) (arguing that judges whose opinions contain factual or legal errors should .freely acknowledge and transparently correct the occasional .goof.); Richard J. Lazarus, The (Non)Finality of Supreme Court Opinions, 128 *Harv. L. Rev.* 540 (2014) (discussing the Supreme Court's practice of revising its opinions to correct errors before the opinions. bound publication).

authorised by the same constitution like the courts. Is the legal "arbitral authority" of arbitrators less legal than the one attributed to judges? Is it essential arbitrators and judges to have the same legal authority to deal with a dispute in order to have two methods of dispute resolution in a single jurisdiction rather than one central such as courts and a supplementary such as arbitration in its present functioning?

Theories of international arbitration[129] focus on arbitral authority rather on arbitrators' procedural powers. It is argued that if arbitral authority is unrestricted, then arbitral justice is expected to be unpredictable and arbitrary[130]. Are arbitral awards not just unreasonable, but also depart from the rule of law in favour of rule along with the will of the decision-maker? Is not arbitration part of the rule of law?

On the other hand, arbitration is emerged as a quicker and more legally effective alternative to courts dispute mechanism rather than a method to get illegal decisions. Arbitrators' awards are based on the same legal rules applied by courts' judges rather than upon alternative legal rules circulated in the same jurisdiction were both dispute methods are implemented. Is it legal and fair to consider only courts as the sole legal dispute mechanism?

Has arbitration emerged as the bypassing route away from the rule of law? Joshua Karton[131] argues that "resolution of international disputes via arbitration would work in opposition to the rule of law, a concern that is particularly severe with respect to investor-state arbitration." It is worth mentioning that international arbitration has been both praised and criticized for revealing a sort of "lawlessness[132]." On the other hand, in practice arbitrators have issued awards grounded in established legal principles rather than upon illegal grounds[133]. International arbitrators issue awards that are conscientious in their application of the governing law and constrain arbitral behaviour linked to

---

[129] Thomas J. Stipanowich, The Arbitration Penumbra: Arbitration Law and the Rapidly Changing Landscape of Dispute Resolution, 8 *Nev. L.J.* 427, 435-36 (2007) (listing four elements of arbitration as (a) a process to settle disputes between parties; (b) a neutral third party; (c) an opportunity for the parties to be heard; and (d) a final, binding decision, or award by the third party after the hearing.).

[130] Timothy A.O. Endicott, Arbitrariness, 27 *Can. J. L. & Jurisprudence* 49 (2014).

[131] *Joshua Karton,* The Structure Of International Arbitration Law And The Exercise Of Arbitral Authority, 2015, 8(2) *Contemp. Asia Arb. J.* 229 at: http://ssrn.com/abstract=2699477 p 234 "The national and international laws that collectively govern international commercial arbitration do not directly empower international arbitral tribunals, nor do they impose any duties upon arbitrators to exercise their authority over the merits of disputes in any particular manner. Rather, they empower the parties to agree to establish a tribunal and confer powers upon it, and then enforce the express and implied terms of that agreement within certain limits. Accordingly, any determinations as to the proper exercise of international arbitrators' authority must be made based on parties' arbitration agreement in the individual arbitration. Any obligations of arbitrators as to the exercise of their authority arise from the parties' agreement, are owed to the parties, and are enforceable only by the parties."

[132] Phillip J. McConnaughay, The Risks and Virtues of Lawlessness: A "Second Look" at International Commercial Arbitration, 93 *Northwestern L. Rev.* 453, 502 (1999); Delissa A. Ridgway, International Arbitration: The Next Growth Industry, 54 *Disp. Resol. J.* 50, 52 (1999).

[133] Yves Dezalay & Bryant G. Garth, *Dealing in Virtue* 36 (1996) (calling today's leading arbitrators "technically better equipped in procedure and substance"); James R. Faulconbridge & Daniel Muzio, Legal Education, Globalization, and Cultures of Professional Practice, 22 *Geo. J Legal Ethics* 1335, 1349-52 (2009).

arbitrators' management of the dispute resolution procedure in order to avoid the formality of litigation but not against legality[134].

It is argued that arbitral decision-making remains more open to the effect of subjective and contextual factors than judicial decision-making[135]. On the other hand, the arbitral decision-making does not based on illegal rationale but merely there is an interpretation of the same legal rules and principles of law within the context of the rule of law. The legality of awards is specified by the applicable rules of arbitration. The tendency to consider courts and litigation as the sole legal and fair dispute mechanism is very biased against the advancement of courts. The emergence of arbitration as a co-equal and independent to courts dispute mechanism within the same jurisdiction will contribute to a quicker, economically more effective overall justice system.

Commercial parties do not desire "the open-textured discretion of international arbitration's past . . . businesses use international arbitration to provide a neutral, adjudicative dispute resolution process where arbitrators independently apply the law to facts and this in turn promotes the legitimacy of international arbitration[136]."

It is obvious that Arbitrators have to decide in line with precise and rightful characterizations of the applicable legal rules. It has to be taken into account that due to ratifying treaties and enacting statutes, states establish a legal space within which privately-created obligations are supreme which means that there is a legal environment within which arbitration is functioning.

International arbitration law is structurally similar to the contract law found in any national jurisdiction which means that there is a harmonized global legal environment for the functioning of arbitration as an alternative dispute system.

Has it made such an international effort to establish an alternative dispute system as merely supplementary to courts? It is evident that many treaties and international arbitration do attribute a role for national courts concerning arbitration as a safeguard of law. Arbitration seems to be legitimized by a private normative order, by national law, or by a transnational legal order[137].

---

[134] Thomas Schultz & Robert Kovacs, The Law is What the Arbitrator Had For Breakfast: On the Determinants of Arbitrator Behavior, in *Selected Topics In International Arbitration – Liber Amicorum For The 100th Anniversary Of The Chartered Institute Of Arbitrators* (J.C. Betancourt ed., forthcoming 2016) (discussing the incentives that shape international arbitral decision-making); Sergio Puig, Social Capital In the Arbitration Market, 25 *Eur. J. Int'l L.* 387 (2014) (arguing that social networks, rather than work product, are the dominant factor in appointments to investor-state arbitration tribunals).

[135] Joshua Karton, *The Culture Of International Arbitration And The Evolution Of Contract* Law 95-96 (2013) (arguing that "The generational shift should not be taken for more than it is. While modern arbitrators are technocratic compared with the previous generation, the relationship between arbitrator and disputing party is such that arbitral decision-making remains more open to the influence of subjective and contextual factors than judicial decision-making.").

[136] Susan D. Franck, The Role of International Arbitrators, 12 *ILSA J. Int'l & Comp. L.* 499, 504 (2006). Joshua Karton, The Arbitral Role in Contractual Interpretation, 6 *J. Int'l Disp. Settlement* 4, 30-31 (2015).

[137] Stephan W. Schill, Developing a Framework for the Legitimacy of International Arbitration, in Legitimacy: *Myths, Realities, Challenges*, 789, 803-09 (Albert Jan van den Berg ed., 2015).

According to the consensual theory, international arbitral tribunals derive their authority entirely from the parties' agreement as a fully autonomous legal order, with national courts and national laws having no inherent role except as an enforcement mechanism and so it is supposed denying any essential role for states and state laws. On the other hand, national law and states create the legal background which the parties can utilize in order to contract.

The consensual theory is in agreement with the central role of party autonomy in international arbitration law, and the parties' arbitration agreement is indisputably the immediate source of the arbitrators' authority.

Does international arbitration leads to denigration of national courts and legal systems? The parties' agreement to arbitrate grants upon tribunals the authority to deliver legally binding awards because states are employing their judicial machinery to enforce those awards. Litigation concerning civil law disputes occurs after the application of a party to the court. It has to be taken into consideration that, provided that courts have the authority —under their own national laws—to stay arbitrations, to remove arbitrators, to refuse to enforce arbitration agreements and to annul arbitral awards, tribunals cannot be said to derive their power exclusively from the parties' agreement. Regardless that states have moved away from close regulation of international arbitral awards, national courts assert themselves over international arbitral tribunals at various points in the process[138].

Is international arbitration truly autonomous from national legal systems? Are courts autonomous by their own will? The constitution authorizes courts autonomy as an independent legal system. The constitution authorizes arbitration as a dispute system and parties can voluntarily comply without and courts' involvement without attributing real autonomy. The law allows courts' intervention in arbitral procedure signifying the non-autonomous of arbitration as a legal system according to the essence specified above. An international arbitration takes place somewhere existing to the degree that a single national legal order that of the jurisdiction that is the seat of the arbitration authorizes it to exist[139].

The jurisdictional theory portrays arbitral tribunals in effect as adjuncts to the courts of the seat. The New York Convention[140], which provides for the near-global enforceability of arbitration agreements and arbitral awards, is the only codified legal basis on which awards are delocalized but under the New York Convention, all awards are "made" in the jurisdiction where the award was rendered. The Convention applies when an award made in one contracting state is enforced in another state.

---

[138] R. Delaume, Law and Practice of Transnational Contracts 282 (1988) Jan Paulsson, Why Good Arbitration Cannot Compensate for Bad Courts, 30 *J. Int'l Arb*. 345 (2013).

[139] Hong-Lin Yu, Explore the Void – An Evaluation of Arbitration Theories: Part 1, 7(6) *Int'l Arb. L. Rev.* 180 (2004); Hong-Lin Yu, Explore the Void – An Evaluation of Arbitration Theories: Part 2, 8(1) *Int'l Arb. L. Rev.* 14 (2005) at 19-22. . Emmanuel Gaillard, Theory of International Arbitration (2010), published originally in *French as Aspects Philosophiques Du Droit De L'arbitrage* International (2008) at 35-39.

[140] Convention on the Recognition and Enforcement of Foreign Arbitral Awards, June 10, 1958, 21 *U.S.T.* 2517, 330 *U.N.T.S.* 38.

Since the appearance of arbitration as a way for the resolution of international commercial disputes, state court intervention in international arbitrations has been an existential interest —too much interference and the parties' choice to have their dispute resolved by arbitration rather than in court is undermined[141]. The refusal by the courts of one country to enforce an international arbitration agreement thwarts the rationale of such an agreement jeopardizing the motivation and aptitude of businessmen to enter into international commercial agreements which indicate the need for the real autonomy of arbitration as an independent and co-equal to courts as a dispute mechanism.

The parties themselves are the exclusive source of the arbitrators' authority for the reason that states have enacted rules that authorize the parties to confer legal powers and obligations upon arbitral tribunals. In other words, the jurisdiction itself authorizes arbitration but not as an independent dispute mechanism such as courts. Joshua Karton[142] argues that "although international commercial arbitration does not constitute a legal system, the typology of primary and secondary rules can nevertheless be applied to international commercial arbitration to useful effect."

Has arbitration gained its independence via its effectiveness implementing the needs of trade? Arbitrators' authority to bind the parties is not totally dependent upon national courts' enforcement of awards, but before an award has been recognized by a state, it is only binding upon the parties by virtue of their contractual obligations to each other via the arbitration agreement, which compels the parties to conform to the decision of the tribunal.

Does arbitration produce res judicata? Can arbitration by producing res judicata to be considered as a legal system? Has arbitration proven its worthiness as a dispute system? Has arbitration gained characteristics identical to courts in order to be considered as a legal system? What is the foundation of courts? Constitution is the foundation of courts and parties apply to courts for the resolution of their civil law disputes. What is the foundation of arbitration? Constitution is the foundation of arbitration and parties apply to arbitration for the resolution of their civil law disputes by their mutual agreement.

Is there allocation of responsibility between state courts and arbitrators? Arbitrators as private individuals take on the authority to adjudicate the affairs of others and so they bind others with definitive judgments. Where does arbitrators' authority come from? Who makes the decision with regard to the existence or scope of that arbitrators' authority? Arbitrators are more expert better interpreting and applying rules and so inferring that the parties intended the agreement to reflect that understanding/

---

[141] *Scherk v. Alberto-Culver*, 417 U.S. 506, 516-17 (1974).

[142] Joshua Karton, The Structure Of International Arbitration Law And The Exercise Of Arbitral Authority, 2015, 8(2) *Contemp. Asia Arb. J.* 229 at 250 at: http://ssrn.com/abstract=2699477.

perception[143]. Moreover, arbitrators are "well situated" to solve the question of "what *kind of arbitration proceeding* the parties agreed to[144]."

It could be said that the arbitral procedure, as a "matter of contract," rests on a principal finding of "consent," being an issue for judicial determination which means that arbitration from its first beginning is matter for a court's decision plummeting any standpoint about the alternative and independence of the arbitration. On the one hand, the parties by their agreement decide to solve their dispute by arbitration which is supposed to means the whole process. On the other hand, the possibility of courts intervention by law in the whole arbitral process diminishes the parties' agreement for arbitration. The parties' agreement should mean that the whole process has to be solved conclusively by arbitration excluding courts. In reality the parties' agreement authorizes the courts' intervention and the courts' intervention cannot be excluded by parties' agreement.

Can parties by agreement to agree on the exclusion of courts' intervention? Is there any difference in the legality between arbitration and courts? Is the application of law by judges more legal than the application of the same law by arbitrators? Is arbitration less legal than courts? The law by itself identifies the legal status of arbitration by specifically allowing the court's intervention. It is argued that the public nature of appointment of judges means that they bring justice.

In effect, the concept of arbitrability[145] is a public-policy limitation upon the scope of arbitration as a method of settling disputes. The entire "arbitrability" inquiry *unavoidably hinges on—would indeed rationally depend on—* the principal substantive issues of the dispute[146]. The NYC provides for the law of arbitrability only from the perspective of enforcement. The NYC of 1958, by far the most important convention on arbitration, recognizes this desire in Article V(2) (a). Under this provision, courts are directed to apply the laws of their own states when determining the arbitrability of a dispute.[147] Thus,

---

[143] *Howsam v. Dean Witter Reynolds, Inc.*, 537 U.S. 79, 85 (2002).

[144] *Green Tree Financial Corp. v. Bazzle*, 539 U.S. 444, 452–53 (2003). *Blue Cross Blue Shield of Mass., Inc. v. BCS Ins. Co.*, 671 F.3d 635, 639–40 (7th Cir. 2011) (noting post-*Bazzle* authority leaves it to arbitrators to order consolidation remains "in place"; it is for the tribunal to "both interpret the contract and exercise any discretion that the contract allows"); Alan Scott Rau, "Gap Filling" by Arbitrators, in ICCA Congress Series Volume 18: *Legitimacy: Myths, Realities, Challenges* 935, 990 n.185 (Albert Jan van den Berg ed., 2015) (*Bazzle* may be "left intact" with respect to arbitral orders for the consolidation of related arbitrations).

[145] John James Barceló III, Substantive and Procedural Arbitrability in Ad Hoc Investor- State Arbitration—*BG Group v. Argentina*, in *Contemporary Issues in International and Mediation: The Fordham Papers* 355, 360, 362 (Arthur W. Rovine ed., 2015) ("All these and similar preconditions represent 'claims selecting rules' not preconditions to the formation or validity or scope of the arbitration agreement[;] . . . [t]hese issues thus have a 'procedural' cast.").

[146] Thomas Stipanowich, Of "Procedural Arbitrability": The Effect of Noncompliance with Contract Claims Procedures, 40 *S.C. L. Rev.* 847, 861–64 (1989).

[147] Article V(2)(a) applies only when recognition and enforcement of an award is sought. Belgian courts and commentators have suggested that a different conflict of laws rule would apply to the issue of arbitrability under Article II(1) of the NYC, which governs the recognition of arbitration agreements. See Court of Appeals of Brussels, 14 *Y.B. Com. Arb.* 93, 94 (1989); Commercial Court of Brussels, Parbelux c/ Jean Patou Parfums, *Revue du droit commercial belge* 1118, 1119 (1993); Socitti Van Hopplynus c/ socitti Cohrent, *Revue de l'arbitrage* 311, 315–16 (1995); Bernard Hanotiau, "The Law Applicable to arbitrability in Improving the Efficiency of Arbitration Agreements and Awards" 146, 163 (ICCA Congress Series No. 9, 1999). According to this view, when courts are asked to enforce an arbitration agreement (as opposed to an arbitration award) as

the law itself attributes to the courts the supervision and assistance in order arbitration to be workable which means that arbitration is under the inspection of courts. Moreover, in-arbitrability correlates to the natural limitations of arbitration as a dispute resolution mechanism of consensual character rather than to public policy.[148]

The *res judicata* upshot of an arbitral award is significant in international arbitration since parties to a dispute mostly choose arbitration to get a final and binding resolution to their existing or potential disputes. National courts reconcile the issue preclusion in subsequent judgments by applying the traditional elements of preclusion making certain the issue of preclusion in arbitration when it is justified[149].

It is argued that arbitration is in many ways a creature of private law and a force for privatization of law[150] but the foundation of public arbitration laws rests on national courts[151]. Other than supporting arbitration at "the front end" by enforcing arbitration agreements, modern laws necessitated court support in the "middle" and in the "back end" by assisting parties to choose arbitrators or aiding arbitral tribunals with service of process and discovery, and entailing recognition and enforcement of arbitration awards[152]. It is worth mentioning here that without courts, it is implausible international arbitration would operate at all, apart from where reputational incentives avail to coerce losing parties into complying with arbitral awards. That is not to say that arbitration co-operates with courts on a daily basis, but rather, that the prospect of court intervention allows arbitration to function.

3. CHARACTERISTICS OF MODERN ARBITRATION

Arbitration provides significant advantages to parties as compared to litigation[153]. Courts uphold public participation in the development and administration of the rule of

---

an exception to their jurisdiction they should apply to arbitrability the law applicable to the arbitration agreement in general i.e., the law chosen by the parties. The basic argument is that Article II(1), in contrast to Article V(2)(a), is silent on the issue of which law governs the question of arbitrability.

148 Arbitration laws define inarbitrability on the basis that the dispute is "permissible to compromise" (Belgian Judicial Code Art. 1676(1)), or that the legal consequences which "the parties cannot freely dispose" (The Netherlands Arbitration Act Art. 1020(3)) or that the rights in question "cannot be disposed by the parties" (Italian Code of Civil Procedure Art. 806 and Greek Code of Civil Procedure Art. 867). German ZPO Art. 1030 (define arbitrability by reference to "economic interest"), Swiss Private International Law Act (PILA) Art. 177("property"), French Civil Code 2060, Arbitration Fairness Act of 2007/2011 (effort to severely restrict the scope of arbitrability on public policy considerations).

149 Sabrina M. Sudol, 'The U.N. Convention on the Recognition and Enforcement of Foreign Arbitral Awards and Issue Preclusion: A Traditional Collateral Estoppel Determination' (2004) 65 *U. Pitt. L. Rev.* 931, 940.

150 Restatement (Third) U.S. Law of Int'l Comm. Arb. Rep. Mem. TD No 1 (2010) (discussing the international, federal, and state laws that make up the "legal landscape of international commercial arbitration in the U.S.").

151 Ian Macneil, American Arbitration Law: Reformation--Nationalization—Internationalization, Part I (1992). *Buckeye Check Cashing, Inc. v. Cardegna*, 546 U.S. 440, 443 (2006).

152 *Am. Exp. Co. v. Italian Colors Rest.,* 570 U.S. 228, 242 (2013) (Kagan, J., dissenting) (discussing these three stages of arbitration).

153 Nat'l Arbitration Forum, The Case For Pre-Dispute Arbitration Agreements: Effective And Affordable Access To Justice For Consumers: Empirical Studies And Survey Results 1 (2004), available at

law by allowing parties to bring actions to enforce legal rights. Courts endorse equality, due process, and rationality by operating according to particular rules of procedure, evidence, and substantive law that have been enacted pursuant to statutory or administrative prescription, or which have evolved over time at common law. Legal standards are to be used as the basis and course for decisions, with the principle of *stare decisis* providing a principal constraining mechanism on judicial rulings. Judicial proceedings function at the highest level of formality, with the maximum level of procedural due process[154] protection offered at law. Courts determine facts and then apply law to those facts to generate outcomes[155] and if the decision is wrong, the losing party can appeal to a higher court that will set it right. The availability of appellate review reassures that legal rules are correctly applied and permits the advancement of legal standards. Are all these qualities represented by arbitration in a more informal way?

Arbitration is an adjudicatory process and has the power to enhance democratic governance. Arbitration enhances personal autonomy by providing a means of governmentally enforceable dispute resolution to complement public adjudication.

---

http://www.adrforum.com/rcontrol/documents/ResearchStudiesAndStatistics/2004EmpiricalStudies.pdf (finding that "[s]eventy-eight percent of trial attorneys find arbitration faster than lawsuits," "[e]ighty-six percent of trial attorneys find arbitration costs are equal to or less expensive than lawsuits," "[s]eventy-eight percent of business attorneys find that arbitration provides faster recovery than lawsuits," "[e]ighty-three percent of business attorneys find arbitration to be equally or more fair than lawsuits," "[i]ndividuals prevail at least slightly more often in arbitration than through lawsuits," "[m]onetary relief for individuals is slightly higher in arbitration than in lawsuits," "[a]rbitration is approximately 36% faster than a lawsuit," "[i]ndividuals receive a greater percentage of the relief they ask for in arbitration versus lawsuits," "[n]inety-three percent of consumers using arbitration find it to be fair," "[c]onsumers prevail 20% more often in arbitration than in court," "[i]n securities actions, consumers prevail in arbitration 16% more than they do in court," and that "[s]ixty-four percent of American consumers would choose arbitration over a lawsuit for monetary damages."). H.R. Rep. No. 96, 68th Cong., 1st Sess., 1, 2 (1924) ("[T]here is so much agitation against the costliness and delays of litigation. These matters can be largely eliminated by agreements for arbitration, if arbitration agreements are made valid and enforceable.").

154 *Yu Yun Yang v. Holder*, 368 *F. App'x* 214, 215 (2d Cir. 2010) (stating that due process analysis examines whether the procedures at issue denied a party "a full opportunity to present her claims, deprived her of fundamental fairness"); *Wander v. United Ben. Life Ins. Co.*, 905 F.2d 1541 (9th Cir. 1990) (stating that due process examines whether a party had "a full and fair opportunity to develop and present facts and legal arguments in support of its position"); *Andela v. Univ. of Miami*, 692 F. Supp. 2d 1356, 1373 (S.D. Fla. 2010) (stating that due to discovery and other procedural protections, a plaintiff's "due process right was not violated because he had a full and fair opportunity to litigate his claims in the administrative proceeding"); *Palmetto Alliance, Inc. v. S. Carolina Pub. Serv. Comm'n*, 319 S.E.2d 695, 699 (S.C. 1984) (analyzing whether permitted discovery violated due process by "impair[ing] [the party's] ability to prepare and present its evidence").

155 *Bell Atlantic Corp. v. Twombly*, 550 U.S. 544 (2007). *Ashcroft v. Iqbal*, 556 U.S. 662 (2009). Andrew Blair-Stanek, *Twombly Is the Logical Extension of the Mathews v. Eldridge Test to Discovery*, 62 *Fla. L. Rev.* 1, 36 (2010) (Dismissal under plausibility standard is "effectively just the denial of discovery, followed by summary judgment based solely on the facts alleged in the complaint"). Marc Galanter, Why the "Haves" Come Out Ahead: Speculations on the Limits of Legal Change, 9 *Law and Soc'y Rev.* 95, 96 (1974). Stephen N. Subrin, Fishing Expeditions Allowed: The Historical Background of the 1938 Federal Discovery Rules, 39 B.C. L. Rev. 691 (1998) ("Prior to the Federal Rules of Civil Procedure ("Federal Rules"), discovery in civil cases in federal court was severely limited. The Federal Rules discovery provisions dramatically increased the potential for discovery."). Kevin M. Clermont & Stephen C. Yeazell, Inventing Tests, Destabilizing Systems, 95 *Iowa L. Rev.* 821, 823 (2010) ("By inventing a new and foggy test for the threshold stage of every lawsuit, [Twombly and Iqbal] have destabilized the entire system of civil litigation."). Suzette Malveaux, Front Loading and Heavy Lifting; How Pre-Dismissal Discovery Can Address the Detrimental Effect of Iqbal on Civil Rights Cases, 14 *Lewis & Clark L. Rev.* 65 (2010) (arguing that courts should allow limited discovery in civil rights cases at the pleading stage in order to maintain the viability of civil rights claims).

Autonomy and flexibility in dispute resolution enhance democracy. As mentioned earlier what we now call "alternative dispute resolution," was the norm rather than the exception in the colonies[156].

Generally, the parties will need to decide whether the arbitration procedure will be 'Ad hoc', or 'Institutional'. Where the arbitration is 'Ad hoc', the parties themselves decide on the procedure of arbitration proceedings[157]. Where institutional arbitration is chosen, the procedure set by the relevant institution. However, the parties are free to vary them where the institution is agreeable. Where the parties have chosen institutional arbitration, the place of arbitration is usually the seat of the institution. However, in ad hoc arbitration, the parties are able to decide that the arbitral proceedings may be conducted wherever they wish. The parties may choose from a wide selection of rules of procedure, including those of the national jurisdiction. The rules of the arbitral institution can be used either specifically, or by default (depending on the provisions of the agreement for arbitration services), or in amended form by the parties. Ad hoc arbitration remains a prevalent practice in the maritime world, rather than in other sectors of trans-national commercial arbitration.

The use of arbitration expanded rapidly in the second half of the last century because of the rising cost of litigation[158]. Peter R. Sonderby[159] and Robert Coulson[160] consider that arbitration can deliver effective dispute resolution services, while avoiding the cost, delay, hostility and public notice of litigation. The United States Supreme Court validated the use of binding contractual arbitration as a dispute resolution mechanism in many situations in which the parties have neither equal bargaining power nor an ongoing relationship. Consequently, arbitration became common in consumer disputes, employer–employee relations, and practically every other context in which parties order their relations by contract[161]. In fact Amy J. Schmitz[162] says that "Courts developed a "love/hate" relationship with finality in that they hated to give arbitrators final power over cases at the outset, but once arbitrators exercised that power and rendered an award,

---

[156] Susan L. Donegan, ADR in Colonial America: A Covenant for Survival, *Arb. J.*, June 1993, at 15; Bruce H. Mann, The Formalization of Informal Law: Arbitration Before the American Revolution, 59 *N.Y.U. L. Rev.* 443, 468-81 (1984).

[157] A recent research by the University of London School of International Arbitration showed that only 24% of the corporations interviewed opt for ad hoc arbitration, which is perceived as appropriate for "primarily larger corporations with more experience of international arbitration": International Arbitration: Corporate Attitudes and Practices (2006) 12.

[158] Deborah R. Hensler, Our Courts, Ourselves: How the Alternative Dispute Resolution Movement Is Re-Shaping Our Legal System, 108 *Penn St. L. Rev.* 165, 167 n.11 (2003) (citing a report by the American Arbitration Association that "from 1990 to 2002, the AAA's caseload increased 379 percent").

[159] Peter R. Sonderby, Commercial Arbitration: Enforcement of an Agreement to Arbitrate Future Disputes, 5 *J. Marshall J. Prac. and Proc.* 72 (1971).

[160] Robert Coulson, Texas Arbitration: Modern Machinery Standing Idle, 25 *SW. L.J.* 290 (1971).

[161] *Gilmer v. Interstate/Johnson Lane Corp.*, 500 U.S. 20 (1991) (allowing arbitration for an employer–employee relationship); *Rodriguez de Quijas v. Shearson/ American Express, Inc.,* 490 U.S. 477 (1989) (allowing arbitration for an investor– broker relationship); *Shearson/American Express, Inc. v. McMahon*, 482 U.S. 220 (1987) (allowing arbitration of RICO claims).

[162] Amy J. Schmitz, Ending A Mud Bowl: Defining Arbitration's Finality Through Functional Analysis, 2002, *Georgia Law Review* Vol. 37:123, p 133-4.

they loved to enforce the award to avoid burdensome and uncomfortable reassessment of equitable proceedings."

It has to be taken into account that inherent powers of arbitrators are those powers which are considered indispensable to let arbitrators to cope with situations that arise before them so as to empower them to accomplish their adjudicatory functions, but which are not conferred by the rules from which their ability depends and so such rules are contained in the law of the seat of the arbitration, the institutional rules and the agreement of the parties[163]. Moreover, arbitrators need not act like national judges, also when it comes to identifying the rules applicable to the merits[164]. To that extent, party autonomy is eventually subordinate to national law, and that the parties are free to govern their arbitration – and for that matter even to resort to arbitration in the first place – only insofar as that is permitted by State law[165].Moreover, national laws grant the parties discretion with regard to matters pertaining to their arbitration[166]. On the other hand, the Supreme Court[167] acknowledges that party autonomy eventually governs arbitration clauses and "parties remain free to alter arbitration procedures to suit their tastes," including choosing collective arbitration" but courts may not let a contract defense to

[163] Article 187 of the Swiss Private International Law Act, Article 1511 of the French Code of Civil Procedure, Section 46 of the English Arbitration Act, Article 28(2) of the UNCITRAL Model Law, Article 21(1) of the ICC Rules, Article 22.3 of the Arbitration Rules of the LCIA and Article 35(1) of the UNCITRAL Arbitration Rules. Article 187 of the Swiss PILA: "1. The arbitral tribunal shall rule according to the law chosen by the parties or, in the absence of such choice, according to the law with which the action is most closely connected. 2. The parties may authorize the arbitral tribunal to rule according to equity." Article 1511 of the French Civil Procedure Code: "*Le tribunal arbitral tranche le litige conformément aux règles de droit que les parties ont choisies ou, à défaut, conformément à celles qu'il estime appropriées. Il tient compte, dans tous les cas, des usages du commerce.*" Section 46 of the English Arbitration Act 1996: "(1) The arbitral tribunal shall decide the dispute— (a) in accordance with the law chosen by the parties as applicable to the substance of the dispute, or (b) if the parties so agree, in accordance with such other considerations as are agreed by them or determined by the tribunal. (2) For this purpose the choice of the laws of a country shall be understood to refer to the substantive laws of that country and not its conflict of laws rules. (3) If or to the extent that there is no such choice or agreement, the tribunal shall apply the law determined by the conflict of laws rules which it considers applicable." Article 28 of the UNCITRAL Model law: "(2) Failing any designation by the parties, the arbitral tribunal shall apply the law determined by the conflict of laws rules which it considers applicable." Article 21 of the ICC Rules: "1) The parties shall be free to agree upon the rules of law to be applied by the arbitral tribunal to the merits of the dispute. In the absence of any such agreement, the arbitral tribunal shall apply the rules of law which it determines to be appropriate." Article 22.3 of the LCIA Arbitration Rules: "The Arbitral Tribunal shall decide the parties' dispute in accordance with the law(s) or rules of law chosen by the parties as applicable to the merits of their dispute. If and to the extent that the Arbitral Tribunal determines that the parties have made no such choice, the Arbitral Tribunal shall apply the law(s) or rules of law which it considers appropriate." Article 35(1) of the UNCITRAL Arbitration Rules: "1. The arbitral tribunal shall apply the rules of law designated by the parties as applicable to the substance of the dispute. Failing such designation by the parties, the arbitral tribunal shall apply the law which it determines to be appropriate."

[164] L.G. Radicati di Brozolo, Party Autonomy and the Rules Applicable to the Merits in International Arbitration, in *Limits to Party Autonomy in International Commercial Arbitration* (F. Ferrari ed., 2016), 331-362.

[165] L.G. Radicati di Brozolo, The impact of National Law and Courts on International Commercial Arbitration: Mythology, Physiology, Pathology, Remedies and Trends, *Les Cahiers De L'arbitrage - The Paris International Arbitration Journal* 663 (2011).

[166] L.G. Radicati di Brozolo, The impact of National Law and Courts on International Commercial Arbitration: Mythology, Physiology, Pathology, Remedies and Trends, *Les Cahiers De L'arbitrage - The Paris International Arbitration Journal* 663 (2011).

[167] *Epic Systems v. Lewis*, 138 S. Ct. 1612 (2018).

redesign traditional individualized arbitration by mandating class wide arbitration procedures without the parties' agreement.

Does arbitration bring reallocation of jurisdiction over various disputes from civil courts and administrative agencies to privately selected arbitrators? Does arbitration transform a system of public law into a system of private justice? Is arbitration a solely private good or one that falls within public jurisdiction? Arbitration is not a simply private good, but one that falls within public jurisdiction. Martin H. Malin[168] argues that the courts' involvement in an arbitration procedure makes this arbitration a system of public law and otherwise arbitration will be transformed into a private justice system. The Legislative Assembly in Canada specified that the law and the courts will make certain that the parties stick to their agreement to arbitrate, do not proceed unlawfully, and put up with the result when it is given[169] which shows clearly that arbitration is under the mercy and control of litigation instead of being an independent and co-equal to courts dispute mechanism. Exclusive arbitration clauses activate a "private jurisdiction" that point to the beating of jurisdiction of state chosen forums for dispute resolution, such as ordinary courts and administrative tribunals, rendering contractual arbitration both different and exclusive of the later entities and so "contractual arbitration has also been described as creating a "private justice system" for the parties:..."From a theoretical standpoint, arbitration is a private justice system that ordinarily arises out of an agreement. Thus, it has a contractual source and an adjudicative function[170]." Arbitration cannot be a replica of courts. In addition, this author thinks that arbitration by the establishment of an appellate arbitral tribunal as it will be analysed later in the thesis will transform arbitration into a fully self-contained method, co-equal to courts and a parallel civil dispute mechanism.

Will the unique role of arbitration as an effective alternative to litigation be achieved if arbitration does not gain its total independence from courts as a dispute mechanism? The universal decision to enforce arbitration awards without significant review amounts to a policy choice. A party does not relinquish the substantive rights afforded by a statute, it only submits to their resolution in an arbitral, rather than a judicial, forum[171]. Courts

---

[168] Martin H. Malin, Privatizing Justice—But by How Much? Questions Gilmer Did Not Answer, 16 *Ohio St. J. On Disp. Resol.* 589, 627 (2001) (positing that "[i]f courts do not review employment arbitration awards for errors of law, we risk transforming a system of public law into a system of private justice"); ("De novo judicial review of arbitral interpretations of law is necessary to . . . ensure that arbitration does not result in contracting out of statutory compliance.").

[169] Ontario, Legislative Assembly, *Official Report of Debates (Hansard),* (5 November 1991) at 1550 (Hon. Howard Hampton). "Further policy debates leading to the enactment of these powerful legislative tools belie many legislators' intentions to increase the use of arbitration as a way to off-set the use of public resources in resolving certain civil matters as well as some legislators' views that arbitration should even be mandated for some commercial circumstances."

[170] *Dell Computer Corp. v. Union des consommateurs,* 2007 SCC 34, at paras. 132- 133 (references omitted) at para. 200 Bastarache and LeBel JJ state that "the effect of exclusive arbitration clauses is to create a 'private jurisdiction' that implicates the loss of jurisdiction of state-appointed authorities for dispute resolution, such as domestic courts and administrative tribunals." *Rogers Wireless Inc. v. Muroff,* 2007 SCC 35.

[171] *Mitsubishi Motors Corp. v. Soler Chrysler-Plymouth, Inc.,* 473 U.S. 614, 628 (1985).

respect party autonomy and they see intense deference to arbitral awards as needed to protect the parties' choice of arbitration as an alternative to adjudication. The US Supreme Court[172] specified that arbitration procedure should not be subject to delay and impediment in the courts. Otherwise arbitration remains vulnerable to traditional judicial distrust that hindered enforcement of arbitration agreements under common law[173]. The drafters of FAA sought to enclose judicial oversight by intentionally crafting a uniform state and federal remedial scheme based on a unique brand of finality defined through limited judicial review which is very doubtful that brings finality in order to preserve independence of arbitration[174]. In the U.S., policy choices concerning the appropriate use of arbitration have been made judicially, not legislatively. These judicial policy choices appear to reflect the interest of the courts in reducing the judicial caseload[175] but not letting arbitration free to manage its own affairs.

Errors in law are significant and arbitration opinions and awards should be subject to some sort of review. This author will argue in this work for the establishment of an appellate arbitral tribunal that can review an award and it is not imperative a court to review an award. Finality of awards is also important and so an appellate arbitral tribunal can expedite the whole process.

Arbitration should be made into a parallel system co-equal to courts and the second pole by keeping its own characteristics. David S. Schwartz[176] argues that "...[t]he analogy between federal labor policy and the FAA is faulty Arbitration pursuant to collective bargaining agreements is a part of a substantive national labor policy. It is a quid pro quo for a union's giving up the right to strike, and therefore a 'stabilizing' and 'therapeutic' influence that promotes 'industrial stabilization' and 'industrial peace' nationwide. Arbitration pursuant to the FAA is simply an alternative to litigation." The following analysis will show if arbitration is practically a co-equal alternative to litigation.

---

[172] *Prima Paint Corp. v. Flood and Conklin Mfg. Co.,* 388 U.S. 395, 404 (1967) (deferring to "the unmistakably clear congressional purpose that the arbitration procedure, when selected by the parties to a contract, be speedy and not subject to delay and obstruction in the courts"). Jean R. Sternlight, Panacea or Corporate Tool? Debunking the Supreme Court's Preference for Binding Arbitration, 74 *Wash. U. L.Q.* 637, 684 (1996) ("One of the company's chief goals in selecting arbitration over litigation is generally to avoid a jury trial.").

[173] *EEOC v. Waffle House, Inc.*, 122 S. Ct. 754, 761 (2002) (reiterating that FAA's "purpose was to reverse the longstanding judicial hostility to arbitration agreements that had existed at English common law and had been adopted by American courts").

[174] *IDS Life Ins. Co. v. SunAmerica, Inc.,* 103 F.3d 524, 528 (7th Cir. 1996) (Posner, J.) (noting "Congress's emphatically expressed support for facilitating arbitration in order to effectuate private ordering and lighten the caseload of the federal courts"). Stephen L. Hayford, Federal Preemption and Vacatur: The Bookend Issues Under the Revised Uniform Arbitration Act, 2001 *J. Disp. Resol.* 67, 84-85 (reporting the drafters' concern that expanded review "effectively eviscerates arbitration as a true alternative to traditional litigation," and that opt-in provisions "virtually guarantee that, in cases of consequence, losers will petition for vacatur, thereby robbing commercial arbitration of its finality and making the process far more complicated, time consuming, and expensive").

[175] Marc Galanter, In The Hundred Year Decline of Trials and the Thirty Years War, 57 *Stan. L. Rev.* 1255, 1264, 1270 (2005).

[176] David S. Schwartz, Correcting Federalism Mistakes in Statutory Interpretation: The Supreme Court and the Federal Arbitration Act, 67 *Law and Contemp. Prob.* 5, 17 (2004) at 43-44.

Like public trial, arbitration is an adjudicatory process in which a third-party neutral decides the dispute. It differs largely in that the proceeding is informal rather than formal, and is not bound by traditional rules of evidence or procedure. Thus, arbitrators are free from the constraints of substantive law in either the procedures by which they conduct their hearings, or in the standards they use to resolve disputes[177.] It has to be taken into account that following formal rules does not necessarily bring justice because justice can be brought by the balanced application of rules and customs in specific disputes bringing a fair outcome. It is argued that judicial inspection limits the extent to which arbitration providers can favour their business customers, and in fact may create pressure to increase the level of "due process" afforded clients[178]. In present practice arbitral tribunals require courts to view their procedures as fair, and businesses want assurances that courts will respect an arbitration provider's rules and enforce awards issued by its arbitrators. Accordingly, providers may file amicus briefs defending their procedures, and they may adjust their procedures in response to judicial censure[179]. According to Christopher R. Drahozal[180] "An institution that develops a reputation for unfairness or biased arbitrators risks losing credibility, which courts rely on to recognize and enforce arbitral awards." Therefore, it becomes obvious that arbitration needs courts in order to get credibility for its awards, which means that presently arbitration is not an independent and co-equal to courts dispute mechanism.

Legal scholars have generally attributed the remarkably swift change of judicial heart concerning the use of ADR to the interest of judges in reducing their workloads, rather than new doctrinal insights[181]. According to Richard C. Reuben[182] "ADR represents only a change in forum, not in the substantive rights of the parties." Although the process used in arbitration is adjudicatory, it is a much more flexible process than traditional litigation[183]. As mentioned above, arbitration advantages include neutrality of forum,

---

[177] Soia Mentschikoff, Commercial Arbitration, 61 *Colum. L. Rev.* 846, 861 (1961) (citing a study demonstrating that while 80% of arbitrators believed their decisions should be based on substantive legal principles almost 90% considered themselves free to ignore these principles if justice required).

[178] *Veliz v. Cintas Corp.*, No. C 03-1180 SBA, 2004 WL 2452851 at * 15 (N.D. Cal. Apr. 5, 2004) (rejecting challenge to confidentiality requirement under AAA rules: "The AAA is a reputable arbitration body and the reasons for confidentiality are designed to protect all parties in a dispute").

[179] Susan Randall, Judicial Attitudes toward Arbitration and the Resurgence of Unconscionability, 52 *Buffalo L. Rev.* 185, 222 (2004) (generally describing and critiquing courts' use of unconscionability doctrine to police arbitration agreements). *Ting v. ATandT*, 319 F3d 1126 (9th Cir 2003) (holding that agreement that, among other things, prevented consumer from bringing class action was unconscionable); *Shankle v. B-G Maint. Mgmt.*, 163 F.3d 1230, 1235 (10th Cir. 1999) (refusing to enforce agreement that required employee to pay half of arbitration expenses).

[180] Christopher R. Drahozal, "Unfair" Arbitration Clauses, 2001 *U. Ill. L. Rev.* 695, 741 at 752.

[181] Ian R. Macneil, American arbitration law: reformation, nationalization, internationalization 172-73 (1992) (arguing that judicial policy on ADR is motivated by judicial self-interest in reducing caseloads); Jonathan R. Macey, Judicial Preferences, Public Choice and the Rules of Procedure, 235 *J. Legal Stud.* 627 (1994) (arguing that judicial behavior is likely to conform to judges' rational self-interest rather than to the interest of economic efficiency).

[182] Richard C. Reuben, Public Justice: Toward A State Action Theory Of Alternative Dispute Resolution, 85 *Cal. L. Rev.* 577 p 579.

[183] Kenneth J. Rigby, Family Law: Alternative Dispute Resolution, 44 *La. L. Rev.* 1725, 1733 (1984). Once an arbitrator renders a decision, the parties have available to them only very limited grounds for appeal.

speed, lower cost, informality, enforcement, language, and confidentiality[184]. By contrast, Margaret L. Moses[185] thinks that "Arbitration does not provide the same level of protection as the courts, because, *inter alia*, there is less discovery, an inadequate record of the proceedings, and the awards are unreviewable on the merits. Moreover, because an arbitration award is confidential, it does not develop the law or serve as a deterrent to other potential violators." Arbitration is an attractive alternative to litigation because parties choose their own neutral dispute resolution forum. Moreover, Richard C. Reuben[186] argues that "the arrival of ADR should be recognized as an expansion of public justice, rather than the establishment of a private alternative to public justice." In other words arbitration as a co-equal to courts dispute mechanism will be a real expansion of public justice. Does arbitration allow parties to privatize law[187]? Government supervises and control dispute resolution through the process of judicial review and courts' involvement in the whole arbitration as it will be analysed in the following chapters[188]. Heinrich Kronstein[189] wrote that "[n]o theory in support of organized arbitration can conceal the essential 'lawlessness' of this form of 'private government.'" On the other hand, as mentioned earlier historically in arbitration not only laws are applicable but also commercial customs and norms which are part of soft law recognised by various formal

---

[184] Stephen B. Goldberg Et Al., Dispute resolution: negotiation, mediation, and other processes, 210 (4th ed. 2003) (discussing potential advantages for choosing arbitration over litigation, including having an expert as an arbitrator, knowing the decision of the arbitrator is binding; having a confidential procedure, proceeding in an informal manner, and having the opportunity to save time and money).

[185] Margaret L. Moses, Statutory Misconstruction: How The Supreme Court Created a Federal Arbitration Law Never Enacted by Congress. 2006 www.ssrn.com at 68. Jean R. Sternlight, Rethinking the Constitutionality of the Supreme Court's Preference for Binding Arbitration: A Fresh Assessment of Jury Trial, Separation of Powers, and Due Process Concerns, 72 *Tul. L. Rev.*1 (1997) (critiquing arbitration case-law for increasingly favouring arbitral forums without regard for basic fairness or rule of law norms).

[186] Richard C. Reuben, Public justice: toward a state action theory of alternative dispute resolution, 85 *Cal. L. Rev.* 577 p 641. Frank E.A. Sander, Varieties of Dispute Processing, in *The pound conference: perspectives on justice in the future* (A. Leo Levine and Russell R. Wheeler eds., 1976) "multi-door courthouse." at 65.

[187] Stephen J Ware, Default Rules from Mandatory Rules: Privatizing Law through Arbitration, 1999 *Minnesota Law Review* 703, at 711 "The enforcement of arbitration agreements effectively converts what would otherwise be mandatory law into default law" at 754 "Arbitration privatizes the creation of law."

[188] Kenneth R. Davis, When Ignorance of the Law is No Excuse: Judicial Review of Arbitration Awards, 45 *Buffalo L. Rev.* 49, 130 (1997) remarking that "Arbitration agreements ... diminish the reach of government to supervise and control dispute resolution through the process of in-court adjudication. By carving out spheres of "private government," parties establish their own tribunal, and shape their own decision making process. They do not appear in court and thus do not participate in the state's legal institution. Rather than following the directions of a judge, a state official, they entrust the dispute to private citizens, the arbitrators of their choice." Edward Brunet, Toward Changing Models of Securities Arbitration, 62 *Brooklyn L. Rev.* 1459 (1996). Edward Brunet, Replacing Folklore Arbitration with a Contract Model of Arbitration, 74 *Tulane L. Rev.* 38, 52-61 (1999); Edward Brunet states that "securities arbitration remains lawless.... While securities arbitration surely operates in the 'shadow of the law,' it is clear that the arbitrators need not apply law." Barbara Black and Jill I. Gross, Making It Up as They Go Along: The Role of Law in Securities Arbitration, 23 *Cardozo L. Rev.* 991, 1040 (2002) ("While it seems that an investor may have difficulty prevailing in court under the established law, arbitration panels, on more than an occasional basis, are reaching decisions favorable to investors even where the 'law is clear' that there is no basis for imposing liability on the broker."); Jennifer J. Johnson, Wall Street Meets the Wild West: Bringing Law and Order to Securities Arbitration, 84 *N.C. L. Rev.* 123, 140 (2005) ("there is no meaningful oversight to ensure that arbitrators are applying the law, and limited evidence on the ground suggests that SRO panels may not in fact apply the law").

[189] Heinrich Kronstein, Business Arbitration—Instrument of Private Government, 54 *Yale L.J.* 36, 66 (1944). Heinrich Kronstein, Arbitration is Power, 38 N.Y.U. L. Rev. 661, 699-700 (1963).

laws are applicable as well. A co-equal and fully independent arbitration might cause government courts to improve their efficiency and consequently increasing their legitimacy[190]. In other words, arbitration enhances access to justice by permitting claimants to bring claims they could not afford to bring in court[191]. Furthermore, arbitration is an alternative dispute resolution mechanism permitting parties to settle disputes before a neutral panel in a pseudo-judicial setting rather than a courtroom[192]. The question is to transform arbitration from a pseudo-judicial setting into a fully alternative mechanism co-equal to courts. In fact, the process of arbitration is a mechanism to avoid national court systems. Arbitration is developed as an alternative to the national court systems and has evolved into central method of dispute resolution for contractual issues[193]. Nevertheless, the judiciary is not excluded from the dispute entirely because enforcement of an arbitral award requires confirmation by a domestic court and so this confirmation alone could successfully overthrow the speed advantage. To that extent an arbitral award could become the first step in lengthy national litigation, for a party and so evoking the entire national legal system at the enforcement stage[194]. Hence, enforcement may hinder the finality of the dispute and may damagingly influence the alleged cost-cutting advantage of arbitration. Consequently in the enforcement stage a court may increase its role in the arbitration process as it deems suitable and controlling arbitration at the enforcement stage.

Arbitration is distinguishable from litigation for the reason that its procedures may be tailored to an individual dispute and may produce determinations based not on strict legal rules, but on equity, norms, and customs. Arbitration is a creature of contract[195]. Courts state that arbitrators need not follow the law which has been described as involving decisions based on equity and fairness rather than legal obligation[196].

---

[190] E. Gary Spitko, Judge Not: In Defense of Minorityculture Arbitration, 77 *Wash. U. L.Q.* 1065, 1082 (2000).

[191] Theodore Eisenberg and Elizabeth Hill, Arbitration and Litigation of Employment Claims: An Empirical Comparison, *Disp. Resol. J.*, Nov. 2003/Jan. 2004, at 44, 45. *Allied-Bruce Terminix Cos. v. Dobson*, 513 U.S. 265 (1995) "arbitration's advantages often would seem helpful to individuals, say, complaining about a product, who need a less expensive alternative to litigation." *Circuit City Stores, Inc. v. Adams*, 532 U.S. 105, 123 (2001) ("Arbitration agreements allow parties to avoid the costs of litigation, a benefit that may be of particular importance in employment litigation, which often involves smaller sums of money than disputes concerning commercial contracts."). Charles B. Craver, The Use of Non-Judicial Procedures to Resolve Employment Discrimination Claims, 11 *Kan. J.L. & Pub. Pol'y* 141, 158 (2001) ("Fair arbitral procedures can provide a more expeditious and less expensive alternative that may benefit workers more than judicial proceedings.").

[192] 4 *Am. Jur.* 2D § 70 *Alternative Dispute Resolution* (1995).

[193] Thomas E. Carbonneau, The Ballad of Transborder Arbitration, 56 *U. Miami L. Rev.* 773, 773-75 (2002).

[194] William H. Knull and Noah D. Rubins, Betting the Farm on International Arbitration: Is it Time to Offer an Appeal Option?, 11 *Am. Rev. Int'l Arb.* 531, 547-550 (2000) at 547 (noting that in numerous jurisdictions an arbitral decision may only initiate the process of national court litigation because addressing appeals regarding the arbitral award itself are still be unavoidable).

[195] Claude R. Thomson and Annie M.K. Finn, Managing an International Arbitration: A Practical Perspective, 60-JUL. *Disp. Resol. J.* 74, 76 (2005) (noting "arbitration is a creature of contract, [and] it can be customized to meet the parties needs").

[196] Stephen J. Ware, Default Rules from Mandatory Rules: Privatizing Law Through Arbitration, 83 *Minn. L. Rev.* 703, 720 n.82 (1999) at 711 ("Contracting out of law through arbitration agreements does not necessarily mean that such law will be under-enforced in the sense that plaintiffs 'do worse' in arbitration than they would

On the other hand, justice can be achieved not only by the application of formal law but by applying customary usages that have not been formalised being part of the law of a society. In the United Kingdom arbitration has on occasion been defined quite differently: "The law of private arbitration is concerned with the relationship between the courts and the relationship between the courts and the arbitral process."[197] Moreover, Ian R. Macneil says that the word alternative means[198] alternative to dispute resolution processes of the State -- the judges, juries, administrative dispute resolvers, and the like of the State legal system. Consequently, the term ADR presupposes that the main, fundamental dispute resolution system is that provided by the State, alternative methods being secondary, supplemental, and probably suspect. This author considers that an alternative dispute method does not mean that it has to be secondary and not co-equal and consequently it has to have different characteristics but not to be guarded by any other dispute mechanism such as courts. A dispute system as long as it is guarded by another one is not an alternative dispute system but it is rather an assessment dispute method.

Adjudication differs from arbitration in following: First, adjudication is public, while arbitration is private[199]. Second, adjudication is reviewable by courts of competent jurisdiction to minimize the likelihood of legal error[200]. Third, adjudication is bound by rules of *stare decisis*, ensuring that like cases will be treated alike and providing predictability for actors in the commercial bargaining process[201]. Fourth, arbitration is and has been designed for the resolution of factual disputes, not legal disputes or disputes involving significant issues of public policy[202]. This author argues that arbitration as an alternative dispute mechanism should be able to deal with all legal matters and arbitration as the second pole in a sovereign could vest the power of the state in officials and could be viewed as a form of social ordering as well.

Courts are open and accessible for the settlement of disputes but when there is a parties' agreement to arbitrate then courts should remain out of the scene and let the

---

have done in court. In some cases, arbitrators reach a more 'pro-plaintiff' result than a court would have reached ....").

[197] M.J. Mustill and S.C. Boyd, The Law and Practice of Commercial Arbitration in England, 2nd ed., (London: Butterworths, 1989) at 3.

[198] Ian R. Macneil, American arbitration law at 4 (Oxford Univ. Press 1992).

[199] Llewellyn Gibbons, Private Law, Public "Justice": Another Look at Privacy, Arbitration and Global E-Commerce, 15 *Ohio St. J. on Disp. Resol.* 769, 771 (2000) ("The possibility of keeping the arbitral process and award private is one of the elements of alternative dispute resolution that separates it from the public courts, which are presumptively open to the public.").

[200] Owen Fiss, Against Settlement, 93 *Yale L. J.* 1073 (1985) ("Adjudication is more likely to do justice than conversation, mediation, arbitration, settlement ... or any other contrivance of ADR, precisely because it vests the power of the state in officials who act as trustees for the public, who are highly visible, and who are committed to reason.") at 1077 (describing the "guiding presence" of the judge in ameliorating inequalities between the parties, a presence not, well, present in the arbitral forum).

[201] Lon Fuller, The Forms and Limits of Adjudication, 92 *Harv. L. Rev.* 353, 357 (1978) ("It is customary to think of adjudication as a means of settling disputes or controversies ... More fundamentally, however, adjudication should be viewed as a form of social ordering.").

[202] *Atcas v. Credit Clearing Corp. of America*, 197 N.W.2d 448 (1972) ("When the making of the agreement itself is put in issue, that issue is more properly determined by those trained in the law. Issues involving a breach or violation of the agreement, which are primarily issues of fact, can be more properly left to the expertise of those trained in the respective fields of arbitration.").

arbitral tribunal to deal with the dispute from the commencement to the enforcement of the award. It is argued that in private arbitration there is the possibility of "capture" of the arbitrator by commercial interests, and concomitant bias in the arbitral forum[203]. The question is if this suggestion can be easily applicable to courts in another scale and dimension as well. According to O Fiss[204] judges ameliorate inequalities between the parties. By contrast, Andrew W. McThenia and Thomas L. Shaffer[205] argue that arbitration leads to reconciliation of the parties rather than litigation.

Margaret L. Moses[206] indicates that "The FAA would only apply when arbitration was voluntarily agreed to by the parties. According to Cohen, its leading proponent and principal drafter, the legislation was to apply to disputes involving facts and simple questions of law, not statutory or constitutional issues, since arbitration was simply not a proper method for deciding points of law of major importance." Thus, arbitration lacks the status of a system to deal with the interpretation of the law. Besides, Amy J. Schmitz[207] suggests that "Arbitration developed as a means for providing private and self-contained dispute resolution. It was similar to judicial resolution in that it culminated in a third-party determination, but was independent from the judiciary and therefore free to be more efficient and flexible than litigation." Has practice proved this view or arbitration has become merely auxiliary to courts?

The finality of arbitration under the FAA is defined by the limited judicial review provisions in the act[208]. According to Amy J. Schmitz[209] "Finality as defined by the judicial review limitations of the FAA sought to insulate arbitration from courts'

---

[203] James L. Guill and Edward A. Slavin, Jr., Rush Unfairness: The Downside of ADR, *Judges' J.*, Summer 1989, at 8, 11 (1989)("[A]n arbitrator's decision might be influenced by the desire for future employment by the parties.... Some arbitrators openly solicit work. They write to parties noting their availability, sometimes enclosing samples of their awards."); Kirby Behre, Arbitration: A Permissible Or Desirable Method for Resolving Disputes Involving Federal Acquisition and Assistance Contracts? 16 *Pub. Cont. L.J.* 66 (1986) (discussing possibility "that an arbitrator will make a decision with an eye toward his role in future disputes involving one or both of the parties–that is, an arbitrator's decision might be influenced by the desire for future employment by the parties.").

[204] Owen Fiss, Against Settlement, 93 *Yale L. J.* 1073 (1985) at 1077 (describing the "guiding presence" of the judge in ameliorating inequalities between the parties, a presence not, well, present in the arbitral forum).

[205] Andrew W. McThenia and Thomas L. Shaffer, For Reconciliation, 94 *Yale L. J.* 1660 (1985) (responding to Fiss by arguing that ADR techniques are more likely to lead to reconciliation of the disputing parties than litigation). Alan Scott Rau, Edward R. Sherman and Scott R. Peppet, *Processes of Dispute Resolution: The Role of Lawyers* 601 (3rd ed. 2001) ("...the privacy of the process may also contribute to a lessening of hostility and confrontation. An arbitration hearing (unlike a trial) is not open to the public..."). Stephen Goldberg, Frank Sander, Nancy Rogers, Sarah Cole, *Dispute Resolution: Negotiation, Mediation, And Other Processes* 210 (4th ed.2003) ("privacy" of the process one of the "theoretical advantages of arbitration"; Andre R. Imbrogno, Arbitration as an Alternative to Divorce Litigation: Redefining the Judicial Role, 31 *Cap. U. L. Rev. 413*, 418–19 (2003) (noting that arbitration provides "the opportunity for resolution of sensitive matters in a private and informal forum").

[206] Margaret L. Moses, *Statutory Misconstruction: How The Supreme Court Created a Federal Arbitration Law Never Enacted by Congress*. 2006 www.ssrn.com p18.

[207] Amy J. Schmitz, Ending A Mud Bowl: Defining Arbitration's Finality Through Functional Analysis, 2002, *Georgia Law Review* Vol. 37:123, p 132.

[208] *O.R. Sec., Inc. v. Prof'l Planning Assocs.*, 857 F.2d 742, 747-48 (11th Cir. 1988) (highlighting importance of finality to effectuate functions of modern arbitration).

[209] Amy J. Schmitz, Ending A Mud Bowl: Defining Arbitration's Finality Through Functional Analysis, 2002, *Georgia Law Review* Vol. 37:123, p 150.

"Monday morning quarterbacking" and protect the allocation of power in the Act between arbitrators and courts." This allocation of power does not establish co-equal dispute systems but merely arbitration as a semi-independent and assisting to courts system. The conception of finality in the FAA directed courts to take for granted enforcement of arbitration awards with limited procedural review. Additionally Amy J. Schmitz[210] says that 'the independence of arbitration from substantive judicial review preserves its self-contained process, which eases judicial caseloads and fosters the efficiency of arbitration by protecting flexibility of proceedings and limiting judicial appeals." Has current practice produced finality regarding arbitral awards or courts are called to deal with judicial review of awards very often?

Arbitration of commercial and maritime disputes can be a workable alternative to litigation[211]. According to Steven J. Burton[212] "In principle, allowing contract parties to agree to settle disputes by arbitration enhances party autonomy. It expands freedom of contract by allowing parties to contract for an arbitral forum, thus making litigation merely a default method of settling disputes...Arbitration might in fact be more effective than litigation at achieving accuracy of results... Even if there is not greater accuracy of results in arbitration, the parties should be empowered to trade off their interests in procedural fairness and efficiency." It has to be taken into account that civil litigation system has a one-size-fits-all procedure, in each jurisdiction, embodied in generally applicable procedural rules sacrificing procedural fairness and accuracy in some cases in the name of judicial efficiency. In judging the qualities of arbitration and courts as dispute systems has to be taken into account the view of Edward A. Dauer[213] who argues that "The trade-off between efficiency and justice is not in itself necessarily a bad thing. . . . The far bigger problem comes . . . from the difference between justice and satisfaction. . . . What seems fair depends upon what one expects." Does satisfaction bring justice or does justice bring satisfaction? It is obvious that nobody should expect arbitration to become a duplicate of courts following the footsteps of litigation. Has arbitration become an autonomous method of settling disputes since courts have got the last word in arbitration with the judicial review of awards?

---

[210] Amy J. Schmitz, Ending A Mud Bowl: Defining Arbitration's Finality Through Functional Analysis, 2002, *Georgia Law Review* Vol. 37:123, p 157.

[211] *Berkovitz v. Arbib and Houlberg, Inc.*, 130 N.E. 288, 290 (1921) (*Cardozo, J.*) ("Arbitration is a form of procedure whereby differences may be settled.").

[212] Steven J. Burton, The New Judicial Hostility to Arbitration: Federal Preemption, Contract Unconscionability, and Agreements to Arbitrate, 2007 University of Iowa Legal Studies Research Paper Number 07-01, p13,16.

[213] Edward A. Dauer, Justice Irrelevant: Speculation on the Causes of ADR, 74 *S.C. L. Rev.* 83, 98 (2000).

Chapter 2

INTERNATIONAL COMMERCIAL ARBITRATION

1. INTRODUCTION

Taking into account the character of international trade relation, which is "organically" exemplified by speed and the necessity for fast solution and naturally cannot wait for the long and complicated judicial process, that is why arbitration, as a trial that takes place "outside the state judicial sphere" is more attractive and a better prospect for the international business,

An agreement by the parties to submit any dispute between them to arbitration is the foundation stone of modern international commercial arbitration. International commercial arbitration is consensual: arbitration only occurs pursuant to an arbitration agreement between the parties. International arbitration is a consensual means of dispute resolution, by a non-governmental decision–maker, that produces a legally binding and enforceable ruling. It is argued that International Arbitration, being a successful mechanism in international trade, established by the will of the parties in conflict and guaranteed by the national legal orders. Additionally, the U.S. Supreme Court, stated that "an agreement to arbitrate before a specified tribunal [is], in effect, a specialized kind of forum-selection clause that posits not only the situs of suit but also the procedure to be used in resolving the dispute."[214] Moreover, there are many other definitions of international commercial arbitration[215]. Most arbitration agreements are included as standard clauses in commercial contracts and provide for the arbitration of any dispute that may arise in the future between the parties within a defined category. It is also possible for parties to an existing dispute to agree to settle their disagreement through

---

[214] *Scherk v. Alberto-Culver* 417 US 506.

[215] G Wilner, Domke on Commercial Arbitration, Sec 1.01 Rev. Ed. 1992 "process by which parties voluntarily refer their disputes to an impartial third person, an arbitrator, selected by them for a decision based on the evidence and arguments to be presented before the arbitration tribunal." H Brown and A Marriot, *ADR Principles and Practise*, 1993 at 56-57.

arbitration. This agreement must be in writing and includes an arbitration clause in a contract or an arbitration agreement signed by the parties or contained in an exchange of letters or telegrams.

Arbitration conventions and national arbitration laws by their terms apply to the 'parties' to the arbitration agreement and arbitration rests on consent[216]. In other words, Arbitration is based on the consent of the parties to the arbitration agreement[217]. To that extent, the Panama Convention[218] provides that '[a]n agreement in which the parties undertake to submit to arbitral decision any differences that may arise or have arisen between them with respect to a commercial transaction is valid.' National arbitration laws infrequently address when non-signatories are a party to an international arbitration agreement.

International arbitration is a fruitful and valuable tool in international commercial dispute resolution due to: (a) neutrality and the autonomy of the forum and (b) the enforcement of the arbitral award (New York Convention) that characteristics of international arbitration are both guaranteed by the national legal order and supervised by the domestic judicial system.

Article II (1) of the New York Convention explicitly states that the dispute referred to arbitration does not need to be contractual. Pursuant to Article II (2) NYC, there is only one formal requirement for the validity of the arbitral agreement: it must be in writing. In fact, article II (2) lays down both maximum and minimum requirements as to the form of arbitration agreements. Moreover, technology makes it crucial to interpret article II (2) in a less restrictive manner so as to take account of other means of telecommunication providing a record of the agreement. As recent case law relating to the NYC shows, the development is to accept arbitration agreements: 1) concluded by the exchange of telexes and facsimiles, 2) in cases of renewal of agreement and other connected contracts, 3) contained in the bill of lading and charter party, 4) concluded through an agent, 5) based on sales or purchase confirmation or by reference to general conditions, 6) concluded pursuant to trade usages and 7) entered into by e-mail or other means of electronic contact [219].

[216] Christopher F. Dugan et al., Investor-State Arbitration 219 (2008) ('The consent of the parties is the basis of the jurisdiction of all international arbitration tribunals.'), *Stolt-Nielsen S.A. v. AnimalFeeds Int'l Corp.*, 559 U.S. 662, 684 (2010) (citing 'the foundational [Federal Arbitration Act] principle that arbitration is a matter of consent'). *Dang v. Samsung Electronics Co.*, No. 14-CV-00530-LHK, 2015 WL 4735520 (N.D. Cal. Aug. 10, 2015) (enforcing arbitration agreement by compelling named plaintiff to submit individual claims to arbitration).

[217] Gary B. Born, International Commercial Arbitration 1446 (2d ed. 2014). Alan Redfern et al., *Law & Practice of International Commercial Arbitration* 145 (4th ed. 2004) ('The general rule is that any natural or legal person who has the capacity to enter into a valid contract has the capacity to enter into an arbitration agreement. Accordingly, the parties to such agreements include individuals, as well as partnerships, corporations, states and state agencies.').

[218] Inter-American Convention on International Commercial Arbitration, art. 1 (30 Jan. 1975).

[219] *Shipowner v. Time Charterer*, *YCA*, Vol. 25 (2000), pp. 714-716. *Chloe Z Fishing Co., Inc (US) and others (US) v. Odyssey Re (London) Limited*, Decision of 26 April 2000, No. 99-2521-IEG RBB, *YCA*, Vol. 26 (2001), pp. 910-938. *Richard Bothell and others v. Hitachi Zosen and others, YCA*, Vol. 26 (2001), pp. 939-948, the court

An arbitration agreement does not merely serve to evidence the consent of the parties to arbitration and to establish the obligation to arbitrate but it is the basic source of the powers of the arbitral tribunal. Arbitration offers the parties the opportunity to choose their own judge, in a way which is not possible in court proceedings. A major weakness of the arbitral process is the limited powers which the arbitral tribunal may exercise. An arbitral tribunal must depend for its full effectiveness upon underlying national systems of law. Powers possessed by arbitrators, whilst adequate for the purpose of resolving the matters in dispute, fall short of those conferred upon a court of law. If it becomes necessary for an arbitral tribunal to take coercive action in order to deal with the case before it, such action must be taken indirectly, through the machinery of the courts, rather than directly, as a judge can do. The arbitral tribunal cannot bring multi-party disputes together before it because only courts of law have power to order consolidation of actions. The *lex mercatoria* is utilized primarily by international arbitral tribunals. State-established courts, for their part, must apply state law. State courts only refer to the *lex mercatoria* in cases to enforce awards made by arbitration tribunals[220].

It is worth mentioning that finality is an essential value in international arbitration, and to give the unsuccessful party the prospect to litigate[221] the same issue time and again around the world does not appear to be along the lines of this central objective. To that extent, Lord Mance[222] has recommended that in today's internationalized legal order, there is a need for better coordination and consistency between various legal systems—more, rather than less, reciprocal recognition and enforcement of each other's decisions. Moreover, the Chief Justice of Singapore Sundaresh Menon[223] has said that "[r]ecognising issue estoppel in this context seems eminently sensible, both from the perspective of harmonising the treatment of awards and perhaps even more importantly, the overarching public policy of finality":

2. International Commercial Arbitration and National Courts

International arbitration differs from international litigation in that arbitrating parties determine to a large extent what procedural rules will govern the resolution of their dispute and who will decide their dispute. The legal basis for arbitration lies in an

ruled that no valid arbitration agreement existed since it could not unequivocally establish the intention of the parties to that effect from the documents exchanged among them.

220 G Stoecker, The *Lex Mercatoria*: To What Extend doe sit Exist?, 1990 *Journal of Int'l Arbitration* 101.

221 Renato Nazzini, *Enforcement of International Arbitral Awards: Res Judicata, Issue Estoppel, and Abuse of Process in a Transnational Context* https://ssrn.com/abstract=3249060

222 Lord Mance, Arbitration—A Law Unto Itself? Speech at the 30th Annual Lecture, School of Int'l Arb. & Freshfields Bruckhaus Deringer 1, 14 (Nov. 4, 2015) https://www.supremecourt.uk/docs/speech-151104.pdf

223 Sundaresh Menon, Patron's Address, 81 *Arbitration* 413, 424 (2015).

agreement by parties to submit disputes to an arbitral tribunal specifying not only the issues to be addressed by arbitration but also the jurisdiction of the tribunal evidencing the consent of the parties to arbitrate.

It has to be taken into consideration that the international appeal of arbitration does not eliminate the submission of its regulation to a specific national legal order which means that legal national competent order that will regulate some aspects of this arbitration will be just that of the state in which will be held the activity of the institute of arbitration, or of the state established on the basis of free will of the parties of a contract. Thus, legal regulations of a national legal order would have a deep value for the definition of a range of issues related to arbitration.

International commercial arbitration is similar in important respects to national arbitration. However, international arbitration has several characteristics that distinguish it from national arbitration. Although international arbitration is a consensual means of dispute resolution, it has binding effect only by virtue of a complex framework of national and international law[224]. Much of international commercial arbitration occurs pursuant to institutional arbitration rules. The leading international arbitration institutions are the International Chamber of Commerce, the American Arbitration Association, and the London Court of International Arbitration, each of which has adopted its own set of rules governing the procedural aspect of arbitration. All of these institutes, as well as another dozen or so less-widely known bodies, supervise arbitrations when parties agree to dispute resolution under its auspices. Finally, the UNCITRAL Commercial Arbitration Rules are widely used in so-called ad hoc arbitrations. It is worth mentioning that in recent years, a race towards procedural law has characterized the world of "general" international commercial arbitration[225].

International arbitration proceedings are a close substitute for proceedings in public court systems and the main reason parties choose to arbitrate international commercial disputes is because neither party is comfortable litigating in the public courts of the other's home country and arbitration awards are easier to enforce than court judgments. It is argued that international commercial arbitration is becoming more and more like public court litigation, particularly public court litigation as practiced in the United States. In other words arbitration is turned into a more legalistic process. Yves Dezalay and Bryant Garth[226] consider that:

The legitimacy of international commercial arbitration is no longer built on the fact that arbitration is informal and close to the needs of business; rather legitimacy now comes more from a recognition that arbitration is *formal* and close to the kind of resolution that would be produced through litigation—more precisely, through the

---

[224] Jack J. Coe, Jr., *International Commercial Arbitration: American Principles and Practice in A Global Context* 59–60 (1997) (noting the ability of parties to customize arbitration proceedings, pertaining to both substantive and procedural issues).

[225] Bruno Oppetit, Philosophie de l'arbitrage commercial international, *J. De Droit Int'l* 819 (1993).

[226] Y Dezaley and B Garth, Fussing about the forum, 1996 *L and Soc. Inq* 285, 299.

negotiation that takes place in the context of U.S.-style litigation. It seems that Yves Dezalay and Bryant Garth relate the legitimacy of arbitration with its closeness to litigation and not its individuality and complete independence. Which is the legitimacy of arbitration? The foundation for arbitration is the agreement between the parties to submit their dispute to an arbitrator, and both the power of the arbitrator and the legitimacy of the arbitration proceeding are based on this agreement which is based on parties' right which is constitutional as well[227].

It is worth mentioning that there are some national laws that do not permit at all or tolerate a very limited interference, making certain more independent arbitration systems as, on the other hand, there are other domestic laws that stipulate a much greater control of the judicial system over arbitration. Moreover, the category of not allowing courts' intervention has been formed from the former socialist countries, where the arbitration was based on precise organisms connected with the chambers of commerce of the countries concerned. However, the nature of these arbitration courts was such that excluded in any consideration of arbitral issues, ordinary courts of these countries. It was as such the centralized arbitration system in Albania until the end of 1993[228], which does not allow judicial intervention in any case. Besides, the category of national laws permitting intervention is a characteristic in Latin American states[229], where the arbitrator is legally subjected to a close judicial protection, at all the stages of the arbitral proceedings. Nevertheless, most of the developed countries legislations stipulate a moderate intervention of the state court and in it there are encompassed the legislation of almost all western European nations, and those states which have accepted the New York Convention of 1958.

Are there unjustified interferences of courts with the arbitral process? Despite the central role of the New York Convention, arbitration is still not subject to a far reaching mandatory harmonization and remains unregulated at the international level which means that States therefore preserve a broad freedom to favor it but, equally, also to treat it with distrust. In contrast to court litigation that is influenced by national peculiarities difficult to understand or to cope with for foreigners, arbitration provides a more neutral venue than national courts permitting parties to mold the proceedings to their needs and operates with rules and procedures that are now to a large extent harmonized. It could be said that arbitration has now become almost a transnational system of justice but it has not been transformed into a co-equal to courts dispute system which means a courts'

---

[227] Derek Roebuck & Bruno De Fumichon, Roman Arbitration (2004); Derek Roebuck, Ancient Greek Arbitration (2001). *Green Tree Fin. Corp. v. Bazzle*, 539 U.S. 444 (2003); Gilmer v. Interstate/Johnson Lane Corp., 500 U.S. 20 (1991); *Volt Info. Scis., Inc. v. Bd. of Trs. of Leland Stanford Junior Univ.*, 489 U.S. 468 (1989); *Shearson/Am. Express Inc. v. McMahon*, 482 U.S. 220 (1987); *Rachal v. Reitz*, 403 S.W.3d 840 (Tex. 2013). *Bowater N. Am. Corp. v. Murray Mach., Inc.*, 604 F. Supp. 821, 822-23 (E.D. Tenn. 1984) ("As a matter of black letter law arbitration is a matter of contract, and the contours of the arbitrator's authority in a given case are determined by reference to the arbitral agreement.").

[228] Decree nr.5009 dt.10.11.1972 and later with the law no. 7424 dt.14.11.1990 "On state arbitration."

[229] Kalia Ardian, *E Drejta Ndërkombëtare Private,* 2nd edition 2010, FLESH Publication.

intervention in all stages of the arbitral process. On the one hand, this is not only because private parties systematically have recourse to it, but also because States acknowledge the significance of arbitration in the interests of promoting international business transactions and to a greater or lesser extent favor it, as is witnessed by the almost universal acceptance of the New York Convention on the Recognition and Enforcement of Foreign Arbitral Awards of June 9, 1958[230]. On the other hand, the Convention is very far from enforcing a harmonized regime, since many of the concepts which are vital to its function are not spelled out in detail and remain receptive to diverse interpretations and applications. As well, the Convention does not offer for a judicial or other mechanism able to guaranteeing its harmonized application.

It could be argued that depending on the conditions and the perspective, almost any type of intervention by national courts concerning arbitration is an interference which is the case when a court dismisses an arbitration exception and exercises jurisdiction on the merits of a dispute alleged to be covered by an arbitration agreement on grounds regarding the existence, validity or form of the arbitration agreement or to its effects in the case at hand or to the arbitrability of the subject matter. Moreover, there is interference when a court issues an injunction against the parties or the arbitrators prohibiting the holding or the continuation of the proceedings or adopts a measure removing the arbitrators or when it declares an award null and void or inexistent, not mentioning the case when a court refuses to recognize or enforce an award. To that extent, State courts utilize their prerogatives with regard to an arbitration in ways and for reasons that are not generally shared and that may even be difficult to classify as bona fide. Similarly, given the opportunity, litigants will attempt to leverage on these divergences intentionally by seeking to obtain from State courts measures favorable to them, even if they run counter to what could be regarded as "arbitration orthodoxy."

It is worth mentioning that timely and effective interim measures are an essential element of robust arbitration proceedings permitting to protect parties' rights, property, from prejudice to the process, and to take other actions pending resolution of the dispute with the intention to make certain effective relief in the final award[231]. There are two concurrent ways to obtain interim measures in arbitration: (1) national courts or (2) an arbitral tribunal[232]which means that such concurrence is an exception to a well-

---

[230] L.G. Radicati Di Brozolo, The impact of national law and courts on international commercial arbitration: mythology, physiology, pathology, remedies and trends, (2011) *Paris J. of Int'l Arbitration/Cahiers de l'Arbitrage* 663.

[231] Nigel Blackaby, Constantine Partasides, et al., *Redfern and Hunter on International Arbitration*, 6th edition, Oxford 2015 at 313.

[232] Gary B. Born, *International Commercial Arbitration*, 2nd edition, Kluwer Law International 2014 at 2457; Peter J.W. Sherwin and Douglas C. Rennie, *Interim Relief under International Arbitration Rules and Guidelines: A Comparative Analysis, American Review of International Arbitration*, Vol. 20, p. 317, 2010 at 317; Donald Francis Donovan, The Allocation of Authority Between Courts and Arbitral Tribunals to Order Interim Measures a Survey of Jurisdictions, the Work of UNCITRAL and a Model Proposal, in Albert Jan van den Berg (ed), *New Horizons in International Commercial Arbitration and Beyond, ICCA Congress Series*,

established principle that an arbitration agreement transfers all the disputes within its scope from a national court to exclusive jurisdiction of an arbitral tribunal. Besides, the deviation is rationalized by the fact that in certain situations an arbitral tribunal is unable to offer effective and speedy interim relief, which is the "Achilles` heel" of arbitration illustrating that courts and arbitration as not co-equal dispute systems. It has to be taken into account that involvement of courts prevents the parties from enjoying certain benefits of arbitration such as neutrality and confidentiality[233]but at the same time may generate duplicative proceedings with contradictory results. Moreover, it may also delay the arbitration process particularly in jurisdictions with high corruptive risks.

The Ukrainian legislation[234] for a long time did not prescribe court-ordered interim measures in aid of international arbitration. Nevertheless, with the new edition of the Civil Procedure Code of Ukraine[235] having come into force, it has become reality. Simultaneously, a recent practice of Ukrainian courts inclines towards enforcement of interim measures granted by arbitral tribunals under the New York Convention[236]. Furthermore, the new arbitration rules of the International Commercial Arbitration Court at the Ukrainian Chamber of Commerce and Industry ("ICAC") entered into force on January 1, 2018[237], which include an updated framework of interim measures. Under the Civil Procedure Code the Ukrainian courts are now empowered to grant interim measures in aid of arbitration before and during arbitral proceedings[238].

The effectiveness of private international arbitration, however, is dependent "on substantial and predictable governmental and intergovernmental support."[239] The decision of an arbitrator, however, does not necessarily result in the resolution of a dispute. Parties to an arbitral proceeding will often resort to domestic proceedings in local courts to enforce either the agreement to arbitrate or the award decision reached by the arbitrator[240] which underlines the inefficiency of an arbitral tribunal to produce a directly enforceable award. The place of arbitration determines the procedural law applicable to the arbitration and the extent of the intervention of national courts[241].

Volume 12, 2005 at 203; Grant Hanessian & E. Alexandra Dosman, Songs of Innocence and Experience: Ten Years of Emergency Arbitration, *American Review of International Arbitration* Vol. 27 p. 215, 2016 at 235.

233 Peter J.W. Sherwin and Douglas C. Rennie, Interim Relief under International Arbitration Rules and Guidelines: A Comparative Analysis, *American Review of International Arbitration*, Vol. 20, p. 317, 2010 at 317.

234 Mykhailo Soldatenko, Ukrainian Legal Framework for Interim Measures In International Commercial Arbitration, January | 2018 *YAR* 12 *Young Arbitration Review* https://ssrn.com/abstract=3118553.

235 The Civil Procedure Code of Ukraine, *Law of Ukraine* № 1618-IV dated 18 March 2004 as amended, the last revision on December 15, 2017 on the basis of the Law of Ukraine № 2147-19 ("Civil Procedure Code").

236 Olena Perepelynska, Chapter 10: Ukraine, in Kaj Hober and Yarik Kryvoi, Law and Practice of International Arbitration in the CIS Region, *Kluwer Law International* 2017 at 419-420.

237 *The new arbitration rules of the ICAC* available http://arb.ucci.org.ua/icac/docs/ICAC_Rules_New_en.pdf, Articles 25-29 of the ICAC Rules.

238 https://www.unian.info/society/2300259new-editions-of-three-codes-put-into-force-new-supreme-court-launches-work-in-ukraine.html; Article 116 (7), Article 149 (3) of the Civil Procedure Code.

239 W. Michael Reisman, *Systems of control in International Adjudication and Arbitration* 107 (1992).

240 Andreas Bucher, Court Intervention in Arbitration, *In International Arbitration in The 21st Century: Towards "Judicialization" And Uniformity?* 29, 29–44 (Richard B. Lillich and Charles N. Brower eds., 1994).

241 Model Law (article 1.2): "The provisions of this Law, except for articles 8, 9, 35 and 36, apply only if the place of arbitration is in the territory of this State."

Lord Mustill[242] compared the relationship between the courts and arbitrators to a relay race: Ideally, the handling of arbitrable disputes should resemble a relay race. In the initial stages, before arbitrators are seized of the dispute, the baton is in the grasp of the court: for at that stage there is no other organization which could take steps to prevent the arbitration agreement from being ineffectual. When the arbitrators take charge they take over the baton and retain it until they have made an award. At this point, having no longer a function to fulfil, the arbitrators hand back the baton so that the court can lend its coercive powers to the enforcement of the award.

Therefore, Mustill's view shows that arbitration commences by a court's involvement and ends up by a court's enforcement which means that the parties' cannot avoid the court's jurisdiction for the resolution of their dispute regardless of their arbitration agreement, thus showing a major disadvantage even of international commercial arbitration. According to Thomas E. Carbonneau[243] judicial intervention, in matters of trans-border or domestic arbitration, is antagonistic to the autonomy and functionality of arbitration.

The goal of reducing judicial intervention in matters of arbitration has been the central objective of modern legislation on arbitration[244]. Judicial interference with arbitration, therefore, thwarts the pursuit of international business itself. The ruling of an arbitral tribunal is usually fair and final and so undoing the effectiveness of this process through judicial supervision could eventually result in a society-wide denial of justice. Local court intervention in international commercial arbitration seems to defeat the purpose of choosing a more neutral alternative means of dispute resolution. Experience shows that it is the unnecessary and untimely referral to municipal courts that has resulted in many frustrated arbitrations.

Is there any conflict between courts and the private world of arbitration? The relationship between courts and arbitration should not give rise to any significant conflict. International commercial arbitration depends for its effectiveness upon the support of the law of the place of arbitration, which might be a local law or a national law. There is an interchange between the arbitral process and national law, which is fundamental to a proper appreciation of international arbitration. Such an interchange can take place at any phase of the arbitral process. At the beginning of arbitration, it may be necessary to ask a court to enforce an arbitration agreement because a party seeks to avoid it by commencing legal proceedings, or to appoint the tribunal. After an award has been made, national courts can be asked by the parties to intervene. The losing party may seek to challenge the award before the courts of the place in which it was made, for instance on the basis that the tribunal exceeded its jurisdiction or that there was a fundamental

---

[242] Lord Mustill, Comments and Conclusions, in Conservatory and Provisional Measures in International Arbitration, *9th Joint Colloquium* (ICC Publication 1993).

[243] Thomas E. Carbonneau, The Exercise of Contract Freedom in the Making of Arbitration Agreements, *Vanderbilt Journal of Transnational Law* Vol. 36:1189.

[244] Hans Smit and Vratislav Pechota, *International Commercial Arbitration and the Courts* (3d ed. 2002).

miscarriage of justice in the course of the proceedings. Besides, the winning party may need to apply to national courts for recognition and enforcement of the award.

States assist international commercial arbitration and they are bound to do so by the international conventions to which they are parties. Are states entitled to exercise control over arbitration? A state's control is exercised on a territorial basis, first, over arbitrations conducted in a state's territory concerned and secondly, over awards brought into the territory of the state concerned for the purpose of recognition and enforcement. A state lends its support to an arbitral tribunal operating within its jurisdiction by claiming some degree of control over the arbitral process. States that may be called upon to recognise and enforce international arbitral awards are entitled to ensure that certain minimum standards have been observed in the making of an award. The subject matter of the award should be arbitrable in terms of national laws and that the award itself should not offend public policy[245]. States can apply their own criteria as to the arbitrability of a dispute and as to public policy grounds for refusing recognition of an arbitration agreement or award. As a means of limiting court control of the arbitrability of a dispute, more and more countries are making a distinction between the arbitrability of domestic and of international disputes. According to Gaillard and Savage, such a distinction enables "a dispute to be found non-arbitrable under a country's domestic law, without necessarily preventing the recognition in that country of a foreign award dealing with the same subject matter"[246]. If arbitration is to take place outside of the territory of the court ordering the parties to arbitrate, the country where the ordering court sits will not exercise set-aside jurisdiction. Set-aside jurisdiction is generally vested in the courts of the seat of arbitration. Thus, even if the ordering court's law provides for de novo review, that law will not apply in set-aside proceedings. The final award will also not necessarily come within the ordering court's jurisdiction, because the award creditor may choose to seek recognition and enforcement elsewhere[247].

The dependence of international commercial arbitration upon national systems of law is clearly understood in the context of the recognition and enforcement of international awards. A series of reforms have made international commercial arbitration noticeably

---

[245] S.I. Strong, Enforcing Class Arbitration In the International Sphere: Due Process and Public Policy Concerns, 30 *U. PA J. Int'l L.* 1, 6, 84 (2008) (stating that "[i]nternational commercial arbitration developed primarily as a means of enforcing bilateral contracts, and the vast majority of its policies and procedures reflect that tradition." Many arguments for the benefits of multiparty arbitration "have not been universally adopted as a means of overcoming the traditional view of arbitration as a bilateral, contractual construct."). S.I. Strong, The Sounds of Silence: Are U.S. Arbitrators Creating Internationally Enforceable Awards when Ordering Class Arbitration in Cases of Contractual Silence or Ambiguity? 30 *Mich. J. Int'l L.* 1017, 1086 (2009) ("[P]roponents of international arbitration have long touted its ability to keep proceedings private and confidential.").

[246] Gaillard, Emmanuel and Savage, John (eds.), *Fouchard Gaillard Goldman on International Commercial Arbitration, Kluwer Law International, The Hague* (1999), p. 995.

[247] *Compagnie de Navigation et Transports SA v. Mediterranean Shipping Co. SA*, 21 *Y.B. Int'l Arb.* 690, 694-95 (DTF 1996).

more transparent, meaning that the rules that regulate decision-making are more ready availability to "interested parties," who in this instance are the users of the system[248].

National legislation and international instruments, particularly the New York Convention 1958 and the UNCITRAL Model Law on International Commercial Arbitration 1985, require arbitration agreements and clauses to be recognized and given effect to by courts and the resulting awards to be enforced internationally by national courts. An arbitral tribunal is limited in the powers it can exercise and these powers fall short of the coercive powers possessed by national courts. A state is reluctant to confer on a private arbitral tribunal the powers it confers on the judges in its own courts. The power to enforce an award against a reluctant party is a power that forms part of the prerogative of the state and it is not a power that is possessed by an arbitrator, which shows that arbitration has not established itself as a co-equal to courts' dispute mechanism. The enforcement of awards must take place through the national court at the place of enforcement operating under its own procedural rules, which vary from state to state.

On August 15, 2010, the amendments to the 1976 Arbitration Rules came into effect. The 2010 Amendments to the UNCITRAL Arbitration Rules Regarding Expert Testimony is one of the largest changes to the UNCITRAL Arbitration Rules which permit parties to object to expert witnesses appointed by the tribunal. Article 27(1) of the 1976 Rules and Article 29(1) of the 2010 Rules permit for an arbitrational tribunal to employ experts to submit reports on the issue being determined, after consultation with the parties. Moreover, the 2010 Arbitration Rules are intended at creating a competent arbitral process. UNCITRAL has made adjustments that should tolerate arbitration to uphold its system of efficiency and usefulness when adopted into arbitration agreement.

The effect of the international conventions has been to secure a considerable degree of uniformity in the recognition and enforcement of awards. The reciprocity reservation has the effect of narrowing the scope of application of the NYC instead of applying to all foreign awards whenever they are made. The NYC applies to commercial relationships, which means that relationships that are regarded as commercial by one state are not necessarily so regarded by others and this does not assist in obtaining a uniform interpretation of the NYC. The party seeking recognition and enforcement is required to produce to the relevant court firstly the duly authenticated original award or a duly certified copy thereof and secondly the original agreement referred to in article II or a

[248] William Want, International Arbitration: The Need for Uniform Interim Measures of Relief, 28 *Brook. J. Int'l L.* 1059 (2003) (reviewing rule revisions to make interim relief procedures more predictable and transparent, but calling for more significant reforms). Christopher R. Drahozal, Contracting Out of National Law: An Empirical Look at the New Law Merchant, 80 *Notre Dame L. Rev*. 523 (2005) (reporting results of empirical research that demonstrates parties overwhelmingly choose national law and hypothesizing that national law is preferred because it is more predictable than alternative transnational legal rules). Darlene S. Wood, International Arbitratoin and Punitive Damages: Delocalization and Mandatory Rules, 71 *Def. Couns. J.* 402 (2004) (noting that the ICC arbitration rules are routinely updated to adjust to changes in the "business climate"); Michael P. Malloy, Current Issues in International Arbitration, 15 *Transnat'l Law*. 43 (2002) (noting that "competition among arbitration institutions for the growing number of international commercial arbitrations has moved their respective technical details closer to conformity").

duly certified copy thereof. The task of enquiry before the court in which the award is sought to be enforced is limited and does not enable a party to the said proceedings to impeach awards on the merits. Once the above-mentioned documents have been supplied, the court will grant recognition and enforcement unless one or more of the grounds for refusal listed in the NYC are present. The NYC does not permit any review on the merits of an award to which the convention applies. Even if grounds for refusal of recognition and enforcement of an award are proved to exist, the enforcing court is not obliged to refuse enforcement[249].

The grounds for refusal of enforcement have to be construed narrowly by national courts. As mentioned earlier, the majority of the awards in international arbitrations are honoured and enforced by national courts. Recognition and enforcement may be refused if the national court of the state in which enforcement is sought finds that the subject matter of the dispute is not arbitrable under the law of the state and the recognition and enforcement of the award would be contrary to the public policy of that state. Hence, the public policy exception to enforcement is an acknowledgement of the right of the State and its courts to put into effect ultimate control over the arbitral process. There is a tension between the wish to lend the State's authority to enforcement of awards which contravene domestic laws and values and the desire to respect the finality of foreign awards. Arbitration has customarily been subjected to extensive supervision by courts, even allowing reviews of an arbitrator's decisions on the ground of an error in substantive law[250].

International arbitration is a wholly voluntary and consensual means of resolving disputes by non-state decision-makers, which are empowered to generate a final and binding decision, which is able to find applicability across national courts. Being considered as a private process, arbitration is only an alternative of the lawsuit, but arbitration does not replace the national judicial machinery in all aspects, but it rather coexists with it. Moreover, International commercial arbitration was principally a compromise-oriented process in which "strictly legal considerations [can be] pushed aside for the sake of achieving unanimity among the arbitrators and giving something to both sides.[251]" It has to be taken into account that high rates of voluntary compliance

[249] *Chromalloy Aeroservices Inc v. Arab Republic of Egypt* 939 Fsup 907, *China Agribusiness v. Balli Trading* [1988] 2 LR 76, *Parsons Whittmore v. Societe Generale* 508 F2d 969.

[250] Justice Mason K, Changing attitudes in the common law's response to international commercial arbitration, 18(2) *The Arbitrator* 73 (1999). In *Excelsior Film TV, srl v. UGC-PH*, the French Cour de Cassation (Supreme Court) denied Excelsior's appeal and affirmed the lower court's decision to refuse enforcement of the arbitral award rendered in Rome on grounds of public policy for lack of impartiality of one of the arbitrators. Published in *YCA*, Vol. 24 (1999), p. 644. "The court drew the conclusion that this disloyalty of an arbitrator, who was connected to one of the parties – as revealed in the award, so that it cannot be inferred from UGCPH's failure to challenge this arbitrator that it waived its right to rely on this irregularity – created an imbalance between the parties, amounting to a violation of due process, so that the award rendered in Italy under such conditions violates French public policy in the sense of both Articles mentioned above" [Art. V(2)(b) NYC and Art. 1502(5) of the new French CCP]."

[251] Fredrick A. Mann, The Aminoil Arbitration, 54 *Brit. Y.B. Int'l L.* 213, 214 (1983). Christopher R. Drahozal, Contracting Out of National Law: An Empirical Look at the New Law Merchant, 80 *Notre Dame L. Rev.* 523

ensured that national courts would not be able to glimpse inside the system during enforcement proceedings[252].

What is the appropriate definition of public policy in the context of enforcement of arbitral awards? There is a need for a harmonious international definition of the context of public policy[253]. International public policy is understood to be narrower than domestic public policy: not every rule of law which belongs to the *ordre public interne* is necessarily part of the *ordre public externe* or *international*[254]. Within the broad concept of public policy, the following sub-categories of rules and norms can be identified: (1) mandatory laws/*lois de police*; (2) fundamental principles of law; (3) public order/good morals; and (4) national interests/ foreign relations. International public policy provides the forum judge with a mechanism for the exceptional exclusion of those provisions of

(2005) (reporting results of empirical research designed to test the frequency with which parties contract out of national law by selecting transnational legal principles to govern their dispute). Fulvio Fracassi, Confidentiality and NAFTA Chapter 11 Arbitrations, 2 *Chi. J. Int'l L.* 213, 221 (2001) ("Arbitrations that have broad and far-reaching public policy implications tend to draw attention from media and nongovernmental organizations. Maintaining a shroud of confidentiality over proceedings and documentation simply draws intense criticism and does harm to the legitimacy of the process.").

252 Thomas E. Carbonneau, Rendering Arbitral Awards with Reasons: The Elaboration of a Common Law of International Transactions, 23 *Colum. J. Transnat'l L.* 579, 606 (1985). Alexis C. Brown, Presumption Meets Reality: An Exploration of the Confidentiality Obligation in International Commercial Arbitration, 16 *Am. U. Int'l L. Rev.* 969 (2001); ("In order for the requested court to perform its task of vacating or confirming an award, a party's adversarial opposition to the award generally yields a relatively comprehensive account of the arbitral proceeding and of the basis for the arbitrators' rulings.").

253 *Egerton v. Brownlow* (1853) 4 HLC 1."that principle of law which holds that no subject can lawfully do that which has a tendency to be injurious to the public, or against public good." Cheshire and North, *Private International Law* (13th ed., Butterworths, 1999), p. 123 "some moral, social or economic principle so sacrosanct ... as to require its maintenance at all costs and without exception" *Deutsche Schachtbau-und Tiefbohrgesellscaft mbh v. Ras Al Khaimah National Oil Company* [1987] 2 *Lloyd's Rep.* 246 at 254. "Considerations of public policy can never be exhaustively defined, but they should be approached with extreme caution. ... It has to be shown that there is some element of illegality or that the enforcement of the award would be clearly injurious to the public good or, possibly, that enforcement would be wholly offensive to the ordinary reasonable and fully informed member of the public on whose behalf the powers of the State are exercised." *Parsons and Whittemore Overseas Co., Inc. v. Société Générale de l'Industrie du Papier RAKTA and Bank of America* 508 F. 2d 969 "only where enforcement would violate the forum state's most basic notions of morality and justice." BGH, 12 July 1990 - III ZR 174/89, NJW 1990 at p. 3210. "A violation of essential principles of German law (ordre public) exists only if the arbitral award contravenes a rule which is basic to public or commercial life, or if it contradicts the German idea of justice in a fundamental way. A mere violation of the substantive or procedural law applied by the arbitral tribunal is not sufficient to constitute such violation." *Lew, Applicable Law in International Commercial Arbitration* (Oceana, 1978), p. 532. "... it is clear that [it] reflects the fundamental economic, legal, moral, political, religious and social standards of every State or extra-national community. Naturally public policy differs according to the character and structure of the State or community to which it appertains, and covers those principles and standards which are so sacrosanct as to require their maintenance at all costs and without exception."

254 Sanders, Commentary" in *60 Years of ICC Arbitration - A Look at the Future* (ICC Publishing, 1984). "international public policy, according to a generally accepted doctrine is confined to violation of really fundamental conceptions of legal order in the country concerned." Articles 1498 and 1502 of Title V of the New Code of Civil Procedure (1981). See Mayer, "La sentence contraire a l'ordre public au fond," (1994) *Rev. Arb.* 615. Fouchard, Gaillard and Goldman on International Commercial Arbitration (ed. Gaillard and Savage) (Kluwer, 1999), para. 1648. "The international public policy to which Article 1502.5 refers can only mean the French conception of international public policy or, in other words, the set of values a breach of which could not be tolerated by the French legal order, even in international cases." Decision dated 4 December 1992, reported in (1997) XXII *Yearbook* 725. The Milan Court of Appeal may have had in mind a more transnational concept when it described international public policy as a "body of universal principles shared by nations of similar civilisation, aiming at the protection of fundamental human rights, often embodied in international declarations or conventions."

the applicable law that are incompatible with the legal system of the forum. The arbitrator, who does not deliver justice on behalf of any State, does not have a national *lex fori* and, as a result, does not have to defend the international public policy of a given State against a foreign law. International public policy requires that no effect be given to contracts involved in setting up corrupt transactions or traffic in human beings or organs. Thus, public policy performs a constructive function and affects the reasoning of the arbitrator separately of the applicable law. The international commercial arbitrator has to pay attention to the public policy of the national judge, as is shown by the effect of mandatory rules of law. It should be taken into account that the public policy in question is that of the national judge, not that of the arbitrator. Nonetheless, the arbitrator has to foresee this public policy which constitutes indistinct threat to his/her award.

An arbitral award which violated a mandatory rule of law that was applicable to the contract in question could be set aside or deprived of any effect due to its breach of international public policy. It is not easy to make certain whether the practice of courts is less accurate when asked to recognise/enforce a foreign award than they are when asked to set aside an award made in their own jurisdiction[255]. Doubt and inconsistencies regarding the interpretation and application of public policy by State courts support the losing party to rely on public policy to resist, or at least delay, enforcement. This author considers that international public policy for arbitration between private parties should contain only the fundamental principles of human rights and principles of law such as *due process* which have to be considered as the basis for national public policy as well in order to have a harmonious application of the rule in arbitration and only exceptional morals could be part of national policy in national cases. In the decision 595/2014 the Athens Court of Appeals (*Efetion*) annulled the ICC award as contradicting to the national public policy grounds due to acts of corruption.

Twenty years ago, arbitration was an *ad hoc* compromise-oriented process characterized by its informality and stress on fairness[256].The arbitrator was expected to render a just and equitable result, even if that sometimes meant disregarding the express terms of the contract or the apparent provisions of chosen law authorizing arbitrators to act as *amiable compositeur* and *ex aequo et bono* disregarding the strictures of so-called auxiliary rules, such as statutes of limitations, in order to justice[257]. Professor David[258]

---

[255] *Omnium de Traitement et de Valorisation SA v. Hilmarton Ltd* (1999) [1999] 2 QB 222.

[256] Yves Dezalay and Bryant Garth, Fussing About the Forum: Categories and Definitions as Stakes in Professional Competition, 21 *L. Soc. Inq.* 285, 295 (1996).

[257] Christine Lecuyer-Thieffry and Patrick Thieffry, Negotiating Settlement of Dispute Provisions in International Business Contracts: Recent Developments in Arbitration and Other Processes, 45 *Bus. L.* 577 (2000). John Beechey, International Commercial Arbitration: A Process under Review and Change, Aug/Oct *Dis. Res. J.* 32 (2000). The doctrine of *amiable composition*, which is often translated to mean "author of friendly compromise," has been described as: allowing arbitrators to decide cases in accordance with customary principles of equity and international commerce. This power permits arbitrators to arrive at an award that is fair in light of all circumstances, rather than in strict conformity with legal rules [, but] . . . generally [they] may not disregard mandatory provisions of substantive law or the public policy of the forum state. The doctrine of ex aequo et bono is very similar to *amiable compositeur*, except that the powers of arbitrators are

perceived ad hoc arbitration as "a diffuse, unsupervised, and casuistic process, and harboured no hope that it could foster the development of international arbitration as a discipline "*tant vaut l'arbitre, tant vaut l'arbitrage.*" Nowadays, the legality of international commercial arbitration is no longer built on the fact that arbitration is informal and close to the needs of commerce; rather, legality now comes more from an acknowledgment that arbitration is formal and close to the kind of resolution that would be produced through courts[259]. Arbitral awards are being published and are even making an appearance as influential authority cited to other arbitration panels. International arbitration has emerged as the paramount means for resolving disputes that arise in the ever-expanding international arena. Hence, arbitration is the *normal* way of settlement of international commercial disputes developed into a fully operational transnational adjudicatory process[260].

So the Italian Code of Civil Procedure (Art. 832. (1) (Rinvio a regolamenti arbitrali)) provides that the arbitration agreement may refer to another procedural arrangement of the arbitration, distinct from that of the institution of arbitration where the parties are addressed and in this case the arbitration agreement prevails. Moreover, the legal basis is found in the recognized principle of the autonomy of the parties will in the regulation of international trade relations, autonomy which is sanctioned by many national laws and international conventions[261].

---

slightly broader, enabling them to disregard even mandatory provisions of substantive law in order to reach an equitable outcome. Nicholas de B. Katzenbach, Business Executives and Lawyers in International Trade, in *Sixty Years Of Icc Arbitration: A Look At The Future* 67-68 (1984) (explaining that while arbitration might be a choice for domestic disputes, because there exists in national courts a reliable alternative, the unpredictability and risks of failure in domestic litigation of international business disputes makes international arbitration the only real option).

[258] Sanders (ed), *International Arbitration: Liber Amicorum for Martin Domke* (1967) 57 at 63.

[259] Yves Dezalay and Bryant Garth, Fussing About the Forum: Categories and Definitions as Stakes in Professional Competition, 21 *L. Soc. Inq.* 285, 299 (1996). International Arbitration in The 21st Century: Towards "Judicialization" and Uniformity" (Richard B. Lillich and Charles N. Brower, eds. 1993).

[260] Thomas E. Carbonneau, Rendering Arbitral Awards with Reasons: The Elaboration of a Common Law of International Transactions, 23 *Colum. J. Transnat'l L.* 579, 580 (1985). Martin Hunter, Ethics of the International Arbitrator, 53 *Arbitration* 219, 220 (1987) (concluding that the world of commercial arbitration to be no longer a club of gentlemen, but one that needs explicit guidelines for conduct). W. Michael Reisman Et Al., *International Commercial Arbitration: Cases, Materials And Notes On The Resolution Of International Business Disputes* 1215 (1997) ("Arbitral awards as a whole enjoy a higher degree of transnational certainty than judgments of national courts."); W. Michael Reisman, Systems Of Control In International Adjudication and Arbitration: Breakdown And Repair 113 (1992) (noting that the international arbitration system intentionally minimizes the role of national courts "may shift the real decision-making from the arbitral tribunal to the courts"). Saul Perloff, The Ties that Bind: The Limits of Autonomy and Uniformity in International Commercial Arbitration, 13 *U. PA Int'l Bus. J.* 323, 324 n.11 (1992). Desiree A. Kennedy, Predisposed with Integrity: The Elusive Quest for Justice in Tripartite Arbitrations, 8 *Geo. J. Legal Ethics* 749, 765 (1995) (criticizing arbitration that permits party communication with arbitrators as incompatible with the principle that adjudicators should be impartial).

[261] European Convention "On international commercial arbitration" (Geneva Convention), 1961, article IV / 1 / b / iii - "...in this case, they (parties) shall be free inter alia ....to lay down the procedure to be followed by the arbitrators"; UNCITRAL model law, Article 19 "Determination of rules of procedure": "(1) Subject to the provisions of this Law, the parties are free to agree on the procedure to be followed by the arbitral tribunal in conducting the proceedings."

It has to be taken into account that the role of common state courts in relation to the arbitration consists of two functions: a) Supporting function for arbitration and b) The control function of the arbitration. State courts, as part of the state power, advance the process of arbitration, when this process for any reason remains in place. Moreover, UNCITRAL model law[262] states that every state that adopts the model law into its domestic law, defines in the latter the competent authority that will intervene to meet several functions of the supporting or supervisory character in the arbitration process. In other words, the essence of the model law permits the judicial intervention to support the purpose of the arbitration procedure, when the arbitrators themselves face barriers in critical moments of the process. In Line the Code of Civil Procedure (CCP) of Albania stipulates the intervention of the Albanian national court in aid of the normal continuity of the arbitration process due to the fact that the power vested to the arbitrator does not have the strength of the state court jurisdiction[263]such as the arbitrators cannot obligate a testimony to vow in front of them. Nonetheless, the Code offers several strict criteria to legitimize this intervention. If the parties cannot come to an agreement to fix or solve the problem that has arisen with the arbitration procedure, is permitted court intervention. Accordingly, when there is no agreement between the parties concerning the number of arbitrators, it may be made by the national courts (Article 405)[264]. Furthermore, the exclusion of the arbitrator may be by the national court at the demand of the parties, when there is no agreement between the parties and when the arbitral tribunal cannot decides itself (Article 409). For that reason the Civil Procedure Code requires the intervention of the court, on request, not *ex officio* to take the appropriate evidences for the process, or to call the witnesses and experts, when arbitration is incompetent to execute in practice these important procedural elements. It is worth mentioning that the state court does not judge the opportunity of the security measures (Article 418 of the Civil Procedure Code), given by the arbitrators, but merely rules on its execution[265]. It cannot be excluded a priori the ordinary civil court jurisdiction from the consideration of disputes arising on the basis of the performance of a contract, pursuant to which the parties have agreed to address to an arbitral tribunal. It has to be taken into account that the international jurisprudence is already accepted that the domestic courts have the authority and so play an imperative role in taking temporary measures, based on the

---

[262] UNCITRAL Model Law, Article 6 "Court or other authority for certain functions of arbitration assistance and supervision": The functions referred to in articles 11(3), 11(4), 13(3), 14, 16(3) and 34(2) shall be performed by ... [Each State enacting this model law specifies the court, courts or, where referred to therein, other authority competent to perform these functions.].

[263] Brati, A. *Procedura Civile*, 1st edition 2008, DUDAJ Publication.

[264] Article 405 of the Civil Procedure Code (CCP): "In case of disagreement between the parties and with their prior consent, the arbitration court is formed by an arbitrator or more arbitrators in the odd number, set by the court."

"The Company "International Colliers" ltd v. "City Park" ltd, addressed by the Supreme Court of the Republic of Albania in the decision No. 92/2010. "....the request for insurance of the lawsuit cannot be judged by the Tirana District Court, but by the court of arbitration, referring to the Article 414/2 of the Code of Civil Procedure."

demand of a party, in some limited cases, such as the issuance of intermediate orders, conservation measures (guarantee), etc., which are assessed by the court as fair and suitable[266]. To that extent, Indian Supreme Court on the case of Olex Focas Pvt. Ltd against Skoda Export Co Ltd[267] stated that the state court has jurisdiction and authority to offer interim measures in appropriate matters and in this case, the provisional measure was concerned on the assurance of an ownership dispute lawsuit. Thus, the national courts play an imperative role in supporting international commercial arbitration tribunals, solving critical issues on their activity which means that without the intervention of the state court in this regard, international commercial arbitration cannot be operative.

It is worth mentioning here that Albanian Code of Civil Procedure stipulates the intervention of the state court in the arbitration process for satisfying two functions: that of supporting and controlling towards arbitration. Thus, the supporting function is demonstrated in the power of the court for appointment of the arbitrator, his replacement, supplementing the number of arbitrators, taking the evidence, call of witnesses and experts. The court has the power to take measures to secure the lawsuit raised before an arbitration forum. Moreover, national judicial jurisprudence has clarified the boundaries of this power, stating that to apply to the national court to get a temporary measure concerning a conflict which belongs to the arbitration jurisdiction, established in the arbitration agreement, and is not deemed a breach of this legitimate jurisdiction. Furthermore, the judicial control purpose, in line with the Civil Procedure Code, is completed through (a) the judicial assessment of the jurisdiction of the arbitral forum, not directly as specified by international acts, but indirectly; (b) the state court control of the legality of the award, through judicial review in an appeal against such award; and (c) the state court control on the arbitration process instigated by the judicial recognition and enforcement of foreign arbitral awards. It has to be taken into account that the judicial control, by the Albanian CCP, is offered restrained, only for well-defined causes and only at the demand of the parties, apart from the judicial assessment of arbitral jurisdiction when the national courts can assess even *ex officio* if the arbitration agreement is manifestly invalid. Indeed, it is required a judicial interpretation concerning the "manifestly invalid" term. Additionally, where are seen clear infringements of the settings of the arbitration agreement validity, such as the capacity of the parties to sign the arbitration agreement, the legal principles of this agreement form and content, and the arbitrability of conflict. However, through the supportive and control function is comprehended the assistance of the state courts towards the arbitration course /procedure which it really needs. Besides, the gradually market expansion and international

---

[266] UNCITRAL Model Law, Article 9: "Arbitration agreement and interim measures by court" - It is not incompatible with an arbitration agreement for a party to request, before or during arbitral proceedings, from a court, an interim measure of protection and for a court to grant such measure."

[267] AIR 2000 Delhi 161.

investment in Albania necessitate active presence of international commercial arbitration, to resolve disputes, which are an exceptionally vital part of the market and international trade. Artan Spahiu[268] argues that "There is a need to sensitize the national courts to support the arbitration process, because without this support the international arbitration will remain ineffective."

International commercial arbitration awards are being voluntarily published with ever-greater frequency[269]. It could be argued that the international arbitration community's movement toward greater transparency is part of the system's demonstrable move toward the Rule of Law[270] which contains the danger of arbitration becoming more formal than litigation as a rule-based system. This author argues that a summary of the award containing the legal reasoning should be published enabling the emergence of arbitration precedent[271].

---

[268] Artan Spahiu, International Arbitration, The Advantages And The Role Of The State Courts In The Development Of This Institute An Overview On The Albanian Legislation And Jurisprudence, *International Journal of Social Science and Economic Research*, Volume:01, Issue:09 Page 1300 at Page 1315 www.ijsser.org.

[269] Dora Marta Gruner, Accounting for the Public Interest in International Arbitration: The Need for Procedural and Structural Reform, 41 *Colum. J. Transnat'l L.* 923, 959 (2003) ("Today, several arbitral institutions, as well as independent publishers, have started to regularly publish arbitral awards.").Tom Ginsburg, The Culture of Arbitration, 36 *Vand. J. Transnat'l L.* 1335, 1340 (2003)("Although certain sources for arbitral decisions exist ...they are but the tip of the iceberg of all the cases produced ... and ... the ICC awards are an explicitly biased sample as the ICC seeks to publish particularly interesting or unusual awards."). Michael D. Goldhaber, Madame La Présidente, *American Lawyer/Focus Europe*/Summer 2004 http://www.americanlawyer.com/focuseurope/arbitration04.html (last visited January 12, 2006) ("Because arbitration has traditionally been confidential, the appointing parties and institutions have not, until now, been subject to pressure from the media [to diversify along gender lines].").

[270] Catherine A. Rogers, Transparency in International Commercial Arbitration, 54 *Kan. L. Rev.* 1301, 1314–17, 1319–20 (2006).Richard H. Fallon, Jr., "The Rule of Law" as a Concept in Constitutional Discourse, 97 *Colum. L. Rev.* 1 (1997) (identifying four ideal types of the Rule of Law, none of which captures the nuance and complexity of the concept, but each of which are invoked by various constituencies in arguing for particular constitutional approaches or outcomes). Catherine A. Rogers, The Vocation of International Arbitrators, 20 *Am. U. Int'l L. Rev.* 957, 972 (2005). Donald P. Arnavas and Rt. Hon. Lord David Hacking, Using ADR to Resolve Contract Disputes, 04-11 Briefing Papers 1 (2004) ("Reasoned awards have always been the norm in international arbitration, but with the shift to more formalized and rule -based decision making, awards have necessarily become longer and more detailed."). William W. Park, Income Tax Treaty Arbitration, 10 *Geo. Mason L. Rev.* 803 (2002) ("The marketplace has pushed international arbitration toward reasoned awards."). Christopher B. Kaczmarek, Public Law Deserves Public Justice: Why Public Law Arbitrators Should Be Required to Issue Written, Publishable Opinions, 4 *Emp. Rts. and Emp. Pol'y J.* 285, 287–88 (2000) (arguing for written, publicly available opinions in cases involving issues of public law).

[271] John Beechy, International Commercial Arbitratiion: A Process Under Review and Change, 55-Oct *Disp . Resol. J.* 32, 34 (2000) ("Not long ago, I heard an eminent international arbitrator suggest that recourse to what he described as 'constructive ambiguity' in the drafting of an arbitral award was appropriate and justified if the arbitrator felt that it might bring about a position in which the parties settled their differences."). Bernardo M. Cremades and Steven L. Plehn, The New *Lex Mercatoria* and the Harmonization of the Laws of International Commercial Transactions, 2 *B.U. Int'l L.J.* 317, 336-37 (1984) (suggesting "the formation of institutions which give arbitrators access to prior arbitration awards and require them to follow a more or less strict rule of *stare decisis*"). Thomas E. Carbonneau, Arbitral Adjudication: A Comparative Assessment of its Remedial and Substantive Status in Transnational Commerce, 19 *Tex. Int'l L. J.* 33, 39 (1984); Kenneth Michael Curtin, Redefining Public Policy in International Arbitration of Mandatory National Laws, 64 *Def. Couns. J.* 271, 279 (1997) ("Publication of arbitral awards...is becoming more common, thus alleviating the difficulties associated with a lack of precedent."); Klaus Peter Berger, Internaitonal Arbitration Practice and the Unidroit Principlces of International Commercial Contracts, 46 *Am. J.. Com. L.* 129 (1998) (stating that "arbitral awards more and more assume a genuine precedential value within the international arbitration process"), William Tetley, Mixed Jurisdictions: Common Law v. Civil Law (Codified and Uncodified), 60 *La. L. Rev.* 677 (2000) ("With each passing year there is an ever-increasing volume of reported arbitral awards (particularly in civil

It is worth mentioning here that in the application of the control function of the arbitration, state courts control particular aspects of the process which means that the national courts finally decide concerning issues of jurisdiction of the arbitral forum, when there is no consensus, or when parties oppose the arbitral jurisdiction. Thus, when the arbitrators set aside the contestation of a party involving the jurisdiction of the arbitral forum, then the party addresses to the state court to finally decide on this issue which is against the original parties' agreement to solve the dispute via arbitration and setting arbitration in a second class of dispute mechanism.

To that extent, the power of the state court to decide on the jurisdiction of arbitration is specified in the model law along with in the Geneva Convention[272]. The Albanian CCP specifies the judicial control of the jurisdiction of the arbitral forum, but this control is provided indirectly firstly when a jurisdiction conflict is raised and the state court assesses, with the demand of the parties or *ex officio*, that the arbitration agreement is noticeably null and secondly when the arbitral award is appealed in the state court and one of the reasons for this appeal is the unlawfully statement by the arbitral tribunal of its own jurisdiction[273]. The state court examines the legality of the arbitral award in the case of appeal against this award and the authority of the state court to review the legality of the arbitral award, because of a complaint filed by one of the parties, is stipulated by all the national legal orders and international acts. Nonetheless, these national or international legal acts have taken care to restrain this authority, through comprehensively determining the grounds for which an arbitral award is annulled by a national court, at the demand of the interested party[274]. Moreover, orders are not usually reviewable by a prior court to the rendering of the final award, although they are subject

law jurisdictions, as well as in the United States), and arbitrators are tending more and more to refer to previous awards rendered in similar cases, thus developing a system of arbitral precedent."),. Cindy G. Buys, The Tensions Between Confidentiality and Transparency in International Arbitration, 14 *Am. Rev. Int'l Arb.* 121, 137 (2003) (arguing for a presumption in favor of publication that can on ly be overcome by objection by both parties); Dora Marta Gruner, Accounting for the Public Interest in International Arbitration: The Need for Procedural and Structural Reform, 41 *Colum. J. Transnat'l L.* 923, 960 (2003) (proposing establishment of an official international regulatory body to require and oversee award publication except in those cases involving exclusively "issues of a private, consensual nature"); Christopher r. Drahozal, Contracting Out of National Law: An Empirical Look at the New Law Merchant, 80 *Notre Dame L. Rev.* 523, 549-50 (2005) (positing that "by publishing books and articles and speaking at conferences on transnational law, prospective arbitrators may be signaling that they have what Stephen R. Bond calls 'legal internationalism'"). Bernard H. Oxman, International Decisions, 96 *Am. J. Int'l L.* 198 (2002) (noting that with regard to non -commercial contexts "the [ICJ] has invoked other international arbitral awards ... on [some] occasions, and has even brought some within the ambit of "precedents" that it will consider on a par with its own prior decisions"); Gabrielle Kaufmann-Kohler, Arbitral Precedent: Dream, Necessity or Excuse? *Arbitration International,* 23 - No. 3 (2007), pp. 357 – 378.

272 UNCITRAL Model Law, article 16/3: "....If the arbitral tribunal rules as a preliminary question that it has jurisdiction, any party may request, within thirty days after having received notice of that ruling, the court specified in article 6 to decide the matter, which decision shall be subject to no appeal...." European Convention "On international commercial arbitration" (Geneva Convention), 1961, article V / 3, article VI.

273 Albanian Code of Civil Procedure, article 414/2. 434 / b, 402/2 404/1.

274 UNCITRAL Model Law, article 34: "(1) Recourse to a court against an arbitral award may be made only by an application for setting aside in accordance with paragraphs (2) and (3) of this article. (2) An arbitral award may be set aside by the court specified in article 6 only if:...."; Albanian Code of Civil Procedure, article 434. Geneva Convention, 1961, article 9; Albanian Code of Civil Procedure, article 434.

to review by the tribunal. Orders that are considered sufficiently final to enable judicial review can be contested in courts. Above all, orders for prehearing security have been found to be reviewable by some courts due to adequate finality[275]. The term "final award" refers to the award by the tribunal that resolves all disputes between the parties but the term "interim award" is used one and the same with "partial award." Nonetheless, partial awards refer to substantive claims, while interim awards refer to issues such as jurisdiction or applicable law which do not resolve all of the issues in dispute between the parties. In addition, issuance of the final award ends the duties of the arbitral tribunal, which becomes *functus officio* – without further jurisdiction and so only a final award is challengeable by the losing party, who may annul or vacate it under the laws of the seat of the arbitration.

Furthermore, the competent national court intervene on recognition and enforcement of the arbitral award, if this award is not executed voluntarily by the parties which means that state courts assure the applicability of the arbitral award, for the reason that otherwise this alternative of the dispute resolution would not have been valuable. Enforcement of the arbitral award, in the case of domestic arbitration is regulated by the national legislation[276] and in the case of Albania, the CCP stipulates that the Court of first instance to issue the order of execution of the arbitral award, upon the request of the parties or arbitrators. Against the decision of the state court that issues this order the appeal is not permitted, while against the decision of the state court refusing issuing the execution order, the appeal is permitted which means that the legislator favors the aid that the judicial system assures the arbitral awards, authorizing the forced execution, by court decision, of these awards.

It is worth mentioning that the domestic law stipulates that recognition of a foreign arbitral award is nothing but a course of evaluation, and control of the national court over the fulfillment of the legal rations by the award, sought to be recognized. There is a worldwide consent that backs the role of national courts on the recognition and enforcement of arbitral awards, without which arbitration would be unproductive. Nonetheless on the other hand, the same consensus stays even for the fact that the state courts also protect the integrity of an arbitration process, not recognizing arbitral awards based only on well-defined grounds which are thoroughly stated in the national and international laws. Besides, this involvement of courts in the whole arbitral process diminishes the advantages of an independent dispute mechanism which is worthwhile to be utilized as an alternative method for solving civil disputes which means that arbitration suffers from courts' intervention rather than offering better justice because there is a need for the existence of two co-equal dispute mechanisms producing the same standard of justice in a single jurisdiction giving the choice to the parties in dispute.

---

[275] Margaret L. Moses, *Principles and Practice of International Commercial Arbitration*, Cambridge University Press, 2008, p.179.

[276] New York Convention, Article 5; Model Law, article 36; Code of Civil Procedure, Article 394.

Specifically after the signing of the New York Convention, the courts recognize and enforce an award, except in cases when procedural infringement, or public policy issues, are found.

The state court decisions either in fulfilling the function of supporting or in fulfilling the function of controller when become final, are binding on the forum of arbitration and for the parties. Accordingly, when the state court makes a decision for expulsion of an arbitrator, the latter will be discharged in spite of arbitration forum will. Then again if the court rejects the demand of one party for expulsion, the arbitrator will prolong to adjudicate the case notwithstanding the contestation or the will of one party in the procedure.

Can parties expand courts' grounds for awards review? Expanding the grounds for attacking arbitration awards makes arbitration more like litigation which means the deficiency of arbitration's finality advantages, for the reason that the appeals are going to become endless. Additionally the courts' increased involvement detaches more of the process's confidentiality. It is worth mentioning here that parties have no right to tell the courts how to do their business in contrast that of arbitration. On the other hand, it is argued that to have an expanded judicial review so that the parties have courts and judges who can bring the legal expertise in the event the arbitrator's got it wrong. Moreover the arbitrator concerns about scrutiny augments the quality of awards rendered by arbitrators who know those awards are going to be reviewed by the courts. If somebody supports the light or the deep courts' involvement in arbitration then it might be better to have only courts dealing with civil disputes rather than supporting arbitration being a non-autonomous dispute mechanism and so wasting money and time to have the perplexing jurisdiction of two methods to deal with the same civil dispute.

Nonetheless, national legislations and international acts have been shown cautious to reduce the judicial intervention within the stringently defined framework with the rationale that the arbitration mechanism has to uphold its strategic features towards the international trade disputes resolution, that individualize it from the trial.

Chapter 3

CONSTITUTION AND ARBITRATION

1. INTRODUCTION

The appearance of alternative dispute resolution/arbitration has been one of the most considerable movements as a part of conflict management and judicial reform, and it has become a global requirement. Arbitration is commended as an economical and speedy alternative to judicial recourse[277]. Equal access to justice is one of the fundamental bases upon which any legal system is founded. Stephen J. Ware[278] and others describe arbitration as a type of adjudication and the variation between the two is that arbitration is private adjudication, while litigation is government adjudication. Since the system of arbitration is essentially conflicting with the availability of the judiciary to hear claims, it initially operated against judicial jealousy. Early public policy favoured non-binding and less definite results, in actual fact ensuring that dissatisfied arbitrating parties received a second bite at the apple if the first[279] was unlikeable. It is argued that arbitration is

---

[277] *Plymouth-Carver Reg'l Sch. Dist. v. J. Farmer and Co.*, 553 N.E.2d 1284, 1285 (Mass. 1990) (citing Marino v. Tagaris, 480 N.E.2d 286, 288 (Mass. 1985)) (claiming "predictability, certainty, and effectiveness" intertwined with voluntary arbitration). Celeste M. Hammond, A Real Estate Focus: The (Pre)(As)sumed "Consent" of Commercial Binding Arbitration Contracts – An Empirical Study of Attitudes and Expectations of Transactional Lawyers, 36 *J. Marshall L. Rev.* 589, 591 (2003) (commenting on the widespread use of arbitration provisions in commercial contracts). Paul H. Dawes, Alternative Dispute Resolution, 1136 *PLI/CORP* 599, 603 (1999) ("The risks [of arbitration], broadly speaking, can be grouped into three major concerns: lack of appeal rights, waiver of other procedural and substantive rights and, ironically, a perception that like jurors, arbitrators can be unpredictable, under-qualified and swayed by emotion.").

[278] Stephen J. Ware, Default Rules from Mandatory Rules: Privatizing Law Through Arbitration, 83 *Minn. L. Rev.* 703 (1999), Stephen J. Ware, Alternative Dispute Resolution §2.1 at 19 (West Group 2001) ("Arbitration is private adjudication."); Ian R. Macneil, Et Al., *Federal Arbitration Law: Agreements, Awards, And Remedies Under The Federal Arbitration Act, § 2.1.2*, at 2:5 (Little Brown and Co. 1999 Supp.) ("Arbitration is generally understood to be a kind of adjudicatory process . . . .").

[279] Amy J. Schmitz, Ending a Mud Bowl: Defining Arbitration's Finality through Functional Analysis, 37 *GA L. Rev.* 123, 132 (2002) at 137 (criticizing early courts' view of arbitration as threat to own power). Margaret M. Maggio and Richard A. Bales, Contracting Around the FAA: The Enforceability of Private Agreements to Expand Judicial Review of Arbitration Awards, 18 *Ohio St. J. On Disp. Resol.* 151, 152 (2002) (observing potential litigants' favoritism of simple, speedy alternate dispute resolution process); at 160 (acknowledging

preferable as a consequence of its lower accent on strictly applying the law and its greater weight on the parties' dispute. On the other hand, arbitration is defined in the Halsbury's Laws of England[280] as "the reference of a dispute or difference between not less than two parties for determination, after hearing both sides in a judicial manner, by a person or persons other than a court of competent jurisdiction." Hence, it is recognized that arbitration is a dispute mechanism of a "judicial manner" and not a lawlessness mechanism. Arbitration is in most jurisdictions practiced in accordance with law made by the state[281].

The public's trust and confidence in the courts is their most valued and fundamental asset[282]. Can arbitration gain public's trust as well? Does arbitration advance the objectives of democratic governance? Arbitration has the aptitude to augment democratic governance in numerous important ways[283]. Arbitration achieves effectiveness for the public justice system because having disputes resolved by arbitration will lessen the number left for resolution by public courts. Voluntary arbitration improves personal autonomy by providing a means of governmentally enforceable dispute resolution to add to public adjudication.

Anthropologists and sociologists have told that informal dispute resolution operates within systems of state law, and consequently is better portrayed on latitude of overlapping "legalities" rather than as merely an alternative to formal law and state regulation[284]. Ethical values exist and are preserved in authoritative texts. Do only judges formulate public values? Owen Fiss argued that ADR is powerless to promote, and in addition is expected to undermine, popular commitments to public values[285]. Moreover, Fiss portrayed public values as moral ideals about justice, rights, and social cohesion that a public should want to uphold, and which, in any event, the state is obligated to enforce. Besides, Arbitration generates exactly the kinds of public values that public judicial institutions could consistently provide for[286]. The dogmatic approach that only courts

---

suspicion of early jurists regarding arbitration as undermining authority); Kenneth R. Davis, When Ignorance of the Law is No Excuse: Judicial Review of Arbitration Awards, 45 *Buff. L. Rev.* 49, 53-60 (1997) (drawing distinctions between arbitration and litigation); at 60-63 (recalling need to protect citizens from agreements that prevented access to judicial forum).

[280] *Halsbury's Laws of England*, 3rd Edition, Volume 2 at pg.2 para 2.

[281] The Arbitration and Conciliation Act Cap 19, Laws of Nigeria 1990, Arbitration Act of England, 1996.

[282] Wayne D. Brazil, Court ADR 25 Years after Pound: Have We Found a Better Way? 18 *Ohio St. J. On Disp. Resol.* 93, 97 (2002).

[283] Carrie Menkel-Meadow, Deliberative Democracy and Conflict Resolution, 12 *Disp. Resol. Mag.* 18, 19 (2006) (Meadow has argued that there are strong connections between deliberative democracy theory and the ADR movement including a shared appreciation for "constitutional experimentalism . . . in which there are feedback mechanisms for sharing and coordinating local outcomes with the broader polity."). Carrie Menkel-Meadow, The Lawyer's Role(s) in Deliberative Democracy, 5 *Nev. L. J.* 347, 348 (2004) (exploring "the use of alternative, legal, political and social problem solving institutions that draw on conflict resolution theory and practice.").

[284] Christine B. Harrington, Informalism as a Form of Legal Ordering, in *The Oxford Handbook Of Law And Politics* 378, 389-90, (Keith E. Whittington et al. eds., 2008).

[285] Owen M. Fiss, Against Settlement, 93 *Yale L. J.* 1073, 1085-87 (1984).

[286] Susan Sturm, Law's Role in Addressing Complex Discrimination, in *Handbook of Employment Discrimination Research: Rights and Realities* 35, 54-55 (Laura Beth Nielsen and Robert L. Nelson eds., 2005) ("The worry

produce law and justice cannot be accepted because all actions of society produce norms and principles.

Rules and laws are created ahead and must be suitably precise both in terms of defining the conduct to which they apply and the consequences that they will entail. R. H. Mnookin and L. Kornhauser[287] argued that the law acts “not as imposing order from above, but rather as a providing a framework within which [parties] can themselves determine their . . . rights and responsibilities...individuals in a wide variety of contexts bargain in the shadow of the law.”” Thus, the authenticity/ legitimacy of adjudication is dependent on the degree it maximizes parties’ participation because adjudication or any other dispute mechanism such as arbitration is “a device which gives formal and institutional expression to the influence of reasoned argument in human affairs.[288]” Fiss’ critique of ADR processes is rooted in his view that adjudication is a mainly public function that derives its legitimacy from an exact process and for Fiss[289] the court’s power to resolve cases is based on a “conception of the judicial function [that] sees the judge as trying to give meaning to our constitutional values” and a view that “adjudication is the process through which that meaning is revealed or elaborated.” It should be taken into account that independence is a significant ingredient in the process that legitimates judicial function or arbitration expressing and developing the meaning of constitutional values.

The central role of adjudication is to generate public policy through the creation of rules and standards by this means creating behavioural norms for those similarly situated and so courts provide guidance for future disputes. Could this role be played by a co-equal and independent arbitration? Fiss[290] argued that, unlike adjudication, dispute resolution derives its legitimacy from the principle of individual consent.

[of Fiss and others] is that ADR... is necessarily private, non-norm generating ... However, it is important to separate critiques of current practice from normative theories ... With judicial involvement in assessing and publicizing adequacy criteria, [ADR] has the potential to be norm generating ... (citations omitted)); Susan Sturm and Howard Gadlin, Conflict Resolution and Systemic Change, 2007 J. Disp. Resol. 1, 3 (disputing the assumption of Fiss and others "that informal conflict resolution is necessarily non-normative, and that it cannot yield more general public values"); Georgios I. Zekos, Maritime Arbitration and the Rule of Law, 39 *J. Mar. L. and Com.* 523, 543 (2008) (discussing "ADR's power to produce responsible public norms").

[287] Robert H. Mnookin and Lewis Kornhauser Bargaining in the Shadow of the Law: the Case of Divorce, 88 *Yale L. J.* 950, 997 (1979) at 950.

[288] Craig Scott and Patrick Macklem, Constitutional Ropes of Sand or Justiciable Guarantees? Social Rights in a New South African Constitution, 141 *U. PA L. Rev.* 1, 22 (1992) (“The resistance to constitutionally entrenched social rights on the grounds of institutional competence is often summarized in the view that social rights are said to be positive rights and therefore requiring time to realize; vague in terms of the obligations they mandate and involving complex polycentric, and diffuse interests in collective goods.”).

[289] Fiss, Foreword: The Forms of Justice, 93 *Harv. L. Rev.* 1, 12-13 (1979).

[290] Owen M. Fiss, Against Settlement, 93 *Yale L. J.* 1073, 1085-87 (1984), Owen Fiss, Law Is Everywhere, 117 *Yale L. J.* 256, 259 (2007) (describing the U.S. Constitution as "the embodiment of the public morality of the nation.., laden with a special normative value that derives from the role it plays in defining our national identity-what it means to be American-and in articulating the governing principles of our society").

Constitution and all public laws[291] are in force as long as they have the consent and acceptance of the governed people and their legitimacy and legality do not gained by their formality and written type. Arbitration is based on the consent of parties as expressed in an accepted contract and so arbitration is constitutionally valuable. Courts are legitimate, not because those who come before them accept to their procedural rules and/or substantive outcomes, but because they distribute justice[292]. Courts are legitimate provided that they hand out justice within the confines of a democratic political system. It is not certain that only judges distribute justice because it is well know that litigation has not become a superior system.

Taking into account that the authority of judgment arises from the law, arbitration awards arise from the same laws than judgment as well[293]. Ohio Supreme Court Chief Justice Thomas Moyer[294] writes, "Courts exist as forums for the resolution of disputes. Ideally, parties involved in litigation are able themselves to negotiate a settlement of their disputes, through mediation or otherwise. When that does not occur, it is the responsibility of the court to render a final judgment."

State legislators granted individuals the right to resort to alternative methods to resolve their disputes, of which the most important method is commercial arbitration[295]. Moreover, the reason for the dominance of commercial arbitration is the prevalent acceptance and recognition of it by civil society institutions and the three powers of the state; the legislative power, judicial and executive, as a suitable method that matches up to judicial action[296]. Furthermore, the courts have become more and more responsive toward permitting civil rights disputes to be decided by arbitration[297].

---

[291] Margaret L. Moses, Arbitration Law: Who's in Charge? 40 *Seton Hall L. Rev.* 147, 181 (2010) ("[W]hen arbitrators are deciding claims under public law, there is a high potential for negative externalities. For example, if an arbitrator makes a wrong decision in a matter arising under the antitrust laws, that decision may negatively affect not only the claimants but the rights of everyone else affected by the anti-competitive behavior.").

[292] William L. Ury, Jeanne M. Brett and Stephen B. Goldberg, *Getting Disputes Resolved: Designing Systems to Cut the Costs of Conflict* 17 (1988) ("Although reconciling interests is generally less costly than determining rights, only adjudication can authoritatively resolve questions of public importance."). Lawrence Susskind and Jeffrey Cruikshank, *Breaking the Impasse: Consensual Approaches to Resolving Public Disputes* 17 (1987) ("When fundamental constitutional rights are at stake, we properly turn to our judicial system.").

[293] Judith Resnik, For Owen M Fiss: Some Reflections on the Triumph and the Death of Adjudication, 58 U. Miami L. Rev. 173, 176 (2003) (arguing that our contemporary generation of judges is "suspicious of adjudication" and prefers "processes sometimes styled 'alternative dispute resolution' (ADR) and sometimes 'dispute resolution' (DR)," which are "committed to the utility of contract and look to the participants to validate outcomes through consensual agreements").

[294] *DeRolph v. State*, 780 N.E.2d 529, 536 (Ohio 2002) (Moyer, C.J., dissenting).

[295] Lowenfeld, Andreas F., Can Arbitration Coexist with Judicial Review? A Critique of *LaPine v. Kyocera*, *ADR Current, American Arbitration Association*, Vol. 3, 1998, p.1.

[296] Riskin, Leonard L. and James E. Westbrook., *Dispute Resolution and Lawyers*, St. Paul West Publishing Company, 1987, p 250.

[297] Linda J. Demaine and Deborah R. Hensler, "Volunteering" to Arbitration through Predispute Arbitration Clauses: The Average Consumer's Experience, 67 *Law and Contemp. Probs.* 55, 56 (2004) (citing *Circuit City Stores, Inc. v. Adams*, 532 U.S. 105, 132 (2001)).

ADR was envisioned as an alternative to litigation, with its own manifest substantive and procedural characteristics[298]. In other words the aim was to create a less formal forum than litigation. Arbitration has been gradually institutionalized over the past five decades and rules and procedures have been to a large extent codified by the key arbitration institutions[299]. The legitimacy of arbitral power is based on an act of delegation to which the parties have unreservedly consented.

Further, the authority of the arbitrator is restricted to the area of activity administered by the contract itself interpreting contractual terms in light of some law of contract, applying these interpretations to settle the dispute. An arbitrator makes law by way of interpretation, reason-giving, and application and this lawmaking is retrospective applying only to a dispute involving a pre-existing contract between two parties.

Is arbitration constitutional or unconstitutional? Do only courts provide and promote justice or ADR award justice as well? Chief Justice Burger[300] redefining "justice" observed that: In order to "fulfil our traditional obligation means that we should provide mechanisms [ADR] that can produce an acceptable result in the shortest possible time, with the least possible expense and with a minimum stress on the participants. That is what justice is all about." Moreover, Chief Justice Burger said that the US legal system is too expensive, destructive, and inefficient[301]. Besides, arbitration cannot violate public policy[302]. Under the FAA, a court may not enforce a contract that is illegal or contrary to public policy. Some jurisdictions reject the public-policy defense in state proceedings for the reason that the local arbitration statute has no such grounds[303]. Judith Resnik[304] argues that "The cumulative effect of the Supreme Court's jurisprudence on arbitration has been to produce an unconstitutional system that undermines both the legitimacy of arbitration and the functions of courts." In contrast, it has to be taken into account that parties are not forced to arbitrate but under their free will they agree to arbitration which is a constitutional right. Moreover, it is worth mentioning that Congress does not constitutionally authorize private litigants to launch authoritative statutory policy in indeed the same way as a public administrative agency that is authorized to engage in rulemaking and adjudication. Besides, Section 553 of the Administrative Procedure

[298] Caroline Harris Crowne, Note, The Alternative Dispute Resolution Act of 1998: Implementing a New Paradigm of Justice, 76 *N.Y.U. L. Rev.* 1768, 1772 (2001); Alexander J.S. Colvin, An Empirical Study of Employment Arbitration: Case Outcomes and Processes, 8 J. Empirical Legal Stud. 1, 2 (2011) Carrie Menkel-Meadow, the Trouble with the Adversary System in a Postmodern, Multicultural World, 38 *Wm. and Mary L. Rev.* 5, 12 (1996); (The intention was to create a less formal forum than litigation.).

[299] Alec Stone Sweet, Arbitration and Judicialization, *Oñati Socio-Legal Series*, v. 1, n. 9 (2011).

[300] Warren E. Burger, Isn't There A Better Way? 68 *A.B.A. J.* 274, 275 (1982).

[301] Warren E. Burger, The State of Justice, 70 *A.B.A. J.* 62, 66 (1984).

[302] *Escobar v. Celebration Cruise Operator, Inc.*, 805 F.3d 1279, 1290 (11th Cir. 2015) (a party seeking to oppose arbitration cannot raise a public policy defense at the arbitration-enforcement stage).

[303] *Nat'l Ass'n of Gov't Emp.'s v. Nat'l Emergency Med. Servs. Ass'n*, 84 F. Supp. 3d 43, 49-50 (D. Mass. 2015) (quoting *W.R. Grace & Co.*, 461 U.S. at 766) (excellent summary). *Warbington Constr., Inc. v. Franklin Landmark, L.L.C.*, 66 S.W.3d 853, 857-58 (Tenn. Ct. App. 2001) (citing Supreme Court decisions).

[304] Judith resnik Diffusing Disputes: The Public in the Private of Arbitration, the Private in Courts, and the Erasure of Rights, 2015 *Yale Law Journal* 124:2804 p2804.

Act[305] establishes a procedure through which agencies enact "legislative" rules that have the "force and effect of law" and the Supreme Court[306] has held that an agency charged with administering a statute can launch binding administrative policy through case by-case adjudication when Congress explicitly or implicitly assigns regulatory authority to the agency. Moreover, the Supreme Court[307] nullified a statute that offered the force of law to "labor agreements negotiated by coal producers and labor unions as an impermissible delegation of Congress's lawmaking power and described the statute as "legislative delegation in its most obnoxious form.""

Finally, it has to be taken into consideration here that legal rights come from doctrines that first ascended in arbitrations centuries ago and common law courts gave these private rights a more public character by adopting privately adjudicated commercial doctrines[308].

2. Constitutions' Background and Arbitration

The United States has participated in international tribunals since the founding era. Even though international adjudication is traced from ancient times, approximately every account of modern international adjudication begins with the Jay Treaty of 1794[309], in which Britain and the United States agreed to set up arbitration commissions which could be considered alike arbitration tribunals to settle boundary disputes and claims by British and American citizens whose property had been damaged or seized during the War of Independence[310]. Therefore, arbitration was the dispute method utilized at the beginning and a difficult turn of the modern US democracy instead of any formal courts and of course arbitration brought justice in society. Moreover, ad hoc arbitrations were common all the way through the nineteenth century. The peace treaty between Great Britain and France in 1815, at the end of the Napoleonic Wars, incorporated a provision for

[305] 5 U.S.C. § 553 J. Maria Glover, Disappearing Claims and the Erosion of Substantive Law, 124 *Yale L. J.* 3052, 3066 (2015) (arbitration clauses permit contract drafters "to frustrate or altogether eliminate claiming in any forum").

[306] *Chrysler Corp. v. Brown*, 441 U.S. 281, 295 (1979) *United States v. Mead Corp.,* 533 U.S. 218, 227–28 (2001).

[307] *Carter v. Carter Coal Co.,* 298 U.S. 238, 311 (1936), See *Am. Express Co. v. Italian Colors Rest*., 133 S. Ct. 2304, 2310 (2013); *Carnival Cruise Lines, Inc. v. Shute*, 499 U.S. 585, 595–96 (1991) Daniel T. Deacon, *Agencies and Arbitration Columbia Law Review* Vol. 117:991

[308] William C. Jones, An Inquiry into the History of the Adjudication of Mercantile Disputes in Great Britain and The United States, 25 U. *Chi. L. Rev*. 445, 447 (1958).

[309] Peter Malanczuk, *Akehurst's Modern Introduction to International Law* 20 (7th rev. ed. 1997) (stating that the modern history of arbitration began with the Jay Treaty, while earlier concepts of peaceful settlement originated with the Peace of Westphalia).

[310] Jenny S. Martinez, International Courts and The U.S. Constitution: Reexamining The History, 2011 *University of Pennsylvania Law Review* Vol. 159: 1069. Henry Paul Monaghan, Article III and Supranational Judicial Review, 107 *Colum. L. Rev*. 833, 842 (2007) (arguing that international trade tribunals "raise no serious problems under Article III" because they are "only a recent instantiation of an age-old practice: the use of arbitration to resolve disputes by American nationals against foreign states and their nationals"); at 851 ("Since the Jay Treaty of 1794, it has been clear that claims of American nationals . . . against foreign sovereigns could be adjudicated by state-state mixed arbitration commissions.").

arbitration of public and private claims linked to the conflict. Thus, instead of a court, arbitration was chosen to solve disputes concerning not only private issues but also public nature ones. The United States was party to many of these nineteenth-century arbitrations[311]. George Washington himself gave authority to arbitration owing to his decision to include an arbitration clause in his last will and testament[312].

Constitution describes rights for people in addition the workability of a state in order people to have rights and be protected. Owen Fiss[313] describes the U.S. Constitution as "the embodiment of the public morality of the nation.., laden with a special normative value that derives from the role it plays in defining our national identity-what it means to be American-and in articulating the governing principles of our society."

In addition, the Constitution is premised on the doctrine of separation of powers[314]. The Constitution verifies a tripartite system of government in which the legislative, executive, and judicial branches are equal and must in general abstain from intruding upon each other's sphere[315]. For instance, no citizen of the United States may be denied the equal protection of the laws[316].

The US Constitution vests the judicial power in Article III courts by this means strictly restricting Congress's capacity to choose the individuals and kind of institutions by which its laws will be applied[317]. The issue of governments' relationships to courts is distinct, not only because of the constitutional charter running to courts but also because of the dependence of the state on courts to order its society[318]. Moreover, Article III of the

---

[311] Arthur Nussbaum, *A Concise History of the Law of Nations* 218-19 (rev. ed. 1954) (examining the 1872 arbitration between Great Britain and the United States regarding the building of the ship Alabama in English shipyards to be used by the Confederacy, which was regarded as proof that arbitration was a viable option for resolving controversial disputes).

[312] Bales, Richard C., *Compulsory Arbitration: The Grand Experiment in Employment*, Ithaca, NY: Cornell University Press, 1997. Steven A. Certilman, Throw Down the Muskets, Seek Out the Town Elders This Is a Brief History of Arbitration in the United States, *NYSBA New York Dispute Resolution Lawyer* | Spring 2010 | Vol. 3 | No. 1, 10.

[313] Owen Fiss, Law Is Everywhere, 117 *Yale L. J.* 256, 259 (2007).

[314] John E. Nowak and Ronald D. Rotunda, Constitutional Law § 3.5, at 129 (5th ed. 1995). The Declaration of Independence para. 1 (U.S. 1776). U.S. CONST. amend. XIV, § 1. (From the Declaration of Independence's claim that "all men are created equal" to the Fourteenth Amendment's guarantee of "equal protection of the laws," our democracy has displayed a deep commitment to the principle of equal treatment. By adhering strictly to their own precedents, the courts help to strengthen that commitment.).

[315] Raoul Berger, Standing to Sue in Public Actions: Is It a Constitutional Requirement? 78 *Yale L. J.* 816, 816 (1969) (arguing that "it is hardly to be doubted that the Framers contemplated resort to English practice for elucidation" of Article III). Robert J. Pushaw, Jr., Justiciability and Separation of Powers: A Neo-Federalist Approach, 81 *Cornell L. Rev.* 393, 400–07 (1996) (relying extensively on Blackstone and English legal authorities in exploring Founding-era attitudes toward the separation of powers and the judicial role).

[316] U.S. Const. amend. XIV ("[N]or shall any State . . . deny to any person within its jurisdiction the equal Protection of the laws.").

[317] U.S. Const. art. III, § 1. As Justice Marshall long ago recognized in *Marbury v. Madison*, "The very essence of civil liberty certainly consists in the rights of every individual to claim the protection of the law, whenever he receives an injury." 5. U.S. 137, at 163 (1803). .Edward Brunet, Arbitration and Constitutional Rights, 71 *N.C. L. Rev.* 81, 102 (1992) (arguing that commercial arbitration involves state action because courts' enforcement of arbitration agreements and awards implicates constitutional rights).

[318] Judith Resnik, Fairness In Numbers: A Comment On *ATandT v. Concepcion*, *Wal-Mart v. Dukes*, and *Turner v. Rogers*, 2011 *Harvard Law Review* [Vol. 125:78. Angela D. Morrison, Dukeing Out Pattern or Practice After Wal-Mart: The EEOC as Fist, 63 *Am. U. L. Rev.* 87 (2013) (exploring ways in which EEOC can step in to protect employees who can no longer participate in nation-wide class actions after Wal-Mart); Dustin Massie,

by Israeli courts in a great number of decisions[336] corresponding to the Israeli approach on the right of access to courts. This right is acknowledged as a constitutional right and by this means accorded the highest position in the hierarchy of civil rights[337]. Moreover, the existence of an arbitration agreement does not by itself preclude any party from breaching the agreement and beginning judicial proceedings in court. Besides, Israeli law provides a single remedy for a party's breach of agreements to arbitrate: The staying of court proceedings. As a result, an Israeli court will never state that it lacks jurisdiction, nor will it grant an injunction for the enforcement of the arbitration agreement. As an alternative, the court will investigate the agreement and the underlying conditions to find out the existence of consent and then either recognize enforcing the arbitration by staying the proceedings in court, or ignore the arbitration agreement and proceed with resolving the dispute[338]. On the other hand, arbitration too, is part of the legal system, and should be first and principally there for the advantage of the public. While the court can repeal all laws that are in conflict with the constitution, the arbitration law of 1968 is the exception. The Constitutional Court said that there is no doubt that an arbitration tribunal is a judicial authority in terms of law. Besides, Supreme Court Judge Dalia Dorner said that "the privatization of the Israeli judicial system. I don't believe this law will shorten proceedings, but it will be a further burden on the system. It's a disaster[339]."

In Brazil, one case generally held that the constitutional principle of universal access to justice in state courts could not be abrogated by an arbitration clause[340]. On the other hand, in December 2001, the debate on the constitutionality of the Brazilian Arbitration Law was finally over, when the Brazilian Supreme Court issued a decision holding the constitutionality of the Brazilian Arbitration Law[341]. As soon as the constitutionality of the Brazilian Arbitration Law was confirmed, there was an obvious growth in the number of arbitration clauses incorporated into contracts with Brazilian parties and consequently a momentous upsurge of national and international arbitration proceedings involving Brazilian parties.

In Hungary, the right to secondary participation in arbitral proceedings is not one of the constitutionally guaranteed fundamental rights that would have to be respected in

---

[336] CA 6796/97 *Berg Jacob and Sons v. Berg E. Import* [2000] IsrSC 54(1) 697, 705.

[337] CA 6450/01 *Simha Urielli and Sons v. Inst. for Treatment of Ashkelon Sewage* [2001] IsrSC 56(5) 769, 773. Shlomo Levin, *The Theory Of Civil Procedure — Introduction And Basic Principles* 6–7 (1999); Yoram Rabin, *Access To The Court As A Constitutional Right* (1998).

[338] Pursuant to §§ 5 and 6 of the Arbitration Law, 5728-1968, 22 LSI 210 (1967-1968).

[339] Prof. Moshe Cohen-Eliya, the dean of the law school at the Academic Center of Law and Business also argued against the bill. "It is actually the privatization of the judicial system, and it violates the fundamental right to go to court, particularly for the weaker members of the public."

[340] *AES–Uruguaiana Empreendimentos Ltda v. CBEE Companhia Estadual de Energia Elétrica*, TJCivRGS-2, Ags. Ins. No. 70004506424, 70004535662, and 70003866258, Relator: Tresinha de Oliveira Silva (Judgment, November 13, 2002).

[341] S.T.F., SE 5206 AgR, Relator: Min. Sepulveda Pertence, 12.12.2001, D.J. 30.04.2004, S.T.F.J. [referred to as *M.B.V. Commercial and Export Management Establishment v. Resil Industria e Comercial Ltda*].

every given case[342]. Consequently, a person who is not authorized to participate in arbitral proceedings as a secondary participant may not ask for participation by means of legal action. On the other hand, arbitration is the only alternative instrument to judicial litigation that provides binding awards. By choosing arbitration, the parties make the crucial decision to divest the courts of the jurisdiction over their dispute[343]. Awards rendered by arbitral tribunals have the same legal force as court judgments from both the material and procedural viewpoints in Hungarian law[344].

Matters in respect of which an arbitral award has been delivered are subject to the principle of *res iudicata.* Once decided, a matter cannot be the subject of another complaint.

Mandatory arbitration breached the Constitution of Malta[345]. Muscat did not attack the legality of *voluntary* arbitration but only *compulsory* arbitration since according to him the Arbitration Tribunal does not present standard guarantees of independence and impartiality as required by the Constitution and the European Convention of Human Rights. Consensual arbitration is not contrary to the European Convention of Human Rights. The constitutional concept of courts as a basic public service provided by government is under siege. Parallel challenges can be found in Europe, where Article 6 of the Convention for the Protection of Human Rights and Fundamental Freedoms expressly endows "everyone" with a right to a "fair and public hearing[346]." Like the terms of Article 6, the three 2011 Supreme Court decisions (*AT&T v. Concepcion*, *Wal-Mart v. Dukes*, and *Turner v. Rogers)*[347] revolve around questions of fairness and of the relationship between fairness and public adjudicatory processes. Is there hegemony of arbitration over federal statutory claims[348]? Today, challenges to arbitration primarily focus on

---

[342] Ruling of the Supreme Court of Hungary (Magyar Koztarsasag OJ Legfelslibb Birosag) Ref. No. Gfv. XI.30.003/2008 delivered in 2009.

[343] Nadia Milone, Arbitration: the Italian perspective and the finality of the award, *Oñati Socio-Legal Series*, v. 1, n. 6 (2011) Italian provisions on arbitration are contained in Articles 806 through 840 of the Italian Code of Civil Procedure, which was most recently amended by means of Legislative Decree no. 40 of 2 February 2006. Arbitration in Austria is in general governed by the ZPO. §§ 577 to 618 ZPO provide a basic framework governing just the most important issues. State courts are in principle only involved in arbitration procedures if an arbitral award is challenged according to §§ 611, 612, 617 para 6 and 7 ZPO (Austrian Code of Civil Procedure).

[344] Ruling of the Supreme Court of Hungary (Magyar Koztarsasag Legfelslibb Birosag) Ref. No. Gfv. XI.30.003/2008 delivered in 2009: Source: (Complex legal information system) No. BH 2009.182. Ruling of the Supreme Court of Hungary (Magyar Koztarsasag Legfelsobb Birosag) Ref. No. Gfv. XI.30.075/2009 delivered in 2009: Source: (Complex legal information system) No. IBH 2009.1969.

[345] *Anthony Grech v. Claire Calleja and Attorney General of the Republic* October 19, 2007 (Application No.11/2007), per Tonio Mallia J. 2 Jotham Scerri-Diacono, "Mandatory Arbitration in Malta versus the European Convention on Human Rights: *Anthony Grech v. Claire Calleja and the Attorney General of the Republic*" (2008) 74 Arbitration 204. The Constitutionality of Mandatory Arbitration in Malta by Jotham Scerri-Diacono and Rachel Mamo (2009) 75 Arbitration 4.

[346] Convention for the Protection of Human Rights and Fundamental Freedoms art. 6.1, Nov. 4, 1950, 213 *U.N.T.S.* 221.

[347] *Turner v. Rogers*, 131 S. Ct. 2507, 2512 (2011). *AT&T Mobility LLC v. Concepcion*, 131 S. Ct. 1740, 1750–52 (2011) *Wal-Mart Stores, Inc. v. Dukes*, 131 S. Ct. 2541, 2559 (2011).

[348] Myriam Gilles, Opting Out of Liability: The Forthcoming, Near-Total Demise of the Modern Class Action, 104 *Mich. L. Rev.* 373, 393-96 (2005) (describing the ascendancy of an "arbitration hegemony" over federal

contractual theories, particularly unconscionability[349]. The *Concepcion* Court held that the FAA preempts California's case-law rule permitting an unconscionability defense that allows the consumer to bypass a class-action waiver to an arbitration clause[350].In other words, Judges repeatedly strike down one-sided arbitration clauses under the contract defense of unconscionability[351]. Courts refused to allow arbitrators to decide whether the agreement to arbitrate the merits of the lawsuit was unconscionable. Some courts perceive no difference between the procedural unconscionability of a delegation clause and the procedural unconscionability of an agreement to arbitrate the merits and so if a drafter gives a consumer or employee a short period of time to opt out of arbitration, a delegation clause cannot be procedurally unconscionable[352]. For instance, in *Ontiveros v.*

---

statutory claims).Sarah Rudolph Cole, Fairness in Securities Arbitration: A Constitutional Mandate? *Pace Law Review* Issue 1 Fall 2005 73.

[349] John E. Murray, Jr., The Judicial Vision of Contract: The Constructed Circle of Assent and Unconscionability, 52 *Duq. L. Rev.* 263, 265 (2014) ("the current fashion inevitably describes unconscionability as 'procedural' or 'substantive.'"("Substantive unconscionability is concerned with whether a contract, or a term of a contract, is overly harsh, one-sided, or manifests an outrageous degree of unfairness"). ("'Procedural' unconscionability is concerned with the circumstances under which the contract was negotiated and formed including the conspicuous or inconspicuous form in which the allegedly unconscionable term is found and, in particular, whether a genuine negotiation occurred, versus a take-it-or-leave-it demand that precluded any choice by the party with inferior bargaining power. Where only one party dictates the terms, the agreement is a 'contract of adhesion' which is 'procedurally' unconscionable.") J. Maria Glover, Beyond Unconscionability: Class Action Waivers and Mandatory Arbitration Agreements, 59 *Vand. L. Rev.* 1735, 1737 (2006) ("Prominent among these challenges is that class action waivers in contracts of adhesion are unenforceable under state-law doctrines of unconscionability. This strategy has met with some success") Cheryl B. Preston & Eli McCann, Llewellyn Slept Here: A Short History of Sticky Contracts and Feudalism, 91 *Or. L. Rev.* 129, 162–65 (2012) (arguing that economists co-opted the judiciary by overstating the benefits of adhesive contracts without accounting for their harms, and this resulted in a decline in the application of the doctrine of unconscionability to form contracts).

[350] *AT&T Mobility LLC v. Concepcion* 563 U.S. 333 (2011); *Sonic-Calabasas A, Inc. v. Moreno*, 311 P.3d 184, 217 (Cal. 2013) (similar argument). *Dean v. Draughons Junior Coll., Inc.*, 917 F. Supp. 2d 751, 762-63 (M.D. Tenn. 2013) (holding that the FAA preempts any argument that arbitration about arbitration is cost prohibitive). Jean R. Sternlight, Tsunami: *AT&T Mobility LLC v. Concepcion* Impedes Access to Justice, 90 *Or. L. Rev.* 703, 725 (2012) ("If we allow companies to insulate themselves from class actions, we are effectively allowing companies to escape many legal regulations and thereby eliminating a great deterrent to company misconduct."). Aaron-Andrew P. Bruhl, The Unconscionability Game: Strategic Judging and the Evolution of Federal Arbitration Law, 83 *N.Y.U. L. Rev.* 1420, 1429 (2008) (explaining that arbitration is "a phenomenon that pervade[s] virtually every corner of the daily economy"). (observing that the unconscionability doctrine gives trial courts great flexibility to target arbitration agreements for voiding); David Horton, Unconscionability Wars, 106 *NW U. L. Rev.* 387, 388 (2012).

[351] *Puleo v. Chase Bank USA*, N.A., 605 F.3d 172, 183 (3d Cir. 2010) ("[t]his is a question of [substantive] arbitrability for the court to resolve"); *Wiley v. Advance Am.*, No. 3:07-3533-TLW-TER, 2008 WL 4179652, at *10 (D.S.C. Sept. 5, 2008) ("[w]hether the agreements to arbitrate are unconscionable . . . are issues of substantive arbitrability"). *Vector Elec. & Controls, Inc. v. ABM Indus. Inc.*, No. 3:15-00252-JWD-RLB, 2016 WL 126752, at *5 (M.D. La. Jan. 11, 2016) ("[S]o long as (1) a valid agreement to arbitrate is tendered, (2) the relevant dispute falls within that agreement's ambit, and (3) none of the general contract defenses subsumed into the Savings Clause have been presented, arbitration must follow, and a federal case either stayed or dismissed.").

[352] *Mohamed v. Uber Techs., Inc.*, 836 F.3d 1102, 1111 (9th Cir.), amended in other part by 848 F.3d 1201 (9th Cir. 2016); *Bruster v. Uber Techs. Inc.*, 188 F. Supp. 3d 658, 664 (N.D. Ohio 2016) (holding that an opt-out provision was fatal to the plaintiffs' procedural unconscionability argument). *Halliday v. Beneficial Fin. I, Inc.*, No. 2:12-cv-708, 2013 WL 693022, at *4(S.D. Ohio Feb. 26, 2013) ("The speculative possibility that threshold issues may require more than one day of arbitration, and that plaintiffs may be forced to spend some uncertain amount of money to continue arbitration[,] does not render the delegation clause unconscionable.").

DHL Express (USA), Inc[353]., the California court of appeals stated that the delegation clause itself was unconscionable under those circumstances, reasoning that "the arbitrator has a unique self-interest in deciding that a dispute is arbitrable" and discovery procedures limited the parties to a request for production of documents and the deposition of one individual and any expert witness[354]. On the other hand, The Supreme Court[355] by deeming delegation clauses to be industrial-strength arbitration clauses, Rent-A-Center extended the parity principle from arbitration about the merits of a lawsuit to arbitration about arbitration. Thus it could not be argued that arbitration is inferior to litigation in court even if it simply allocates jurisdiction between judges and arbitrators to decide whether arbitration is warranted[356]. Moreover, arbitrators will continue to interpret "silent" arbitration provisions which is an away for the independence of arbitration from courts[357]. It is argued that delegation clauses permit arbitrators to decide whether the

---

[353] *Ontiveros v. DHL Express (USA), Inc.*, 79 *Cal. Rptr.* 3d 471, 482 (Ct. App. 2008), abrogated by *Tiri v. Lucky Chances, Inc.*, 171 *Cal. Rptr.* 3d 621 (Ct. App. 2014), and *Malone v. Superior Court*, 173 Cal. Rptr. 3d 241 (Ct. App. 2014). *Lloyd v. BRSI, LLC*, No. CIV-15-964-M, 2016 WL 234861, at *2 (W.D. Okla. Jan. 19, 2016) (enforcing a delegation clause in arbitration agreement); *Williams v. Omainsky*, No. 15-0123-WS-N, 2015 WL 8056142, at *6 (S.D. Ala. Dec. 3, 2015) (enforcing a delegation clause in arbitration agreement). *Vargas v. Delivery Outsourcing, LLC*, No. 15-cv-03408-JST, 2016 WL 946112, at *7 (N.D. Cal. Mar. 14, 2016) ("[D]espite clear language delegating arbitrability to the arbitrator, the issue of delegation is made ambiguous by the language of the arbitration provision that permits modification of the . . . [a]greement should 'a court of law or equity' hold any provision of the [a]greement unenforceable. The [a]greement cannot be read as providing a 'clear and unmistakable' delegation to [the] arbitrator."); *Cobarruviaz v. Maplebear, Inc.*, 143 F. Supp. 3d 930, 940 (N.D. Cal. 2015) (holding that the purported delegation clause "is inconsistent with the severability clause . . ., which states that 'any arbitrator or court' could declare or determine that a provision of the [a]greement is invalid or unenforceable").

[354] *Venture Cotton Cooperative v. Freeman*, No. 11-11-00093-CV, 2011 WL 7452136 (*Tex. App.* Dec. 21, 2011) (arguing discovery limitations in arbitration clause were unconscionable); Venture Cotton Cooperative v. Freeman, 395 S.W.3d 272 (*Tex. App.* 2013) (affirming trial court's order finding arbitration agreement to be substantively unconscionable), rev'd on other grounds by *Venture Cotton Cooperative v. Freeman*, No. 13-0122, 2014 WL 2619535 (*Tex.* June 13, 2013).

[355] *Rent-A-Ctr., W., Inc. v. Jackson*, 561 U.S. 63, 68-70 (2010).See *Gonzalez v. Ceva Logistics U.S., Inc.*, No. 16-CV04282-WHO, 2016 WL 6427866 (N.D. Cal. Oct. 31, 2016) ("if the class waiver is found unenforceable, the court cannot compel arbitration of the class claims under the Supreme Court's holding in Stolt-Nielsen"), *McElrath v. Uber Techs., Inc.*, No. 16-CV-07241-JSC, 2017 WL 1175591 (N.D. Cal. Mar. 30, 2017) ("excising the class action waiver does not cure the . . . NLRA problem because . . . if the class action waiver is found unenforceable, the Agreement is silent as to whether Plaintiff can arbitrate on behalf of a class"), and *Mims v. Adecco USA, Inc.*, No. 1-16-3366, 2017 WL 5202949 (Ill. Ct. App. Nov. 9, 2017) (noting that striking the class arbitration waiver "renders the [a]greement silent as to class action proceedings and absent an express provision, the parties cannot submit to class action arbitration") It is held that waivers of the right to collective redress in employment contracts violate the National Labor Relations Act (NLRA).

[356] *THI of New Mexico at Hobbs Ctr., LLC v. Patton*, 741 F.3d 1162, 1165 (10th Cir. 2014). *Phillips v. Bestway Rental, Inc.*, No. 4:12CV48, 2013 WL 832306, at *3 (N.D. Miss. Mar. 6, 2013), aff'd, 542 F. App'x 410 (5th Cir. 2013) (per curiam); accord Tiri, 171 *Cal. Rptr.* 3d at 635.

[357] *Robinson v. J&K Administrative Management Services, Inc.*, 817 F.3d 193, 194 (5th Cir. 2016), *Rossi v. SCI Funeral Servs. of New York, Inc.*, No. 15CV473ERKVMS, 2016 WL 524253, at *13 (E.D. N.Y. Jan. 28, 2016); *Hedrick v. BNC Nat'l Bank*, 186 F. Supp. 3d 1189, 1195-96 (D. Kan. 2016) ("However, even assuming that the availability of class arbitration is a 'question of [substantive] arbitrability,' the Court finds that the arbitrator must determine this question because the Employment Agreement provides 'clear and unmistakable evidence' that the parties intended the arbitrator to determine questions of arbitrability."). *Dish Network, L.L.C. v. Ray*, 226 F. Supp. 3d 1168, 1172 (D. Colo. 2016) ("As to the parties' broad agreement regarding matters to be submitted to arbitration, there is nothing in the language used expressly delegating authority to the arbitrator to decide issues of [substantive] arbitrability.").

President, Congress, or an agency has precluded the arbitration of a particular grievance[358].

It could be said that the parity principle is not only concerned with the wills of the parties, but also aids a larger aim, through judicial reasoning and publicity and statutory interpretation, of counter balancing business power and transferring power back to diffuse economic parties[359] so as to confirm their social welfare which means that the parity principle is established on an ideal of regulation rather than privatization and so in sequence forms its ability to confine arbitration law. Moreover, the parity principle is deep-rooted into the diffusion of public law into the domain of private law being set up on an ideal of distributive justice. It seems that the rejection of arbitration, where parity was missing, was only to some extent about the less powerful party's aptitude to agree to arbitrate. Taking into consideration that government was regulating great power disparities in part through litigation that is why it is argued that the FAA was litigation-promoting for parties where parity was so absent. To that extent, unconscionability is regarded not only as a contract defense but also an "equitable safety valve" and so the Supreme Court in *AT&T Mobility LLC v. Concepcion*[360] focused on the FAA's "purposes and objectives" to ask whether it preempted the California unconscionability doctrine[361].

Does arbitration weaken regulatory enforcement? The parity principle manifests an insistence that the disputes between parties whose power is so unequal remain in courts. While the parity paradigm indicates the advantages of legislative and administrative efforts to protect statutory rights from arbitration and initially the court held that arbitration could interfere with the vindication of statutory rights and supervised the enforcement of arbitration agreements[362], the post-Mitsubishi "arbitration-valorization" approach permits the presumed priority of contract to interfere with the capacity of economically less powerful parties to require public justice and so the Supreme Court[363] has permitted the FAA to preempt state laws that are impediments to accomplishing the statute's rationales such as contract enforcement goals.

---

[358] *Green v. SuperShuttle Int'l, Inc.*, 653 F.3d 766, 769 (8th Cir. 2011) (holding that an arbitrator should decide whether a lawsuit falls under section 1 of the FAA); see also 9 U.S.C. § 1 (2016) (exempting "contracts of employment of . . . any . . . class of workers engaged in foreign or interstate commerce").

[359] Batya Goodman, Note, Honey, I Shrink-Wrapped the Consumer: The Shrink-Wrap Agreement as an Adhesion Contract, 21 *Cardozo L. Rev.* 319, 323–24 (1999) ("Today, the typical agreement consists of a standard printed form prepared by one party in the superior bargaining position and adhered to by the other party, who has little or no opportunity for bargaining.").

[360] 563 U.S. 333, 352 (2011) (quoting *Hines v. Davidowitz*, 312 U.S. 52, 67 (1941)).

[361] David Horton, Federal Arbitration Act Preemption, Purposivism, and State Public Policy, 101 *Geo. L. J.* 1217, 1223 (2013) (stating that, because the FAA is only meant to preempt state rules that subvert its goals and policies, "preemption should hinge on what lawmakers wanted to accomplish with the statute, not a hyper technical parsing of its text").

[362] *Wilko v. Swan*, 346 U.S. 427, 438 (1953). The Court considered (the lack of parity between the parties, the advantages of public process that the less powerful party gives up, and how the "protective provisions of the Securities Act require the exercise of judicial direction to fairly assure their effectiveness.") Correspondingly, in *Alexander v. Gardner-Denver Co.*, 416 U.S. 36 (1974), the Court stated that arbitration was a "comparatively inappropriate forum for the final resolution of rights created by Title VII."

[363] *Southland Corp. v. Keating*, 465 U.S. 1, 16 (1984).

The first law to broadly regulate arbitration in the Slovak Republic according to international standards was Act No. 218/1996 Coll. on arbitration facilitating the establishment of permanent arbitration courts by means of a law, i.e., a separate law expressly enabling legal persons set up an arbitration court. In practice, this meant several years of de facto "domination" by a single court in the settlement of arbitration disputes. Certain shortcomings were tackled by an amendment (Act No. 448/2001 Coll.) which makes clear a number of issues concerning arbitrators, objections of bias, remedies, the right of the enforceability and legality of rulings, embracing a modification of the opportunities for a review of an arbitral award Under the settled case-law of the Constitutional Court of the Slovak Republic (the "Constitutional Court"). Arbitration is an alternative to proceedings before the ordinary courts, compared to which it presents the major advantages of flexibility and speed of procedure, informality and lower costs. However, the Constitutional Court has held that, although arbitration can be illustrated as a less complex procedure than proceedings before courts, it is essential to comply with the *principles of justice and legality*. One of the conditions for the establishment of an arbitration court's jurisdiction is its contractual basis (Section 3 of the Arbitration Act)[364].

In Australia, the *Constitution* is more concerned with the structural protection of federalism rather than rights protection[365]. Section 71 of the *Constitution* invests only the 'judicial power *of the Commonwealth*' solely in Chapter III courts raising the question of whether an international arbitral tribunal can probably exercise the judicial power 'of the Commonwealth' when foreign law governs the dispute before them[366]. The constitutional uncertainty of the *IAA has* to be resolved by assessing the scheme in light of the underlying objects and purposes of section 71 of the *Constitution*[367]. In *Hi-Fert Pty Ltd v Kiukiang Maritime Carriers (No 5)*[368], Emmett J, in *obiter*, said that international arbitral tribunals could not be exercising the judicial power of the Commonwealth as their determinations did not have an enforceable nature comparable to that of a court. The

[364] Decision of the Constitutional Court of the Slovak Republic III. US 95/2010 or II. US 173/2010. (the Constitutional Court focused on the nature and substance of the arbitration). Decision of the Constitutional Court of 21 September 2010 III. US 335/2010-16.

[365] *Brown v. The Queen* (1985) 160 CLR 171, 214 *Kruger v. Commonwealth* (1997) 190 CLR 1, 167 James Stellios, The Constitutional Jury: A Bulwark of Liberty? (2005) 27 *Sydney Law Review* 113, 127; Peter Gerangelos, The Decisional Independence of Chapter III Courts and Constitutional Limitations on Legislative Power: Notes from the United States (2005) 33 *Federal Law Review* 391, 395. Bruce Kercher, An Unruly Child: A History of Law in Australia xvii (Allen and Unwin 1995) ("[I]n the competition for fees each [court] sought to expand its jurisdiction to cover the most lucrative business.").

[366] *Kruger v. Commonwealth* (1997) 190 CLR 1, 109. *Attorney-General (Cth) v. Breckler* (1999) 197 CLR 83 (arbitral tribunals are not exercising judicial power, as they are creating rights, as opposed to enforcing existing ones).

[367] As section 71 of the Constitution embodies the doctrine of the separation of judicial power - a doctrine itself possessed of a number of objects and purposes - it is instead logical for. *Grollo v. Palmer* (1995) 184 CLR 348, 376. William Gwyn, *The Meaning of the Separation of Powers: An analysis of the Doctrine from its Origin to the Adoption of the United States Constitution* (1965).

[368] (1998) 90 FCR 1. *Comandate Marine Corp v. Pan Australia Shipping Pty Ltd* (2006) 157 FCR 45, 95 (suggests that a court today would be more willing to give effect to the purpose of the New York Convention in interpreting the IAA). Michael Polkinghorne and Jean-Claude Najar, An Introduction to ICC Arbitration in Australia: Some Current Issues in International Arbitration (1991) 3 *Bond Law Review* 43, 44.

preservation of the rule of law to protect the federal compact is of fundamental importance to the Australian concept of the separation of judicial power. This could not be waived by parties, as the outcome of a waiver could have consequences beyond the immediate dispute that could undercut the federation or the rule of law[369]. Parties can select to surrender the opportunity to have their controversy determined by an independent and impartial judiciary but they cannot do so, if it were to undercut the structural objective, of Chapter III[370]. Prima facie, an arbitral tribunal applies existing law to a set of established facts and awards remedies as a matter of legal entitlement. The arbitrator applies law to existing facts, but this can reliably be done by a non-judicial body as a process incidental to the creation of new rights. The arbitrator's decision is simply a 'factum upon which the law operates to create the right or duty[371].'

Arbitration can merely be seen as a dispute method for the contractual rights as between the parties. The only legislative powers available to the Commonwealth Parliament are those contained in the Constitution. Although the arbitration power has been relied upon by successive federal governments as the key source of constitutional authority to enact legislation regulating Australian industrial relations, there is nothing new in the use of the corporations' power, namely section 51 (xx) of the Constitution, for the same general purpose[372].

The Bulgarian Constitution[373] does not require a three-instance judicial system as an overriding mandatory constitutional principle. Moreover, there is no constitutional barrier preventing the resolution of particular selected civil and criminal matters within the framework of another system rather than only system of court instances. The jurisdiction of courts in civil cases can be excluded by an arbitration agreement pursuant to Section 9(3) of the CPe. The existence of such an arbitration agreement constitutes a procedural impediment, which prevents the court from ruling on any substantive issues, including such issues on which the court would otherwise be obliged to rule *(sua sponte)*[374].

---

[369] Jesse Kennedy, Arbitrate This! Enforcing Foreign Arbitral Awards and Chapter III of the Constitution, 2008 ANU College of Law Research Paper No. 09-04.

[370] Schor, 478 US 833, 850 (1986).

[371] Re Cram; Ex parte The Newcastle Wallsend Coal Co Pty Ltd (1987) 163 CLR 140, 149. Alexander's Case (1918) 25 CLR 434, 464 (Isaacs and Rich JJ).

[372] W.J. Ford, Politics, The Constitution, And Australian Industrial Relations: Pursuing A Unified National System, 2005 *Comp. Labor Law and Pol'y Journal* [Vol. 26:161. A. Stewart, Federal Labor Law and New Uses for the Corporations Power, 14 *Austl. J. Lab. L.* 145 (2001);

[373] Decision of Constitutional Court of Republic of Bulgaria No.9, Constitutional Case No. 15/2002 of October 24, 2002. CCP [BUL], Article 9 -(Paragraph 1, amended [by an act promulgated in:] 55 *State Gazette* (1992) (approximate translation, ciL) The parties to a dispute over property can agree that the dispute will be submitted to arbitration; this shall not apply to disputes over rights in rem or ownership of real property, maintenance or rights arising from labor relationships. Judgment of Bulgarian Supreme Court No. 327, Civil Case No. 257/92 of January 14, 1993: APIS 7 PRAVO legal information system]; Case law, 2 (14) *Bulletin of Supreme Court of Republic of Bulgaria* J2 (1993).

[374] Judgment of Bulgarian Supreme Court No. 508, Civil? Case No. 817/95 of June 6, 1995: APIS 7 PRAVO Case law, 9 *Bulletin of Supreme Court of Republic of Bulgaria*, 20 (1995). Judgment of Bulgarian Supreme Court No. 630, Civil Case No. 1832/2003 of July 28, 2004 (in *H.T.E.K.Co.V.L.L., [Kuwait] v. T. EAD [BUL]*): APIS 7 PRAVO, 4 *Bulgarski Zakonnik Magazine* 93 (2005).

In *Teléfonos de México, S.A. de C.V. ("Telmex")* the Supreme Court indicates that arbitration is a jurisdiction /domain of its own and according to article 1435 is but part of an integral law which, if analyzed in its entirety, met the said Constitutional requirements. Moreover, the First Chamber of the Supreme Court of Justice of the Nation in connection with the association between arbitration and Mexican courts ruled that arbitration is a constitutionally valid legal method to resolve disputes among private parties[375]. Moreover, it is constitutionally permissible for private parties to submit their disputes to an arbitrator for resolution and the arbitral tribunal is not a special court, consequently article 13 of the Political Constitution of the United Mexican States is not violated.

Arbitral tribunals are not part of the Russian court system and are not courts according to Article 45 of the Russian Constitution. While arbitral tribunals do not utilize state (judicial) power and are not part of the Russian court system, parties may willingly waive their constitutional right to recourse to a state court for resolution of a dispute based on the principles of free disposition of rights, autonomy of will and freedom of contract[376]. Moreover, arbitral tribunals have the right to hear disputes involving real property, including disputes to levy the execution on real property. Furthermore, a system of *state arbitration courts* on the one hand and on the other hand various *nongovernmental courts of arbitration* ("arbitrage"). The nongovernmental arbitration proceeding is carried out on the basis of Federal Statutes of 07 July 1993 on International Commercial Arbitrage, no. 5338-1, and of 24 July 2002 on Arbitration Courts in Russian Federation, no. 102-FS[377].

Early Confucian society illustrated an inclination for resolving interpersonal conflict outside the confines of formal law through relational networks. Informal mechanisms, rather than formal legal rules, were applied to resolve most civil disputes in traditional China[378]. By adopting the 1994 Arbitration Law, the Chinese domestic system was unified, and somewhat independent arbitration commissions were set up in more than 140

---

[375] I.a. CLXXXVI/2004, of the First Chamber of the Supreme Court of Justice of the Nation, Ninth Period. Amparo in Review No. 237/2004, Emilio Francisco Casares Loret de Mola (April 28, 2004).

[376] On May 26, 2011, the Constitutional Court of the Russian Federation (the "Constitutional Court") issued Ruling No. 10-P. The referral of civil law disputes to arbitral tribunals for resolution is provided for in Art. 1.2 of Law of the Russian Federation No. 5338-I on International Commercial Arbitration, (the "ICA Law") and Art. 1.2 of Federal Law No. 102-FZ on Arbitration in the Russian Federation (the "Arbitration Law"). The legal provisions in question did not contravene the Constitution.

[377] Federal Statute on International Commercial Arbitrage, no. 5338-1, July 07, 1993, Federal Statute on Arbitration Courts in Russian Federation, no. 102-FS, July 24, 2002.

[378] Folsom, R.H. and Minan, J.H., 1989. *Law in the People's Republic of China: Commentary, Readings and Materials*. Dordrecht: Martinus p. 5(Through the rule of "just men" rather than "just laws," officials qualified to maintain Confucian ideals of social harmony and proper rule were selected to both govern and administer law. The guiding principle was "men govern law, law does not govern man" (ren guan fa, bu shi fa guan ren). Legal structures were thus founded on the belief that ideal social order could be obtained, "not by strict regulation or severe punishment, but by the rule of good men, whose virtuous example was the most effective form of persuasion.") Ross, L., 1990. The Changing Profile of Dispute Resolution in Rural China: The Case of Zouping County, Shandong. *Stanford Journal of International Law* 26, p. 16 (Confucian philosophy viewed virtuous deeds as a higher expression of righteousness than merely following a set of legal sanctions).

municipalities around the country. Lately established arbitration commissions have broad jurisdiction over contractual or property disputes, excluding labor and farming contract disputes[379]. In China, the final say over arbitral jurisdiction, such as ruling on the existence and validity of an arbitration agreement, belongs to the national court, which is considered as one of the two branches of supervisory powers of courts versus arbitration. The court's supervisory power over arbitration is exercised in two ways (1) to examine the effectiveness of the arbitration agreement and (2) to review the arbitral award[380]. Commercial arbitration disputes are classified as economic cases and are commonly processed by the economic division in a court[381]. In japan[382], courts have the power to supervise arbitration and as the Japanese court preserves the pro-arbitration stance, they firmly confine themselves from over-interfering with the arbitration process. Hereafter, arbitration institutions are free from direct or indirect pressure from the judiciary which means that judicialisation of the arbitration has not taken place in the country[383].

Settlement of disputes by arbitration has been performed in India a long time ago and historical legal literature reports the ancient system of arbitration for resolving disputes regarding the family or a social group or in the domain of trade. Characteristically the Indian Constitution also specifies settlement of international disputes by arbitration as a Directive Principle of State Policy [(Article 51(d)][384]. The materialization of alternative dispute resolution has been one of the most momentous movements as a part of conflict management and judicial reform, and it has become a global need[385]. The principles of natural justice have been developed by the courts, in order to secure fairness in judicial functions being the Common Law counterpart of the "due process of law" in the Constitution of the United States. The violation of principles of natural justice would amount to be contrary to the public policy of India[386]. An arbitral tribunal discharging quasi-judicial functions is expected to be fair and impartial in the arbitral proceedings. In

---

[379] Katherine L. Lynch, Chinese Law: The New Arbitration Law, 26 *Hong Kong L. J.* 104, 105. Civil Procedure Law of PRC, art. 18-21, adopted on April 9, 1991 at the Fourth Session of the Seventh National People's Congress (available in Lexis' China law info library, PRCLEG 19) Enacted in 1991, the Civil Procedure Law of the PRC is another important piece of arbitration-related legislation separating arbitral awards into domestic, foreign-related, and foreign awards, with each receiving a dissimilar standard of judicial review.

[380] Dr.Weixia Gu, *Judicial Review Over Arbitration In China: Assessing The Extent Of The Latest Pro-Arbitration Move By The Supreme People's Court In The People's Republic Of China*, Vol. 27, No. 2 *Wisconsin International Law Journal* 221.

[381] Daniel C.K. Chow, *The Legal System of The People's Republic of China In A* Nutshell 201 (2003).

[382] Nobumichi Teramura and Luke Nottage, *Arbitration Reform in Japan: Reluctant Legislature and Institutional Challenges*. http://ssrn.com/abstract=3252270

[383] Japan to Open Center for International Business Arbitration, *Nikkei Asian Review*, 18 May 2017, http://asia.nikkei.com/Politics-Economy/Policy-Politics/Japan-to-open-center-for-international-business-arbitration.

[384] Kd Raj, *Alternate Dispute Resolution System: A Prudent Mechanism of Speedy Redress in India* 1 www.ssrn.com p2, "When we go to court, we know that we are going to win all or lose all. Whereas, when we go to any method of ADR or for informal settlement with different expectations, we know that we may not get all that we want, but we will not lose everything. In India, arbitration and domestic or in-house tribunals are alternatives to formal courts."

[385] KD Raj, *Alternate Dispute Resolution System: A Prudent Mechanism of Speedy Redress in India*, www.ssrn.com p2.

[386] Seth JC, "Efficacy of Arbitration – Measures to Streamline the Law and Procedure," 2004 (1) *Arb L. R.* 7.

R. S. Dass v. Union of India[387], the Supreme Court observed that: "It is well established that rules of natural justice are not rigid rules, they are flexible and their application depends upon the setting and background of statutory provisions, nature of the right which may be affected and the consequences which may entail, its application depends upon the facts and circumstances of each case." It could be said that arbitration applies rules of natural justice as well.

Section 34 of Chapter 2 on Bill of Rights of the South African Constitution Act No. 108 of 1996 provides "Everyone has the right to have any dispute that can be resolved by the application of law decided in a fair public hearing before a court or, where appropriate, another independent and impartial tribunal or forum." Correspondingly section 6 of Nigeria's 1999 Federal Constitution presents that the judicial powers of the Federation shall be vested in the courts but parties to a contract can select to resolve any dispute which arises between them without reference to the regular courts. Moreover, Bolaji Owasanoye[388] argues that "arbitration is part of the legal system and if the law allows awards to be final by not allowing judicial review, then it has merit."

3. CONSTITUTIONALITY OF ARBITRATION

Does arbitration violate Article III? Is there "arbitration hegemony" over federal statutory claims[389]? The "jurisdictional ouster" claim found its roots in contract law and in essence treating the arbitration agreement as a void contract that offended public policy[390]. Congress made available a quasi-judicial mechanism through which willing parties may, at their option, choose to resolve their differences[391]. Article III unreservedly authorizes substantial private ordering. Indeed, historical treatments of the pre-Revolutionary period imply that what we now call "alternative dispute resolution," was the norm rather than the exception in the colonies[392]. It has to be remembered that arbitration as the central dispute mechanism brought justice and contributed into the

---

[387] AIR 1987 SC 593: 1986 Supp SCC 617.

[388] Bolaji Owasanoye, *Dispute Resolution Mechanisms and Constitutional Rights in Sub-Saharan Africa* (Article Reference: Document No.14, Chapter 2, March 2001).

[389] Myriam Gilles, Opting Out of Liability: The Forthcoming, Near-Total Demise of the Modern Class Action, 104 *Mich. L. Rev.* 373, 393-96 (2005) (describing the ascendancy of an "arbitration hegemony" over federal statutory claims). *Scherck v. Alberto-Culver Co.*, 417 U.S. 506 (1974) *Rodriguez de Quijas v. Shearson/American Express, Inc.*, 490 U.S. 477 (1989), *Shearson/American Express, Inc. v. McMahon*, 482 U.S. 220 (1987), *Mitsubishi Motors Corp. v. Soler Chrysler-Plymouth, Inc.*, 473 U.S. 614 (1985), Gilmer v. Interstate/Johnson Lane Corp., 500 U.S. 20 (1991).

[390] Macneil, Speidel, and Stipanowich, Federal Arbitration Law § 4.3.2.2 (Supp. 1999). *Nebraska v. Nebraska Ass'n of Public Employees*, 477 N.W.2d 577 (Neb. 1991) (holding that state authorizing binding arbitration violated "open courts" provision of Nebraska Constitution).

[391] *CFTC v. Schor* 478 U.S. 848.

[392] Richard C. Reuben, Democracy And Dispute Resolution: The Problem Of Arbitration, Winter/Spring 2004 *Law and Contemporary Problems* Vol. 67:279, Peter B. Rutledge Arbitration and Constitution Advocate 2011 www.law.uga.edu.

establishment of modern democracies. In other words, arbitration brought justice and contributed in the emergence and establishment of all the principles expressed by constitutions in modern states. Judith Resnik[393] said that, "federal judges who once had declined to enforce *ex ante* agreements to arbitrate federal statutory rights now generally insist on holding parties to such bargains, thereby outsourcing an array of claims." There is criticism for cutting off the production of law, for challenging the role of Article III courts, for narrowing access to law by enforcing bans on the collective pursuit of claims and so the rationalization of disputes through the FAA to non-public service providers reveals a shadow conflict over public subsidies for litigants[394]. It is characteristic that Justice Scalia has questioned the extent to which the Constitution requires governments to aid individuals seeking to use the courts[395] by requiring single-file arbitrations[396] and Justice Thomas concurred in upholding class bans[397] and objected to constitutional obligations to subsidize litigants[398].

Rule 38 of the Federal Rules of Civil Procedure provides that "[t]he right of trial by jury as declared by the Seventh Amendment to the Constitution or as given by a statute of the United States shall be preserved to the parties inviolate.[399]" The Supreme Court has considered the right to trial by jury in a civil action as a "basic and fundamental" right that is "sacred to the citizen" and therefore "should be jealously guarded by the court.[400]" Mandatory binding arbitration threatens a basic principle of any justice system: the constitutional right to take a dispute to court[401] but parties to a contract can agree that, in

---

[393] Resnik J, Procedure as Contract, 80 *Notre Dame L. Rev*. 593, 597 (2005).

[394] J. Maria Glover, Feature, Disappearing Claims and the Erosion of Substantive Law, 124 *Yale L. J*. 3052 (2015). Peter B. Rutledge, Arbitration And The Constitution 15-53 (2012); Roger J. Perlstadt, Article III Judicial Power and the Federal Arbitration Act, 62 *Am. U. L. Rev*. 201 (2012). Burt Neuborne, Ending Lochner Lite, 50 Harv. *C.R.-C.L. L. Rev*. 183 (2015). Judith Resnik, Fairness in Numbers: A Comment on *AT&T v. Concepcion*, *Wal-Mart v. Dukes*, and *Turner v. Rogers*, 125 *Harv. L. Rev*. 78, 118-133 (2011); Myriam E. Gilles, The End of Doctrine: Private Arbitration, Public Law and the Anti-Lawsuit Movement (Benjamin N. Cardozo Sch. of Law, Jacob Burns Inst. for Advanced Legal Studies Research Paper No. 436, 2014), http://ssrn.com/abstract=2488575.

[395] *Lewis v. Casey*, 518 U.S. 343, 349-350 (1996).

[396] *Am. Express Co. v. Italian Colors Rest*., 133 S. Ct. 2304 (2013); *AT&T Mobility LLC v. Concepcion*, 131 S. Ct. 1740 (2011).

[397] *Italian Colors*, 133 S. Ct. at 2312-13-*AT&T v. Concepcion*, 131 S. Ct. at 1753-56.

[398] *Turner v. Rogers*, 131 S.Ct. 2507, 2521 (2011)- *M.L.B. v. S.L.J. ex rel. M.L.J*., 519 U.S. 102, 130 (1996).

[399] Fed. R. Civ. P. 38.

[400] *Jacob v. New York City*, 315 U.S. 752, 752–53 (1942); *Beacon Theatres, Inc. v. Westover*, 359 U.S. 500, 501 (1959) (stating that the right to jury trial "is of such importance and occupies so firm a place in our history and jurisprudence that any seeming curtailment of the right to a jury trial should be scrutinized with the utmost care").

[401] Sen. Russell D. Feingold, Mandatory Arbitration: What Process is Due, 39 *Harv. J. On Leg*. 281, 288 (2002) ("One reason that mandatory, binding arbitration has become so troubling is because it threatens a fundamental principle of our justice system: the constitutional right to take a dispute to court.") Christine M. Reilly, Comment, Achieving Knowing and Voluntary Consent in Pre-Dispute Mandatory Agreements at the Contracting Stage of Employment, 90 *Cal. L. Rev*. 1203, 1210 (2002). Reilly explains that in addition to waiving their right to trial by judge or jury, individuals who agree to submit disputes to arbitration waive (1) their rights under Article I and Article III of the Constitution;(2) their rights under the 5th, 7th, and 14th Amendments; (3) their rights to demand that [federal statutory claims] be adjudicated in a federal district court under the Federal Rules of Civil Procedure and the Federal Rules of Evidence by a judge, appointed under Article III of the Constitution, who will provide instruction as to the applicable law to a jury chosen in a fair, objective, and non-discriminatory manner; and (4) their right to appeal an adverse verdict to a U.S. Court of

the event a dispute arises, they waive their right to a jury. Democratic theory commands that power be only exercised with the consent of the governed. It thus legitimizes the power of arbitrators to settle the dispute, at least as far as the parties are concerned. It should be taken into account that arbitrators are private individuals exercising a power which is generally assigned to state officials acting with publicly accepted authority.

It is worth mentioning that consent to arbitration "may be implied in fact"[402] and so under the doctrine of direct benefits estoppel, a party can establish agreement to arbitrate by exercising rights under an instrument that contains an arbitration provision[403]. Thus, it could be said that the consent to arbitration is itself an exercise of sovereignty, signifying that arbitral tribunals firmly apply the law[404]. Locke and Cohen believed that public authority was needed to make arbitration more effective[405]and this author argues that arbitrators should be attributed the public authority to deal with arbitration. Moreover, in 1697, Locke drafted two legislative proposals to consolidate the functioning and autonomy of arbitration. One proposal made private arbitration agreements enforceable in courts and a "submission"— a private agreement to present a dispute to arbitration— would function like a court reference, a procedure by which courts ordered arbitration[406]. It is worth mentioning that John Locke recognized that arbitration was valuable for resolving trade disputes needed to be "decisive without appeal" and so final and binding[407]. Thus, the need of an independent arbitration is reiterated by Locke and Cohen. Freedom of contract was presented as a sort of philosophical counterweight and a justification with constitutional connotation for limiting parties' right to bring suit in court, and that Congress was in reality principally motivated by its practical concern for judicial efficiency. Moreover, freedom of contract is a party's "power to decide whether to contract and to establish the [contract] terms" and a "fundamental" policy of

---

Appeals or to petition for certiorari to the U.S. Supreme Court. Jean R. Sternlight, The Rise and Spread of Mandatory Arbitration as a Substitute for the Jury Trial 38 *U.S.F. L. Rev*. 17, 19 (2003).

[402] *Pinnacle Museum Tower Ass'n. v. Pinnacle Mkt. Dev. (US), LLC*, 282 P.3d 1217, 1231 (Cal. 2012). Maureen A. Weston, The Death of Class Arbitration After Concepcion? 60 *Kans. L. Rev*. 767, 772 (2012) ("A fundamental principle underlying the FAA is to respect freedom of contract.").

[403] *Damon v. StrucSure Home Warranty, LLC*, 338 P.3d 123, 128 (N.M. 2014). *Jansen v. Salomon Smith Barney, Inc*., 776 A.2d 816, 821 (N.J. Super. Ct. App. Div. 2001). *Herbert v. Superior Court*, 215 *Cal. Rptr*. 477, 481 (Ct. App. 1985). *Rachal v. Reitz*, 403 S.W.3d 840, 842 (Tex. 2013) (holding that beneficiary who argued the trustee breached his fiduciary duty had "accept[ed] the benefits of the trust" and thus was bound to arbitrate); see also *McArthur v. McArthur*, 168 *Cal. Rptr*. 3d 785, 795 (Ct. App. 2014) (finding that party did not consent to arbitration when she challenged the validity of a trust amendment that contained an arbitration provision). E. Gary Spitko, The Will As An Implied Unilateral Arbitration Contract, 68 *Fla. L. Rev*. 49 (2016).

[404] W. Michael Reisman, *Reflections on Economic Development, National Sovereignty and International Arbitration* 16–20 (Apr. 13, 2006) (unpublished manuscript, available at http://www.law.yale.edu/documents/pdf/Bogota.4.13.06.pdf) (observing that the consent to arbitration is itself an exercise of sovereignty, suggesting that arbitral tribunals strictly apply the law, and commenting that countries can then take steps to accommodate concerns about sovereignty through the normal political process).

[405] Julius Henry Cohen, The Law of Commercial Arbitration and the New York Statute, 31 *Yale L. J*. 147, 147 (1921) ("For over three hundred years, a dictum of Lord Coke has held sway over the minds of America. It is now on its fair way to a decent burial.").

[406] Henry Horwitz and James Oldham, John Locke, Lord Mansfield and Arbitration during the Eighteenth Century, 36 *The Historical J*. 137, 138 (1993).

[407] Henry Horwitz and James Oldham, John Locke, Lord Mansfield and Arbitration during the Eighteenth Century, 36 *The Historical J*. 137, 138 (1993).

arbitration[408]. Some rights, however, are alienable. The jury-trial right, like many other rights, is alienable. Consent is a common way of alienating, or "waiving," one's rights[409]. While consent is a way of waiving rights in many areas of law, these areas fluctuate in their standards of consent. For example, the standards of consent governing jury-waiver clauses in general tend to be higher than those governing contracts[410]. A contractual right to arbitrate may be waived explicitly or unreservedly[411]. Courts[412] must scrutinize the entirety of the circumstances and "determine whether based on all the circumstances, the party against whom the waiver is to be enforced has acted inconsistently with the right to arbitrate." There is a common, three-part test for determining whether a right to arbitrate has been waived. A party knew of an existing right to arbitration; (2) acted

[408] *Jones v. U-Haul Co. of Mass. & Ohio*, 16 F. Supp. 3d 922, 942 (S.D. Ohio. 2014); *Cable Connection, Inc. v. DIRECTV, Inc.*, 190 P.3d 586, 604 (Cal. 2008) (noting that "freedom of contract . . . is fundamental to arbitration"); *United States v. Alabama*, 691 F.3d 1269, 1293 (11th Cir. 2012) ("The ability to contract is not merely an act of legislative grace; it is a capability that, in practical application, is essential for an individual to live and conduct daily affairs."); *Chavez v. Sargent*, 339 P.2d 801, 835-37 (Cal. 1959) (McComb, J., concurring) ("The citizen's rights of liberty, property, and the pursuit of happiness . . . apply as fully to his right to contract, unlimited by unnecessary regulation, as they do to the individual's freedom from arrest or restraint of person."). Carolyn Edwards, Freedom of Contract and Fundamental Fairness for Individual Parties: The Tug of War Continues, 77 *UMKC L. Rev.* 647, 654 (2009). *Kona Vill. Realty, Inc. v. Sunstone Realty Partners, XIV*, 236 P.3d 456, 458 (Haw. 2010) (citing the "recognized autonomy of parties to enter into an arbitration agreement" that stems from the "right of freedom to contract"). (The public has an interest that individuals entering arbitration have "broad powers to order their own affairs by making legally enforceable promises"); *State v. Nakanelua*, 345 P.3d 155, 172 (Haw. 2015) ("[A]rbitration is a consensual process in which autonomy of the parties who enter into arbitration agreements should be given primary consideration.").

[409] *Grafton Partners L.P. v. Price Waterhouse Coopers L.L.P.*, 116 P.3d 479, 490–93 (Cal. Super. Ct. 2005) (breaking from the majority of courts in refusing to enforce a pre-dispute jury waiver). 1 Thomas H. Oehmke, *Commercial Arbitration §§ 23:11*, 23:56 (3d ed. 2008) (stating submitting claim does not waive right to arbitration); Michael D. Fielding, Navigating the Intersection of Bankruptcy and Commercial Arbitration, 27 No. 2 *Banking and Fin. Services Pol'y Rep.* 13, 16 (2008) (noting "courts have effectively elevated the statutory right to compel arbitration above the constitutional right to a jury trial"); Fred Neufeld, Enforcement of Contractual Arbitration Agreements Under The Bankruptcy Code, 65 *Am. Bankr. L. J.* 525, 544–45 (1991) (discussing bankruptcy courts could hold party which has filed proof of claim has waived its right to arbitrate). *Shaffer v. Heitner*, 433 U.S. 186, 207 (1977) (explaining when exercising in rem jurisdiction over property, same test applied for exercise of in personam jurisdiction); *Int'l Shoe Co. v. Washington*, 326 U.S. 310, 316 (1945) (stating to subject defendant to in personam jurisdiction minimum contacts must exist). *Cent. Va. Cmty. Coll. v. Katz*, 546 U.S. 356, 362 (2006) at 369 ("Bankruptcy jurisdiction, as understood today and at the time of the framing, is principally in rem jurisdiction."); (interpreting Constitution to support Congress' authority to intrude upon state sovereign immunity in context of bankruptcy legislation) at 370 (discussing courts adjudicating disputes have historically had power to issue ancillary orders to enforce their in rem adjudications).

[410] Jean R. Sternlight, Mandatory Binding Arbitration and Demise of the Seventh Amendment Right to a Jury Trial, 16 *Ohio St. J. on Disp. Resol.* 669, 674 (2001).

[411] *Ernst and Young LLP v. Baker O'Neal Holdings, Inc.*, 304 F.3d 753, 756 (7th Cir. 2002) (affirming lower court decision denying motion to compel arbitration finding appellant had impliedly waived its right to arbitrate). *Fisher v. A.G. Becker Paribas Inc.*, 791 F.2d 691, 694 (9th Cir. 1986) (setting out three requirements party seeking arbitration must demonstrate in order to successfully compel arbitration); *Carcich v. Rederi A/B Nordie*, 389 F.2d 692, 696 (2d Cir. 1968) (reaffirming strong "federal policy favoring arbitration" and thus finding waiver "is not to be lightly inferred").

[412] *Sharif v. Wellness Int'l Network, Ltd.*, 376 F.3d 720, 726 (7th Cir. 2004) (emphasis added) (quoting *Cabinetree of Wis., Inc. v. Kraftmaid Cabinetry, Inc.*, 50 F.3d 388, 391 (7th Cir. 1995)). *Cabinetree of Wis., Inc.*, 50 F.3d at 390 (supporting finding party has implicitly waived its right to arbitrate when it has chosen judicial, rather than arbitrary forum, to adjudicate matter). —"did that party do all it could reasonably have been expected to do to make the earliest feasible determination of whether to proceed judicially or by arbitration?" *SW Indus. Imp. and Exp., Inc. v. Wilmod Co., Inc.*, 524 F.2d 468, 470 (5th Cir. 1975) (finding "[p]articipation in settlement negotiations" does not "preclude the right to arbitrate").

contradictorily with that right; and (3) prejudiced the other party by these incoherent acts[413]. Moreover, courts routinely decide that a party has waived its right to arbitrate, even though this issue involves a flexible, multi-factored balancing test[414].

One way to alienate the jury-trial right is to consent to a contract containing an arbitration clause—that is, a clause asserting to waive[415] the right to have disputes resolved in litigation and to generate the right to have them resolved by arbitration. An enforceable arbitration clause[416] involving a dispute denotes that arbitration replaces litigation with regard to that dispute. The term "waiver" is utilized to refer only to *giving* away one's rights. Standard accounts of contract law cautiously differentiate the "waiver" of contractual rights, which does not demand consideration, from the "modification" of contractual rights, which does[417]. It is argued that by agreeing to arbitration, parties in fact waive the right to assert upon procedural due process and other constitutional rights that would be involved if a state actor were involved[418]. It has to be taken into account that arbitration allows parties to accomplish the due process ideal of procedure tailored to the stakes of disputes that are expected to arise between the contracting parties[419]. It is worth mentioning here that where the benefits of an alternative procedure outweighed[420] its costs was a specific procedure needed as a matter of constitutional due process. Thus, arbitration has the capacity to overcome perceived pathologies of civil litigation in the United States[421]. It seems that judges understand that arbitration has to take its place in

---

[413] Thomas H. Oehmke, *Commercial Arbitration § 23:30* (3d ed. 2008) (illustrating constraints and limitations of waiving one's right to arbitration). *Gay v. Credit Inform*, 511 F.3d 369, 379 (3d Cir. 2007) ("A party seeking to avoid arbitration for a statutory claim has the burden of establishing that Congress intended to preclude arbitration of the claim."); *Mintze v. Am. Gen. Fin. Servs., Inc.* (In re Mintze), 434 F.3d 222, 229 (3d Cir. 2006) (finding arbitration enforcement can be overcome when "party opposing arbitration" establishes congressional intent to create exception to FAA mandate regarding statutory claims). *Mirant Corp. v. The Southern Co.*, 337 B.R. 107, 121 (N.D. Tex. 2006) (noting "the court will not presume that a litigant has knowingly and willfully surrendered its constitutional right to a jury trial for the resolution of disputes that are only incidentally related to the bankruptcy process").

[414] *Capitol Const. Services, Inc. v. Farah, LLC*, -- N.E. 2d --, 2011 WL 1119023, at *4 (Ind. Ct. App. 2011).

[415] Charles Alan Wright et Al., Federal Practice And Procedure § 3721, at 97 (2009) ("The modern view . . . is that, in advance of suit, a defendant can contractually waive his right to remove to federal court an action brought against him in a state court, unless the Constitution or a federal statute grants the federal courts exclusive jurisdiction over that action.").

[416] *Duran v. J. Haas Grp., LLC*, 531 Fed. App'x 146 (2d Cir. 2013) (enforcing arbitration clause that required New York plaintiff allegedly defrauded by defendant to travel to Maricopa County, Arizona, to challenge validity of arbitration clause). *Am. Express Co. v. Italian Colors Rest.*, 133 S. Ct. 2304, 2316 (2013) (Kagan, J., dissenting) (observing that American Express's arbitration provision "prevents [plaintiff] from informally arranging with other merchants to produce a common expert report").

[417] E. Allan Farnsworth, *Contracts § 8.5* (3d ed. 1999).

[418] Carole J. Buckner, Due Process in Class Arbitration, 58 *Fla. L. Rev.* 185, 216 (2006).

[419] *AT&T Mobility LLC v. Concepcion*, 563 U.S. 333 (2011) (No. 09-893) (stressing that arbitration is the only cost-effective means of resolving disputes over "minor charges or adjustments to monthly bills").

[420] *Mathews v. Eldridge*, 424 U.S. 319, 335 (1976).

[421] *Stolt-Nielsen S.A. v. AnimalFeeds International Corp.* 559 U.S. 662, 685 (2010). *Volt Info. Scis., Inc. v. Bd. of Trs. of Leland Stanford Jr. Univ.*, 489 U.S. 468, 476 (1989) ("There is no federal policy favoring arbitration under a certain set of procedural rules; the federal policy is simply to ensure the enforceability, according to their terms, of private agreements to arbitrate."). *Oxford Health Plans LLC v. Sutter*, 133 S. Ct. 2064 (2013) (recognizing arbitrator's authority to conduct class proceedings where parties agree that correct interpretation of the arbitration agreement is a question for the arbitrator and the contract implicitly authorizes class proceedings by giving arbitrators all powers of a court).

the dispute system in a single jurisdiction by becoming independent than courts to have a say on all matters of an arbitral procedure.

There is no due process[422] in arbitration? It could be said that an arbitration agreement means waiving many of the procedural rights guaranteed in litigation which does not mean luck of due process[423]. Arbitration agreements have need of workers to waive their right to sue, and substitute a court with arbitration[424]. Additionally an arbitration agreement means a waiver of many of the procedural rights assured in litigation[425]. Apparently, in arbitration, the parties waive first their rights to fact finding by a jury of their peers, second a trial presided over by a judge who is an elected or appointed public official and third a full-blown discovery[426].

Parties who consent by contract to arbitration explicitly waived their constitutional rights by opting out of the judicial system with its rigid substantive rules[427]. It is a constitutional right of parties to choose their dispute mechanism such as arbitration which is established by law and it is not an illegal creation. It is worth mentioning that no

---

[422] *Flores v. Evergreen at San Diego, LLC*, 55 *Cal. Rptr.* 3d 823, 832 (Ct. App. 2007) ("arbitration agreements waive important legal rights."). Carole J. Buckner, Due Process in Class Arbitration, 58 *Fla. L. Rev.* 185, 216 (2006) ("[C]ourts addressing this issue hold that, by agreeing to arbitration, parties effectively waive the right to insist upon procedural due process and other constitutional rights that would be required if a state actor were involved.").

[423] Stephen J. Ware, Domain-Name Arbitration in the Arbitration-Law Context: Consent to, and Fairness in the UDRP, 6 *J. Small and Emerging Bus. L.* 129, 153 (2002).

[424] Jean Sternlicht, Creeping Mandatory Arbitration, 57 *Stan. L. Rev.* 1631, 1654 (2005), *Baldeo v. Darden Rest., Inc.*, 2005 WL 44703 (E.D.N.Y. 2005), at * 2. *Gold v. Deutsche Aktiengesellschaft*, 365 F.3d 144, 146 (2d Cir. 2004). David B. Lipsky Et Al., Emerging Systems for Managing Workplace Conflict (2003). Carole J. Buckner, Due Process in Class Arbitration, 58 *Fla. L. Rev.* 185, 216 (2006) ("[C]ourts addressing this issue hold that, by agreeing to arbitration, parties effectively waive the right to insist upon procedural due process and other constitutional rights that would be required if a state actor were involved.") Edward Brunet, Arbitration and Constitutional Rights, 71 *N.C. L. Rev.* 81, 102 (1992) ("The orthodox view holds that parties who consent by contract to arbitration expressly waive their constitutional rights. The parties opt out of the judicial system with its rigid substantive rules."); Stephen J. Ware, Domain-Name Arbitration in the Arbitration-Law Context: Consent to, and Fairness in the UDRP, 6 *J. Small and Emerging Bus. L.* 129, 153 (2002) ("An arbitration agreement . . . is a waiver of many of the procedural rights guaranteed in litigation."); *Flores v. Evergreen at San Diego, LLC*, 55 *Cal. Rptr.* 3d 823, 832 (Ct. App. 2007) ("arbitration agreements waive important legal rights.").

[425] Stephen J. Ware, Domain-Name Arbitration in the Arbitration-Law Context: Consent to, and Fairness in the UDRP, 6 *J. Small and Emerging Bus. L.* 129, 153 (2002). Paul H. Dawes, Alternative Dispute Resolution, 1136 PLI/CORP 599, 603 (1999) ("The risks [of arbitration], broadly speaking, can be grouped into three major concerns: lack of appeal rights, waiver of other procedural and substantive rights and, ironically, a perception that like jurors, arbitrators can be unpredictable, under-qualified and swayed by emotion."). *Clerk v. First Bank of Del.*, 735 F. Supp. 2d 170, 183 (E.D. Pa. 2010) (noting that "the presence of an opt-out clause does not automatically spare the arbitration provision from a finding of procedural unconscionability" and collecting cases).

[426] Mark E. Budnitz, Arbitration of Disputes between Consumers and Financial Institutions: A Serious Threat to Consumer Protection, 10 *Ohio St. J. on Disp. Resol.* 267, 283 (1995), Ryan Griffitts, Stearing Clear of the Runaway Jury 68 *Tex. B. J.* 320, 320 (2005) ("By executing arbitration agreements, the parties waive their right to have their case decided by a judge, and, more important, a jury.").

[427] Edward Brunet, Arbitration and Constitutional Rights, 71 *N.C. L. Rev.* 81, 102 (1992). Mark E. Budnitz, Arbitration of Disputes between Consumers and Financial Institutions: A Serious Threat to Consumer Protection, 10 *Ohio St. J. On Disp. Resol.* 267, 283 (1995) ("Obviously, in arbitration, the parties waive their rights to fact finding by a jury of their peers . . . . to a trial presided over by a judge who is an elected or appointed public official . . . . [and] to full-blown discovery."); Ryan Griffitts, Stearing Clear of the Runaway Jury 68 *Tex. B. J.* 320, 320 (2005) ("By executing arbitration agreements, the parties waive their right to have their case decided by a judge, and, more important, a jury.").

ing federal and state dockets in the wake of the Industrial Revolution[444]. Is tutional? The constitutionality of the Federal Arbitration Act is beyond A, which provides for the enforceability of arbitration agreements, derives nality from Congress' Article I power to regulate interstate commerce[445]. other national arbitration laws do not strip courts of jurisdiction entirely but ers their consideration of the dispute limiting the extent of their review. If ict courts striped of their power to review[446] arbitral awards will a l infirmity arise? It is argued that constitutionality of arbitration based on the ederal courts to conduct *de novo* review of questions of law[447]. other hand, arbitration is a voluntary process. Moreover, federal courts are rom conducting *de novo* review of the arbitrator's legal errors448. Arbitration, tutionally guaranteed adjudication method, is subject to the primary rules of g/due process, neutrality and impartiality of arbitrators, which apply to state Furthermore, the capacity of parties to choose their judge brings arbitration as a

---

. No. 96, at 1 (1924) *Preston v. Ferrer*, 128 S. Ct. 978, 986 (2008) ("A prime objective of an agreement rate is to achieve 'streamlined proceedings and expeditious results.'" (quoting Mitsubishi Motors Corp., S. at 633)); *Rich v. Spartis*, 516 F.3d 75, 81 (2d Cir. 2008) (indicating plaintiffs are helped by general nd "'twin goals of arbitration'" which include "'settling disputes efficiently and avoiding long and sive litigation'") *Houdstermaatschappij v. Standard Mircrosystems Corp*., 103 F.3d 9, 12 (2d Cir. 1997) fying review of arbitration awards in order to avoid "'undermining'" aims of arbitration).

Owners Ass'n v. Satomi, L.L.C., 159 P.3d 460, 467 (*Wash Ct. App.* 2007). "[The Congress shall have the r t]o regulate commerce with foreign nations, and among the several states . . . ." U.S. Const. art. I, § 8, *Satomi Owners Ass'n v. Satomi, L.L.C.*, No. 80480-0, 2009 WL 4985689, at *16 (Wash. Dec. 24, 2009). *ton v. Ferrer*, 552 U.S. 346, 359 (2008) ("When parties agree to arbitrate all questions arising under a ract, the FAA supersedes state laws lodging primary jurisdiction in another forum, whether judicial or inistrative.") *Nitro-Lift Tech., L.L.C. v. Howard*, 133 S. Ct. 500 (2012) (preempting Oklahoma Supreme rt rule that a court, not an arbitrator, determines the validity of a covenant not to compete in a contract aining an arbitration clause).

44 *son v. Robinson*, 415 U.S. 361 (1974) (precluding judicial review of certain Veteran's Administration erminations), *Morris v. Gressette*, 432 U.S. 491, (1997) (finding that Attorney General's failure to make ely objection under the Voting Rights Act of 1965 is not subject to judicial review), Block v. Community trition Institute, 467 U.S. 340 (1984) (consumers of dairy products could not obtain judicial review of milk rket orders), *Webster v. Doe*, 486 U.S. 592 (1988) (holding CIA director's decision to discharge employee as not subject to judicial review). *Crowell v. Benson*, 285 U.S. 22 (1932). *United States v. Raddatz*, 447 U.S. 57 (1980), *Commodity Futures Trading Commission v. Schor*, 478 U.S. 833 (1986).

447 on, Of Legislative Courts, Administrative Agencies and Article III, 101 *Harv. L. Rev*. 915, 918-26 (1988) *Inited States v. Meade*, 533 U.S. 218 (2001) (discussing degrees of judicial deference to agency statutory nterpretations). D Schwartz, The federal Arbitration Act and the power of Congress over state courts, 2004 Ore L Rev 541. "FAA preemption is unconstitutional" Jean R. Stemlight, Rethinking the Constitutionality of he Supreme Court's Preference for Binding Arbitration: A Fresh Assessment of Jury Trial, Separation of Powers, and Due Process Concems, 72 *Tul. L. Rev.* 1, 1 (1997) (arguing that the current pro-arbitration policy neglects the contractual principle of consent and often leads to the violation of constitutional rights); J. Douglas Uloth and J. Hamilton Rial, III, Equitable Estoppel as a Basis for Compelling Nonsignatories to Arbitrate—A Bridge Too Far?, 21 *Rev. Litig.* 593, 632 (2002) ("Since 1999, courts have arguably reached too far to find an agreement to arbitrate.").

48 Norman Posner Judicial Review of Arbitral Awards: Manifest Disregard of the Law 64 *Brook. L. Rev*. 471, 506 (1998) ("Consequently, although most circuit courts have adopted "manifest disregard of the law" as a non-statutory ground for vacating or modifying an award, until recently there have been few cases in which a court has set aside an arbitral award on this ground."), Noah Rubins, Manifest Disregard of the Law' and 'Vacatur of Arbitral Awards in the United States, 12 *Am. Rev. Int'l Arb.* 363 (2001).

449 T. Carbonneau, Arbitral Justice: The Demise of Due Process in American law, 70 *Tulane L Rev* 1945 (1996); F. Kessedjian, Principe de la contradiction et arbitrage, *Rev Arb* 381 (1995). *ATandT and Another v. Saudi Cable Company*, [2000] 2 *Lloyd's Rep* 127 (CA).

country shall adopt any law impairing the obligations of contract[428]. Professor Rubin[429] said that "the contract standard cannot be used to justify those waivers that involve constitutional rights since such rights necessarily take precedence over the contract policy of honoring private agreements" but his argument was not directed at section 2 of the FAA specifically. The traditional theory used to rationalize arbitration's compatibility with Article III rests on the principle of waiver. Parties entering into an arbitration agreement have waived their right to a federal forum, by this means eliminating any Article III point. Even if an arbitration clause has been inserted in a contract of adhesion on a 'take-it-or-leave-it' basis, its acceptance means consent. It should be taken into account that enforcement of adhesive arbitration[430] agreements benefits society by reducing procedure costs, by this means benefiting consumers, employees and other adhering parties[431]. Moreover, simple disproportion in bargaining power does not make

---

[428] U.S. Const. art. I, § 10. Max Helveston & Michael Jacobs, The Incoherent Role of Bargaining Power in Contract Law, 49 *Wake Forest L. Rev.* 1017, 1054 (2014) ("Examples abound of laws and regulations aimed at resolving the very concerns that have led courts to turn to bargaining-power analysis. In a number of different areas, legislatures and agencies have prohibited contracts from including terms deemed abusive to one of the parties"). Robert W. Emerson, Franchising and the Parol Evidence Rule, 50 *Am. Bus. L. J.* 659, 680-81 (2013) ("most state statutes regulating franchise relationships prohibit franchisors from requiring their franchisees to waive the franchisor's liability for a violation of those state franchise laws when entering into a franchise agreement"); Daniel B. Kelly, The Right to Include, 63 *Emory L. J.* 857, 912 (2014) ("Although similar to contracts, franchises differ because franchise law entails certain mandatory rules (e.g., limitations on termination) and attempts to deter renegotiation in ways that contract law generally does not.").

[429] Edward L. Rubin, Toward a General Theory of Waiver, 28 *UCLA L. Rev.* 478 (1981).

[430] *AT&T Mobility LLC v. Concepcion*, 131 S.Ct. 1740, 1753 (2011) (holding that Federal Arbitration Act preempts California law refusing to enforce adhesive arbitration agreement requiring claims to be brought on an individual, rather than class, basis while acknowledging that California law would not, under similar circumstances, enforce such a requirement in a non-arbitration agreement) (citing *Am. Online, Inc. v. Superior Court*, 90 *Cal. App.* 4th 1, 18, 108 *Cal. Rptr.* 2d 699, 712 (2001) ("The unavailability of class action relief in this context is sufficient in and by itself to preclude enforcement of the TOS forum selection clause.")). *Stolt-Nielsen S.A. v. AnimalFeeds International Corp.*, 559 U.S. 662 (2010), *American Express Co. v. Italian Colors Rest.*, 133 S. Ct. 2304 (2013), (which held that an enforceable adhesive arbitration agreement prohibited class arbitration or class litigation under conditions in which a non-arbitration agreement purporting to have that effect would not likely have been enforced).

[431] Stephen J. Ware, The Case for Enforcing Adhesive Arbitration Agreements— With Particular Consideration of Class Actions and Arbitration Fees, 5 *J. Am. Arb.* 251 (2006) Todd D. Rakoff, Contracts of Adhesion: An Essay in Reconstruction, 96 *Harv. L. Rev.* 1173, 1177 (1983). Tom W. Bell, Graduated Consent in Contract and Tort Law: Toward A Theory of Justification, 61 *Case W. Res. L. Rev.* 17, 50 (2010) ("most courts, regard even take-it-or-leave-it, standard form agreements, formed between powerful legal entities and relatively powerless natural persons, as not only prima facie valid, but moreover as boons for social utility"); Steven J. Burton, The New Judicial Hostility to Arbitration: Federal Preemption, Contract Unconscionability, and Agreements to Arbitrate, 2006 *J. Disp. Resol.* 469, 479 (2006) (stating that "[a]dhesion contracts are ubiquitous" and "generally are enforced"); (arguing that courts are still hostile to arbitration and are using the doctrine of unconscionability as a broad principle of fairness to circumvent arbitration contracts); Juliet M. Moringiello, Signals, Assent and Internet Contracting, 57 *Rutgers L. Rev.* 1307, 1314-15 (2005) ("courts routinely enforce standard form contracts unless they give no notice of the fact that they contain terms that could affect the offeree's legal rights, or contain unconscionable or objectively unexpected terms"); Raymond T. Nimmer, Breaking Barriers: The Relation Between Contract and Intellectual Property Law, 13 *Berkeley Tech. L. J.* 827, 848 (1998) ("Contracts of adhesion are routinely enforced. A contract of adhesion analysis typically indicates that a court enforces the contract, but scrutinizes its terms more closely for terms that are procedurally or substantively unconscionable"); *Gatton v. T-Mobile USA, Inc.*, 61 *Cal. Rptr.* 3d 344, 355 (2007) ("contracts of adhesion are well accepted in the law and routinely enforced"); Restatement (Second) Of Contracts § 211 cmt. a (1981) ("Standardization of agreements serves many of the same functions as standardization of goods and services; both are essential to a system of mass production and distribution.").

the contract necessarily unconscionable[432]. According to the Supreme Court the FAA's preemption of inconsistent state law leaves little room for state courts to enforce state law opposing enforcement of adhesive arbitration agreements[433].

In cases of voluntary (contractual) arbitration the FAA reduces the power of the federal judiciary by ordering that federal courts confirm arbitral awards as judgments conditional on a few non-substantive exceptions. Article III of the Constitution makes available protection to federal judges by providing them with life tenure, by this means eliminating salaries and job security as means for influence by the other branches of government[434]. Has job security concerning judges brought a powerful justice worldwide or still society has to be on alert? Can the co-existence of a co-equal and independent alternative dispute mechanism to courts such as arbitration augment justice?

Reilly[435] makes clear that in addition to waiving their right to trial by judge or jury, people who agree to submit disputes to arbitration waive "(1) their rights under Article I and Article III of the Constitution;(2) their rights under the 5th, 7th, and 14th Amendments; (3) their rights to demand that federal statutory claims be adjudicated in a federal district court under the Federal Rules of Civil Procedure and the Federal Rules of Evidence by a judge, appointed under Article III of the Constitution, who will provide instruction as to the applicable law to a jury chosen in a fair, objective, and non-discriminatory manner; and (4) their right to appeal an adverse verdict to a U.S. Court of Appeals or to petition for certiorari to the U.S. Supreme Court." Arbitration-law standards of consent are contract-law standards of consent. As a result, as the Supreme Court explained in *Doctor's Associates v. Casarotto*[436] in general applicable contract defenses, such as

---

[432] *Faber v. Menard, Inc.*, 367 F.3d 1048, 1053 (8th Cir. 2004), Susan Randall, Judicial Attitudes toward Arbitration and the Resurgence of Unconscionability, 52 *Buff. L. Rev.* 158, 194 (2004) ("[A]s the use of arbitration agreements has increased, claims of unconscionability have also increased . . . ."). Edith R. Warkentine, Beyond Unconscionability: The Case for Using "Knowing Assent" As the Basis for Analyzing Unbargained-for Terms in Standard Form Contracts, 31 *Seattle U. L. Rev.* 469, 547 (2008) (California courts "equate the finding of a contract of adhesion with the finding of procedural unconscionability"); Russell Korobkin, Bounded Rationality, Standard Form Contracts, and Unconscionability, 70 *U. Chi. L. Rev.* 1203, 1258 (2003) ("In some cases, courts point to the adhesive nature of form contracts as evidence that the terms therein are 'involuntary' and thus procedurally unconscionable"); id. at 1295, n.201 ("The majority of courts, however, find that the fact that a contract is adhesive is not alone enough for a finding of procedural unconscionability"); Catherine Riley, Signing in Glitter or Blood?: Unconscionability and Reality Television Contracts, 3 *NYU J. Intell. Prop. & Ent. L.* 106, 120 (2013) ("Habitually, courts assume procedural unconscionability in contracts of adhesion").

[433] *Doctor's Associates, Inc. v. Casarotto*, 517 U.S. 681 (1996); *Southland Corp. v. Keating*, 482 U.S. 483 (1984); *Allied-Bruce Terminix Companies, Inc. v. Dobson*, 513 U.S. 265 (1995).

[434] U.S. Const. art. III, § 1. ("The Judges . . . shall hold their Offices during good Behavior, and shall . . . receive for their Services, a Compensation, which shall not be diminished during their Continuance in Office.").

[435] Christine M. Reilly, Comment, Achieving Knowing and Voluntary Consent in Pre-Dispute Mandatory Agreements at the Contracting Stage of Employment, 90 *Cal. L. Rev.* 1203, 1210 (2002). *ENSCO Int'l, Inc. v. Certain Underwriters at Lloyd's*, 579 F.3d 442, 443–44 (5th Cir. 2009) ("There are three ways in which a party may clearly and unequivocally waive its removal rights: '[1] by explicitly stating that it is doing so, [2] by allowing the other party the right to choose venue, or [3] by establishing an exclusive venue within the contract.'") (quoting City of New Orleans v. Mun. Admin. Servs., Inc., 376 F.3d 501, 504 (5th Cir. 1991)).

[436] 17 U.S. 681 (1996). *Southland Corp. v. Keating*, 465 U.S. 1 (1984) (holding that FAA requires state court to compel arbitration of claim despite state law to the contrary), *Perry v. Thomas*, 482 U.S. 483 (1987), *Gilmer v. Interstate/Johnson Lane Corp.*, 500 U.S. 20 (1991) (enforcing adhesive arbitration agreement against

unconscionability, duress or fraud, may be applied to invalid without contravening § 2 section 2 of the Federal Arbitratior general considers consent as an objective, rather than a subj particular, formation of a contract entails, not mutual assent, but m assent[438]. There is consent to arbitrate according to FAA if the co mutual assent is satisfied. According to David S. Schwartz[439] "If an been inserted in a contract of adhesion on a 'take-it-or-leave-it' ba characterize it as the product of 'consent,' 'agreement' or 'bargaining Sternlight[440] argues for a standard "sufficient to protect ignoran consumers from unwittingly waiving their rights to a jury trial, an Arti due process." Moreover, if a claim is appropriately before an arbitral fo an arbitration agreement, the jury trial right vanishes[441].

4. THE FAA AND CONSTITUTIONALITY

The FAA requires courts to apply contract-law standards of consent agreements, but certain commentators argue that courts are instead co required to apply the higher standards of consent governing jury-waiver clau Ware argues that the FAA's contract-law standards of consent are const Waivers of constitutional rights not only must be voluntary but must be deliber acceptance of an arbitration agreement encloses both of them[443].

The legislative history of the FAA suggests that Congress intended it to purposes: first, to affirm the validity of arbitration agreements as binding provisions in their own right; and second, to curb costly and time-consuming

---

employee seeking to sue employer), *Allied-Bruce Terminix Companies, Inc. v. Dobson*, 513 U.S. 2 (FAA preemption of state law encompasses full scope of Constitution's Commerce Clause), *Associates, Inc. v. Casarotto*, 517 U.S. 681 (1996) (FAA preempts state law requiring adhesive a agreements to be on contract's first page and in large font) and *Buckeye Check Cashing, Inc. v. Card* U.S. 440 (2006) (FAA preempts state law holding consumer finance arbitration agreement unenforc to usury).

[437] *First Options of Chi., Inc. v. Kaplan*, 514 U.S. 938, 944 (1995) ("When deciding whether the parties arbitrate a certain matter . . . courts generally . . . should apply ordinary state law principles that go formation of contracts.").

[438] Stephen J. Ware, Employment Arbitration and Voluntary Consent, 25 *Hofstra L. Rev.* 83, 113 (1996).

[439] David S. Schwartz, Enforcing Small Print to Protect Big Business: Employee and Consumer Rights Clai Age of Compelled Arbitration, 1997 *Wis. L. Rev.* 33, 58.

[440] Jean Sternlight, Rethinking the Constitutionality of the Supreme Court's Preference for Binding Arbitra *Tul. L. Rev.* 1, 59 (1997).

[441] *Am. Heritage Life Ins. Co. v. Orr*, 294 F.3d 702, 711 (5th Cir. 2002), *Cremin v. Merrill Lynch, Pierce, and Smith, Inc.*, 957 F. Supp. 1460, 1471 (N.D. Ill. 1997)).

[442] Stephen J. Ware, *Arbitration Clauses, Jury-Waiver Clauses, And Other Contractual Waivers of Consti Rights* Winter/Spring 2004 http:// www.law.duke.edu/ journals/67LCPWare.

[443] Jean R. Sternlight, Mandatory Binding Arbitration and Demise of the Seventh Amendment Right to a Jur 16 *Ohio St. J. On Disp. Resol.* 669, 674 (2001). *Brady v. United States*, 397 U.S. 742, 748 (1970).

that was clogging federal and state dockets in the wake of the Industrial Revolution[444]. Is FAA unconstitutional? The constitutionality of the Federal Arbitration Act is beyond doubt; The FAA, which provides for the enforceability of arbitration agreements, derives its constitutionality from Congress' Article I power to regulate interstate commerce[445]. FAA and the other national arbitration laws do not strip courts of jurisdiction entirely but it simply defers their consideration of the dispute limiting the extent of their review. If federal district courts striped of their power to review[446] arbitral awards will a constitutional infirmity arise? It is argued that constitutionality of arbitration based on the chance for federal courts to conduct *de novo* review of questions of law[447].

On the other hand, arbitration is a voluntary process. Moreover, federal courts are precluded from conducting *de novo* review of the arbitrator's legal errors448. Arbitration, as a constitutionally guaranteed adjudication method, is subject to the primary rules of fair hearing/due process, neutrality and impartiality of arbitrators, which apply to state courts[449]. Furthermore, the capacity of parties to choose their judge brings arbitration as a

---

[444] H.R. Rep. No. 96, at 1 (1924) *Preston v. Ferrer*, 128 S. Ct. 978, 986 (2008) ("A prime objective of an agreement to arbitrate is to achieve 'streamlined proceedings and expeditious results.'" (quoting Mitsubishi Motors Corp., 473 U.S. at 633)); *Rich v. Spartis*, 516 F.3d 75, 81 (2d Cir. 2008) (indicating plaintiffs are helped by general rule and "'twin goals of arbitration'" which include "'settling disputes efficiently and avoiding long and expensive litigation'") *Houdstermaatschappij v. Standard Mircrosystems Corp.*, 103 F.3d 9, 12 (2d Cir. 1997) (qualifying review of arbitration awards in order to avoid "'undermining'" aims of arbitration).

[445] *Satomi Owners Ass'n v. Satomi, L.L.C.*, 159 P.3d 460, 467 (*Wash Ct. App.* 2007). "[The Congress shall have the power t]o regulate commerce with foreign nations, and among the several states . . . ." U.S. Const. art. I, § 8, cl. 3 *Satomi Owners Ass'n v. Satomi, L.L.C.*, No. 80480-0, 2009 WL 4985689, at *16 (Wash. Dec. 24, 2009). *Preston v. Ferrer*, 552 U.S. 346, 359 (2008) ("When parties agree to arbitrate all questions arising under a contract, the FAA supersedes state laws lodging primary jurisdiction in another forum, whether judicial or administrative.") *Nitro-Lift Tech., L.L.C. v. Howard*, 133 S. Ct. 500 (2012) (preempting Oklahoma Supreme Court rule that a court, not an arbitrator, determines the validity of a covenant not to compete in a contract containing an arbitration clause).

[446] *Johnson v. Robinson*, 415 U.S. 361 (1974) (precluding judicial review of certain Veteran's Administration determinations), *Morris v. Gressette*, 432 U.S. 491, (1997) (finding that Attorney General's failure to make timely objection under the Voting Rights Act of 1965 is not subject to judicial review), Block v. Community Nutrition Institute, 467 U.S. 340 (1984) (consumers of dairy products could not obtain judicial review of milk market orders), *Webster v. Doe*, 486 U.S. 592 (1988) (holding CIA director's decision to discharge employee was not subject to judicial review). *Crowell v. Benson*, 285 U.S. 22 (1932). *United States v. Raddatz*, 447 U.S. 667 (1980), *Commodity Futures Trading Commission v. Schor*, 478 U.S. 833 (1986).

[447] Fallon, Of Legislative Courts, Administrative Agencies and Article III, 101 *Harv. L. Rev.* 915, 918-26 (1988) *United States v. Meade*, 533 U.S. 218 (2001) (discussing degrees of judicial deference to agency statutory interpretations). D Schwartz, The federal Arbitration Act and the power of Congress over state courts, 2004 Ore L Rev 541. "FAA preemption is unconstitutional" Jean R. Stemlight, Rethinking the Constitutionality of the Supreme Court's Preference for Binding Arbitration: A Fresh Assessment of Jury Trial, Separation of Powers, and Due Process Concems, 72 *Tul. L. Rev.* 1, 1 (1997) (arguing that the current pro-arbitration policy neglects the contractual principle of consent and often leads to the violation of constitutional rights); J. Douglas Uloth and J. Hamilton Rial, III, Equitable Estoppel as a Basis for Compelling Nonsignatories to Arbitrate—A Bridge Too Far?, 21 *Rev. Litig.* 593, 632 (2002) ("Since 1999, courts have arguably reached too far to find an agreement to arbitrate.").

[448] Norman Posner Judicial Review of Arbitral Awards: Manifest Disregard of the Law 64 *Brook. L. Rev.* 471, 506 (1998) ("Consequently, although most circuit courts have adopted "manifest disregard of the law" as a non-statutory ground for vacating or modifying an award, until recently there have been few cases in which a court has set aside an arbitral award on this ground."), Noah Rubins, Manifest Disregard of the Law' and 'Vacatur of Arbitral Awards in the United States, 12 *Am. Rev. Int'l Arb.* 363 (2001).

[449] T. Carbonneau, Arbitral Justice: The Demise of Due Process in American law, 70 *Tulane L Rev* 1945 (1996); F. Kessedjian, Principe de la contradiction et arbitrage, *Rev Arb* 381 (1995). *ATandT and Another v. Saudi Cable Company*, [2000] 2 *Lloyd's Rep* 127 (CA).

unconscionability, duress or fraud, may be applied to invalidate arbitration agreements without contravening § 2 section 2 of the Federal Arbitration Act[437]. Contract law in general considers consent as an objective, rather than a subjective, phenomenon. In particular, formation of a contract entails, not mutual assent, but mutual *manifestations* of assent[438]. There is consent to arbitrate according to FAA if the contract law doctrine of mutual assent is satisfied. According to David S. Schwartz[439] "If an arbitration clause has been inserted in a contract of adhesion on a 'take-it-or-leave-it' basis, it is difficult to characterize it as the product of 'consent,' 'agreement' or 'bargaining.'" Moreover, Jean Sternlight[440] argues for a standard "sufficient to protect ignorant employees and consumers from unwittingly waiving their rights to a jury trial, an Article III judge, and due process." Moreover, if a claim is appropriately before an arbitral forum pursuant to an arbitration agreement, the jury trial right vanishes[441].

4. THE FAA AND CONSTITUTIONALITY

The FAA requires courts to apply contract-law standards of consent to arbitration agreements, but certain commentators argue that courts are instead constitutionally required to apply the higher standards of consent governing jury-waiver clauses. Stephen Ware argues that the FAA's contract-law standards of consent are constitutional[442]. Waivers of constitutional rights not only must be voluntary but must be deliberate and the acceptance of an arbitration agreement encloses both of them[443].

The legislative history of the FAA suggests that Congress intended it to serve two purposes: first, to affirm the validity of arbitration agreements as binding contract provisions in their own right; and second, to curb costly and time-consuming litigation

---

employee seeking to sue employer), *Allied-Bruce Terminix Companies, Inc. v. Dobson*, 513 U.S. 265 (1995) (FAA preemption of state law encompasses full scope of Constitution's Commerce Clause), *Doctor's Associates, Inc. v. Casarotto*, 517 U.S. 681 (1996) (FAA preempts state law requiring adhesive arbitration agreements to be on contract's first page and in large font) and *Buckeye Check Cashing, Inc. v. Cardegna*. 546 U.S. 440 (2006) (FAA preempts state law holding consumer finance arbitration agreement unenforceable due to usury).

437 *First Options of Chi., Inc. v. Kaplan*, 514 U.S. 938, 944 (1995) ("When deciding whether the parties agreed to arbitrate a certain matter . . . courts generally . . . should apply ordinary state law principles that govern the formation of contracts.").

438 Stephen J. Ware, Employment Arbitration and Voluntary Consent, 25 *Hofstra L. Rev*. 83, 113 (1996).

439 David S. Schwartz, Enforcing Small Print to Protect Big Business: Employee and Consumer Rights Claims in an Age of Compelled Arbitration, 1997 *Wis. L. Rev*. 33, 58.

440 Jean Sternlight, Rethinking the Constitutionality of the Supreme Court's Preference for Binding Arbitration, 72 *Tul. L. Rev*. 1, 59 (1997).

441 *Am. Heritage Life Ins. Co. v. Orr*, 294 F.3d 702, 711 (5th Cir. 2002), *Cremin v. Merrill Lynch, Pierce, Fenner and Smith, Inc*., 957 F. Supp. 1460, 1471 (N.D. Ill. 1997)).

442 Stephen J. Ware, *Arbitration Clauses, Jury-Waiver Clauses, And Other Contractual Waivers of Constitutional Rights* Winter/Spring 2004 http:// www.law.duke.edu/ journals/67LCPWare.

443 Jean R. Sternlight, Mandatory Binding Arbitration and Demise of the Seventh Amendment Right to a Jury Trial, 16 *Ohio St. J. On Disp. Resol*. 669, 674 (2001). *Brady v. United States*, 397 U.S. 742, 748 (1970).

the contract necessarily unconscionable[432]. According to the Supreme Court the FAA's preemption of inconsistent state law leaves little room for state courts to enforce state law opposing enforcement of adhesive arbitration agreements[433].

In cases of voluntary (contractual) arbitration the FAA reduces the power of the federal judiciary by ordering that federal courts confirm arbitral awards as judgments conditional on a few non-substantive exceptions. Article III of the Constitution makes available protection to federal judges by providing them with life tenure, by this means eliminating salaries and job security as means for influence by the other branches of government[434]. Has job security concerning judges brought a powerful justice worldwide or still society has to be on alert? Can the co-existence of a co-equal and independent alternative dispute mechanism to courts such as arbitration augment justice?

Reilly[435] makes clear that in addition to waiving their right to trial by judge or jury, people who agree to submit disputes to arbitration waive "(1) their rights under Article I and Article III of the Constitution;(2) their rights under the 5th, 7th, and 14th Amendments; (3) their rights to demand that federal statutory claims be adjudicated in a federal district court under the Federal Rules of Civil Procedure and the Federal Rules of Evidence by a judge, appointed under Article III of the Constitution, who will provide instruction as to the applicable law to a jury chosen in a fair, objective, and non-discriminatory manner; and (4) their right to appeal an adverse verdict to a U.S. Court of Appeals or to petition for certiorari to the U.S. Supreme Court." Arbitration-law standards of consent are contract-law standards of consent. As a result, as the Supreme Court explained in *Doctor's Associates v. Casarotto*[436] in general applicable contract defenses, such as

---

432 *Faber v. Menard, Inc.*, 367 F.3d 1048, 1053 (8th Cir. 2004), Susan Randall, Judicial Attitudes toward Arbitration and the Resurgence of Unconscionability, 52 *Buff. L. Rev.* 158, 194 (2004) ("[A]s the use of arbitration agreements has increased, claims of unconscionability have also increased . . . ."). Edith R. Warkentine, Beyond Unconscionability: The Case for Using "Knowing Assent" As the Basis for Analyzing Unbargained-for Terms in Standard Form Contracts, 31 *Seattle U. L. Rev.* 469, 547 (2008) (California courts "equate the finding of a contract of adhesion with the finding of procedural unconscionability"); Russell Korobkin, Bounded Rationality, Standard Form Contracts, and Unconscionability, 70 *U. Chi. L. Rev.* 1203, 1258 (2003) ("In some cases, courts point to the adhesive nature of form contracts as evidence that the terms therein are 'involuntary' and thus procedurally unconscionable"); id. at 1295, n.201 ("The majority of courts, however, find that the fact that a contract is adhesive is not alone enough for a finding of procedural unconscionability"); Catherine Riley, Signing in Glitter or Blood?: Unconscionability and Reality Television Contracts, 3 *NYU J. Intell. Prop. & Ent. L.* 106, 120 (2013) ("Habitually, courts assume procedural unconscionability in contracts of adhesion").

433 *Doctor's Associates, Inc. v. Casarotto*, 517 U.S. 681 (1996); *Southland Corp. v. Keating*, 482 U.S. 483 (1984); *Allied-Bruce Terminix Companies, Inc. v. Dobson*, 513 U.S. 265 (1995).

434 U.S. Const. art. III, § 1. ("The Judges . . . shall hold their Offices during good Behavior, and shall . . . receive for their Services, a Compensation, which shall not be diminished during their Continuance in Office.").

435 Christine M. Reilly, Comment, Achieving Knowing and Voluntary Consent in Pre-Dispute Mandatory Agreements at the Contracting Stage of Employment, 90 *Cal. L. Rev.* 1203, 1210 (2002). *ENSCO Int'l, Inc. v. Certain Underwriters at Lloyd's*, 579 F.3d 442, 443–44 (5th Cir. 2009) ("There are three ways in which a party may clearly and unequivocally waive its removal rights: '[1] by explicitly stating that it is doing so, [2] by allowing the other party the right to choose venue, or [3] by establishing an exclusive venue within the contract.'") (quoting City of New Orleans v. Mun. Admin. Servs., Inc., 376 F.3d 501, 504 (5th Cir. 1991)).

436 17 U.S. 681 (1996). *Southland Corp. v. Keating*, 465 U.S. 1 (1984) (holding that FAA requires state court to compel arbitration of claim despite state law to the contrary), *Perry v. Thomas*, 482 U.S. 483 (1987), *Gilmer v. Interstate/Johnson Lane Corp.*, 500 U.S. 20 (1991) (enforcing adhesive arbitration agreement against

country shall adopt any law impairing the obligations of contract[428]. Professor Rubin[429] said that "the contract standard cannot be used to justify those waivers that involve constitutional rights since such rights necessarily take precedence over the contract policy of honoring private agreements" but his argument was not directed at section 2 of the FAA specifically. The traditional theory used to rationalize arbitration's compatibility with Article III rests on the principle of waiver. Parties entering into an arbitration agreement have waived their right to a federal forum, by this means eliminating any Article III point. Even if an arbitration clause has been inserted in a contract of adhesion on a 'take-it-or-leave-it' basis, its acceptance means consent. It should be taken into account that enforcement of adhesive arbitration[430] agreements benefits society by reducing procedure costs, by this means benefiting consumers, employees and other adhering parties[431]. Moreover, simple disproportion in bargaining power does not make

---

[428] U.S. Const. art. I, § 10. Max Helveston & Michael Jacobs, The Incoherent Role of Bargaining Power in Contract Law, 49 *Wake Forest L. Rev.* 1017, 1054 (2014) ("Examples abound of laws and regulations aimed at resolving the very concerns that have led courts to turn to bargaining-power analysis. In a number of different areas, legislatures and agencies have prohibited contracts from including terms deemed abusive to one of the parties"). Robert W. Emerson, Franchising and the Parol Evidence Rule, 50 *Am. Bus. L. J.* 659, 680-81 (2013) ("most state statutes regulating franchise relationships prohibit franchisors from requiring their franchisees to waive the franchisor's liability for a violation of those state franchise laws when entering into a franchise agreement"); Daniel B. Kelly, The Right to Include, 63 *Emory L. J.* 857, 912 (2014) ("Although similar to contracts, franchises differ because franchise law entails certain mandatory rules (e.g., limitations on termination) and attempts to deter renegotiation in ways that contract law generally does not.").

[429] Edward L. Rubin, Toward a General Theory of Waiver, 28 *UCLA L. Rev.* 478 (1981).

[430] *AT&T Mobility LLC v. Concepcion*, 131 S.Ct. 1740, 1753 (2011) (holding that Federal Arbitration Act preempts California law refusing to enforce adhesive arbitration agreement requiring claims to be brought on an individual, rather than class, basis while acknowledging that California law would not, under similar circumstances, enforce such a requirement in a non-arbitration agreement) (citing *Am. Online, Inc. v. Superior Court*, 90 *Cal. App.* 4th 1, 18, 108 *Cal. Rptr.* 2d 699, 712 (2001) ("The unavailability of class action relief in this context is sufficient in and by itself to preclude enforcement of the TOS forum selection clause.")). *Stolt-Nielsen S.A. v. AnimalFeeds International Corp.*, 559 U.S. 662 (2010), *American Express Co. v. Italian Colors Rest.*, 133 S. Ct. 2304 (2013), (which held that an enforceable adhesive arbitration agreement prohibited class arbitration or class litigation under conditions in which a non-arbitration agreement purporting to have that effect would not likely have been enforced).

[431] Stephen J. Ware, The Case for Enforcing Adhesive Arbitration Agreements— With Particular Consideration of Class Actions and Arbitration Fees, 5 *J. Am. Arb.* 251 (2006) Todd D. Rakoff, Contracts of Adhesion: An Essay in Reconstruction, 96 *Harv. L. Rev.* 1173, 1177 (1983). Tom W. Bell, Graduated Consent in Contract and Tort Law: Toward A Theory of Justification, 61 *Case W. Res. L. Rev.* 17, 50 (2010) ("most courts, regard even take-it-or-leave-it, standard form agreements, formed between powerful legal entities and relatively powerless natural persons, as not only prima facie valid, but moreover as boons for social utility"); Steven J. Burton, The New Judicial Hostility to Arbitration: Federal Preemption, Contract Unconscionability, and Agreements to Arbitrate, 2006 *J. Disp. Resol.* 469, 479 (2006) (stating that "[a]dhesion contracts are ubiquitous" and "generally are enforced"); (arguing that courts are still hostile to arbitration and are using the doctrine of unconscionability as a broad principle of fairness to circumvent arbitration contracts); Juliet M. Moringiello, Signals, Assent and Internet Contracting, 57 *Rutgers L. Rev.* 1307, 1314-15 (2005) ("courts routinely enforce standard form contracts unless they give no notice of the fact that they contain terms that could affect the offeree's legal rights, or contain unconscionable or objectively unexpected terms"); Raymond T. Nimmer, Breaking Barriers: The Relation Between Contract and Intellectual Property Law, 13 *Berkeley Tech. L. J.* 827, 848 (1998) ("Contracts of adhesion are routinely enforced. A contract of adhesion analysis typically indicates that a court enforces the contract, but scrutinizes its terms more closely for terms that are procedurally or substantively unconscionable"); *Gatton v. T-Mobile USA, Inc.*, 61 *Cal. Rptr.* 3d 344, 355 (2007) ("contracts of adhesion are well accepted in the law and routinely enforced"); Restatement (Second) Of Contracts § 211 cmt. a (1981) ("Standardization of agreements serves many of the same functions as standardization of goods and services; both are essential to a system of mass production and distribution.").

coercion dispute system into line with the constitution of any state[450]. It is worth mentioning that in *Henderson v. Beaton*[451] the constitutionality of a Texas statute enacted in 1879 upheld that provided for a board of referees or arbitrators to dispose of civil actions by the consent of parties.

Will the United States increasingly have a privatized system of justice[452] by favoring the right of parties to choose arbitration? The Courts' interpretation of the FAA[453] has ignited an "arbitration war": "a battle over whether the United States will increasingly have a privatized system of justice." Do not arbitrators possess legal expertise[454]? The Supreme Court in *Marbury v. Madison*[455] stated that the interpretation of constitutional provisions was the province of judges[456]. A. Marmor argues that[457] "courts tend to possess legal expertise, they are the best kind of institution to be entrusted with constitutional interpretation." The constitutional system of federalism assigns powers to state and federal government officials not for their own benefit, but for that of the people of the entire nation. As discussed earlier arbitration is deep-rooted in ancient Greek and Roman laws and since the French Revolution, arbitration was considered a *droit naturel*[458] but in modern days the established *fora* for all disputes are national courts existing and maintained by the state to offer a dispute settlement service for parties. States make certain that courts exist as an expression of state prerogative and power. Arbitration is not a national court procedure but arbitration is a private proceeding with public consequences.

---

450 The Greek constitution is an illustration of modern standards where the constitutional text makes positive reference to the rights of persons to waive or oust the jurisdiction of national courts. Article 8 Greek Constitution (1975/1986/2001) provides "No person shall be deprived of the judge assigned to him by law against his will" Article 20(1) provides "Every person shall be entitled to receive legal protection by the courts and may plead before them his views concerning his rights or interests, as specified by law." Lindsay Melworm, Note, Biased? Prove It: Addressing Arbitrator Bias and the Merits of Implementing Broad Disclosure Standards, *22 Cardozo J. Int.L & Comp. L.* 431, 464 (2014) (explaining that .too much knowledge or exposure in any particular area can lend itself to generating conflicts of interest or may necessarily involve prior relationships that compromise the independence and impartiality of the arbitrator.).

451 52 *Tex.* 29 (*Tex.* 1879).

452 *Moses H. Cone Mem'l Hosp. v. Mercury Constr. Corp*., 460 U.S. 1, 24-25 (1983). *Soutland Corp. v. Keating*, 465 U.S. 1, 11 (1984). *Mitsubishi Motors Corp. v. Soler Chrysler-Plymouth, Inc*., 473 U.S. 614, 627 (1985).

453 The Arbitration War, *N.Y. Times*, Nov. 26, 2010, at A18.

454 *Alexander v. Gardner-Denver*, 415 U.S. 36, 57 (1974) (stating that parties select a particular arbitrator "because they trust his knowledge and judgment concerning the demands" and customs of the field from which the dispute originates); Ian Macneil Et Al., *Federal Arbitration Law § 2.6.2* (1994) (stating that an arbitrator is expected to be an expert in the norms governing the resolution of the dispute). Michael Pryles, Reflections on Transnational Public Policy, 24 *J. Int'l Arb.* 1, 4 (2003) ("Arbitrators have an obligation to apply internationally accepted norms of procedure. . . .").

455 5 U.S. (1 Cranch) 137 (1803).

456 David Boies, Judicial Independence and the Rule of Law, 22 *Journal of Law and Policy* 57.

457 Andrei Marmor, Constitutional Interpretation, USC Public Policy Research Paper No. 04-4, p10.

458 "Le droit des citoyens de terminer définitevement leurs contestations par la voie de l'arbitrage, ne peut recevoir aucune atteinte par les acts du Pouvoir législatif." (The legislative power [Parliament] cannot by any means hinder the right of the citizens to settle their disputes by means of arbitration). Title III, Chap V, Article 5, Constitution of 3 September 1791. "Il ne peut être porté aucune atteinte au droit de faire prononcer sur les différends par les arbitres du choix des parties," Constitution, 22 August 1795. See Constitution of Greece 1827, Article 139.

It is worth mentioning here that according to Fiss[459] only a judge articulates public values by the legal reasoning. In line, Resnik[460] argues that the arbitrator is prospective threat to the state, as lawmaker. Moreover, according to John O. McGinnis and Ilya Somin[461] "Judges thus often put aside their political and public policy preferences to enforce the law according to a set of rules." On the other hand, voting patterns in the Supreme Court back a "political" or "attitudinal" model which posits that judicial votes abide by political ideology[462]. Moreover, according to R. C. Reuben[463] "Courts have a vested institutional interest in managing the size of their dockets, and individual judges may have ideological preferences that would cause them to steer certain cases or classes of cases in to arbitration rather than permitting them to proceed before judges or juries." It could be argued that in line arbitrators put aside their political preferences and enforce the law and customs as well.

Do judges make errors? Professor Chris Guthrie argues that judges *Misjudge*[464]. Wrong judging/misjudge implicates such things as incompetence, bias, and corruption[465]. Is it possible to predict the frequency or consequences of judges' errors in the real world? It could be said that parties underestimate judges' fallibility expecting that judges would

---

[459] Owen M. Fiss, Against Settlement, 93 *Yale L. J.* 1073, 1085–87 (1984).

[460] Judith Resnik, Many Doors? Closing Doors? Alternative Dispute Resolution and Adjudication, 10 *Ohio St. J. On Disp. Resol.* 211, 224 (1995) (noting that under the Wilko standard, "[t]he arbitrator as dispute resolver was posited as a potential hazard to the state, as lawmaker").

[461] John O. McGinnis, Ilya Somin, Federalism vs. States' Rights: A Defense of Judicial Review in a Federal System, Research Paper No. 04-08, p48.

[462] Daniel R. Pinello, Linking Party to Judicial Ideology in American Courts: A Meta-Analysis, 20 *Justice Sys. J.* 219 (1999) (citing studies and concluding that voting patterns support a "political" or "attitudinal" model which posits that judicial votes follow political ideology). Harry T. Edwards, The Effects of Collegiality on Judicial Decision making, 151 *U. PA L. Rev.* 1639, 1640-41 (2003) ("These scholars invariably ignore the many ways in which collegiality mitigates judges' ideological preferences and enables us to find common ground and reach better decisions."). Theodore W. Ruger, et al., The Supreme Court Forecasting Project: Legal and Political Science Approaches to Predicting Supreme Court Decision-making, 104 *Colum. L. Rev.* 1150, 1162 (2004) ("Because our study does not account for the content [of judicial decisions] there is much is does not, and cannot, say about the judicial process.").

[463] Richard C. Reuben, Process Purity and Innovation in Dispute Resolution: A Response to Professors Stempel, Cole, and Drahozal, Legal Studies Research Paper Series, Research Paper No. 2007-14 at 36-37. Ian R. Macneil, American Arbitration Law: Reformation, Nationalization, Internationalization 172-73 (1992) at 172-73 (U.S. Supreme Court's arbitration jurisprudence based on its vested interest in "docket-clearing pure and simple."); Richard A. Posner, What Do Judges and Justices Maximize? (The Same Thing Everybody Else Does), 3 *S. Ct. Econ. Rev.* 1, 2 (1993) "[J]judges have a vested interest in reducing the workload of the courts, and they may attempt to advance that agenda without sensitivity to the impact on the system as a whole, particularly the impact on the attorney-client relationship."

[464] Chris Guthrie, Misjudging, 7 *Nev. L. J.* 420 (2007), Chris Guthrie et al., Inside the Judicial Mind, 86 Cornell L. Rev. 777 (2001); Andrew J. Wistrich et al., Can Judges Ignore Inadmissible Information? The Difficulty of Deliberately Disregarding, 153 *U. PA. L. Rev.* 1251 (2005). Chris Guthrie, Panacea or Pandora's Box? The Costs of Options in Negotiation, 88 *Iowa L. Rev.* 601 (2003). Martha J. Dragich, Justice Blackmun, Franz Kafka, and Capital Punishment, 63 *Mo. L. Rev.* 853, 904–05 (1998) (we expect judges, as unbiased arbiters, to set personal beliefs aside). Andrew D. Bradt & D. Theodore Rave, The Information-Forcing Role of the Judge in Multidistrict Litigation, 105 *Calif. L. Rev.* 1259, 1288-92 (2017) (arguing judges should use multidistrict litigation process to force disclosure of information to allow parties to make informed decisions in deciding whether to settle).

[465] Geoffrey P. Miller, Bad Judges, 83 *Tex. L. Rev.* 431, 432-33 (2004), Thomas A. Lambert, Two Mistakes Behavioralists Make: A Response to Professors Feigenson et al. and Professor Slovic, 69 *Mo. L. Rev.* 1053, 1054 n.6 (2004) (collecting criticisms of over-generalization of research on decision making).

not make any mistakes. Guthrie[466] thinks that "there is a "still-dominant assumption that the courthouse is the proper locus of dispute resolution" and the "legal system implicitly assumes that judicial error is infrequent, random, and often 'harmless.'" According to J. Lande[467] "Many judges, lawyers, and other knowledgeable observers …discover that judges are fallible as they would be to find out that gambling takes place in casinos." Even though judges were perfect or made only few or unsystematic errors, some parties value particular things more than decision accuracy[468]. While judges aim to arrive at a correct interpretation, arbitrators do the same as well[469]. Judges cannot be seen as angels and gods. Guthrie[470] argues that "disputants might decide to place a primacy on other values in disputing, like self-determination, creativity, improved relationships, speedier and cheaper resolutions, and so forth." Parties think that arbitration instead of court adjudication shows the diversity of values that may outweigh technical decision making.

Constitutional prohibitions apply only to state action. If state action arises when a plaintiff is required to use arbitration process, that process must satisfy the constitutional requirements of due process and equal protection. Federal courts concluded that there is no state action present in either securities or contractual arbitration[471]. No state courts have found state action in contractual arbitration as well[472]. According to the view expressed in the courts private party use of a private dispute resolution system does not create state action nor is state action present when one arbitral party seeks to enforce an arbitration agreement or award.

On the one hand, it is argued that arbitrators are not compelled to determine the dispute according to legal precedents or principles. On the other hand, arbitrators can apply not only legal precedents or principles[473] but also standards of the industry, their contractual understanding, or merely what they regard as appropriate and fair. In addition, standards of the industry, contractual understanding, and various norms create precedent and legal principles.

---

[466] Chris Guthrie, Misjudging, 7 *Nev. L. J.* 420 (2007), at 448, 421.

[467] John Lande, Judging Judges and Dispute Resolution Processes, 2007 *Nevada Law Journal* 457 at 461.

[468] John Lande and Gregg Herman, Fitting the Forum to the Family Fuss: Choosing Mediation, Collaborative Law, or Cooperative Law for Negotiating Divorce Cases, 42 *Fam. Ct. Rev.* 280 (2004); Frank E. A. Sander and Stephen B. Goldberg, Fitting the Forum to the Fuss: A User-Friendly Guide to Selecting an ADR Procedure, 10 Neg. J. 49 (1994).

[469] Owen Fiss, Between Supremacy and Exclusivity, 57 *Syracuse L. Rev.* 187, 204 (2007) (arguing that judges aim "to arrive at a correct interpretation [, not] the one that most or all people agree with.... [or] accept").

[470] Chris Guthrie, Misjudging, 7 *Nev. L. J.* 420 (2007), at 448.

[471] *Perpetual Secs., Inc. v. Tang*, 290 F.3d 132, 137-39 (2d Cir. 2002); *Davis v. Prudential Secs., Inc.*, 59 F.3d 1186, 1190-92 (11th Cir. 1995); One federal district court states in dicta that it "respectfully doubts that the rationale for the result set forth in Davis . . . that an arbitration award involves no state action is well-founded." *Commonwealth Assocs. v. Letsos*, 40 F. Supp. 2d 170, 177 n.37 (S.D.N.Y. 1999) (citing Davis, 59 F.3d at 1191).

[472] *Hadelman v. Deluca*, 876 A.2d 1136, 1138 (Conn. 2005).

[473] Luca G. Radicati di Brozolo, Res Judicata and International Arbitral Awards, *ASA Special Series* 2011.

Are arbitrators state actors[474]? Presently arbitration does not exist without statutory authorization and the right to force arbitration and enforce the resulting award clearly derives from state authority[475]. In other words the parties' right to choose arbitration instead of litigation derives from the law and the constitution and so the parties' right does not appear from a vacuum. According to Paul F. Kirgis [476]"Arbitration is a substitute for public adjudication, at least in cases involving mandatory legal rules, and public adjudication is beyond doubt a traditional government function."

Does the Federal Arbitration Act supplant juries with arbitrators whenever possible[477]? Is the FAA which provides the mechanism by which such enforcement actions take place a neutral regulatory scheme? Is arbitration customarily a distinctive, if not sole, function of the state? R. Reuben[478] explains that binding dispute resolution, predominantly arbitration, is "traditionally an exclusive public function." The Supreme Court in *Boddie v. Connecticut*[479] stated that the state has a "monopoly over techniques for binding conflict resolution" but then again the state allows arbitration to be utilized as a dispute resolution system. An arbitral award is enforceable only after a judge enters the award as a judgment in accordance with FAA or other national arbitration laws and so arbitration does not operate autonomously from the state. Courts expressed the view that the fact that the court enforces arbitration agreements and awards does not turn the arbitrator or the parties to the arbitration into state actors[480]. Thus, Courts have rejected arguments that either arbitration itself or the judicial confirmation of arbitral awards constitutes state action[481]. On the other hand, the right to compel arbitration and enforce the award derives from state authority. The *raison d'etre* for the FAA was that arbitration could not function successfully with not judicial recognition and enforcement providing governmental assistance and benefits to parties in search of use binding arbitration.

---

[474] Richard C. Reuben, Public Justice: Toward a State Action Theory of Alternative Dispute Resolution, 85 *Cal. L. Rev*. 577, 619, 625 (1997).

[475] *Edmonson v. Leesville Concrete Co*. 500 U.S. 614 (1991). *Lugar v. Edmondson Oil Co*. 457 U.S. 922 (1982).

[476] Paul F. Kirgis, Judicial Review and the Limits of Arbitral Authority: Lessons from the Law of Contract, 2007 *St. John's Law Review* 99, at 108. Amy J. Schmitz, Consideration Of "Contracting Culture" In Enforcing Arbitration Provisions, *2007 St. John's Law Review* 123.

[477] *Southland Corp. v. Keating*, 465 U.S. 1, 11, 16 (1984) (holding Federal Arbitration Act applies in state courts and preempts conflicting state law). Christopher R. Drahozal, In Defense of Southland: Reexamining the Legislative History of the Federal Arbitration Act, 78 *Notre Dame L. Rev*. 101, 103 (2002). "the Court's decision in Southland Corp. is widely held to be an illegitimate exercise in judicial lawmaking, flatly inconsistent with congressional intent in enacting the FAA. Commentators have lined up behind Justice O'Connor, whose dissent derided the [Chief Justice Burger's] majority opinion as an "exercise in judicial revisionism" that ignored the "unambiguous" legislative history of the FAA as a procedural statute applicable only in federal court."

[478] Richard C. Reuben, Constitutional Gravity: A Unitary Theory of Alternative Dispute Resolution and Public Civil Justice, 47 *UCLA L. Rev*. 949 (2000) at 997–98. (arguing that contractual forms of alternative dispute resolution can constitute state action); ("Virtually all of th[e] activity [in ordinary civil litigation] takes place in the public courthouse and is presided over by a judge with plenary power to administer and decide the case as he or she deems appropriate.").

[479] 401 U.S. 371, 375 (1971).

[480] *Flagg Bros. v. Brooks*, 436 U.S. 149 (1978). *Lugar v. Edmonson Oil Co*., 457 U.S. 922 (1982).

[481] *MedValUSA Health Programs, Inc. v. Member Works,* Inc., 872 A.2d 423, 428 (Conn. 2005). *Davis v. Prudential Securities, Inc*., 59 F.3d 1186 (11th Cir. 1995). *Pacific Mutual Life Insurance Co. v. Haslip*, 499 U.S. 1 (1991).

Moreover, according to Richard Reuben[482] arbitrators are state actors. Additionally, Paul F. Kirgis[483] thinks that "Arbitration has existed as a method of dispute resolution for centuries, and for most of that time the formal courts have considered arbitrators to be minor league judges." The Supreme Court moved from suspicion[484] to a whole-hearted acceptance of arbitration as an alternative to the judicial process[485] and so there is a doctrinal change that has enhanced the role of arbitration as a substitute for judicial decision-making.

On the one hand, contractual arbitration gives rise to state action when courts enforce contractual commitments to participate in arbitration and when courts subsequently enforce arbitration awards[486]. Many scholars have argued in favour in the presence of state action in arbitration[487]. On the other hand, courts have rejected a finding of state action in contractual arbitration[488]. According to Sarah Rudolph Cole[489] "the mere fact that the court enforces arbitration agreements and awards does not turn the arbitrator or the parties to the arbitration into state actors. Simply put, the creation of a statutory scheme that "permits but does not compel" private party action does not create state action." It could be argued that in reality the comparison of courts and arbitration brings forward a relation similar to courts of law and courts of equity in the application of law but with arbitration to have a secondary role not equal even to that of courts of equity.

Arbitration is erected on the basis of a statutory allocation of the traditionally sole public function of binding dispute resolution. State action exists in binding arbitration

---

[482] Richard C. Reuben, Public Justice: Toward a State Action Theory of Alternative Dispute Resolution, 85 *Cal. L. Rev.* 577 589–91, 609–10 (1997) (critiquing American courts' consensus that private arbitration does not constitute state action subject to constitutional requirements).

[483] Paul F. Kirgis, Judicial review and the limits of arbitral authority: lessons from the law of contract, 2006 Legal studies research paper series paper #06-0057 p1.

[484] *Wilko v. Swan*, 346 U.S. 427 (1953).

[485] *Southland Corp. v. Keating*, 465 U.S. 1 (1984), Allied-Bruce Terminix v. Dobson, 513 U.S. 249 (1995); *Doctor's Assocs., Inc. v. Casarotto*, 517 U.S. 679 (1995). *Sherk v. Alberto-Culver*, 417 U.S. 506 (1974).

[486] Jean R. Sternlight, Rethinking the Constitutionality of the Supreme Court's Preference for Binding Arbitration: A Fresh Assessment of Jury Trial, Separation of Powers, and Due Process Concerns, 72 *Tul. L. Rev.* 1493 (1997). Stephen J. Ware, Employment Arbitration and Voluntary Consent, 25 *Hofstra L. Rev.* 83, 145–46 (1996) (noting that because "securities laws constitute an occupational licensing scheme that conditions a license to be a securities employee" on an agreement to arbitrate, state action is present.).

[487] Richard C. Reuben, Constitutional Gravity: A Unitary Theory of Alternative Dispute Resolution and Public Civil Justice, 47 *UCLA L. Rev.* 949, 1049 (2000); at 991; Edward Brunet, Arbitration and Constitutional Rights, 71 *N.C. L. Rev.* 81, 109 (1992); at 109; Kenneth R. Davis, Due Process Right to Judicial Review of Arbitral Punitive Damages Awards, 32 *Am. Bus. L. J.* 583 (1995); Jeffery L. Fisher, State Action and the Enforcement of Compulsory Arbitration Agreements Against Employment Discrimination Claims, 18 *Hofstra Lab. and Emp. L. J.* 289, 295-96 (2000); at 295-96; Jean Sternlight, Rethinking the Constitutionality of the Supreme Court's Preference for Binding Arbitration: A Fresh Assessment of Jury Trial, Separation of Powers, and Due Process Concerns, 72 *Tul. L. Rev.* 1 (1997), at 40.

[488] *Perpetual Sec., Inc. v. Tang*, 290 F.3d 132, 138 (2d Cir. 2002); *Desiderio v. Nat'l Ass'n of Secs. Dealers, Inc.*, 191 F.3d 198, 207 (2d Cir. 1999); *Duffield v. Robertson Stephens and Co.*, 144 F.3d 1182, 1200–02 (9th Cir. 1998).

[489] Sarah Rudolph Cole, Arbitration and State Action, 2005 *Brigham Young University Law Review* 1 p47. Maureen A. Weston, Universes Colliding: The Constitutional Implications of Arbitral Class Actions, 47 *Wm. and Mary L. Rev.* 1711, 1745–65 (2006) (noting American courts' conclusion that private arbitration does not involve state action but critiquing this conclusion with respect to arbitral class actions). (arguing that class arbitration constitutes state action).

under the public function and entanglement theories[490]. Disproportionate entanglement occurs because judicial involvement occurs in the whole apparently private process. Court enforcement attributes civil authority on private arbitrators. According to Michael C. Grossman[491] "A "symbiotic relationship" exists between the lucrative arbitration industry and the economizing of judicial resources leading to reciprocal profiting." Court enforcement gives tribunal awards under the FAA *res judicata* effects. This author thinks that access to courts or arbitration has been deemed an essential right guaranteed by the Constitutions. In consensual arbitration, parties have waived their right to court access, precluding due process challenges later[492] but parties' right to conclude arbitration agreements is constitutional. The federal governments, through the FAA, generate a statutory right to a statutory standard of review satisfying the fact that there is a "right" and it is "governmental." FAA review as a statutory right means that courts qualify as state actors, in this manner creating the duty to protect procedural due process.

According to A. Imbrogno[493] "As sophisticated as arbitration and other ADR mechanisms have become, judicial decision-making still possesses unique attributes. Most importantly, judicial decision-making is uniquely public in nature." Moreover, H. Edwards[494] thinks that an asset of adjudication is its aptitude to guarantee the proper resolution and application of public values, and public officers, not private individuals, have to interpret the values of the Constitution and statutes. Judicial adjudication develops substantive law, creates precedent, produces uniform law, educates the public, and forms public values. This development through litigation before state courts of a uniform precedent that educates and informs public values is more likely than arbitration to balance integration of the legal system. Therefore to that extent arbitration has to take off in this point and establish its own precedent, uniform law integrating the legal system as well but not to mimic the stereotype of courts' features relating to followed procedures

---

[490] Sarah Rudolph Cole, Arbitration and State Action, 2005 *BYU L. Rev.* 1, 4 and n.11 at 7 (arguing state action exists under public function and excessive entanglement theories, but noting that symbiotic theory of state action is not relevant to arbitration) (noting that "[c]ourt involvement occurs, if at all, prior to start of arbitration and after the completion of arbitration").

[491] Michael C. Grossman, Is this arbitration?: Religious tribunals, judicial review, and due process, 107 Columbia Law Review 169 p200. Amy J. Schmitz, Mobile-Home Mania? Protecting Procedurally Fair Arbitration in a Consumer Microcosm, 20 *Ohio St. J. On Disp. Resol.* 291, 313–15, 371 (2005) (discussing how manufacturers' use of form arbitration agreements has privatized dispute resolution in the mobile home industry).

[492] *Kovacs v. Kovacs*, 633 A.2d 425, 433 (Md. Ct. Spec. App. 1993) ("[P]arties expressly waived application of Maryland law . . . when they agreed to arbitration under Jewish substantive and procedural law.").

[493] Andre R. Imbrogno, Arbitration As An Alternative To Divorce Litigation: Redefining The Judicial Role, 2003 *Capital University Law Review* 413 at 438. Natalie C. Scott, Note, Don't Forget Me! The Client in a Class Action Lawsuit, 15 *Geo. J. Legal Ethics* 561, 578 (2002) (describing judges as guardians of the class and as responsible to the public). In re [Sealed], 64 F. Supp. 2d 183, 184 (E.D.N.Y. 1999) (noting that "[c]ourts have obligations to the public that private arbitrators do not"); Eagle v. Fred Martin Motor Co., 809 N.E.2d 1161, 1181 (*Ohio Ct. App.* 2004) (recognizing that "generally arbitration forums should be treated differently from courts").

[494] Harry T. Edwards, Commentary, Alternative Dispute Resolution: Panacea or Anathema? 99 *Harv. L. Rev.* 668, 675–82 (1986). Owen M. Fiss, Commentary, Against Settlement, 93 *Yale L. J.* 1073, 1075 (1984) (urging that by resolving disputes through settlements rather than through adjudication, justice is sacrificed for peace).

and why not forcing courts to improve their efficiency by shortening multifaceted processes.

5. Stare Decisis and Precedent

Stare decisis, which is a stricter form of precedent than was conventionally used in common law, necessitates judges to stick to earlier court ruling. Stare decisis as the obligation to follow prior decisions – even those the judge disagrees with, is a function of the common law[495]. From the Latin phrase, "*stare decisis et non quieta movere*," meaning, "[t]o stand by things decided, and not to disturb settled points." Stare decisis is defined as "[t]he doctrine of precedent, under which it is necessary for a court to follow earlier judicial decisions when the same points arise again in litigation.[496] "Modern courts draw cases with high positive externalities through the court-imposed doctrine of stare decisis. Stare decisis is used as a tool to focus adjudication on areas where there are gaps in the law rather than replacing the law but when the stare decisis shapes the law accordingly the wishes of the groups of people who just use rigid rule in order to preserve their status then stare decisis does not bring justice, and as a result expected to be larger positive externalities. Stare decisis works in combination with rationing by waiting as a means to limit demand for court services, by this means conserving judicial resources.

Stare decisis is, at its core, a function of the rules concerning which courts can overturn the decisions of other courts[497]. If a judge does not abide by the appropriate precedent, the appellate court can overturn the decision. It has to be taken into account that since in US a judge's job performance is somewhat measured by the number of their rulings that are overturned, these rules of appellate review function to attach courts to the system of stare decisis.

In ancient Greece, judges relied on past cases to settle commercial disputes, while early Egyptian judges prepared a rudimentary system of law reports to help guide their decisions. Roman judges also displayed a tendency to follow the example of their predecessors, especially in procedural matters. Though courts in Greece, Egypt, or Rome may have consulted past decisions for guidance, they were never bound, even presumptively, by those decisions, and they did not view precedent as a restraint on their

[495] William Blackstone, Commentaries *69–70 ("precedents and rules must be followed, unless flatly absurd or unjust"); James Kent, *Commentaries On American Law*, volume I, 473–76 (New York, 1826), twelfth edition, edited by Oliver Wendell Holmes, Jr. (Boston, 1873) (stating that the best evidence of the common law is found in the decisions of the courts, those decisions are precedents for future cases resting on analogous facts, which judges are bound to follow these decisions, unless it can be shown that the law was misunderstood, and that this is just because when a rule has been deliberately adopted and declared, the community ought to be able to rely upon it to govern their contracts and affairs).

[496] *Black's Law Dictionary* 1443 (8th ed. 2004).

[497] Lewis A. Kornhouser, Adjudication by a Resource-constrained team: Hierarchy and Precedent in a Judicial System, 68 S. *Cal. L. Rev.* 1605, 1606 (1995).

power. In fact, Justinian believed that the judicial practice of consulting past decisions threatened his power because it established the courts as the final arbiter of the law, a role he wanted for himself. "No judge or arbitrator," he declared, "is to deem himself bound by juristic opinions which he considers wrong: still less by the decisions of learned prefects or other judges. . . Decisions should be based on laws, not on precedents"[498]. It could be argued that Judges and arbitrators should have the same status. Thus, a judge or an arbitrator should be equally powerful to decide a case based on their understanding of law. Codification of the law was the basis of Justinian understanding of law. The law has to adjust to the needs of the community as social conditions change[499]. A system of precedent harmonizes the law's performance concerning advancement and handling presenting a uniform method through which judges reach judicial decisions that modify the law in an evolutionary fashion to circumvent generating remarkable instabilities. Consequently, precedent both allows judges to improve the law and controls the abuse of judicial power[500].

Is stare decisis prerequisite to a functioning judicial system? The assurance provided by stare decisis is not a precondition to a functioning judicial system. Under the older system of common law, the law was able to reply and adjust to new economic situations more efficiently. Precedent obliges the courts to treat correspondingly situated parties the same from one case to the next. However, Peters[501] thinks that stare decisis cannot serve the goal of equity because when a court treats on party unjustly, stare decisis would entail that the court also treats similarly situated parties unjustly.

Stare decisis can only generate judicial impartiality if the judge who laid down the original rule was himself free from bias. If the judge is not free from bias, stare decisis results in perpetuating the bias. Caleb Nelson[502] thinks that weak precedent is that it permits amendment when a prior court went outside the acceptable range of indeterminacy in the law and so allowing this type of error-correction would boundary the effect of bias judges and be beneficial to the judicial system. Does reliance on a weak precedent is the basis of arbitration?

The colonists needed a legal system that could be moulded to meet the challenges of a developing society. Therefore, from their earliest years they established a marked preference for adaptability over certainty, for latitude over restraint[503]. Samuel

---

[498] Carleton Kemp Allen, *Law in the Making* 170, 177 n.1 (Clarendon Press 7th ed., 1964), at 171, 175-76, at 172-73.

[499] H.L.A. Hart, *The Concept Of Law* 97-107 (1972).

[500] *United States v. Mason*, 412 U.S. 391, 399-400 (1973) (stating that "people in their everyday affairs [should] be able to rely on [the court's] decisions and not be needlessly penalized for such reliance."); *Planned Parenthood of SE PA. v. Casey*, 505 U.S. 833, 854-55 (1992). ("[W]e recognize that no judicial system could do society's work if it eyed each issue afresh in every case that raised it").

[501] Christopher J. Peters, Foolish Consistency: On Equity, Integrity, and Justice in Stare Decisis, 105 *Yale L. J.* 2031, 2065-73 (1996).

[502] Caleb Nelson, Stare Decisis and Demonstrably Erroneous Precedents, 87 *Va. L. Rev.* 1 (2001).

[503] Paul Samuel Reinsch, The English Common Law in the Early American Colonies, in 1 *Select Essays In Anglo-American Legal* History 367, 369, 411, 414 (1907). Qualified adoption of the common law was a willingness

Livermore, the colony's Chief Justice in the 1780s, "paid little attention to precedent," and when reminded once of his previous decision in a similar case declared that "[e]very tub must stand on its own bottom[504]." Justices in the 19th Century responded to the crisis of legitimacy by strengthening the norm of stare decisis, a legal norm inherited from English common law that encourages judges to follow precedent by letting the past decision stand[505]. The precedent-setting utility relates to the concept that judicial decisions are to be followed in indistinguishable, later cases, absent overruling or abrogation by some superior form of authority[506]. Precedent[507] as a concept has become part of understanding of what law is.

Courts are by no means the only mechanism for dispute resolution but they are the prevailing mechanism of dispute resolution backed by the sovereign power of state. When disputes arise, parties can choose among a number of alternatives to litigation, including mediation, negotiation, rent-a-judge programs and arbitration. Rent-a-judge programs allow parties to consent to a form of compulsory arbitration before an individual, frequently a retired judge whose decision possesses the same binding force that a judgment in a normal court carries[508]. Courts' and legislatures' efforts to focus demand for court services on cases with the highest social value had the effect of pushing high-valued, fact-specific disputes toward other means of dispute settlement.

Precedent, or stare decisis, refers the doctrine under which a court, when deciding a point of law, generally follows to a holding of a prior court on that point if that prior court is equal or superior in the judicial hierarchy[509]. Even the highest appellate court will normally follow its prior decisions on a point of law, apart from exceptional

---

by colonial legislatures to innovate. Craig Evan Klafter, Reason Over Precedents: Origins of American Legal Thought 42 (1993).

[504] *King v. Hopkins*, 57 N.H. 334, *7 (1876) (giving an account of Livermore's statement). at *9.John Dudley, an associate justice in the 1790s, took an equally dim view of precedents, describing Coke and Blackstone as "books that I never read and never will." *King v. Hopkins*, 57 N.H. 334, *7 (1876) (giving an account of Livermore's statement). Morton J. Horwitz, The Transformation Of American Law: 1780- 1860 8-9 (1977).

[505] Friedman, Lawrence M. 1985. *A History of American Law*. 2d ed. New York: Simon and Schuster.

[506] *Harper v. Virginia Dep't of Taxation*, 509 U.S. 86, 97 (1993) ("When this Court applies a rule of federal law to the parties before it, that rule is the controlling interpretation of federal law and must be given full retroactive effect in all cases still open on direct review and as to all events, regardless of whether such events predate or postdate our announcement of the rule."); *Anastasoff v. United States*, 223 F.3d 898, 899–900 ("Inherent in every judicial decision is a declaration and interpretation of a general principle or rule of law. This declaration of law is authoritative to the extent necessary for the decision, and must be applied in subsequent cases to similarly situated parties.") (citation omitted), vacated as moot on reh'g en banc, 235 F.3d 1054 (8th Cir.2000); *Hart v. Massanari*, 266 F.3d 1155, 1168 (9th Cir. 2001) ("The modern concept of binding precedent—where a single opinion sets the course on a particular point of law and must be followed by courts at the same level and lower within a pyramidal judicial hierarchy—came about only gradually over the nineteenth and early twentieth centuries").

[507] Henry P. Monaghan, Stare Decisis and Constitutional Adjudication, 88 *Colum. L. Rev.* 723, 748 (1988) ("Precedent is, of course, part of our understanding of what law is").

[508] Anne S. Kim, Rent-A-Judge and the Cost of Selling Justice, 44 *Duke L. J.* 166 (1994). Kim Karelis, Private Justice: How Civil Litigation is Becoming a Private Institution—The Rise of Private Dispute Centers. 23 *SW U. L. Rev.* 621, 624 (1994).

[509] J.W. Harris, *Legal Philosophies* 168 (1980).

circumstances[510]. The Advocate General of the European Court of Justice has stated that the Court should keep to its previous case-law except where there are strong reasons for not so doing[511].

Judges began to follow precedent for the sake of convenience and stability. Kent[512] argued that "an indigestible heap of laws and legal authorities" would "destroy the certainty of the law, and promote litigation, delay, and subtilty." Adherence to erroneous decisions, at least in the constitutional arena, violates the courts' duty "to say what the law is.[513] "Gary Lawson[514] argues that "at least as a prima facie matter, the reasoning of Marbury thoroughly de-legitimizes precedent. It could be argued that a system apparently committed to justice cannot justify a decision-making process that essentially produces unjust results[515]. The difference between arbitrators and judges was not that one could ignore the substantive law while the other could not, but rather that only the former was permitted to do so openly[516].

A judge's compulsion to consult precedent before deciding a case has been a core element of the Rule of Law in the United States, whether the appropriate source of law at issue is statutory, constitutional, or common law. The Court gives less deference to precedents interpreting the Constitution than to precedents that interpret a statute or involve other, non-constitutional legal norms[517]. In *Harmelin v. Michigan*[518], Justice

---

[510] *Dickerson v. United States*, 530 U.S. 428, 443 (2000) (Rehnquist, C. J.) ("The doctrine [of stare decisis] carries such persuasive force that we have always required a departure from precedent to be supported by some 'special justification'"); *Ariz. v. Rumsey*, 467 U.S. 203, 212 (1984) ("[A]ny departure from the doctrine of stare decisis demands special justification."). J.W. Harris, *Legal Philosophies* 168 (1980).

[511] *Merck v. Primecrown, Ltd.*, Joined Cases C-267/95 & C-268/95, [1996] E.C.R. 1-6285, 139.

[512] James Kent, I *Commentaries on American Law* 474 (14th ed., John M. Gould, ed. 1896) (1826) at 477.

[513] *Planned Parenthood v. Casey*, 505 U.S 833, 868 (1992) ("The Court's concern with legitimacy is not for the sake of the Court, but for the sake of the Nation to which it is responsible").

[514] Gary Lawson, The Constitutional Case Against Precedent, 17 *Harv. J. L. & Pub.* Pol'y 23 (1994) at 28.

[515] Richard A. Wasserstrom, *The Judicial Decision: Toward A Theory Of Legal Justification* 39 (1961). at 42-53.

[516] Hiro N. Aragaki, The Federal Arbitration Act As Procedural Reform 89 *N.Y.U. L. Rev.* 2014 http://ssrn.com/abstract=2421704 *p. 66.*

[517] *Payne v. Tennessee*, 501 U.S. 808, 828 (1991); see also e.g., *Neal v. United States*, 516 U.S. 284, 295 (1996) (stating that the Court gives "great weight to stare decisis in the area of statutory construction" due to "concerns about the relationship of the Judiciary to Congress"). Thomas G. Hansford & James F. Spriggs, Ii, The Politics of Precedent on the U.S. Supreme Court 4 (2006) (describing the "attitudinal model" as the claim that "the justices' votes are exclusively a result of their ideological leanings").

[518] *Harmelin v. Michigan*, 501 U.S. 957, 965 (1991); see also *Clark v. Martinez*, 543 U.S. 371, 401-02 (2005) (Thomas, J., dissenting) ("It is true that we give stronger stare decisis effect to our holdings in statutory cases than in constitutional cases."). Justices elsewhere on the ideological spectrum, such as Justice O'Connor, have expressed similar sentiments:

As we have often noted, "stare decisis is not an inexorable command," but instead reflects a policy judgment that "in most matters it is more important that the applicable rule of law be settled than that it be settled right." That policy is at its weakest when we interpret the Constitution because our interpretation can be altered only by constitutional amendment or by overruling our prior decisions.

Agostini v. Felton, 521 U.S. 203, 235 (1997) (citing Payne, 501 U.S. at 828; Burnet, 285 U.S. at 406 (1932) (Brandeis, J., dissenting)); see also *Hohn v. United States*, 524 U.S. 236, 251 (1998) (Kennedy, J.) (same). Justice Bryer has likewise found that the "Court applies stare decisis more 'rigorously' in statutory than in constitutional cases." *Leegin Creative Leather Prods., Inc. v. PSKS, Inc.*, 127 S. Ct. 2705, 2734 (2007) (Bryer, J., dissenting); see also *Shepard v. United States*, 544 U.S. 13, 23 (2005) (Souter, J.) (same); *Hubbard v. United States*, 514 U.S. 695, 712 (1995) (Stevens, J.) (same). Gary Lawson, The Constitutional Case Against Precedent, 17 *Harv. J.L. & Pub. Pol'y*, 23 (1994) (arguing that judges are bound by the judicial oath to correct errors of constitutional interpretation).

Scalia stated that "the doctrine of stare decisis is less rigid in its application to constitutional precedents."

A stream of consistent case law does not oblige a judge to reach a certain result, but it gives him/her a compelling way of resolving the merits if she/he chooses to rely on it[519]. Precedent never has been considered binding as a norm in civil law courts[520]. A given decision either makes law[521] (law-making) or simply applies the law (dispute resolving) and so a given decision may either: 1) make new law by expanding the range of existing law or writing a new principle into the body of law, or 2) it may merely apply the law without altering it[522]. Richard Cappalli[523] argues that the present system of permitting judges to decide prospectively which of their decisions are law and which are not, "starkly reverses centuries of common law tradition." While the legislature enacts laws, courts "legislate" through their interpretation of legislation, as well as enactment of the "common law." The judge has just enough law-making responsibility to limit the court's interpretive role exercising a substantial law-making choice by deferring to the legislative writer or the statutory text. A judicial decision to assign law-making responsibility to the legislature makes sense when the legislature is aware of a technically multifaceted or politically controversial matter. Judges allocate law-making accountability to the legislature so it may decide whether the intervening judicial or agency interpretation is good law, while the matter is on the legislative agenda.

Court decisions are a form of "state-sponsored dispute resolution" in which judges make decisions to finalize outcomes in disputes. In democratic States, the constant existence of any system of State-sponsored decision making eventually depends on its legality in the eyes of the public. The legality of judicial decision-making, and the

---

519 John Bell, Comparing Precedent, 82 *Cornell L. Rev.* 1243, 1257 (1997)(book review) ("[T]he civilian approach typically gives greater weight to a line of authority (la jurisprudence constante) than to an individual decision. It is the cumulation of authority in a particular direction that is seen as persuasive.") (citations omitted); James L. Dennis, The 21st John M. Tucker, Jr. Lecture in Civil Law: Interpretation and Application of the Civil Code and the Evaluation of Judicial Precedent, 54 *La. L. Rev.* 1, 15 (1993) ("When a series of decisions forms a constant stream of uniform and homogeneous rulings having the same reasoning, [jurisprudence constante] accords the cases considerable persuasive authority and justifies, without requiring, the court in abstaining from new inquiry because of its faith in the precedents.") (citations omitted); Francesco G. Mazzotta, Precedents in Italian Law, 9 *Msu-Dcl J. Int'l L.* 121, 142 (2000) (explaining that not one decision, but "a coherent group of decisions," established "'giurisprudenza costante'" in Italian law).

520 Mary Ann Glendon Et Al., *Comparative Legal Traditions* 130–31 (2d ed. 1999).

521 H. Jefferson Powell, The Modern Misunderstanding of Original Intent, 54 *U. Chi. L. Rev.* 1513, 1537, & n.91 (1987) (asserting Lord Coke's belief that the law was "refined" by "long and continual experience" by judges seeking to ever refine the law further by, "declaring its principles with even greater precision and renewing it by application to the matter at hand.").

522 Frederick Schauer, Precedent, 39 *Stan. L. Rev.* 571, 577 (1987) ("No two events are exactly alike. For a decision to be precedent for another decision does not require that the facts of the earlier and the later cases be absolutely identical. Were that required, nothing would be precedent for anything else.").

523 Richard B. Cappalli, The Common Law's Case Against Non-Precedential Opinions, 76 *S. Cal. L. Rev.* 755 (2003) at 772. Karl Llewellyn, The Bramble Bush 52 (1930) (noting that it is the precedent-applying court that determines the scope of the precedent-writing court's decision notwithstanding the words used by the precedent-writing court).

public's perceptions of such legitimacy, depends on the system's performance[524]. Procedural indicia do not directly evaluate the content of legal rules or of legal outcomes. As an alternative, procedural indicia determine whether the law's processes are functioning appropriately to channel the evolution of rules and the derivation of outcomes towards desirable ends[525].

Although arbitrators in investment treaty arbitration are not officially bound by precedent in the same way as common-law judges, there is an informal, but dominant, system of precedent that compels arbitrators to give a reason for prior published awards and to stabilize international investment law[526].

Investment treaty arbitration is not a substitute for local institutions; rather, it provides a complement to domestic institutional reform[527]. Endorsing the use of arbitration augments contract enforceability. A larger question is whether investment treaty arbitration advances the rule of law and supplies enticements to further fair and legitimate decision making in national institutions.

The accessibility of treaty arbitration assists investment by providing adjudicative independence and/or a model for national courts to follow the rule of law. Investment arbitration has the aptitude to fuel domestic support for the rule of law instilling a belief in the capability of institutions to administer justice impartially. National courts are an imperative counterpart to the resolution of investment disputes. Domestic courts of general jurisdiction have little stimulus to compete with specialist arbitral tribunals for the resolution disputes correlated to international law. Investors select between court litigation and arbitration.

National courts provide critical support to the investment arbitration procedure. While a court's role tends to be limited in ICSID arbitration proceedings, national courts have a role to play in enforcing ICSID arbitration awards[528]. In the context of an ad hoc

---

[524] Thomas Franck, *Fairness in International Law and Institutions* 26 (1998) (noting that in a legal system, "legitimacy validates community" and "promote[s] voluntary compliance by those to whom [its norms are] addressed").

[525] John Finnis, Natural Law and Natural Rights 81-85 (1980) (stating that "values" refer to the basic aspects of each individual's well-being); Tai-Heng Cheng, Power and Authority in International Investment Law, 20 *Am. U. Int'l L. Rev.* 465, 504 (2005) (describing values as "the universe of tangible and intangible benefits, interests and resources").

[526] Tai-Heng Cheng, Precedent and Control in Investment Treaty Arbitration 2006 Fordham International Law Journal Volume 30, Issue 4 Article 3. W. Michael Reisman, The Breakdown of the Control Mechanism in ICSID Arbitration, 1989 *Duke L. J.* 739, 770, 775 (1989) (noting that the annulment of the Kloeckner award had a "constitutive dimension" and was "a precedent"). *Jan Asmus Bischoff*, Just a little bit of "mixity"? The EU's role in the field of international investment protection law, (2011) 48 *Common Market Law Review* 1527–1570, 1534 et seq.

[527] Susan D. Franck, Foreign Direct Investment, Investment Treaty Arbitration, and the Rule of Law 2007 *Global Business & Development Law Journal* 337 / Vol. 19 p 367.

[528] In *Mobil Cerro Negro, Limited v. Bolivarian Republic of* Venezuela 446 and *Micula v. Government of Romania*, 447 *Fed.App'x.* ____, 2017 WL 4772435 (2nd Cir. 2017). The court held that the FSIA provides the exclusive mechanism for enforcing ICSID awards against foreign sovereigns and summary ex parte proceedings are incompatible with the FSIA, since they are, by nature, conducted without the required service on the foreign state. R. Rana, The Enforcement of Awards Set Aside at the Seat: An Asian and European Perspective, 40 *Fordham Int'l L .J.* 813 (2017).

UNCITRAL arbitration, national courts are playing a greater role[529]. The adjudicative fairness and neutrality of treaty arbitration offers a helpful model for national decision makers and conveniently upgrade adherence to the rule of law. Martin Malin[530] argues that the courts' involvement in an arbitration procedure makes this arbitration a system of public law and otherwise arbitration will be transformed into a private justice system.

The question that has to be answered is if a domestic court system following the rule of law provides a valuable backing to the integrity of the investment treaty arbitration process. An autonomous arbitration dealing exclusively with the dispute resolution without the need to have courts to intervene causing confusion, cost rise and time consuming further enhances investor confidence in the resolution of investment-related disputes by arbitration.

A. Daniel[531] argues that "While it is argued that arbitration must be free from courts, in order to be effective, it is also accepted that arbitration needs the support of national courts to be effective." How effective a dispute system could be if it is controlled by another dispute system? What is the use to have an incomplete dispute system such as arbitration as long as it is possible to merely improve courts and eradicate arbitration as it is currently functioning by not be able to deal alone with not even a stage of its whole process? Why is considered that only courts protect the public interest? What is the use of a non-independent dispute system such as arbitration as long as it is not considered to be able to protect the public interests?

A dispute system can be effective only if it is autonomous, complete and independent from commence of its process till the award. Is it time to have arbitration totally independent and complete dispute system co-equal to courts unchained totally from courts' control? Is there a reason for arbitration not be considered co-equal to courts as another independent dispute system in a jurisdiction? Can be suggested that there is a behind the curtain controlling of a single dispute system and so making difficult to allow a totally independent arbitration?

International commercial arbitration is a method by which disputes arising out of international trade and commerce are determined pursuant to the parties' voluntary agreement, through a procedure other than a court of competent jurisdiction. Can we have arbitration an effective dispute system as long as it is under the safeguarding of another supposed superior dispute system such as courts? If courts are the effective dispute

---

[529] United Nations Commission on International Trade Law ("UNCITRAL") Model Law on International Commercial Arbitration, June 21, 1985, *Annex* 1, art. 13, U.N. Doc. A/40/17, 24 I.L.M. 1302. (1985), http://www.uncitral.org/pdf/english/texts/arbitration/ml-arb/ml-arb-e.pdf(permitting courts to hear challenges to arbitrators).

[530] Martin H. Malin, Privatizing Justice—But by How Much? Questions Gilmer Did Not Answer, 16 *Ohio St. J. On Disp. Resol.* 589, 627 (2001) (positing that "[i]f courts do not review employment arbitration awards for errors of law, we risk transforming a system of public law into a system of private justice"); ("De novo judicial review of arbitral interpretations of law is necessary to ensure that arbitration does not result in contracting out of statutory compliance").

[531] Angualia Daniel, *The Role of Domestic Courts in International Commercial Arbitration* September 2010 http://ssrn.com/abstract=1674760 p. 9.

system there is no need to have another dispute system such as arbitration because there is consuming of time and effort against the affectivity of courts to become much more effectual. There is a need to have two totally independent dispute systems such as courts and arbitration with their own characteristics adding to the effectiveness of justice. The basis of arbitration has to be the same of courts in a jurisdiction in order to have two co-equal dispute systems implemented in a single jurisdiction.

As mentioned earlier, arbitration has a judicial function[532]. The only divergence between arbitrators and judges is that arbitrators are appointed by the parties and judges by the state. In view of the fact that the powers and functions of arbitrators and judges are comparable, the arbitral award should be considered as a type of judgment, and should have the same outcome[533]. Angualia Daniel[534] says that "Arbitration is only an alternative to litigation and it does not replace the judicial machinery in all aspects, rather it co-exists with it."

The theory limits the autonomy of arbitrators and emphasizes the power of the state law, entailing the arbitral award to be consistent with the law of the place of enforcement. Cannot the arbitral process be effective without courts support? The recognition of the res judicata of arbitral awards identical to judgments is a further element in recognizing arbitration as a co-equal dispute system.[535]

Nothing in the Convention's *travaux préparatoires* indicates that investment tribunals should apply the doctrine of stare decisis[536]. Judicial decisions are explicitly mentioned in Article 38 of the Statute of the International Court of Justice (ICJ) as 'as subsidiary means for the determination of rules of law.' While customary law, treaties and general principles, also set out in Article 38 of the Statute of the ICJ, are considered as the key or formal sources of international law, doctrine and judicial decisions are classified as subsidiary or material sources.

International law has no doctrine of binding precedent or stare decisis. The wording of Article 38 of the ICJ Statute means that judicial decisions are not a means for the creation of rules of law. Notwithstanding the lack of any rule on binding precedent in international and in international investment law, many investment tribunals very often refer to preceding investment law cases in their decisions[537]. Investment tribunals refer to

---

[532] Lutz, Robert E, International Arbitration and Judicial Intervention, 10 *Loy. L. A. Int'l & Comp. L. J.* 1988, 621.

[533] Klein, F. - E. *Considtions sur 1' arbitrage en droit international priv?* Bale: Heilbing & Lichtenhahn, 1955, para. 105-112.

[534] Angualia Daniel, *The Role of Domestic Courts in International Commercial Arbitration*, September 2010 http://ssrn.com/abstract=1674760 p 5.

[535] Luca G. Radicati di Brozolo, Res Judicata and International Arbitral Awards, *ASA Special Series* 2011. S. Haubold, Res judicata: A tale of two cities, in *Global Arb. Rev.*, 2007, vol 2, issue 3, p. 19.

[536] Michael Waibel, Coordinating Adjudication Processes, Paper No. 6/2014 January 2014 *Law Legal Studies Research Paper Series* http://www.law.cam.ac.uk/ssrn/.

[537] Mohamed Shahabuddeen, *Precedent in the World Court* (Cambridge: Cambridge University Press, 1996), 1.

decisions of courts and tribunals when coping with issues other than international investment law[538].

Regardless of the directness of the subsidiary character of judicial and arbitral decisions as sources of law, judicial and arbitral decisions do play a very imperative role in defining international law[539]. International investment tribunals very often refer to the case-law of other international courts and arbitral tribunals or to their own previous decisions[540]. The practice of arbitral tribunals to rely widely on previous decisions furthers the development of the law relating to foreign investment.

A court or tribunal does not mechanically apply a certain given rule to a case but is often needed to further identify and clarify the applicable law. The law is applied or interpreted by the court or tribunal in a meaning echoing the customary status of the norm or an exception to that norm, or for the reason that the legal reasoning underlying a decision is considered as the accurate interpretation of a treaty rule binding upon a party. The influence of 'binding precedent' extends to the *ratio decidendi* of the decision but also obiter dicta have 'persuasive value[541].'

Jurisprudence constant functions as 'persuasive authority' used in civil law systems but transposed to the international legal system, particularly in international investment arbitration[542]. Investment tribunals very often rely upon previous awards of both investment tribunals and other international courts and tribunals[543]. Investment tribunals cite precedents forms part of the legal reasoning of arbitral tribunals[544]. There is indeed a significant distinction between the de facto use of precedent, the requirement to hold on to and develop a jurisprudence constant, and the 'obligation' to follow precedents.

---

538 Gilbert Guillaume, "The Use of Precedent by International Judges and Arbitrator," 2 *Journal of International Dispute Settlement* (2011): 5-23.

539 Paul Reuter, *Droit international public* (Paris: Presses Universitaires de France, 1958), 85.

540 Ian Brownlie, *Principles of Public International Law* (Oxford: Oxford University Press, 2003), p. 19. Gabrielle Kaufmann-Kohler, Arbitral Precedent: Dream, Necessity or Excuse? *Arbitration International* 23 (2007), p. 361. The Agreement Establishing the Caribbean Court of Justice, which provides in its Article XXII –entitled "Judgment of the Court to Constitute Stare Decisis," that "Judgments of the Court shall be legally binding precedents for parties in proceedings before the Court unless such judgments have been revised in accordance with Article XX." http://www.caricom.org/jsp/secretariat/legal_instruments/agreement_ccj.pdf).

541 James Crawford, "Similarity of Issues in Disputes Arising under the Same of Similarly Drafted Investment Treaties," in Precedent in international arbitration, ed. Yas Banifatemi (Huntington: Juris Publishing, 2008), p. 101 Robert L Henry, Jurisprudence Constante and Stare Decisis Contrasted, 15 *A.B.A. J.* 11 (1929).:11-13 and Vincy Fon and Francesco Parisi, Judicial precedents in civil law systems: A dynamic analysis, 26 *International Review of Law and* Economics (2006).

542 *Willis-Knighton Med. Ctr. v. Caddo-Shreveport Sales & Use Tax Comm'n*., 903 So.2d 1071, at n.17 (La. 2005), p. 26 (footnote 17) at http://www.lasc.org/opinions/2005/04c0473.opn.pdf.

543 J. P. Commission, Precedent in Investment Treaty Arbitration: A Citation Analysis of a Developing Jurisprudence, 24 *Journal of International Arbitration* (2007) and Ole Kristian Fauchal, The Legal Reasoning of ICSID Tribunals – An Empirical Analysis, 19 *European Journal of International Law* 2 (2008): 301.

544 *El Paso Energy International Company v. Argentine Republic*, (ICSID Case No. ARB/03/15) Decision on Jurisdiction (April 27, 2006), para. 39.

It is argued that investment arbitration is an alternate for dysfunctional domestic courts in states with a weak rule of law tradition[545]. Arbitration has seen as a means to achieve greater commercial autonomy and self-governance but not against the rule of law and the FAA promotes private ordering in dispute resolution as free as possible from state interference[546]. Arbitration was supposed to be qualitatively superior adjudicative alternative to the increasingly unworkable public system of civil justice[547]. It could be said that the FAA arose out of debates about the demand for reform in judicial procedure that obsessed the nation in the early twentieth century and arbitration successfully manages justice without rigorous pleading rules[548]. In other words, FAA can be seen as an early procedural reform rendering easier for parties to litigate disputes successfully which means that the idea behind the FAA was that procedure was not an end in itself other than a channel to the more vital purpose of securing substantial justice. To that extent, FAA' section 2 command makes simpler the commercial disputing procedure and so enhancing the administration of justice.

The idea for a federal arbitration law arose out of debates about the need for reform in judicial procedure that it was no longer probable to get justice in the courts, in large part for the reason that practice and procedure had become too complicated, unforgiving, and self-important[549]. Lord Coleridge[550] criticized revocability as "directly contrary to the spirit of later times, which leaves parties at full liberty to refer their disputes at pleasure to public or private tribunals." International commercial arbitration has become the generally utilized means to resolve the inevitable disputes that arise between the parties to international contracts[551].

The publicity of awards is, in itself, one of the critical prerequisites to the likelihood of viewing arbitrators as law makers. A valuable body of case law contributes to strengthen legal predictability in international sports law[552]. In *Saipem v. Bangladesh*[553]

---

[545] Thomas Schultz, Cédric Dupont, Investment Arbitration: Promoting the Rule of Law or Over-Empowering Investors? A Quantitative Empirical Study King's College London Dickson Poon School of Law Legal Studies Research Paper Series, paper no. 2014-16.

[546] *American Express v. Italian Colors Restaurant*, 133 S. Ct. 2304 (2013), and *AT&T Mobility v. Concepcion*, 131 S. Ct. 1740 (2011).

[547] Henry David Thoreau, *Civil Disobedience* 2 (1942). *Wayman v. Southard*, 23 U.S. (10 Wheat.) 1 (1825) (upholding the constitutionality of the Process Act of 1789 and establishing the right of federal courts to set their own procedures).

[548] Charles E. Clark, Procedural Fundamentals, 1 *Conn. B. J.* 67, 71 (1927).

[549] Roscoe Pound, The Causes of Popular Dissatisfaction with the Administration of Justice, 29 *Annu. Rep. A.B.A.* 395 (1906). William H. Taft, The Delays of the Law, 18 *Yale L .J.* 28 (1908). Roscoe Pound, Some Principles of Procedural Reform, 4 *U. Ill. L. Rev.* 388, 391 (1910) (stating that under the "sporting theory of justice . . . judicial administration of justice is a game, to be played to the bitter end as a game of football might be . . . .").

[550] Vynior's case, [1609] 8 Co. Rep. 81b *Scott v. Avery*, [1856] 5 HLC 811, 843, 852–53 (Coleridge, L.J.).

[551] Margaret Moses, Arbitration/Litigation Interface: The European Debate, Public Law & Legal Theory Research Paper No. 2014-013. In *National Report on Switzerland in Klaus Peter Berger, International Handbook on Commercial Arbitration* (permitting party to challenge an arbitrator in court where "circumstances exist that give rise to justifiable doubts as to his independence").

[552] *Anderson v. Int'l Olympic Comm.*, CAS 2008/A/1545, 1 53 (July 16, 2010) http://jurisprudence.tas-cas.org/, Alexis C. Brown, Presumption Meets Reality, 16 *Am. U. Int'l L. Rv.* 969, 1013 (2001) (asserting that "awards made in important and well-known cases are often published with commentaies, and will naturally serve as precedents."). *El Paso Energy Int'l Co. v. Argentine Republic*, ICSID (W. Bank) Case No. ARB/03/15,

the arbitrators wrote, they had "a duty to adopt solutions established in a series of consistent cases." The arbitrators in *Methanex Corp. v. United States*[554] endorsed this approach, insisting that investment treaty tribunals "can set no legal precedent, in general or at all." Arbitration produces law which is not totally a uniform or consistent law which should be the characteristic arbitrations' precedent[555].

By ignoring any line in law interpretation of law means that arbitration loses its credibility as a trustful, quick and effective system. If arbitrators are totally free to interpret law according to dissimilar way based on an effort to please parties in arbitration than a fair interpretation of law then arbitration will be transformed into a distorter of law. An inconsistent arbitration indicates the need for setting it aside as a serious dispute mechanism and allowing courts to be the single dispute mechanism.

Arbitrators do make law, whether they want to or not. Arbitrators regularly cite to prior awards. Lawmaking is defined as the laying down of normative rules of conduct to which a sanction for non-compliance attaches being the kind of law that legislators make, and that the superior courts in common law systems generate. Arbitrators, by contrast, do not generally make that kind of law possessing no imperium, and there is no recognized system of binding precedent in international arbitration or in international law, for that subject. Arbitrators make what might be thought of as "hard law" is *inter partes*[556]. Lesser use of precedent is apparent in the awards of pure commercial arbitration panels[557].

When do arbitrators make law? In order for arbitrators to "make law," there must be either a "gap" in the system of rules being applied, or at least some vagueness in the applicable standard requiring interpretation. Arbitrators[558] make three types of law: procedural law, substantive law (*lex mercatoria*, or general principles of law governing commercial transactions such as good faith, changed circumstances, or abuse of rights) and an emerging international ordre public. The Iran-U.S. Claims Tribunal provided for

---

Decision on Jurisdiction, 82 (2006) (explicitly stating that decision was taken pursuant to "important precedents by Tribunals").

553 *Saipem S.p.A. v. People's Republic of Bangl.*, ICSID Case No. ARB/ 05/7, Decision on Jurisdiction and Recommendation of Provisional Measures, 67 (Mar. 21, 2007) *Tulip Real Estate Inv. & Dev. Neth. B.V. v. Republic of Turk.*, ICSID Case No. ARB/11/28, Decision on Bifurcated Jurisdictional Issue,1 45 (Mar. 5, 2013) *Quiborax S.A. v. Plurinational State of Bol.*, ICSID Case No. ARB/06/2, Decision on Jurisdiction, 46 (Sept. 27, 2012) *Saba Fakes v. Republic of Turk.*, ICSID Case No. ARB/07/20, Award, 1 96 (July 14, 2010).

554 *Methanex Corp. v. United States*, Decision of the Tribunal on Petitions from Third Persons to Intervene as 'Amici Curiae,' 51 (NAFTA Arb. Trib. 2001) Quiborax S.A., ICSID Case No. ARB/06/2, Decision on Jurisdiction, 1 46 (Dec. 27, 2012).

555 Geraldine Szott Moohr, Arbitration and the Goals of Employment Discrimination Law, 56 *Wash. & Lee L. Rev.* 395 (1999).

556 D. Brian King and Rahim Moloo International Arbitrators as Lawmakers 2014 *International Law and Politics* Vol. 46:875.

557 *Dow Chemicals v. Isover Saint-Gobain*, 9 *Y.B. Comm. Arb.* 131, 136 (ICC *Int'l Ct. Arb.* 1984) *Int'l Thunderbird Gaming Corp. v. United Mexican States*, Separate Opinion of Thomas Wilde, 1 128 (UNCITRAL Dec. 1, 2005).

558 M. Ten Cate, The Costs of Consistency: Precedent in Investment Treaty Arbitration, 51 *Colum. J. Transnat'l L.* 418 (2013).

the first time an extensive body of published case law on arbitral procedure and substantive international law topics.

Arbitrations have the ability to harmonize common law and civil law procedures. Arbitrators are more knowledgeable and experienced in certain areas of the law than others. Wesley Sturges[559] characterizes arbitration as a "litigation substitute" and arbitrators in international matters care more than judges about strict legal analysis. Arbitration removes disputes from the perceived vagaries of civil juries aiming to augment the rule of law in its broadest sense, seeking balance between respect for parties' agreement and the correlative judicial duty to monitor fairness in the process[560]. Furthermore, it is argued that arbitration generates an "autonomous legal order"[561].

---

[559] Wesley Sturges, Arbitration-- What is it, 35 N.Y.U. L. Rev. 1031, 1041-45 (1960).

[560] William W. Park, The Predictability Paradox: Arbitrators and Applicable Law, in 11 ICC DOSSIERS (*Institute World Business Law* 2014).

[561] Jan Paulsson, *The Idea of Arbitration* (2013) 39-42. Emmanuel Gaillard, *Legal Theory Of International Arbitration* (2010)

Chapter 4

ARBITRATION, POLITICS AND THE RULE OF LAW

1. INTRODUCTION

Globalization involves countries' institutional structure by the diffusion of social values and individual value creation via interactions with wide range of backgrounds and nationality. Moreover, globalization procedure has been driven by political ideas, economic forces and new technology augmenting the speed but diminishing the cost of transportation and communication.

Politics (πολιτικός/ *politikos*) is the procedure of making decisions applying to all members of each group and so politics refers to accomplishing and exercising positions of governance— organized control over a human community, particularly a state. Additionally, politics is the study or practice of the distribution of power/ authority and resources within a given society on top of the interrelationship(s) between societies. It is very often said that politics is about power/ authority. To that extent, a political system is a framework which expresses adequate political methods within a given society. Globalization has political, social, and cultural dimensions by generating economic networks. International production networks implicate not just inter-industry or inter-company but also intra-industry and intra-company trade.

Due to globalization augmented competition through access to product markets has resulted from the liberalization of cross-border trade in goods and services. This liberalization of trade in goods and services has been supplemented by the parallel liberalization of international movements of capital. To that extent, economic globalization refers to the increasing interdependence of world economies by means of the growing scale of cross-border trade of commodities and services, flow of international capital and wide and rapid spread of technologies. Moreover, the rapid growing magnitude of information in all types of productive activities and marketization are the two key driving factors for economic globalization. Hence, financial globalization and the spreading out of global capital flows bring a number of benefits such as more competent allocation of resources, enhanced risk sharing and more swift technology transfer[562].

States are sovereign and rules are only advantageous to the extent that states agree to follow them. Therefore, the need of the rule of law means that the sovereign state concedes a great deal of legal power to the law and organization that stabilizes the system. In conjunction with the upsurge of new international or transnational institutions and norms, the partial reconfiguration of the state denotes that norms 'created somewhere else' influence daily life in ways which were up to that time out of the question. People continually renegotiate their internal rules on how they should act with regard to each other on a day-to-day.

Law merely reflects a determinate resolution of the controversy as contemplated fitting by those who have the power and authority to resolve the issue within a specific society[563]. Common law and civil law systems are all, to some degree, amalgams in which case law works alongside codes and statutes[564].

Legal authority is a type of power exemplified by a content-independent response to a command or order. Legal authority is more multipart than parental authority, but it is similar in that subjects obey for the reason that an authoritative actor has said what handling is needed.

There is a need to examine the political context in which law operates. Does law apply irrespective of any political context or politics influence the appliance of law? Does politics overrule the rule of law? Is there a tendency to implement a politics of law instead of objective appliance of law? Is there a relationship between Law and politics expressed as politics of law? Has globalization influenced the rule of law and its appliance owing to politics?

2. Globalization and the Law

Globalization embodies a transformation in the spatial organization of social relations and transactions generating transcontinental or interregional flows and networks of activity, interaction, and the exercise of power.[565] The growth of MNEs and international production networks, new technology, changes in the nature and form of work, and the rise of new actors on the international scene have shaped globalization. On the other

---

[562] G Zekos, *Monetary Policy and Risk Management in Financial Globalization*, 2015 Nova Science Publications New York USA. www.novapublishers.com.

[563] Neil MacCormick, *Institutions of Law: An Essay in Legal Theory* (Oxford: Oxford University Press, 2007) 255-61.

[564] M. Roe, Chaos and evolution in law and economics (1996) 109 *Harvard Law Review* 641-668.

[565] Held, D. McGrew, A., Goldblatt, D., and Perraton, J.: *Global Transformations: Politics, Economics and Culture (*Cambridge, England: Polity Press, 1999).

hand, the State remains influential, even prevalent, with the relative strength of different institutions, norms and dispute resolution processes depending often on the particular background[566].

Which forces control the state and how? It has to be taken into account that the legal consequences of economic globalization have implications for law. Moreover, norms of nation-states, or of regional organizations such as the European Union, are founded on or infused by 'international' norms, embracing WTO international trade rules, codes of conduct, standards or the results of international dispute settlement processes. On the other hand, some legal fields have always been more internationalized than others such as areas of law most directly associated with international trade and MNEs. Furthermore, global regulation consists primarily in competitive interaction among various national legal systems which means regulatory competition among public authorities[567]. Nonetheless, in many fields, the legal framework of regulation takes the form of networks of regulatory agencies, often working in cooperation with private actors which means based on decentralized enforcement, rather than international or transnational enforcement[568].

For instance, international commercial arbitration is not wholly independent of the nation-state, either in legal terms or in terms of the questions it raises about the role of law in society. The formation of a constitution is not inevitably in the sense of a written document, but rather in the sense of continuing processes of constitutionalisation. Moreover, local institutions, interest-specific institutions or even personal relationships are more valuable than universalistic norms in providing legal assurance for cross-border or international transactions[569].

It is characteristic that the impressive growth of global economic networks has had conflicting consequences on the development on constitutional systems based on regional integration. In the European Union, globalization produces interests and relationships which destabilize conventional constitutionalism as mode of regional governance requiring the constitutionalisation of global governance.

It is worth mentioning that the horizontality of global governance concerns the fact that international relations and inter-states relations are centered on the principles of

---

566 Jayasuriya, K.: 'Globalization, Sovereignty, and the Rule of Law: From Political to Economic Constitutionalism?', *Constellations*, 8, 2001, pp. 442-460. G. Zekos, 'Constructing a New IPRs index' [2012] 4 *Web JCLI* http://webjcli.ncl.ac.uk/2012/issue4/zekos4.html, G Zekos, *The Impact of IPRs upon FDI*, 2013 PhD Thesis, Economics Department, University of Peloponnese Hellas www.uop.gr G Zekos, *IPRs protection and their impact upon FDI, GDP growth & trade*, 2013 Scholar's Press, www.scholars-press.com www.morebooks.de Germany.

567 Bratton, W, McCahery, J., Picciotto, S., and Scott, C.: eds., *International Regulatory Competition and Coordination: Perspectives on Economic Regulation in Europe and the United States* (Oxford: Clarendon Press, 1996).

568 Jayasuriya, K., 'Globalization, Law and the Transformation of Sovereignty: The Emergence of Global Regulatory Governance', *Indiana Journal of Global Legal Studies*, 6, 1999, pp. 425-455.

569 Gessner, V. and Budak, A.C.: *Emerging Legal Certainty: Empirical Studies on the Globalization of Law.* (Ashgate: Dartmouth, for the Oñati International Institute for the Sociology of Law, 1998).

sovereign equality and non-interference preserved in Article 2 of the UN Charter[570].On the other hand, there is weak institutionalization of global governance and so difficulty to guarantee the equality of all – individuals and states – before global justice. Moreover, the weak institutionalization of global governance is based on character of international law that lacks enforceability and the creation of regulatory mechanisms (soft law, transnational law, private standards) at the global level[571].

States do not have to, nor they should be anticipated to relinquish their national identity but they have to adopt a widespread standard for the interpretation of legislation in accordance with global existential values. Added legitimacy to any global legal system means that it does not only acknowledge the significance of national values, but also emerging global ones. To that extent, significant documents, such as the Universal Declaration of Human Rights 1948, already lay down a global frame of values that apply in all places implemented in domestic legislation making certain an equal global playing field. It has to be taken into account that every state has to approve universal global values in interpreting its national legislation[572] as well. To that extent, there is a transplant of fundamental legal principles developed in some Western countries to the East due to globalization.

Globalization brings up new challenges for law due to the differences among legal systems. The emergence of powerful private or transnational actors creates networks and new spheres of normativity distinct from the nation state causing question of conventional representation of law itself and the related plot of the relationship between the center and the periphery. It is argued that arbitration[573] is blooming into the framework of globalization and international governance which means that arbitration is considered to be the new dispute system suitable to cope with the demands of globalization.

There is a move from the welfare state to the competition state forced to act increasingly resembling a market player molding its policies to uphold, control, and maximize returns from market forces in a global background[574]. Moreover, the competition state encompassed two broad elements: firstly, a persistent belief in national competitiveness as the way for causing economic growth and going up living standards,

---

[570] Article 2 of the UN Charter reads as follows: 'The Organization is based on the principle of the sovereign equality of all its Members […] All Members shall refrain in their international relations from the threat or use of force against the territorial integrity or political independence of any state', UN, Charter of the United Nations, 1 U.N.T.S. XVI, signed in San-Francisco on 26 June 1945, effective on 24 October 1945, art. 2.

[571] Jacques de Ville, Mythology and the Images of Justice, *Law and Literature*, Vol. 23, No. 3, 2011, pp. 325-326. Sophie Harman and David Williams, Conclusion: Governing the World, in Sophie Harman and David Williams eds., *Governing the World? Cases in Global Governance* (London: Routledge, 2013), p. 197.

[572] Ennals, R.; Kathrani, P. *International Human Rights and Globalization: The Dawn of a New Age*. 10th International Conference of Chief Justices of the World, City Montessori School, Lucknow, India; December, 2008. Kant, I. *Critique of Practical Reason*. New York: Dover Publications, 1909, p. 31.

[573] Thomas Hale, *Between Interests and Law: The Politics of Transnational Commercial Disputes* (2015) (placing the evolution of arbitration law in the framework of international politics and governance).

[574] Bob Jessop, *The Future of the Capitalist State* (Cambridge: Polity Press, 2002). Philip. G. Cerny, *The Changing Architecture of Politics: Structure, Agency, and the Future of the State* (London: Sage, 1990), p. 205.

and secondly, the way by which governments carry out competitive policies in a global economic market has moved from mainly demand-side measures to supply-side measures[575].

It is worth mentioning that global commerce relies, considerably, on local laws and national enforcement mechanisms which means that globalism is localized. Human rights movements, on the other hand, attain local policy changes by forming network which means that their localism is globalized. Therefore, globalization is not purely uniformization regardless that increased communication and competition leads towards uniformity of culture, of policies, and of laws which uniformity always remains limited.

It has to be taken into account that for all three notions of globalization—reality, theory, ideology—the role of the state is fundamental in particular with regard to law, for the reason that the state is central to contemporary thinking. On the other hand, the state is constituted by three elements: a territory, a population, and an administrative structure which means that the transformation of the state under conditions of globalization has to be illustrated via a transformation of these three elements[576].

Moreover, it has to be taken into consideration that law is playing an essential role in correcting inequalities that the legal accommodation of industrialism had produced or exaggerated. Taking into consideration that given that law and the state are constitutive of economic life which means that the government is the positive force in the economy and so the government by legislating and via the law of contracts has established and allowed arbitration as an alternative dispute system not mentioning, as described earlier, arbitration was the only dispute system prior to the introduction of the public dispute system.

National laws take in respect of the overwhelming majority of legal areas and states generate their 'own' laws so that they maintain their *imperium* (legal power) over their *territorium* (territory). In other words, law was and still is a symbol of national unity. There is one of overall divergence of legal system to legal system which is achieved via organizations such as the Council of Europe, the European Union, the World Trade Organization and the United Nations. Moreover, there is substance in the modern legal convergence occurring via practicality and economic utility which is derived from the reality that single legal standards apply throughout.

Legal globalization permits for the assortment of national laws, and actually leaves them the right to be different, either by leaving whole disciplines uncovered, to be regulated by State law, or by providing exceptional derogatory measures, or else by applying techniques that abandon spaces, margins and weave networks. Nonetheless, legal globalization is a result of the materialization of problems that no national legal

---

575 Joachim Hirsch, *Der nationale Wettbewerbsstaat: Staat, Demokratie und Politik im globalen Kapitalismus* (Berlin: Edition ID-Archiv, 1995); Ronen Palan and Jason Abbot (with Phil Deans), *State Strategies in the Global Political Economy* (London: Pinter, 1996), p. 4.

576 S Sassen, *Teritory, Authority, Rights: From Medieval to Global Assemblages* (Princeton NJ, Princeton University Press, 2nd ed. 2008).

order can resolve on its own such as the expansion of trade and the demand for a "corpus" of rules to accompany it.

Have the established international criminal tribunals offered applicability of the rule of law or enforcement of political affairs via an international rule of law enveloped with a political color? There is balance being established among national legal systems within the global legal order but introducing several sectoral imbalances. The variability of "international regimes" generates a different form of relativism such as sectoral rather than national aggravating reactions[577].

Which is the role of the rule of law in the global legal order? Has the rule of law applied to the global order? The answer is yes but in fact there is emergence and utilization of politics of law rather than appliance of objective law. Can globalization endure governance without government? Above the States there is now a network of sectoral governments and this network has developed incrementally and has been made possible by the need of a center and by the occurrence of a center – the UN – operating as a "forum." To that extent, Sabino Cassese[578] argues that "A unitary cosmopolitan legal system is not on the horizon nor is it perhaps among current ambitions. Instead a process is under way that affects certain positive principles and branches of law."

It is worth mentioning that while comparative law is facing the matter of what makes up a practice irreducible to the classical conception of a national "legal system" and to a general categorization of "legal families," public international law has to cope with "governance without government," and private international law has to tackle the altering meaning of the linkage between law and territory.

In reality, various legal fields are today reconfiguring around several points of general agreement[579]. Bruno Latour[580] argues that there is "a passage from law as an institution to law as an enunciation." A. Riles[581] says that rather than concentrating on how global private law is or is not an objet d'art of state power, a body of private norms, or a sound legal system, there is a need to view global private law as an array of institutions, actors, doctrines, ideas, documents, that is, as a focused series of knowledge practices. It is worth mentioning that the old concepts of international law, which were all "state centered," are now questioned by the globalization of law[582]. To that extent, the "mobility" of the private actors is altering the notion of territoriality of law, the perception of choice of law, of public order or even the notion of legal order.

---

[577] S. Krasner (ed.), *International Regimes*, Ithaca, Cornell Univ. Press, 1983 (3 rd ed. 1995).

[578] Sabino Cassese, *The Globalization of Law* www.ssrn.com P24.

[579] A. Riles, Comparative Law and Socio-Legal Studies, in M. Reimann, R. Zimmermann, *The Oxford Handbook of Comparative Law*, Oxford, Oxford University Press, 2008, p. 799.

[580] B. Latour, *La fabrique du droit. Une ethnographie du Conseil d'État*, Paris, La Découverte, 2002.

[581] A. Riles, The Anti-Network: Global private law, legal knowledge, and the legitimacy of the state, *American Journal of Comparative Law*, Vol. 56, No. 3, 2008; Cornell Legal Studies Research Paper No 07-025.

[582] G. Lhuilier, *Analysis of Global Law*, http://www.msh-paris.fr/recherche/ aires-geographiques/monde/le-reseau-glsn/; or: http://www.glsn.eu.

It could be said that the state sees itself in competition with other states and private parties in a global market for investors starting to resemble private actors[583] which means that private actors gain a higher role and so private justice in the form of arbitration could gain a co-equal role to state justice via litigation. There is a confluence of public and private international law[584]. In international investment law pairs states and investors on opposing ends having asymmetrical powers such as the state has sovereignty and the investor has assets without being clear, in terms of either power or law, which is superior[585]. Besides, the common law materializes from custom but what makes it law is its recognition by the state. Individuals are restrained not only by law but by multiple other norms. Currently, globalization challenges this distinction and the reason is not simply, as is sometimes proclaimed, a decline in the significance of the state as regulator. If anything, official laws have become more vital than they were in the past: the state regulates more and more affairs.

It is worth mentioning that globalization compels that we re-cast international law into a global public law, and open out the domain of justice from the national into the global, as the underlying normative criterion for international law. Moreover, it is has to be taken into account that via a re-examination of central international legal doctrines and institutions such as boundaries, sovereignty, legitimacy, citizenship, and the territorial control of resources, the international law of a society of states is re- shaped into the global public law of a global institute. Presently, the lack of democratic participation and legitimacy, lack of distributive justice, lack of basic welfare rights and security characterize international law and institutions. Moreover, globalization is altering the character of global social relations by producing the basis for both society and community at the global level. It has to be taken into account that from viewpoint of political theory, globalization is lifting relationships out of the closely territorial into the "global" or meta-territorial era. Thus, the political and legal consequence of this alteration is important and central: as the space in which social relations are handled transform the way of regulating those relations as well. To that extent to be effective, regulatory decisions have to progressively entangle the meta-state level.

The globalization of the law is a development of the 20th and 21st centuries and the rules governing the interpretation of international treaties are to be found in articles 31 and 32 of the Vienna Convention on the Law of Treaties. Moreover, the crucial rule is contained in article 31(1) which stipulates that a treaty shall be interpreted in good faith in line with the ordinary meaning to be given to the terms of the treaty in their context and in the light of its object and rationale.

---

[583] R Michaels and N Jansen, Private Law beyond the State. Europeanization, Globalization, Privatization (2006) 54 *American Journal of Comparative Law* 845. T Büthe and W Mattli, *New Global Rulers: The Privatization of Regulation in the World Economy* (Princeton NJ, Princeton University Press, 2011).

[584] JA Maupin, Public and Private in International Investment Law: An Integrated Systems Approach. (2013) 53 *Virginia Journal of International Law.*

[585] A Mills, *The Confluence of Public and Private International Law* (Cambridge: Cambridge University Press 2009); H Muir Watt, Private International Law Beyond the Schism (2011) 2 *Transnational Legal Theory* 347.

Furthermore, international law and norms formed in the international arena have effect on almost every legal area from human rights law to intellectual property rights, trade, taxation, labor, environmental law, criminal law, government procurement, governance etc. Similarly, there is a mounting stimulus by the international field on national policy and the internal conduct of the state. It has to be taken into account that most areas of law were internal state matters and not subject to state to state relations. Nowadays, in many of law areas, there are agreements on a state to state level, expanding the responsibilities of states towards each other. Nowadays intellectual property rights, human rights, environmental, labor, and criminal laws are influenced by some form of international regime or norm and so many of the international norms no longer have the form of general statements, which are broadly interpreted, and fashioned to affect the national policy when applied nationally. To that extent, the international norms are similar to the one in national legislation and regulations, recording details of the issues, leaving the national legislature with very little guiding prospects, if at all. In other words there is a convergence among national and international norms in various areas of law due to global policy which means that there is interplay among them.

Globalization has forced states to adjust to these modifications in international law. States realize today that many matters that were customarily counted as pertaining to national jurisprudence and policy have now augmented to the international level. Moreover, there are many sorts of international agreements, many of which launch international obligations, embracing duties for variations of national legislation and so any alterations the state has to produce in its national legislation or policy or in its state to state commitments are the result of the state's positive decision to enter into the agreement. Therefore, globalization and increasing interdependency is varying this reality more and more which means that a state has to enter into a new international agreement or accede to an existing one, if a state wants to stay a worthwhile player in the embryonic global community in economic globalization. In other words, the state may not be able to affect the norms set forth in the agreement which means having to put up with those norms "as is" resulting in a requirement to perform alterations in the national legislation and policy in specific fields that if not might not have been contemplated by the state. Owing to the globalization and escalating interdependency, states often are left with no option on whether to join these organizations or not. Hence, there is a growing significance of international and transnational law in the international arena in forming the norms and practices of states in globalization.

The expansion of international law and organizations is a remarkable development of globalization. The European Union has been in the forefront of legalizing inter-state relations, to the point where the national and inter-state legal structures in Europe are broadly undividable. On the other hand, nowadays the undertaking to assemble logic has brought international relations to the intersection of politics and law. Political parties are based on the performance and undertaking of national politicians on national matters such as war and peace, monetary policy and deficit spending.

3. The Advancement of Law

Law is not mere singularity but also it is about unity in coherent wholes. Law is about system, order and discipline and the very *raison d'être* of the nation-State *is* legal unity. Napoleon created the Civil Code in order to *unite* France in law.

Cosmopolitan law is about the forces of legal convergence and divergence coming into one. Cosmopolitan law is not promoted by States but it is *driven* by citizens. The world of post-modernity is characterized by insecurity, choice and indeterminacy. However, cosmopolitan law functions in a close-to-chaotic postmodern setting of global political alliances, economic interests and at-many-times intrinsically centrifugal legal realities. Furthermore, cosmopolitan law has to provide for a new sense of global justice which means that global justice must be served by global institutions. It has to be taken into consideration that the death of the nation State is not an option regardless of the emergence of more powerful movements and there is rise of cosmopolitan law[586]. The cosmopolitan in law does not confirm the democratic successes of the nation State which means that the establishment of cosmopolitan institutions does not come with democratic assurance[587].

It is worth mentioning that privately made rules create "law" only insofar as they're coercively enforced without any real judicial review[588] and so arbitration forgoes the public goods of precedent and transparency only insofar as private parties with authority settle their disputes unsupervised[589].

The law has an internal or external meaning. Internally, people can naturally decide for themselves how to act enabling them to lead their day-to day lives. The internal rules of life continually advance with everyday occurrences. Moreover, the internal rules that a person will acquire will stem from the way in which they construct the world around them. Nevertheless, the law is external when the rules that are directed towards them are not made by them, but come from an outside source, such as the statutes of a legislature, or the common law of the courts. In spite of this, what both internal and external forms

---

586 Ruddall J. A Cartography of Cosmopolitanism: Particularising the Universal // *Cambridge Journal of International and Comparative Law*. 2014. No. 3. Stone Sweet A. A Cosmopolitan Legal Order: Constitutional Pluralism and Rights Adjudication in Europe // *Global Constitutionalism*. 2012. No. 1. Vertovec S., Cohen R. *Conceiving Cosmopolitanism. Theory, Context, and Practice*. OUP, 2002.

587 Dibadj R. Postmodernism, Representation, Law // *University of Hawaii Law Review*. 2006–2007. Vol. 29.

588 Matthew A. Shapiro, Delegating Procedure 2018 *Columbia Law Review* Vol. 118:983.

589 *Rent-A-Center, W., Inc. v. Jackson*, 561 U.S. 63, 78 (2010) (allowing parties to delegate the arbitrability determination to arbitrators). Richard C. Reuben, Democracy and Dispute Resolution: The Problem of Arbitration, 67 *Law & Contemp. Probs*. 279, 296 (2004) (noting that arbitral awards "generally are final, binding, and enforceable by courts, and generally may not be reversed on substantive grounds").

have in common is that they regularize the association between the subject and the other in their world.

The substance of law is to legalize the relationship between the being and the other in their world, external rules do this by positing the rules that people need so as to accomplish their existential lives together. Moreover, the law has a constructive essence. Whether it is internal or external, it lets people to make sense of their own world offering them with a context in which they comprehend/ understand their existential nature, which is to master their world.

Law has to be understood not only in terms of its own 'internal dynamic', but also in empirical, critical and complex interplay of causes and effects[590]. To that extent rules of custom and local legal processes are favored over and above formal legal institutions visualized under liberal notions and positivist thinking in justice delivery mechanisms[591].

There is consideration to norms with the emergence of 'soft law' or rules of conduct which supposedly are not legally binding but which nonetheless have practical and even legal effects. Codes of conduct were developed progressively by private actors, not by international organizations, both as codes among private actors and codes internal to private actors transforming global and corporate governance. Compared to hard law, soft law has the advantages of lower contracting costs and lower sovereignty costs tailored to conditions of uncertainty or those demanding compromise[592].

It has to be taken into account that primary rules are the most fundamental type of law embedded in custom or generalized practice. Besides, secondary rules build upon the first set stipulating for operations to the creation or variation of duties or obligations. To that extent, secondary rules generate, modify, alter or negate primary rules in particular conditions.

Furthermore, it has to be taken into consideration that soft law encompasses non-mandatory or discretionary legal techniques that can nevertheless impact decision-makers[593]. Is soft law as a central threat to the rule of law? Soft law is first, a norm or rule

---

[590] Michael Giudice, Ways of Understanding Diversity among Theories of Law (2005) 24 *Law and Philosophy* 509. Pierre Bourdieu, The Force of Law: Toward a Sociology of the Juridical Field (1987) 38 *Hastings Law Journal* 814; Richard Abel, Law and Society: Project and Practice (2010) 6 *Annual Review of Law and Social Science* 1; Mariana Valverde, The Sociology of Law as a Means against Struggle itself (2006) 15 *Social and Legal Studies* 591; Allan Hutchinson, Judges and Politics: An Essay from Canada (2004) 24 *Legal Studies* 275.

[591] Tanja Chopra, Dispensing Elusive Justice: The Kenyan Judiciary amongst Pastoralist Societies (2010) 2 *Hague Journal on the Rule of Law* 95; Peter Uvin and Charles Mironko, Western and Local Approaches to Justice in Rwanda (2003) 9 *Global Governance* 219; Phil Clark, Hybridity, Holism, and "Traditional" Justice: The Case of the GACACA Courts in Post-Genocide Rwanda (2007) 39 *George Washington International Law Review* 765; Varun Gauri, Customary Law and Economic Outcomes in Indonesia (2010) 2 *Hague Journal on the Rule of Law* 75.

[592] Abbott, K.W. and Snidal, D.: Hard law and soft law in international governance, *International Organization*, 54, 2000, pp. 421-456.

[593] Gabrielle Kaufmann-Kohler, Soft Law in International Arbitration: Codification and Normativity, 1 *J. Int'l Dispute Settlement* 283, 284 (2010). Andrew T. Guzman & Timothy L. Meyer, International Soft Law, 2 *J. Legal Analysis* 171, 174 (2010). Marc Jacob & Stephan W. Schill, Going Soft: Towards a New Age of Soft Law in International Law? 8 *World Arb. & Mediation Rev.* 1 (2014).

that can be used to interpret or inform the understanding of binding legal rules[594]. Second, soft law has a legal influence insofar as it is comparable to a "contractual promise" that changes what parties are entitled to expect[595]. Can soft law offer the most favorable institutional design for governing sensitive matters such as working conditions, human rights, or protection of the environment? The widespread arrays of standards are produced by international standards organizations and other institutions are not legally binding. International standards organizations apply noteworthy powers of 'governance without government' gaining their international leverage from their gate-keeping role.

It is worth mentioning that legalization has three dimensions: the existence of legal obligations, the accuracy with which these obligations are identified, and the extent to which responsibility for dispute resolution is entrusted to third parties. Each dimension is a continuum, composed of differences of degree, and each differs separately of the others. Particular norms or specific procedures are more or less legalized. To that extent interstate dispute resolution and transnational dispute resolution as two idyllic types, differing in independence from actual state interests, admittance by parties other than states and embeddedness in the awareness that decisions can be implemented without governmental action. It could be said that the transnational dispute resolution is more thriving than interstate dispute resolution in controlling caseloads and making certain compliance[596].

The legislature sets how within its jurisdiction people should behave with regards to others. The legislature will advance laws to allow people to live together. In other words, the legislature will settle the desires of all people to create their own world. With respect to the normative sphere, ethics are focused on the meanings and elements of social goods, stemming from several breaches, disturbances, or disorientations in familiar ethical habits and prospects[597].

Internal or external rules are renegotiated on a day-to-day basis which means that as people come across new experiences and dialogues, the values they give to things will adjust[598]. To that extent, the legislature will have to enact external rules in order to make certain that all people carry on making their own individual point of the world around them. Thus, the external rules empower a person to accomplish their reason to be consisting of those norms that the legislature has acknowledged as indispensable to allow

---

594 Richard Collins & María Mercedes Albornoz, On the Dwindling Divide between the Public and Private: The Role of Soft Law Instruments in Global Governance, in *Linkages and Boundaries in Private and Public International Law* 105 (Verónica Ruiz Abou-Nigm et al. eds., 2018).

595 Statute of the I.C.J. art. 38.

596 G Zekos, *The Independence of Arbitration*, 2016 Nova Science Publications New York USA. www.novapublishers.com G Zekos, *Constitution, Arbitration and Courts*, 2013 Nova Science Publications New York USA. www.novapublishers.com G Zekos, *International Commercial and Marine Arbitration*, 2008 Routledge-Cavendish Publishers London www.routledge.com.

597 Critchley, S. *Ethics, Politics, Subjectivity*. London: Verso, 1997.

598 Mill, J. S. *On Liberty*. London: Penguin Books, 1974, p. 59–60; Berlin, I. Two Concepts of Liberty. *Four Essays on Liberty*. Oxford: University Press, 1969; Ed. Hardy, H. *Liberty: Incorporating "Four Essays on Liberty: Isaiah Berlin."* Oxford: University Press, 2002.

people to lead their lives together[599]. Legislature should be able to enforce these rules and it is also vital that these laws are adjudicated in line with the general spirit of the community for the reason that external rules that a community develops are an essential part of an individual's identity. Hence, the goal of any law, whether internal or external, is to make possible a person to make sense of the world around them. Although people do this internally by making their own rules, the legislature interferes to advance these if the fights between people become too much. Nevertheless, in all cases, the purpose is to permit people to survive.

Due to globalization in interpreting any of its external national rules, not just those take on further to positive international law the states take into consideration national values and international ones as well which means that there is a need for striking a balance between national and global values. To that extent, states cannot abandon its national values altogether but there is a need to make certain that the national identity is preserved with an adjustment in accordance with the greater global culture in order to escape tensions evolving from an existential anguish[600].

'Legal pluralism' gets across the reality of a diversity of legal cultures within a society. Thus, globalization and pluralism instruct an understanding of tension generating more inclusive legal knowledge constructive to a diversity of social communities. As globalization prolongs, nations face the challenge of balancing the necessities for global competitiveness against the internal pressure to uphold the cultural identity of the region generating interesting challenges for law and legal structure. The developments in Australia, a federation, were provoked by two High Court decisions[601] and globalization influences the advance of law in nations including US, Australia, and in the supra-national body that is the EU. To that extent, translating and converting policy into law is a complex course which means that the external pressures of globalization have to be squared with the internal pressure to make certain that legal advances are in line with the legal culture of the nation state. Moreover, while 'legal culture' includes its own definitional and abstract problems, it does grant a device for classifying a variety of phenomena upsetting the function of law in society embracing the thoughts, wishes, and ideas of members of society, both generally and particularly.

As an alternative, the distinction begins to disintegrate for the reason that the criteria used in legal positivism to define what should count as law are becoming dubious. Legal positivism calls for an unquestioned starting point such as a constitution, a sovereign people and this starting point is tied to the state. Moreover, there is a need to rationalize this very starting point becoming aware that the starting point itself is a fabrication of the law, not just its forerunner. The result is that we have to comprehend law and society as

---

599 Hegel, G. W. F. (translated by Dyde, S.W.) *Philosophy of Right*. New York: Dover Publications, 2005.

600 Habremas, J. *The Inclusion of the Other: Studies in Political Theory*. Ed. Cronin, C.; De Greiff, P. Cambridge: Polity Press, 2005, p. 124–125, Grotius, H. *On the Laws of War and Peace*. Kessinger Publishing, 2004; Kant, I. *PerpetualPeace*. New York: Cosimo Books, 2005.

601 Re Wakim; Ex Parte McNally (1999) 198 CLR 511. R v. Hughes (2000) 171 ALR 155.

being mutually constitutive: law is shaped by and in society, but law also generates society in the way in which we find it. In other words law and politics are shaped by society and both serve the society but the problem is which is superior in a way that the other has to follow in order to have an agreed order bringing equality and justice.

Legal thought has acted in response to globalization not with a real move but instead by progressive attempts to become accustomed to the methodological nationalism that has provided its paradigm for the last hundred years or so. On the other hand, globalization poses interdisciplinary challenges, and inter-disciplinarity in law and globalization is still lacking by disregarding or downplaying the law as an imperative factor further than an occasional indicate agreement to international law. To that extent, a prevalent understanding of globalization recognizes three features such as economics, culture and politics which means that law is absent.[602] In legal thinking seems that globalization is either simply absent or emerges as a minimal idea of internationalization that in some way affects the law. Alternatively, legal theory and doctrine have functioned with basic concepts of globalization[603].

According to common law legal rules occur from the decisions courts reach and the reasoning they utilize in the course of resolving specific disputes. Moreover, the course of rule formation is by no means entirely unprompted resting on the meta-rule of 'precedent', or *stare decisis*: similar cases have to be decided correspondingly being both a principle of justice, inferring equal treatment under the law, and a basis for allowing the law to advance in response to social alteration. To that extent, the doctrine of precedent is multi-functional permitting both for the establishment of legal rules and also for their amendment. Karl Llewellyn argues that the common law doctrine of precedent by some means achieves 'at once stability and change[604]'. There is a specific complex trade-off between the adaptability and autonomy of the common law. It is argued that the common law is a "catallaxy" for the reason that rules develop unexpectedly from the decisions of courts deciding specific cases and it is supposed that the law is developed via a legal analysis and the need of the emerging rules which of course serve the social needs of the people which is a political standpoint as well.

While legal change is frequently a matter of chance, the direction which the law takes is coordinated in a more organized manner by the path on which existing decisions have formerly set it due to political and social prevailing conditions. Lord Macmillan[605] argues that the law adjusts due to social conditions and standards' changes which means that the "legal principle must 'adjust and adapt itself to the changing circumstances of life." In

---

[602] D Held, A McGrew, D Goldblatt, J Perraton, *Global Transformations: Politics, Economics, and Culture* (Stanford, Stanford University Press 1999) 14-28.

[603] W Twining, *General Jurisprudence—Understanding Law from a Global Perspective* (Cambridge, Cambridge University Press 2009).

[604] K. Llewellyn, *The Bramble Bush* (New York, Oceana: 1930).

[605] *Donoghue* v. *Stevenson* [1932] AC 562. 619.

other words, the law's autonomy, that is to say, its parting from the political and economic environment, is weakened/ undermined/undercut.

Does common law produce objective law? Does civil law by legislation produce objective law? Is there subjectivity in both systems adding to the politics of law? Is there in fact a politics of law in an away to apply some rules or interpretations in order society to follow specific direction based on ethics, norms or social life imposed to society by the economic elite?

Any legal system has to have standards/ principles for judging what is a legal rule and what is not in order to discern between legal norms on the one hand and social or economic policy on the other because there is a need to maintain the continuity of the legal order. A new rule, an 'alteration', is chosen for survival if it is one which is explicated in terms of established doctrinal structures of juridical thought. To that extent, finding a doctrinal justification for a new rule and preserving the autonomy of juridical thought in the face of external political or social forces are two sides of the same coin[606].

There is a need to permit the law maximum flexibility to adjust to social change. Since a legal rule is formed there is a need to be applied objectively without any political intervention in order to be applied objectively which does not mean that the new legal rule will not be formed in a way influenced by political and social changes via globalization. Who decides the social change? Does a change is intact with the interests of the prevailing economic elite?

As mentioned earlier, the common law method is designed by the meta-rule or doctrine of precedent, which has itself advanced, but is a basis of stabilization indeed for the reason that of the consistency it compels on judicial decision making. To that extent, systems which merge the surfacing legal order of judge-made law with periodic statutory interferences have an evolutionary lead over those which are dependent entirely on the courts. On the other hand, judge made law might has less political direct interference rather than statutory law which might serves directly the political interests of a prevailing group promoting their political affairs via a governments legislature. In practice all legal systems of developed states, whether of common law or civil legal origin, conjoin judge-made law with codes or statutes in some manner or another. The common law is characteristically more prospective to generate rules which favour the interests of well-resourced litigants and repeat players such as insurers and business companies than those of society overall[607].

Common law as judge-made law *systems* are, in fact, noticeably shaped by legislative norms, while judicial innovation is, equally, a weighty issue in the development of private law and commercial law in civil law systems. However, common law and civil law methods of reasoning are no identical but merely we have no undoubted justifications

---

[606] *Donoghue* v. *Stevenson* [1932] AC 562. 619 per Lord Buckmaster.

[607] M. Galanter, Why the "haves" come out ahead: speculation on the limits of legal change (1974) 9 *Law and Society Review* 95-151.

for considering that common law methods are *essentially superior* to those of the civil law in reinforcing/ supporting economic development and growth[608].

On the one hand, legal rules are expected to be adaptive in the logic of assisting communal coordination. On the other hand, common law rules are adaptive to their setting or circumstance, but ineffective rules may stay[609], and disequilibria are engendered by lock-in consequences internally and externally which means that within common law systems, rectification of error through legislation is often required, albeit that legislation, sequentially, is often merely an incentive for an extra development of case law. In other words Common law and civil law systems are all, partially, hybrids in which case law work along with codes and statutes.

It is worth mentioning that two inter-related mechanisms function through which legal origin inspire finance etc. Firstly, the "political" contraption underlines that (a) legal traditions vary in terms of the priority they assign to private property vis-à-vis the rights of the State and (b) the protection of private contracting rights materializes the center of financial development[610]. Secondly, the "adaptability" contraption underlines that (a) legal traditions fluctuate in their formalism and capacity to advance with shifting conditions and (b) legal traditions adjust competently to diminish the gap between the contracting requirements of the economy and the legal system's potential cultivate financial development than more inflexible systems[611].

Courts have to enforce private contracts fairly and have both the aptitude and willingness to deal with multipart contracts and substantiate technically complex clauses generating explicit actions. Hayek[612] says that Emperor Justinian employed two substantive modifications in comparison to Roman law. Firstly, while Roman law placed the law above all individuals, the Justinian texts placed the emperor above the law. It could be argued that Justinian tried to abolish the employment of the rule of law and implying a more political utilization of the law by the interests of the Emperor. Secondly, Justinian broke with Roman law by trying to abolish jurisprudence. Roman law had produced over centuries on a case-by-case basis, modifying according to the requirements of a community to the requests of a world empire with only a minor role left for formal

[608] J. Armour, S. Deakin, P. Lele and M. Siems, 'How do legal rules evolve? Evidence from a cross-country comparison of shareholder, creditor and worker protection' (2009) 57 *American Journal of Comparative Law* 579-630.

[609] See Concerning bills of lading precedent. G Zekos, Judicial analysis of the contractual role of bills of lading as it stands in Greek, United States and English law, PhD Thesis, Hull Law School https://hydra.hull.ac.uk/resources/hull:8290.

[610] La Porta, R., Lopez-de-Silanes, F., Shleifer, A., Vishny, R.W., 1999. The Quality of Government. *Journal of Law and Economic Organization* 15, 222-279.

[611] Merryman, J.H., 1985. *The Civil Law Tradition: An Introduction to the Legal Systems of Western Europe and Latin America.* Stanford University Press, Stanford, CA. Merryman, J. H., 1996. The French Deviation. *The American Journal of Comparative Law* 44, 109-119. K. Sabeel Rahman, Domination, Democracy, and Constitutional Political Economy in the New Gilded Age: Towards a Fourth Wave of Legal Realism?, 94 *Tex. L. Rev.* 1329, 1332 (2016) (defining political economy as "how our politics and economics relate to one another, how they are structured by law and institutions, and how they ought to be structured in light of fundamental moral values").

[612] Hayek, F., 1960. *The Constitution of Liberty.* The University of Chicago Press, Chicago, IL.

legislation. Justinian altered this doctrine and "... asserted for himself a monopoly, not only over all lawmaking power, but over legal interpretations[613]" but jurisprudence continued to mold the law. Of course, the French Revolution put the State above the courts abolishing jurisprudence. Codification under Napoleon backed the unification and strengthening of the State downgrading judges to a minor, bureaucratic role. Moreover, in line with the theory underlying the French Civil Code, the legislature drafts laws without gaps, so judges do not make law by interpreting existing laws. On the other hand, the legislature does draft conflicting laws, so that judges do make law by choosing between laws.

Like Justinian, Napoleon required a code that was so apparent, complete, and consistent that there would be no necessity for judges to consider about which laws, customs, and past experiences apply to new, embryonic situations. It could be said that it is chosen the approach that the political head leads the legal development without the need for implementation and law making based on the employment of the laws by courts and the legal system. In addition, this approach needed a high degree of procedural formalism to lessen the freedom of choice of judges in regulating the presentation of evidence, witnesses, arguments, and appeals[614]. Besides, German legal history favored jurisprudence rejecting France's approach which means that the German Code does not get rid of prior law put simply codifies those principles of German law that surface from meticulous historical study of the German legal system[615]. In addition the power of the law vis-à-vis the State, the courts in England were viewed more positively and as supporters of progressive improvement, so that judges were given greater discretion.

In terms of legal formalism, English law compels less rigid and formalistic rations on the presentation of evidence, witnesses, etc., and instead offers judges greater autonomy[616]. In terms of jurisprudence, the English common law tradition is equal with judges having broad interpretation powers and with courts shaping and generating law as state of affairs change. The question to be answered is if the judges' alteration and law making is based on legal terms or on political terms in order to support the new politically prevailing cast against any legal justification. The common law is preoccupied with facts and deciding concrete cases, rather than holding to the logical principles of codified law.

The political contraption is based on firstly on the fact that legal traditions vary in the weight they place on protecting the rights of private investors in relation to the rights of the State and secondly on the fact that private property rights protection materializes the

---

[613] Dawson, J. P., 1968. *The Oracles of the Law*. University of Michigan Law School, Ann Arbor, MI(Reprinted in 1986 by William S. Hein & Co., Inc. Buffalo, New York).

[614] Schlesinger, R., Baade, H., Damaska, M., Herzog, P., 1988. *Comparative Law. Case-Text-Materials*. (New York, NY: The Foundation Press, Inc.).

[615] Merryman, J.H., 1985. *The Civil Law Tradition: An Introduction to the Legal Systems of Western Europe and Latin America*. Stanford University Press, Stanford, CA.

[616] Schlesinger, R., Baade, H., Damaska, M., Herzog, P., 1988. *Comparative Law. Case-Text-Materials*. (New York, NY: The Foundation Press, Inc.).

foundation for financial development. Consequently, firm differences in legal origin make clear existing disparities in financial development along with the viewpoint of the law and finance[617]. Moreover, the political contraption supports that the Civil law maintains the rights of the State, rather than private property rights, to a greater degree than the Common law with undesirable inferences for financial development. It is supposed that judges are freer to follow law making on principles of law rather than legislature that it is influenced by the governmental policy but in reality both players can be more legalistic and less politically influenced in the process of law making or be influenced indirectly by their agents that they appoint them. The more important is the implementation of the endorsed law in any case without any political influence to the detriment of justice and the rule of law.

It is argued that in civil law countries, the State grants judges' tenure by giving court's jurisdiction over cases concerning the government, or permitting judicial review of the constitutionality of laws[618]. Moreover, it is mentioned that a civil legal tradition is taken as a proxy for the aim to build institutions to advance the power of the State[619] which means that an authoritative State with a responsive civil law at its disposal redirects the flow of society's resources toward favored ends, which is antithetical to competitive financial markets etc. On the other hand, it seems that states favor financial markets in order to advance their economies via the legislation of privileged laws.

Incompetent laws are contested in the courts, so that the process of litigation and re-litigation advances the efficiency of the law[620]. Quite the opposite, legal systems that discard jurisprudence essentially count on statutory law changes to update and adjust the law. Moreover, statutory law is slow and costly to modify, so that the lack of jurisprudence deter the efficiency with which laws adjust to altering setting[621]. Besides, courts are expected to comply with the review of constitutional amendment than replacement which means that courts comply with their decisions when they involve in broad interventions in other parts of the polity demanding cooperation with other institutions. Courts' active role in refining politics in line makes it more probable that political actors will value their review of constitutional amendments[622]. In other words,

---

617 La Porta, R., Lopez-de-Silanes, F., Shleifer, A., Vishny, R.W., 1999. The Quality of Government. *Journal of Law and Economic Organization* 15, 222-279.

618 La Porta, R., Lopez-de-Silanes, F., Pop-Eleches, C., Shleifer, A., 2003. Judicial checks and balances. National Bureau of Economic Research Working Paper 9775.

619 La Porta, R., Lopez-de-Silanes, F., Shleifer, A., Vishny, R.W., 1999. The Quality of Government. *Journal of Law and Economic Organization* 15, 222-279.

620 Pistor, K., Keinan, Y., Kleinheisterkamp, J., West, M.D., 2002. The evolution of corporate law. *University of Pennsylvania Journal of International Economics and Law* 23, 791-871.

621 Bailey, M. J., Rubin, P. H., 1994. A positive theory of legal change. *International Review of Law and Economics* 14, 467-477, December 1994.

622 Lee Epstein, Jack Knight & Olga Shvetsova, The Role of Constitutional Courts in the Establishment and Maitnenance of Democratic Systems of Government, 35 *L. & Soc'y Rev.* 117, 156 (2001). Luz Estella Nagle, Evolution of the Colombian Judiciary and the Constitutional Court, 6 *Ind. Int'l & Comp. L. Rev.* 59, 81 (1995) (stating that in Colombia, justices are nominated by the President, the supreme court, and the administrative court and then the Senate selects from those options). Nuno Garoupa & Tom Ginsburg, Reputation,

there is an interrelation between law –making and politics in order to have the rightful law complying with the polity demands of the society. Moreover, constitutional interpretation is a unique endeavor/venture which are taken for granted by legal professionals. Moreover, constitutional law is issue to distinct interpretive methods as linked to other sources of law, such as statutes and common-law precedents[623].

Anyway, the Constitution is not essentially more fixed in practice than all other sources of law[624]. It has to be taken into consideration that the Constitution is specially legitimated which means that it justifies unique interpretive treatment for the reason that it is prepared and ratified through a procedure designed to guarantee that it enjoyed prevalent public support reflecting the whole political approach of a state[625]. Besides, the Constitution diverges from other sources of law because it is written using broad terms so that it could undergo well beyond the classic life of a statute[626]. All legitimate interpretation of the Constitution are categorized as either doctrinal, historical, or what he called responsive[627]. The Constitution *as a whole* is subject to particular interpretive steps that are not validated by features or attributes of the Constitution *as a whole*[628].

Taking into consideration the emergence of cyberspace and its significance in all aspects of social life within globalization, national legislators have chosen to intervene in regulating cyberspace. Accordingly, law of global application has been caught between nation-centred politics and economics. Minimum level of regulation is applied in the area of ecommerce law playing a dominant role in trade itself nowadays[629]. Furthermore, existent law takes in the area of interest of cyberspace matters such as contract law responding successfully not in all occasions needing some amendments in order to apply

---

Information and the Organization of the Judiciary, 4 *J. Comp. L.* 228, 241 (2009). Manoj Mate, The Rise of Judicial Governance in the Supreme Court of India, 33 *B. U. Int'l L. J.* 167, 208–09 (2015).

[623] *District of Columbia v. Heller*, 554 U.S. 570, 625 (2008) (purporting to adopt original understanding of Second Amendment); *People v. Nutt*, 677 N.W.2d 1, 6 (Mich. 2004) ("Our goal in construing our Constitution is to discern the original meaning attributed to the words of a constitutional provision by its ratifiers.").

[624] William Baude, *Is Originalism Our Law?* 115 *Colum. L. Rev.* 2349, 2355 (2015) (justifying originalism on the positive ground that constitutional practice, in fact, makes original meaning "the ultimate criterion for constitutional law"); Keith E. Whittington, *The New Originalism*, 2 *Geo. J. L. & Pub. Pol'y* 599, 599 (2004) ("Originalism regards the discoverable meaning of the Constitution at the time of its initial adoption as authoritative for purposes of constitutional interpretation in the present.").

[625] Christopher Serkin, Public Entrenchment through Private Law: Binding Local Governments, 78 *U. Chi. L. Rev.* 879, 882 (2011).

[626] Bruce Ackerman, *We the People, Volume 3: The Civil Rights Revolution* (2014) (arguing that the civil rights laws of the 1960s have landmark status and constitutional significance). *Shelby County v. Holder*, 133 S.Ct. 2612, 2631 (2013) (invalidating Section 4 of the Voting Rights Act of 1965).

[627] Robert Post, Theories of Constitutional Interpretation, 30 *Representations* 13, 19 (1990). Jeffrey A. Pojanowski, Statutes in Common Law Courts, 91 *Tex. L. Rev.* 479, 482–83 (2013) (applying modalities of constitutional interpretation to statutes).

[628] Larry Alexander & Emily Sherwin, *Demystifying Legal Reasoning* 221–22 (2008) ("interpreting a constitution is not different in any material way from interpreting a statute."). *Burwell v. Hobby Lobby Stores, Inc.*, 134 S. Ct. 2751, 2772 (2014) (stating that "nothing in the text of RFRA as originally enacted suggested that the statutory phrase 'exercise of religion under the First Amendment' was meant to be tied to this Court's pre-*Smith* interpretation of that Amendment").

[629] Lim Y.F., *Cyberspace Law: Commentaries and Materials* (OUP 2007). Forder J. and Svantesson D., *Internet and E-Commerce Law* (OUP 2007).

rightfully. To that extent, the involvedness of cyberspace applications presently is regulated, whilst in other parts of the world is little regulated or not regulated at all.

Nonetheless, a minimum degree of regulation is needed not only at a national level but also at the global level. Information law, data-protection law and freedom of information as a whole as well as the right to cyberspace entrée are perceived as these areas of e-law should be structured on a national basis. Taking into account that technology and innovation are a central element of globalization, it has to be answered how national standards fit in the global phenomenon of technological development which means that there is a need for international regulation of some cyberspace' legal matters such as jurisdiction, applicable law etc.[630].

According to the traditional private international law cyberspace' matters can merely be regulated by choice of law clauses[631]. The 'freedom of contract doctrine approach' and the private international law suggest that such matters are matters falling within the domain of national sovereignty. On the one hand, the 'freedom of contract' approach does not give us an answer as to how inter-national matters are controlled in an international approach. On the other hand, the 'national sovereignty' approach comes from the domain of public law which means that e-traders cannot involve with the *territorium* and the *imperium* of States in international e-Commerce matters in the substance that e-commerce deals involve many jurisdictions at once causing problems of forum shopping etc. Certainly, international trade matters are typically dealt at the national level of litigation but that alone does not solve the dispute being a mere portrayal of the *present status quo*. It could be argued that national sovereignty plays an inconsequential role having little to offer to traders in the area of international e-Commerce.

4. The Rule of Law

It could be said that, the rule of law exists when the law is publicly known, applies equally to ordinary citizens and rulers, and where all are free to test and observe that universal application. To that extent, politics cannot prohibit or manipulate the ordinary application of the law according to who is under consideration and due to the political affairs of state or political ambitions of economic elites upon the outcome of a particular case. The rule of law means equality. Can the rule of law mean equality per occasion or constantly applicable?

---

[630] Goldman D.B., *Globalization and the Western Legal Tradition: Recurring Patterns of Law and Authority* (Cambridge University Press 2007) 25.

[631] Beatson, International Arbitration, Public Policy Considerations, and Conflicts of Law: The Perspectives of Reviewing and Enforcing Courts, 33 *Arb. Int'l* 175 (2017); G.A. Bermann, "International Standards" as a Choice of Law Option in International Commercial Arbitration, 27 *Am. Rev. Int'l Arb.* 423 (2016).

It is worth mentioning that the state has a monopoly on the legitimate violence or authority within a defined territory and administered by some form of logical bureaucracy rule of law existing when the sovereign or ruler is compelled to the same laws set for his subjects. Consequently, the rule of law acts as a restraint against uncontrolled state authority and exists somewhat in opposition to the ability of the modern bureaucratic state which means that this dualism of state authority and its institutionalized control due to the rule of law is required to keep any apt governing order in balance. Does a rule of law exist or to be sure that it does not? How many sovereigns or rulers have declared themselves formally above the law since the French Revolution?

It is questionable how many countries in the current age have a rule of law. Moreover, weak states are further undermined by accountability which means that the Rule of law is not sufficient in powerless states or in the absence of democracy. It has to be taken into account that strong rational states, ruled by leaders bound by the same laws as everyday citizens and subject periodically to elections and other forms of liability, are the most expected to reveal good modern governance. Moreover, it is characteristic that the concept of rule of law is as old as systematic thinking about politics itself. Aristotle promoted laws to rein in the power of rulers. Cicero advised against rule by dictators unrestricted by legal restraints in the days of the Roman Republic. Montesquieu urged for a type of judicial independence.

It is vital that not only does the state enforce external rules so that everyone can accomplish their raison d'être together, but also that they are administered in line with the same social will that people generally obey, otherwise they may reject them. To that extent, it is central that law is not only interpreted impartially, but that it is done in a manner that reveals the general and individual spirit of the public. On the other hand, if law is interpreted unfairly or unjustly to the disadvantage of one group, then it demoralizes one of the foundations of law, which is that people generally accept it for the reason that it settles their interests. Thus, all people in a society have to know that the law is interpreted fairly in line with the social spirit that they are assented for the reason that it is basic where the legal system gets its legitimacy, explicitly that it is instituted to settle the conflicts between people[632]. To that extent, external rules are administered in line with the general will of the society in order to evade existential anguish which means that the state has to make certain that they are enforced against those who are on the outside, or do not come within the social will, if not this may lead to disruption as well.

Borders identify territories within which political communities arise and flourish. Political communities extend beyond borders, but in our world they are directly linked with borders. Thus, political borders play a role in generating a membership in a political

[632] Dworkin, R. *Law's Empire*. Oxford: Hart Publishing, 2007, p. 188. Rousseau, J.-J., ed. Griffith, T. *The Social Contract*. Ware: Wordsworth Editions Limited, 1998, p.15–16: "Each of us puts in common his person and his whole power under the supreme direction of the general will; and in return we receive every member as an individual part of the whole."; Locke, J. *Two Treaties of Government*. Cambridge: University Press, 1990; and Rawls, J. *A Theory of Justice: Revised Edition*. Oxford: University Press, 1999, p. 4.

community[633]. In line it has to be taken into consideration that the nation state has a sole social will that has to be defended at all costs for the reason that this is the only way in which its people accomplish their elemental reason to be. Moreover, due to globalization the world has noticeably transformed and now there are numerous identities that ought to be protected permitting people to make sense of their worlds. Nevertheless, whereas the conservation of national external rules is central for the reason that they allow people to preserve their distinctive cultural identity and heritage to that extent globalization with its global "markets in goods, services and capital," means that individuals rely on people in different countries as well. It could be said that due to globalization not only public institutions but also everyday life is becoming free from the hold of tradition which means that societies are becoming de-traditionalized producing a global cosmopolitan society which means another role for law making as well[634].

In interpreting the law internally the state has to make certain that it does so in a fair way that is harmonious with what people see as part of their identity. If they do not do this, it might lead to larger conflict for the reason that this general will is also part of a person's identity that permits them to accomplish their raison d'être, and if it is not made possible, it may cause them existential anguish. Thus, all legal systems are ranked along one scale in terms of the degree of rule of law present or lacking. Certain legal systems actually exhibit the qualities of a legitimate rule of law to a clear and reliable degree. Nonetheless, apart from the development of internal rules that make people more morally aware of their dependability to those in other parts of the world, and external rules, such as the economic ones by which legislatures augment their people's prospects by take full advantage of their global prospects.

Is the rule of law under threat? The threats against the rule of law are founded on many factors such as the need to combat physical terrorism and cyber-attacks, the need to fulfill public concern about crime, IT-based intrusion into individual privacy, government cut-backs on the legal system, escalating inequality and globalization, and repressive regimes in some countries. Lord Neuberger[635] says that "arbitrators perform an essentially contract-based function for specific parties in private, whereas judges carry out a

---

633 Coleman, J. L. and Harding, S. K. Citizenship, the demand of justice, and the moral relevance of political borders. *Justice in Immigration*. ed. Schwartz, W. F. Cambridge: University Press, 2007, p. 40. Maier, C. S. Being there: place, territory and identity. *Identities, Affiliations and Allegiances*, ed. Benhabib, S.; Shapiro, I.; Petranovic, D. Cambridge: University Press, 2007, p. 78.

634 Garrett, G. *The Causes of Globalization* [interactive]. Yale University, April 2000 http://www.yale.edu/leitner/pdf/2000-02.pdf: "I define globalization somewhat narrowly as the international integration of markets in goods, services and capital." Giddens, A. *Runaway World: How Globalization is Reshaping our Lives*. London: Profile Books, 2002, p.42–43.

635 Lord Neuberger, Arbitration and the Rule of Law, Chartered Institute of Arbitrators Centenary Celebration, Hong Kong, 20 March 2015. Adeline Chong 'Transnational public policy in civil and commercial matters' (2012) LQR 88. Richard T. Ely, Studies In The Evolution Of Industrial Society 406 (1903) ("[C]oercion . . . is largely due to the unequal strength of those who make a contract, for back of contract lies inequality in strength of those who form the contract. Contract does not change existing inequalities and forces, but is simply the medium through which they find expression."). Roscoe Pound, Liberty of Contract, 18 *Yale L. J.* 454, 454 (1909). Morris R. Cohen, The Basis of Contract, 46 *Harv. L. Rev.* 553, 569 (1933).

constitutional function for everyone in public, so the rule of law can be said to be central to the role of judges in a way that it is not for arbitrators.... arbitration is totally dependent on the courts, and therefore on access to justice and the rule of law, for its efficacy...In conclusion, it seems to me that arbitration is not simply compatible with the key features of the rule of law, but that it has an increasingly important role to play in upholding those key features, both nationally and internationally." On the other hand, both judges and arbitrators utilize the rule of law in order to arrive at their decision and so judgment and award should produce precedent. Arbitrators run justice acting in line with the law and are seen to act according to the law. If an arbitrator acts inconsistently with fundamental rights, then his award will be reviewed. Moreover, arbitrators resolve disputes between business people or national entities, and in the commercial and the diplomatic worlds, the rule of law is indispensable. It is worth mentioning that, a foreign arbitral award will not be legalized where the foreign arbitral or award somehow violates English principles of "*natural justice*"[636]. The Swiss Supreme[637] Court's refused to enforce a disciplinary decision by CAS[638] and the Court held that the ban was a breach of a "fundamental" principle which, according to the prevailing view in Switzerland, should form part of *any* legal order. The case is a landmark for the reason that an international arbitral award has now been annulled for breach of substantive public policy. The Federal Tribunal reiterated its distinction between substantive and procedural public policy. To that extent, in order to breach public policy, an international award must be inconsistent with the fundamental values which, according to prevailing opinions in Switzerland, should be the basis of any legal order.

The French law view[639] is that an international arbitral award is "not anchored in any national legal order," but "is a decision of international justice, whose validity must be ascertained with regard to the rules applicable in the country where its recognition and enforcement are sought." French law, and in part Italian law, appears to be even more decisive in favoring arbitration as an alternative and substitute form of civil procedure, once it has been chosen by the parties in concluding a valid arbitration agreement.

5. International Rule of Law

States take into consideration wider global factors in the general interpretation of national rules in their territories as well which is achieved via public international law as

[636] *Adams v. Cape Industries* [1990] Ch 433; *Cukurova Holding AS v. Sonera Holding BV* [2014] UKPC 14.

[637] 30 *ASA Bull* 591 (2012) 138 BGE III 322.

[638] CAS 2008/A/1519 – *FC Shakhtar Donetsk (Ukraine) v. Mr. Matuzalem Francelino da Silva (Brazil) & Real Zaragoza SAD (Spain) & FIFA. CAS* 2008/A/1520 – *Mr. Matuzalem Francelino da Silva (Brazil) & Real Zaragoza SAD (Spain) v. FC Shakhtar Donetsk (Ukraine) & FIFA* (the Panel is satisfied that Shakhtar Donetsk paid the salary of June 2007 to the Player. Accordingly, the Panel shall reject the respective claim raised by the Player.).

[639] Putrabali decision of 29 June 2007.

well. It is worth mentioning that States come together in forums like the United Nations, European Union and other international and regional groups to advance rules to the general good[640]. There is the direct transfer of institutions from one national system to another. In addition, there is the imposition of a global legal principle upon national public administrations which means that the imposition by a global judicial body of a common legal principle, not only upon States, but also within national legal systems. Moreover, legal thought is the first area influenced by the circulation and spreading of law. Globalization[641] influences research approaches, techniques and methodologies not extended to positive law[642]. To that extent, the universal or general legal thought founded on principles common to several systems of positive law including the writings of jurists[643]. A universal law involves a single sovereign and a single, worldwide legal community which means that universality extends to the extent that legal thought and does not influence the relativism of positive legal systems[644]. On the other hand, universality/legal globalization might cause a fundamental interference of politics in order to shape the required politics of law necessary for the satisfaction of the needs of economic elites against a general justice and objectivity in the appliance of the law and the rule of law.

As mentioned earlier, a rule-of-law system is one in which the choices of an actor are made in light of rules that are fixed. To that extent, actors opt to violate the rules, but when they do, they do so knowing what the rules denote and considering the inferences of compliance and breach. In a domestic context, the rule of law tackles problems related with an overly powerful centralized authority illustrating a political system founded on stable public laws and known in advance applying equally to a governments and its citizens without regard to specific status. It is supposes that the rule of law regulates the government power implying equality before the law and favoring judicial justice.

The international rule of law is a derivative function of the domestic rule of law. The "rule of law" portrays a social system that divides society into political and legal domains placing the latter within the former. Moreover, the international rule of law embraces the obligation of states to comply with their legal commitments and states are free to take on

---

[640] Evans, M.; Cerny, P. Globalization and Social Policy. *Developments in British Social Policy 2*. Ed. Ellison N.; Pierson, C. Basingstoke: Palgrave Macmillan, p. 22.

[641] G. Silverstein, Globalization and the rule of law: A machine that runs of itself? in *International Journal of Constitutional Law*, vol. 1, n. 3, 2003, pp. 429-445.

[642] G. Fassò, *La filosofia del diritto dell'Ottocento e del Novecento*, Bologna, Il Mulino, 1988, p. 306.

[643] M. Barberis, John Austin, la teoria del diritto e l'universalità dei concetti giuridici, in *Materiali per una storia della cultura giuridica*, n. 2, December 2003, pp. 407-427. R. Saleilles, Le Code civil et la Méthode historique, in *Le Code Civil 1804-1904* Livre du Centenaire publié par la Societé d'Etudes Législatives, I, Paris, Librairie Edouard Duchemin, 1904, reprinted 1969, p. 127 "all legal thought is necessarily international and universal."

[644] G.D. Romagnosi, *Introduzione allo studio del diritto pubblico universale*, Florence, Piatti, 3rd ed., 1833. P. Grossi, Un diritto senza Stato (la nozione di autonomia come fondamento della Costituzione giuridica medievale), in *Quaderni fiorentini per la storia del pensiero giuridico modern*, n. 25, 1996, pp. 267-284; Il ruolo del giurista nell'attuale società italiana, in *Rassegna forense*, n. 3, 2002, pp.501-515; C. Schmitt, *La condizione della scienza giuridica europea,* Rome, Antonio Pellicani Editore, 1996.

legal obligations as they see them fit requiring complying with them. The idea that states should comply with their legal obligations is primary to conventional accounts of the contemporary international legal-political system. It is central to international law and is almost universally preferred over violation._Compliance is broadly seen as a legal, political, and moral vital for states. Legally, the obligation to comply is institutionalized in the principle of pacta sunt servanda and in the "good faith" clauses that come out in many international treaties, including the Vienna Convention on the Law of Treaties.

Human rights, international stability, and perhaps even the progress of civilization itself are said to be founded on compliance with international law. Is this the rule or politics have proscribed this principle?

The normative preference for compliance over violation is deep-seated in international legal understanding, to some extent for the reason that law is seen as the alternative to power politics. It could be argued that a legal order emerges to be the antidote to force but it seems that in many occasions the law and the rule of law are replaced by use of force in demand of politics which destroys order in the long run despite that in many occasions political groups think that they have imposed their interests upon local or international society. On the other hand, international order based on states' choices to abide by international law and so to track a negotiated common position rather than an individualistic, short-term, and self-interested one. Besides, in many occasions' powerful states seem to try to impose their political position against the well understanding of the rule of law.

In international level the legality of an action is dependent on an actor doing it and it is difficult to assess the legality of an international act without knowing the identity of the agent. Moreover, the international legality of an act depends on which state undertakes it, what that state says about the act, and what it has previously said about its link to the pieces of international law that may apply. International legal obligations so attach to states in an occasional way opposing the factor of equality that is said to be vital for the national kind of the rule of law. In national law, the identity of the actor should not enter into the assessment of how law regulates the act; in international law, it ought to.

It is worth mentioning that states using international law to rationalize their policies. To that extent, states offer explanations for how their conduct is coherent with their international commitments, and accordingly there is a competing diplomatic and legal accounts concerning compliance. In other words there is no likelihood for an objective settling of the differences. It seems that the international rule of law utilizes law to legitimate state policy.

Law is seen as a resource which states and others utilize in the chase of their targets which means that state goals are inseparable from the practices of international law challenging a common assumption that law has to be independent of the preferences of the agents. The conventional view of international law is that it provides a self-imposed set of limits on states so as to better permit those very states to chase their mutual and individual interests[645]. International law as a set of resources acknowledging that law contains the aptitude to legitimate state policy. Moreover, international law presents the resources with which states talk about and comprehend their behavior[646].

In other words, the content of international law is altered in the course of being used to validate state policies due to the practices of diplomacy, as states give legal rationalization for their actions seeing the mutual charter of international law and foreign policy. To that extent, the connotation of international legal rules occurs from how it is used in the diplomacy of states[647].It is characteristic that states give favorable legal interpretations to legalize their own actions, which are inseparably legal and political, being part of the course of international politics[648]. Furthermore, governments and others employ international law to clarify and justify their actions adding to the meaning of the rules they appeal to altering the meaning of the rule of law which is an objective approach of the meaning and content of law in order to have lawful justice and not a lawful justice in accordance with the demands of a politically powerful state of agent against the general good of a society.

It is obvious that the rule of law is not utilized as a solution to the governance challenges in Europe or globally. The rule of law has to alter/ redraft political disputes in legal language. On the other hand, the international examples illustrate that eventually, the rule of law and the international rule of law have become political resources which actors utilize in the political struggle over the legitimation and de-legitimation of their desires which is against the real meaning of the rule of law to the detriment of international peace and progress. However, states utilize international law in order to legalize their actions and those of others against the real legal meaning of the rule by enveloping the meaning of an international rule of law with a lawful context which in fact is the political dress of law in order to achieve any political goals even against a settled legal order and in an effort to change the legal status quo accordingly.

The international rule of law is enveloped/ encircled with the essence of being a political term based on the national rule of law which is shaped by a real law context rather than the political affairs of state sovereignty. To that extent, the prevailed international rule of law makes certain that legal resources carry political weight, and that being seen as acting legally is politically authoritative for states. Legal resources such as national rule of law and international rule of law are an available and socially legitimated pool of such ideas and concepts. National rule of law and international rule of law is utilized as a useful, and dominant, device in the course of "sense-making" for states.

---

[645] *France v. Turkey*, "Judgment of 7 September1927," PCIJ Series A, no. 10, at p. 18.

[646] Martin, Lisa L. *Against Compliance*. Cambridge: Cambridge University Press, 2013.

[647] Hurd, Ian. *International Law and the Practice of Diplomacy*. Edited by Ole Jacob Sending, Vincent Pouliot, and Iver B. Neumann. Cambridge University Press, 2015.

[648] Beaulac, Stéphane. *The Rule of Law in International Law Today*. Edited by Gianluca Palombella and Neil Walker. Portland, OR: Hart, 2009. Patten, Chris. *The Rule of Lawless*. February 23, 2015. http://www.project-syndicate.org/commentary/ international-rule-of-law-by-chris-patten-2015-02.

In addition, the international rule of law is seen as ingredient of the political structure for international relations on top of the agency of actors to maneuver and utilize fundamentals of the legal system with their own interests in mind against the essence of the rule of law itself. The ever-present employment of international law in foreign policy sits at the crossroads of international structure and agency limited by international legal resources[649].

The due process of law in the global legal order is based on the following three features. First, the principle of "procedural fairness" is not acknowledged by international treaties, but is created by judicial bodies. Secondly, the expansion of global law through lateral connections, in particular with trade, is open to further opening out for the reason that of its many ties to such correlated matters as the environment, human rights, health protection, security, and other areas in which "constitutional" principles emerged by global judges are effortlessly transferred. Finally, under global law, both the State and private actors have the right of involvement in their correlation with public administrations. It has to be taken into consideration that there is an escalating number of areas in which a body of fairly uniform rules of universal application is developing. In fact, the escalation of global trade necessitates common standards for product conformity, consumer protection and product liability. To that extent, states' incapacity to manage such phenomena as financial crises, global warming, the exploitation of the seas and maritime resources authorizes that these universal public goods be protected at the global altitude.

Does an international economic consortium accomplish its targets via the international politics of law in harmony with politics of law internally? It is worth mentioning that international organizations consolidate work on various matters, and their decisions, or the rules set by them, converted into binding guidelines or requirements for participation for states in the modeling of their national laws and policy. In other words politics influence the formation of law in international and national level but since its formation the law has to be implemented without any further political influence in order to have application of the rule of law.

6. States and the Law

States make certain that courts exist as an expression of state prerogative and power. Arbitration is not a national court procedure but arbitration is a private proceeding with public consequences[650]. According to John O. McGinnis and Ilya Somin[651] "Judges thus

---

[649] Hurd, Ian. *International Law and the Practice of Diplomacy*. Edited by Ole Jacob Sending, Vincent Pouliot, and Iver B. Neumann. Cambridge University Press, 2015.

[650] G Zekos, *The Independence of Arbitration*, 2016 Nova Science Publications New York USA. www.novapublishers.com.

often put aside their political and public policy preferences to enforce the law according to a set of rules." On the other hand, voting patterns in the Supreme Court back a "political" or "attitudinal" model which posits that judicial votes abide by political ideology[652]. The Supreme Court in *Marbury v. Madison*[653] stated that the interpretation of constitutional provisions was the province of judges[654]. A. Marmor argues that[655] "courts tend to possess legal expertise, they are the best kind of institution to be entrusted with constitutional interpretation." The constitutional system of federalism assigns powers to state and federal government officials not for their own benefit, but for that of the people of the entire nation. The total segregation of the courts from the legislature was itself a departure from an English tradition in which the House of Lords both wrote the laws and served as the supreme appellate court[656]. Courts' decisions cannot be reversed by the legislature[657].

In addition, the Constitution is premised on the doctrine of separation of powers[658]. The Constitution verifies a tripartite system of government in which the legislative, executive, and judicial branches are equal and must in general abstain from intruding upon each other's sphere[659]. For instance, no citizen of the United States may be denied the equal protection of the laws[660].

The US Constitution vests the judicial power in Article III courts by this means strictly restricting Congress's capacity to choose the individuals and kind of institutions by which its laws will be applied[661]. The issue of governments' relationships to courts is

---

[651] John O. McGinnis, Ilya Somin, Federalism vs. States' Rights: A Defense of Judicial Review in a Federal System, Research Paper No. 04-08, p48.

[652] Daniel R. Pinello, Linking Party to Judicial Ideology in American Courts: A Meta-Analysis, 20 *Justice Sys. J.* 219 (1999) (citing studies and concluding that voting patterns support a "political" or "attitudinal" model which posits that judicial votes follow political ideology). Harry T. Edwards, The Effects of Collegiality on Judicial Decision making, 151 *U. PA L. Rev.* 1639, 1640-41 (2003) ("These scholars invariably ignore the many ways in which collegiality mitigates judges' ideological preferences and enables us to find common ground and reach better decisions."). Theodore W. Ruger, et al., The Supreme Court Forecasting Project: Legal and Political Science Approaches to Predicting Supreme Court Decision-making, 104 *Colum. L. Rev.* 1150, 1162 (2004) ("Because our study does not account for the content [of judicial decisions] there is much is does not, and cannot, say about the judicial process.").

[653] 5 U.S. (1 Cranch) 137 (1803).

[654] David Boies, Judicial Independence and the Rule of Law, 22 *Journal of Law and Policy* 57.

[655] Andrei Marmor, Constitutional Interpretation, USC Public Policy Research Paper No. 04-4, p10.

[656] Sotirios A. Barber, *The Constitution Of Judicial* Power 50 (1993).

[657] *Dickerson v. United States*, 530 U.S. 428, 443-44 (2000); *Marbury v. Madison*, 5 U.S. (1 Cranch) 137 (1803).

[658] John E. Nowak and Ronald D. Rotunda, Constitutional Law § 3.5, at 129 (5th ed. 1995). The Declaration of Independence para. 1 (U.S. 1776). U.S. Const. amend. XIV, § 1. (From the Declaration of Independence's claim that "all men are created equal" to the Fourteenth Amendment's guarantee of "equal protection of the laws," our democracy has displayed a deep commitment to the principle of equal treatment. By adhering strictly to their own precedents, the courts help to strengthen that commitment.).

[659] Raoul Berger, Standing to Sue in Public Actions: Is It a Constitutional Requirement?, 78 *Yale L. J.* 816, 816 (1969) (arguing that "it is hardly to be doubted that the Framers contemplated resort to English practice for elucidation" of Article III). Robert J. Pushaw, Jr., Justiciability and Separation of Powers: A Neo-Federalist Approach, 81 *Cornell L. Rev.* 393, 400–07 (1996) (relying extensively on Blackstone and English legal authorities in exploring Founding-era attitudes toward the separation of powers and the judicial role).

[660] U.S. Const. amend. XIV ("[N]or shall any State . . . deny to any person within its jurisdiction the equal Protection of the laws.").

[661] U.S. Const. art. III, § 1. As Justice Marshall long ago recognized in *Marbury v. Madison*, "The very essence of civil liberty certainly consists in the rights of every individual to claim the protection of the law, whenever he

distinct, not only because of the constitutional charter running to courts but also because of the dependence of the state on courts to order its society[662]. Moreover, article III of the United States Constitution states[663]: "The judicial power of the United States shall be vested in a supreme court and in such inferior courts as the congress may, from time to time, ordain and establish." Federal courts have jurisdiction under Article III for cases "arising under" the laws of the United States[664]. To that extent, the Constitution only requires minimal diversity, and it does not employ an amount-in-controversy requirement[665]. Global constitution-making is a highly political and risky exercise in a multiethnic globe, not just for the reason that it might fail but since it tends to presuppose that 'the best comes from the West'.

Is the legislative branch totally independent from the judicial? Can the legislation drive the law towards the political direction and interests of the prevailing group via their economic status in a society? Can the judicial by the interpretation of law drive towards a specific direction? Is there the politics of law? Can law be totally objective? Is there the subjectivity of the objectivity of law? Does the politics of law define the objectivity of law and the depth of its subjectivity? Can the judicial branch by itself produce objective law? A totally independent judicial branch can produce objective law but it is based on a political decision towards the needed substance served by the content of the law. Can the legislative branch control in a way the judicial branch by producing the law serving the demands of interests of specific groups and not the whole society but merely the rest of the society has to adjust to the interests of the prevailing group?

Constitutions refer to both the right to be ruled by law and the right to a fair trial. In national legal systems it has been applied commonly to the relationship between citizens and the government which principle is now applied also globally. It is worth mentioning that while the doctrines and institutions of public law are tied to the State and to the blueprint thereof preserved in State norms, private law institutions like property, family, contract and tort law may actually have common rules. Moreover, public law too resorts to imitation due to transfers from one national legal context to another national legal framework, on top of the universal level embracing the consequences of such transfers in domestic legal systems.

---

receives an injury." 5. U.S. 137, at 163 (1803). .Edward Brunet, Arbitration and Constitutional Rights, 71 *N.C. L. Rev.* 81, 102 (1992).

[662] Judith Resnik, Fairness In Numbers: A Comment On *ATandT v. Concepcion*, *Wal-Mart v. Dukes*, and *Turner v. Rogers*, 2011 *Harvard Law Review* [Vol. 125:78.

[663] U.S. Const. art. III, § 1, cl. 1. Henry Paul Monaghan, Article III and Supranational Judicial Review, 107 *Colum. L. Rev.* 833, 842 (2007) (arguing that international trade tribunals "raise no serious problems under Article III" because they are "only a recent instantiation of an age-old practice: the use of arbitration to resolve disputes by American nationals against foreign states and their nationals").

[664] *Retail Prop. Tr. v. United Bhd. of Carpenters & Joiners of Am.*, 768 F.3d 938, 947 (9th Cir. 2014) ("The well-pleaded complaint rule means that 'a case may *not* be removed to federal court on the basis of a federal defense.'" (quoting *Caterpillar Inc. v. Williams*, 482 U.S. 386, 393 (1987))).

[665] *Exxon Mobil Corp. v. Allapattah Servs., Inc.*, 545 U.S. 546, 584 (2005) (Ginsburg, J., dissenting). The additional requirements are found in 28 U.S.C. § 1332 (2012).

The mutual recognition agreements well point up the transfer of legal institutions from one country to another. Due to such agreements, a product that can be sold in one state can also be sold in another state, on the same conditions. Moreover, mutual recognition agreements do not consist simply in the approval by one State of the law that applies to goods and businesses in another State in a given instant but they also portray that the other State's rules may be modified. Furthermore, with mutual recognition, national laws mix together, escalating the requirement for common standards to be established by multilateral organizations making possible one to choose from among multiple national law regimes. To that extent, labor protection, criminal justice and government-citizen relations exemplify the transfer from the state to the worldwide framework. Thus, a transfer takes place along a vertical alignment rather than a horizontal one which means that universal criminal law protects peace and security, and delineates war crimes, crimes against humanity and genocide as international crimes. In other words, the alternative of establishing non-State tribunals reacts to the objective to prevail over national legal systems by presenting the global one. A "universal" criminal law amalgamates or sometimes counters "parochial" criminal law[666]. To that extent, they have to act as real courts and not as political instruments in order to achieve political targets via the utilization of the law and the rule of law.

The Appellate Body of the WTO held that a State, when limiting imports from other countries, has to give exporting countries the likelihood to be heard, has to offer a reasoned and rational decision acknowledging the right to defense. The International Tribunal for the Law of the Sea (ITLOS) decided that a government which sequesters a ship and takes away the crew's passports has to respect the due process of law and the principle of fairness, informing the ship's owner and the crew and giving them the option to be heard. The European Court of Human Rights (ECHR) held that administrative decisions influencing individual rights are taken only after the interested parties have been heard.

The possibility of a technocratic patron-state and its client companies to exercise over market outcomes has weakened with integration into global markets, and to some extent for the reason that states have fractured in the meaning that state actors and agencies are ever more intertwined with 'trans-governmental networks' – and the neoliberal state has become the established model of the competition state nowadays.

Taking into account that the state, through its government, has the power to lay down binding rules as laws that do not demand the explicit consent of the governed, it means that the state, and only the state, is permitted to enforce its laws which means that it has the monopoly of violence. It is vital to comprehend the contingency of the dual monopoly of lawmaking and of enforcement. The monopoly is an achievement of the modern state, not a feature of every conceivable state because the monopoly did not exist in the middle

666 G.P. Fletcher, Parochial versus Universal Criminal Law, in *Journal of International Criminal Justice*, n. 3, 2005, p. 4.

ages, when multiple institutions competed. Moreover, the monopoly does not mean that state laws are the only binding rules in society for the reason that many non-state institutions are able to make binding rules and to have them enforced via the state's courts or via arbitration. What the monopoly implies is that such powers of non-state institutions get hold of their legally binding force only from assignment or recognition by the state. Besides, the state is not the only lawmaker, but it is the only institution that is free to decide whose rules should be recognized as law[667].

On the one hand, transnational law is appealing in particular from the standpoint of social theory, for the reason that it amalgamates both doctrine and theory and both law and social reality[668].On the other hand, international law embraces non-state actors, in particular Non-Governmental Organizations (NGOs) and MNEs. In addition, international law focused more on individuals such as in human rights law on the one hand and in international criminal law on the other. Thus, international law reaches into what had formerly been considered internal matters of sovereign states fragmenting the initiative of absolute state sovereignty.

National law has had to internationalize, the more it has been faced up to with circumstances that cannot be located evidently within one state. To that extent international and domestic law are no longer as distinct as they once were which nowadays this is a direct outcome of globalization and the decline of the bordered state. Nevertheless, international and national law stay officially distinct, and a theory of transnational law that disregards this prescribed distinction would have to be deficient.

As discussed earlier, public law is the law that governs relations between the state and the individual; private law governs relations between individuals. The distinction between public and private law exists in all national legal systems having different meanings in various legal systems. Besides, even private law depends for its enforcement on the state and its institutions. Insofar as private plaintiffs enforce their private rights, they make use of sovereignty of the state.

Therefore, by linking, in many occasions a state is forced not just by the core documents of the organizations, but also by following decisions, interpretations, and other actions undertaken by organs of that organization which have to be taken into consideration by the state when forming its national policies and laws. Moreover, the capacity of a state to affect the various norms depends on the organization, and its comparative power within it. Furthermore, a member state progressively undergoes a decrease in its capability to affect the decision making processes within the organization's institutions such as WTO because the state is constrained by these decisions as long as it remains a member of the organization.

---

[667] PS Berman, *Global Legal Pluralism: A Jurisprudence of Law Beyond Borders* (Cambridge: Cambridge University Press 2012); S Richards, Globalization as a Factor in General Jurisprudence (2012) 41 *Netherlands Journal of Legal Philosophy* 129.

[668] P Zumbansen, Transnational Legal Pluralism (2010 1 *Transnational Legal Theory* 141.

The key reliance on public law urges the well-ordered state, rather than looking for the well-ordering of the state from other resources and then anticipating that well-ordering to be mirrored in the state's public law. Although public law is considered as qualitatively unique from the rest of municipal law implies a pre-eminence for law in this area which means looking to the law to offer us the idea of the well-functioning.

7. POLITICS AND LAW

As mentioned above constitution is the *grundnorm* or basic norm of any national legal system which means that all other sources of law acquire their legitimacy from the Constitution. All legal systems are placed within their societal and political context having a number of functions. While the passage of law and its interpretation are of remarkable weight, there is a need to look at the interface of law with individuals, with political systems both formal and informal and with society. Furthermore, politicians, judges, administrative decision-makers and the legal profession interlock with their functions within a societal context concerning their impact upon the formation of law and the legal system.

The political contraption asserts that State control of the judiciary generates a system that focuses more on the authority of the State and less on the private contracting rights of individual investors than a legal system portrayed by an independent judiciary. Consequently, the political conduit emphasizes that cross-country differentiations in the independence of the judiciary are decisive for explaining cross-country divergences in financial development due to law application and its interpretation. Quite the opposite, the adaptability conduit underlines that cross-country disparities in the flexibility of the law are essential for explaining cross-country differentiations in financial development. To that extent, the political channel concentrates on the authority of the State while the adaptability channel highlights variations in the capacity of legal systems to go forward with altering circumstances. The impact of Jurisprudence is less in a system in which the State controls the judiciary than in a system where the judiciary benefits from greater independence[669]. Anyway, it is obvious that there is an impact of the elite economic interest groups upon the formation of laws especially in fields such as finance and trade in order to safeguard their interests. Moreover, elite economic interest groups (business and industry) make up the majority of interest groups and spend the most money on lobbying[670]. Economic elites have uneven impact over public policy[671]. Martin Gilens[672]

---

[669] Glaeser, E., Shleifer, A., 2002. Legal origins. *Quarterly Journal of Economics* 117, 1193-1230.
[670] Kay Lehman Schlozman, Sidney Verba & Henry E. Brady, *The Unheavenly Chorus* (2012).
[671] Benjamin I. Page & Lawrence R. Jacobs, *Class War?* 14 (2009) (describing public opinion and concluding that "Majorities of Americans of all economic and political stripes actually agree that economic inequality has widened, that this is worrisome, and that the government should respond.").

argues that government policy across all policy areas echoes the policy preferences of the well-off but is untouched by the views of the poor and middle class. It is worth mentioning that global governance is escalating fast and in different directions, frequently without a clear or principled agenda to direct institutional formation and alteration. Moreover, formal international institutions, intergovernmental networks and private authority run alongside, sometimes in harmony, sometimes in divergence, and all of them have close relations with a range of national political actors[673].

It is has to be taken into account that political influence is tilted in support of the wealthiest members of society in all states[674]. In addition, economic matters and their political lobbying is a fundamental ingredient of the conversation at the macro-level in constitutional law[675] which means an impact upon law making as well[676]. Business and industry interest groups are not only more engaged in politics, but also their interests better elucidate effects than the views of other interest groups[677]. It is questionable how much affect those with economic power have over politics and public policy in all states[678]. It is worth mentioning that the majority only gets its way when, by coincidence, their liking happen to line up with the standpoint of economic elites[679].

On the one hand, states have assigned progressively power to international institutions and international courts. On the other hand, many international bodies have developed well beyond preliminary prospects and new types of transnational and private authority have materialized unlikely of formal assignment compositions altogether[680]. It has to be taken into consideration that the global elite economic interest groups formed due to economic globalization influence global politics and governance which means an impact upon the global law making as well. In addition, global governance has criticized

---

[672] Martin Gilens & Benjamin I. Page, Testing Theories of American Politics: Elites, Interest Groups, and Average Citizens, 12 *Persp. on Pol.* 564, 573 (2014).

[673] Andreas Follesdal, The principle of subsidiarity as a constitutional principle in international law, 2 Glob. Const. 37–62 (2013).

[674] Benjamin I. Page, Larry M. Bartels & Jason Seawright, Democracy and the Policy Preferences of Wealthy Americans, 11 *Persp. on Pol.* 51 (March 2013). Martin Gilens & Benjamin I. Page, Testing Theories of American Politics: Elites, Interest Groups, and Average Citizens, 12 *Persp. On Pol*. 564, 573 (2014).

[675] Randy E. Barnett, *Restoring The Lost Constitution* (2013); David E. Bernstein, *Rehabilitating Lochner* (2012); Richard A. Epstein, *The Classical Liberal Constitution* (2014).

[676] Joseph Fishkin & William E. Forbath, The Anti-Oligarchy Constitution, 94 *B. U. L. Rev.* 669 (2014); David S. Grewal & Jedediah Purdy, Introduction: Law and Neoliberalism, 77 *L. & Contemp. Problems* 1 (2015).

[677] Andrew Gelman, Red State, Blue State, Rich State, Poor State (2010) (explaining how economic class, and state wealth, and ideology are related); Jeffrey A. Winters & Benjamin I. Page, Oligarchy in the United States? 7 *Persp. on Pol.* 731 (2009) (suggesting that the United States might be better considered an oligarchy).

[678] Larry Bartels, Rich People Rule! *Wash. Post. Monkey Cage Blog*, Apr. 8, 2014, http://www.washingtonpost.com/blogs/monkeycage/wp/2014/04/08/rich-people-rule/ (noting that this turn in political science is relatively recent). G. William Domhoff, *Who Rules America?* (7th ed. 2013).

[679] Martin Gilens & Benjamin I. Page, Testing Theories of American Politics: Elites, Interest Groups, and Average Citizens, 12 *Persp. on Pol.* 564, 573 (2014).

[680] *Who Governs The Globe?* (Deborah D. Avant, Martha Finnemore, & Susan K. Sell eds., 2010).

for its democratic deficit, weak accountability mechanisms, and absence of judicial control in analogous way than national models have grown over the years[681].

It is supposed that legal authority is a form of authority distinguished by a content-independent reaction to an instruction or order which means that the reply is content-independent for the reason that the order is not tailored to the recipient's interests[682].

It is worth mentioning that subsidiarity needs in global governance have turned into practice in certain areas of international politics, such as the European human rights regime, while they have exercised in other areas, such as trade and investment[683]. On the other hand, informal institutional settings generate fewer needs for subsidiarity not suited to the application of the principle as more formal decisional procedures[684].

It has to be taken into account that legal systems do not occur from thin air. While law and legal systems have a "relative autonomy," law and legal systems are shaped by citizens' engagement with the political system, on top of the values and practices of legislators, judges and the legal profession. Moreover, it has to be taken into consideration that legal systems are influenced by their institutions whose task it is to generate law, their courts' interpretation and contribution in the application of law and the rules emerging from legal systems[685] assisting persons to comprehend what they can or cannot do. In other words, law enjoys a "relative autonomy" as long as its content is shaped and written down until it is repelled or modified by new rules formed by the above mentioned influence[686].

All players in legal systems are no different and it is central to reflect their effect on the concept, contestation and application of legal rules and norms. It is essential to focus on the principle of legality, equality before the law, the need for an independent judiciary, and for law to be public, precise and accessible. Have these principles followed by international courts?

The law alone proscribes in a way state interference in the administration of justice[687]. Hence, legal decision-making has to be uncovered of political considerations and concentrated to a course of categorizing the facts into the appropriate legal categories which means that law could and should exclude political impacts.

---

681 Michael Zürn, Martin Binder & Matthias Ecker-Ehrhardt, *International authority and its politicization*, 4 *Int. Theory* 69–106 (2012). Benedict Kingsbury, Nico Krisch & Richard B. Stewart, The Emergence of Global Administrative Law, 68 *Law Contemp. Probl.* 15–61 (2005).

682 Andrei Marmor, An Institutional Conception of Authority, 39 *Phil. & Pub. Aff.* 238–40, 240 n.3 (2011).

683 Sanford Levinson, *Our Undemocratic Constitution: Where the Constitution Goes Wrong (And How We The People Can Correct It)* 167–80 (2006) (discussing the need for the American people to retake control of their constitutional order through formal constitution-making).

684 Michael Zürn, Global governance and legitimacy problems, 39 *Gov. Oppos.* 260–287 (2004).

685 J. Raz, *The Concept of a Legal System* (Oxford: Clarendon, 1967); and L.M. Friedman, *The Legal System: A Social Science Perspective* (New York: Russel Sage, 1975). J. Raz, The Identity of Legal Systems (1971) 59(3) *California Law Review* 795.

686 I.D. Balbus, Commodity Form and Legal Form: An Essay on the "Relative Autonomy" of Law (1977) 11(3) *Law & Society Review* 571.

687 Mirjan Damaška, The Reality of Prosecutorial Discretion: Comments on a German Monograph. *American Journal of Comparative Law* 29 (1981): 125.

It has to be taken into account that all law in basically bound up with politics and so its practice carries both political and wider social influences and implications which means that States with closed or fixed polities are governed by stable elite coalitions that are not at immediate risk of losing or having to share power. Besides, the rule of law means that since the law is formed it has to be applied and interpreted in the same way in all cases regardless of who is under consideration or what economic or political interests are at stake.

Legal regimes with low intervention into the adjudication of specific cases are formally rational democratic. Besides, legal regimes in which political actors interfere dynamically and often into the adjudication of individual cases end up as apparatus or conservatory of politics, rather than fully functional legal systems in their own right. On the one hand, when legal institutions adjudicate cases without significant intervention by other actors, they function according to the rule of law. On the other hand, when legal institutions are subject to intervention in their adjudication of individual cases, they function under the order of authoritarian leaders, or other contenders for power seek to mobilize justice in support of revolutionary, transformational, or other political agendas. Where intervention is high, but the polity is closed or fixed, neo-traditional legal systems can be found which means that in such systems, well-established elites use law energetically as a means to uphold their positions of political, economic, and social power. Besides, where established elites abstain from intervention, leaving legal institutions to adjudicate cases in a properly rational manner even in anticipation of augmenting their political legitimacy or assisting undeniable types of economic relationships and development, they are categorized as rule by law regimes.

Which is the place of law in a globalized terrain of politics and economics? It is worth mentioning that law and politics are intensely interrelated in the space beyond the state. In other words, regarding the creation and application of law, politics is a force that has to be controlled via legislative and juridical action. It could be argued that politics intervene when law fails which means that rules are a means to political ends, both in words of a policy agenda, on top of provisions of political concession. On the other hand, law is needed for political success, but it seems that law is not always the first movement towards an orderly international system.

Furthermore, politics considered as a way to an end by altering rules and practices regarded detrimental to the public good. Moreover, both politics and law are medians for social advancement and restructuring. It is argued that politics and law are discrete fields of "ontological and epistemological" peculiarities, but they are utilized by governments in order to produce institutional and juridical grounds modeling the rationality of political agency that commands the new world of global economic law. In other words, global politics more and more take place in a legal framework and so alike in the national milieu, international legal environments are arenas at which governments and private entities pursue political contests over procedure and outcome. It worth mentioning here that the impact of politics over the formation of law and vice versa is productive in many occasions as long as the written law is applied as a rule of law without any effort to manipulate the interpretation of law in order to serve specific economic affairs against the equality and justice in the essence of the rule of law' applicability.

On the one hand, political economists regard institutions and their attendant rules and practices as establishing the modern form of global economic governance. On the other hand, lawyers talk about the escalating institutionalization of market governance mechanisms as international economic law. In other words, global economic governance is achieved via international economic law but this does not means that the international economic law as an international rule of law has not to be applied objectively which means not accepting a case by case different application of the international economic law in accordance with the economic interests of the specific economic elite.

The question to be answered is if the political targeting influences directly the law and the rule of law rather than a good law works nicely with the political targets implementing them? The political goals should not twist the implementation of the rule of law in order to achieve and implement the interests of a particular group against the essence of justice and fairness. However, political and legal practices converge towards a future of legal interconnection but political deliberations over the future of the global economy occur via legal networks and in institutional arenas. To that extent, law counted less in international relations than did the eternal effort over wealth and power designating the equilibrium of power by which politics molds legal frames. It could be said that the fight for international law is a fight to restrain politics.

It has to be taken into account that politics covers a wide ground of activity, while the law remains a confined ground where the rules of politics are generated and questioned. Nonetheless, politics is not external to law and international politics takes place within a legal environment. Any political activity by an individual or business, or a government that takes place within the modern state is regulated to some degree. Global politics is ruled as much by the law as by the ethos of diplomats. States are the subject of international law commanding the use of violence undermining the question of legal legitimacy.

States have developed a noteworthy legal system in order to utilize economic law moving from politics and law to the politics of law in the realm of international economic regulation. State action is based upon a rationale rooting in some form of planning process signifying the strategic and political intent of governments.

It is worth mentioning here that legitimacy is a variable concept in law and politics denoting the way in which social and political players experience a system of governance regarding as creditable, loyalty, and respect. Along these lines, legitimacy delivers a degree of stability and resilience to forms of social organization and rule. So, legitimacy offers an analytical encounter to anyone paying attention in the link between legal and political alteration and their sociopolitical, socio-cultural foundations. For instance, there is a varying character of the legitimacy of a 'constitutional' legislature as opposed to a simply 'administrative' body or an independent agency.

In current governance, both sorts of institutions are qualified as legitimate producers of rules of general and potential application, notwithstanding in separate settings and under different limitations. To that extent, the rules generated by administrative bodies are, legally at least, considered as inferior to, indeed even dependent upon, the rules produced by legislatures but the legitimacy cannot be challenged[688]. The national legislature is the apparent source of legitimacy, a privileged role often written in the constitution itself[689] generating the law and so the need for the application of the rule of law free from any influence of politics during the appliance of the law.

8. The Politics of Law

Legal scholars frequently talk about the politics of law meaning that the design and application of law is not a direct procedure of applying reason to produce rules. It is worth mentioning that the values and beliefs of decision makers have to be taken into account concerning the setting of the decision-making procedure.

Law is stated as a set of rules that rule relations between members of society involving a basis in obligation and contains enforcement measures together with a procedure for establishing violation. Moreover, the materialization of law occurs in a political arena in which ideas and interests are disputed which means that the politics of law articulates a phenomenon incorporating the essence of the way of forming and implementing law in order to achieve the political goals for which the law is made to serve which is explored across international relations and international law.

Politics of law embrace the role of ideology in legal processes. The aim of law is to advance social life which is the aim of politics as well which means that politics is the background upon which the law is shaped and so politics is indispensable for law and law is for politics for the reason that politics is arena for law to develop and advance. It has to be taken into account that the politics of law may be identified as political belief over the way that rules are formulated and applied. In other words, politics of law is the frame/ setting in which politics takes place beyond the state. Moreover, it could be argued that politics of law is about politics in the context of law because any written law not only encompasses the prevailed political aspect of social life on the regulated matter but also the written law is interpreted in accordance with the political environment prevailed in the regulated jurisdiction. Furthermore, there is politics of international economic law for the reason that the place of law has to be taken into account due to the conception of the

---

688 Peter L Lindseth, *Power and Legitimacy: Reconciling Europe and the Nation-State* (OUP 2010).

689 Peter L Lindseth, The Paradox of Parliamentary Supremacy: Delegation, Democracy, and Dictatorship in Germany and France, 1920s-1950s (2004) 113 *Yale L. J.* 1341.

rule of law beyond the state since international law is a tool of state authority, and so international economic law considered as a means to politics and diplomacy that governments exploit when it suits them.

Politics of law is the utilization of law in such a way that it promotes the interests of the prevailing group with all governments which in fact is the one holding the economic resources. The legislature produces the right law to implement the interests of the prevailing group but not being obviously against the rights of a society and the society is shifting by law towards the direction decided by the leading economic syndicates. In other words it is given the interpretation and approach by courts the one helpful towards the prevailing syndicates producing the politics of law. Globalization adds to the politics of law as well implementing the interests of the international economic syndicates. The law has to be objective but in fact there is a subjective objectivity which is formulated via the politics of law in order to comply with the interests of the prevailing economic group being behind all governments. Is the politics of law context clear from the wording of the law? The answer is no and on first sight it seems that the law expresses the whole society but the combination of various laws and their interpretation or implementation in practice identifies the direction chosen to be followed by the prevailing economic group within a society. Does politics of law affect politics? There is an interrelation between them utilized by governments to achieve their goals. Is politics of law illegal? No it is a fair way to achieve with a typically legal way the interest of the prevailing group. Does this happen with all laws? No it takes place in topics essential for the dominant economic syndicate with in a society.

9. Politics, Law and Courts

A range of normative principles have been projected to direct the allocation of global authority and the classical norm is the *consent* of contracting states. To that extent, if states consensually choose to use right in a given subject area jointly, their consent also determines the aptness of the newly constituted international authority[690]. *Besides, Utilitarian* considerations founded on the principle of "comparative benefit," the idea of global public goods, or the Pareto principle offering an option which means that decisions are allocated to an institution that can make certain the most valuable stipulation of welfare[691]. Moreover, a third standpoint puts up conceptions of *justice* which means the emergence of cosmopolitan justice stressing moral obligations beyond borders backing global authority. Furthermore, cosmopolitan justice rationalizes the formation of strong

[690] Tom Christiano, *The Legitimacy of International Institutions*, *in* The Routledge Companion To Philosophy Of Law (Andrei Marmor, Ed.) 380–393 (2012). Nico Krisch, The Decay of Consent: International Law in an Age of Global Public Goods, 108 *Am. J. Int. Law* 1–40 (2014).

[691] Allen Buchanan & Robert O. Keohane, The legitimacy of global governance institutions, 20 *Ethics Int. Aff.* 405–437 (2006). Wallace E. Oates, Fiscal Federalism (1972).

supra-state institutions as instrumentally needed so as to guarantee compliance with trans-boundary obligations of justice, together with obligations of distributive justice[692].

Subsidiarity is a principle entailing decision-making to take place at a lower level if not good reasons are for shifting it upwards[693]. Subsidiarity favors local action becoming a justification for higher-level decision-making[694]. Which is to the relations between national and international institutions? Subsidiarity is a principle for assigning authority to various levels of governance presenting assistance on how powers are to be implemented. Moreover, subsidiarity is "the soul of federalism" which means preference for the local leaving open how this is to be accomplished being the list of powers for each level of government[695]. To that extent, in the EU subsidiarity has dominated a prominent place which is introduced as a formal rule for the first time in the 1992 Maastricht Treaty. Furthermore, subsidiarity deals with political questions of power-sharing which should be left to the political procedure but in general not be used by constitutional courts to review legislative endeavor. Besides, it could be said that courts should play a role in reviewing formal, written constitution-making which means constitutional amendment and replacement.[696]

Forceful types of judicial review have developed that have enhanced the politics of constitution-making suggesting that courts might be able to defend individual rights and political competition from the dangers of majoritarian constitution-making in embryonic democracies[697]. Courts are often unable to advance constitution-making politics allowing

---

692 Simon Caney, Justice Beyond Borders: A Global Political Theory (2005). ch. 5. Michael Blake & Patrick Taylor Smith, International Distributive Justice, in *Stanford Encyclopedia of Philosophy* (2013), http://plato.stanford.edu/archives/win2013/entries/international-justice/.

693 Andreas Follesdal, Subsidiarity and International Human Rights Courts, 79 *Law Contemp. Probl.* (2016). Loren King, Cities, Subsidiarity, and Federalism, in *Federalism and Subsidiarity* (James E. Fleming & Jacob T. Levy, Eds.) 291–331 (2014).

694 Michelle Evans, The Principle of Subsidiarity as a Social and Political Principle in Catholic Social Teaching, 3 *Solidar. J. Cathol. Soc. Thought Secul. Ethics* 4, 54 (2013).
David Golemboski, *Federalism and the Catholic Principle of Subsidiarity, EarlyView PUBLIUS* (2015).

695 Gareth Davies, Subsidiarity: The Wrong Idea, in the Wrong Place, at the Wrong Time, 43 *Common Mark. Law Rev*. 63–84 (2006).

696 Jenna Bednar, Subsidiarity and Robustness. Building the Adaptive Efficiency of Federal Systems, in *Federalism and Subsidiarity* (Nomos Lv) 231, 231 (James E. Fleming & Jacob T. Levy eds., 2014). Steven G. Calabresi & Lucy D. Bickford, Federalism and Subsidiarity: Perspectives from U.S. Constitutional Law, in *Federalism and Subsidiarity* (James E. Fleming & Jacob T. Levy, Eds.) 123–189 (2014). Paul Craig, Subsidiarity: A Political and Legal Analysis, 50 *J. Common Mark. Stud.* 72–87, 80 (2012). Laurence H. Tribe, A Constitution We Are Amending: In Defense of a Restrained Judicial Role, 97 *Harv. L. Rev.* 433, 435–36, 436 n.13 (1983) (arguing that courts should play a highly limited role in reviewing the substance and procedure of constitutional change).

697 Katherine Glenn Bass & Sujit Choudhry, *Democracy Reporting Int'l, Constitutional Review In New Democracies* 7 (Michael Meyer-Resende & Duncan Pickard eds., 2013), http://www.democracy-reporting.org/files/dri-bp-40_en_constitutional_review_in_new_democracies_2013-09.pdf (citing South Africa and Colombia as the examples of places demonstrating the benefits of robust judicial review); Helen M. Stacy, *Human Rights For The 21st Century: Sovereignty, Civil Society, Culture* 128–31, 167–68 (2009) (looking at Colombian, Indian, and South African courts as powerful guardians of judicially protected human rights); Jackie Dugard & Theunis Roux, The Record of the South African Constitutional Court in Providing an Institutional Voice for the Poor: 1995–2004, in *Courts And Social Transformation in New Democracies: An Institutional Voice For The Poor?* 107–52 (Roberto Gargarell et al. eds., 2006) (describing India, South Africa, and Colombia as having courts that could help provide a voice for the poor in the consolidation of democracy); Daniel Bonilla Maldonado, *Introduction to Constitutionalism of the Global South: The Activist*

abuse by the elite of formal constitutional alteration[698]. Moreover, formal, written constitution-making whether it is constitutional amendment or replacement can be risky to individual rights demonstrating institutionalized political competition in weak and inadequately institutionalized democracies. Formal institutionalization of presidential rule through the constitution-making procedure is considered to be "abusive constitutionalism[699]."

It is worth mentioning that there is an escalating role of courts in regulating constitution-making politics. Taking into account that "new constitutionalism" has spread around the globe constitutions have allowed courts significant formal power to mediate in politics. Moreover, it seems that courts perform a vital task in protecting democratic outcomes in constitution-making[700]. Andrew Arato[701] argues that judicial review makes certain that the principles of constitutionalism apply not just to the resulting constitution but also to "the democratic *process* of constitution making." President Morsi striped the courts of jurisdiction eventually diluting deliberation and turning constitution-making

---

Tribunals of India, South Africa, and Colombia 21 (Daniel Bonilla Maldonado ed., 2013) (discussing how the Indian Supreme Court, the South African Constitutional Court, and the Colombian Constitutional Court are seen as "activist tribunals" that contribute to the "public and private spheres of their countries"); Nick Robinson, Expanding Judiciaries: India and the Rise of the Good Governance Court, 8 *Wash. U. Global Stud. L. Rev. 1*, 67 (2009) (discussing "a global shift to check representative institutions with increasingly broad principles of good governance"). (discussing the role of the Indian Supreme Court in the constitutional amendment process as "a court of good governance over the rest of the government."); Andrew Arato, Redeeming the Still Redeemable: Post Sovereign Constitution Making, 22 *Int'l J. Pol. Culture Soc'y* 427, 429, 433 (2009) (describing the importance of judicial review in a post-sovereign form of constitution-making); Aharon Barak, Unconstitutional Constitutional Amendments, 44 *Isr. L. Rev.* 321, 336 (2011) (discussing the possibilities of judicial review in improving constitution-making politics).

698 Samuel Issacharoff, Constitutional Courts and Democratic Hedging, 99 *Geo. L. J.* 961, 965 (2011) (discussing the possibilities of judicial review in improving constitution-making politics); Samuel Issacharoff, Constitutionalizing Democracy in Fractured Societies, 82 *Tex. L. Rev.* 1861, 1870–83 (2004) (looking at the South African constitutional example and noting that there is great significance to "the provisions that reaffirmed limitations on government and those that were struck down [by the court] for what may be termed an excess of majoritarianism"); Yaniv Roznai, Unconstitutional Constitutional Amendments—The Migration and Success of a Constitutional Idea, 61 *Am. J. Comp. L.* 657, 718 (2013); Po Jen Yap, The Conundrum of Unconstitutional Constitutional Amendments, 4 *Global Constitutionalism* 114, 136 (2015) (arguing that courts should declare constitutional amendments unconstitutional in response to attempts by dominant parties to use constitutional rules to entrench power or abuse rights).

699 David Landau, Constitution-Making Gone Wrong, 64 *Ala. L. Rev.* 923 (2013) (describing how extra-parliamentary process has given charismatic executives a democratic tool to circumvent parliamentary opposition in Venezuela and Bolivia). David Landau, Abusive Constitutionalism, 47 *U.C. Davis L. Rev.* 189, 191 (2013);

700 Ran Hirschl, Towards Juristocracy: The Origins and Consequences Of The New Constitutionalism 169–70 (2004). William Partlett, The Dangers of Popular Constitution-Making, 38 *Brook. J. Int'l L.* 193 (2012) (discussing such occurrences in Russia, Belarus, and Kazakhstan).

701 Andrew Arato, Constitution-Making under Occupation: The Politics of Imposed Revolution in Iraq, at viii (2009). Victor Ferreres Comella, The Consequences of Centralizing Constitutional Review in a Special Court: Some Thoughts on Judicial Activism, 82 *Tex. L. Rev.* 1705, 1730 (2004) (arguing that specialized constitutional courts will tend to be relatively less deferential because "[a] constitutional court is not likely to earn its own space in the institutional system if it regularly upholds the statutes that are challenged before it"). David M. Jaros & Adam S. Zimmerman, Judging Aggregate Settlement, 94 *Wash. U. L. Rev.* 545, 552 (2017) ("[J]udicial review would mean . . . demanding more information about the parties' competing interests in settlement . . . .").

into a divisive assignment of majoritarian imposition[702]. Besides, judicial review is most common in the review of constitutional amendment.

On the one hand, some constitutions explicitly ascertain that parts of the constitution un-amendable. On the other hand, other constitutions clarify the majority required for the amendment to be backed up by referendum or delegate the determination of the majority to a particular law. In addition, many new constitutions clearly award constitutional courts the formal power to review constitution-making[703]. It has to be taken into account that courts perform a positive role in improving constitution-making when the judges on these courts being part of a community which has a broad role in advancing the performance of democracy. Judges of such as specialized constitutional courts are expected to build up an attitudinal duty which is developed in contexts with historically entrenched respect for judicial review where courts have control over who is appointed to the court.

Likewise, various countries across the globe use changing and intersecting ideologies and practices in the administration of justice[704]. There are primary constitutional and political reasons for separating state from community but certain local agency employees are forming part of "community" throughout the restorative procedure. To that extent, state representatives though *politically* separated from the community, in *reality* form an imperative component of any local social milieu.

Further, most International Courts (ICs) gain formal legal authority (de jure authority) due to an act of delegation from states creating a court's formal right to rule on disputes falling within its jurisdiction[705]. The legal right to rule exists even if the moral or ethical basis of that right continues to be disputed. ICs acquire unquestioned power merely by asset of delegation which means that delegation awards formal authority on ICs denoting their purpose in vital manner.

To that extent, the act of delegation grants upon a court a defined authority to rule on disputes that fall within its jurisdiction[706]. International judges supposed to decide cases

---

[702] Nathan Brown, Decoder: Morsi, the Judiciary, and Acts of Sovereignty, *ARABIST* (Nov. 25, 2012), http://arabist.net/blog/2012/11/25/decoder-morsi-the-judiciary-and-acts-of-sovereignty.html (discussing the acts of sovereignty doctrine that Morsi relied on to raise the constituent assembly above judicial review).

[703] European Commission for Democracy Through Law (Venice Commission), *Report on Constitutional Amendment*, Study No. 720/2008, CDL-AD (2010)001 (Jan. 19, 2010), http://www.venice.coe.int/webforms/documents/default.aspx?pdffile=CDL-AD%282010%29001-e. Tom Ginsburg & Mila Versteeg, Why Do Countries Adopt Constitutional Review? 30 *J. L. Econ. & Org*. 587, 587 (2014) ("[B]y 2011, 83% of the world's constitutions had given courts the power to supervise implementation of the constitution and to set aside legislation for constitutional incompatibility.").

[704] Baker, Estella, and Roberts, Julian B. 2005. Globalization and the New Punitiveness. In *The New Punitiveness: Current Trends, Theories and Perspectives,* edited by John Pratt, David Brown, Mark Brown, Simon Hallsworth and Wayne Morrison, Devon: Willan Publishing. Vogler, Richard. 2005. *A World View of Criminal Justice*, Aldershot: Ashgate.

[705] David A. Wirth, Reexamining Decision-Making Processes in International Environmental Law, 79 *Iowa L. Rev.* 769, 779 (1994) ("Notwithstanding a meritorious legal claim . . . , one State may be reluctant to initiate a third-party dispute settlement process against another State for fear of jeopardizing other strategic or economic bilateral relationships."). Andrei Marmor, An Institutional Conception of Authority, 39 *Phil & Pub Aff.* 238–40, 240 n.3 (2011).

[706] Curtis A. Bradley & Judith G. Kelley, The Concept of Delegation, 71 *Law &Contemp Probs* no. 1, 2008.

based on the reasoned interpretation and application of international law irrespective of any political interference. It has to be taken into account that ICs by being new institutions, their rulings may conflict with and ousting well-established or presumed interpretations of legal rules or social norms which means that replacing established ideas and practices is challenging. For international judges, doing so is particularly insubordinate for the reason that ICs function in a milieu of compound authoritative decision makers. Officially, ICs are the premier judicial interpreters of the international rules within their jurisdictions but other international and national legal and political players compete over their respective jurisdictions and over the meanings of laws. The judicial nature of ICs makes them a marked kind of international institution having the right to rule applying the rule of law which means turn their formal mandate into de facto authority provoking political, legal, and practical encounter. Moreover, delegation alone is inadequate for the reason that a court may have de facto authority in some of the disputes that it adjudicates but still not be a politically commanding institution since many legal violations are never brought to court or are the theme of rulings that are disregarded[707]. Besides, authoritative ICs have power in reality stretching out across a wide array of matters, states, and types of cases[708].

10. Criminal Law and Politics

The establishment of globalized society throughout the post-modern period has had numeral of noteworthy implications on the ways in which individual states now react to crime. Especially, the explosion of international human rights law together with the creation of international governing bodies such as the United Nations has produced the forefront for a developing and improving policy basis for the internationalization of crime regulation.

The growth in international justice mechanisms is a system of justice placing emphasis on imposing *deserved* punishments while upholding defendant rights within a framework of proportionate sentencing[709]. Any international justice mechanism has to be employed according to the rule of law not influenced by any political targeting. Has the international justice implemented without any political intervention either direct or indirect via the tools of criminal procedure codes?

---

707 Walid Ben Hamida, The First Arab Investment Court Decision, 7 *J. World Invest. & Trade* 699 (2006) (discussing the Arab Investment Court). Joseph Weiler, The Transformation of Europe, 100 *Yale L. J.* 2403, 2447–48 (1991) (discussing how the ECJ built its authority incrementally through its interactions with national judges, government officials, and private litigants).

708 Eric A. Posner & Alan O. Sykes, Efficient Breach of International Law: Optimal Remedies, "Legalized Noncompliance," and Related Issues, 110 *Mich. L. Rev.* 243, 280 (2011).

709 Findlay, Mark J. 2008. *Governing through Globalised Crime: Futures for international criminal justice*, Devon: Willan Publishing. Ashworth, Andrew. 2010, *Sentencing and Criminal Justice,* 5th ed. Cambridge: Cambridge University Press.

The Organization for Security and Co-operation in Europe (OSCE) has been influential in internationalizing both the concept of hate crime and its legal proscription[710]. ODIHR's work has been instrumental in proliferating hate crime laws internationally. The international policy domain for hate crime has been focused mostly on neo-liberal and punitive approaches to dealing with the problem. Article 4 of the European Union Framework Decision on Racist and Xenophobic Crime (2008) states that member states "shall take the necessary measures to ensure that racist and xenophobic motivation is considered an aggravating circumstance, or, alternatively that such motivation may be taken into consideration by the courts in the determination of the penalties." All members of the EU must have provisions in law that count hate-motivation as an exacerbating factor for any offence or member states must punish hate-motivated offenders more strictly.

According to the Council of the EU's conclusions on combating hate crime members to make certain that they have transferred the provisions of the Framework Decisions 2008 and to "consider the experience of other Member States in extending within their criminal legislation, the scope of punishable hate crime offences." Nonetheless, legislating to combat hate crime cannot, by itself, immobilize the globalization of hate and there is an increase in the number of hate-motivated offences across Europe[711].

Prosecutors have suppressed exculpatory evidence, applied the law selectively and used their sentencing leverage to force plea bargains[712]. To that extent, prosecutors lack of accountability, non-transparent decision-making processes, and prosecutors' desire for political gain due to the inefficiency of elections[713].

It has to be taken into account that by increasing transparency and strengthening prosecutors' democratic responsibility we reduce the inequitable exercise of prosecutorial discretion and so restricting prosecutorial misconduct.[714] Moreover, in corporate corruption cases weak laws and personnel constraints lead prosecutors to assume weak "confession agreements" with influential corporate interests which means the there is an impact of politics upon prosecutors [715]. There is a need to upgrade fairness and advance

---

710 Goodall, Kay. 2013. Conceptualising "racism" in criminal law. *Legal Studies*, 33 (2): pp. 215-238. http://www.legislationline.org/topics/subtopic/79/topic/4.

711 Home Office, Office for National Statistics and Ministry of Justice 2013. *An Overview of Hate Crime in England and Wales*, London: Home Office, Office for National Statistics and Ministry of Justice.

712 Angela J. Davis, *Arbitrary Justice: The Power of the American Prosecutor* (New York: Oxford University Press, 2007), 4.

713 "Federal Prosecutor Range Criticizes 'Political Influence' on Investigation," *Deutsche Welle*, August 4, 2015. http://www.dw.com/en/federal-prosecutor-range-criticizes-political-influence-on-investigation/a-18625429. Hon. Alex Kozinski, "Criminal Law 2.0," *Georgetown Law Journal Annual Review Criminal Procedure*. 44 (2015): iii, viii. http://georgetownlawjournal.org/files/2015/06/Kozinski_Preface.pdf.

714 Ronald F. Wright, "How Prosecutor Elections Fail Us," *Ohio State Journal of Criminal Law* 6 (2009): 509-606. Glenn Harlan Reynolds, "Ham Sandwich Nation: Due Process When Everything Is a Crime," *Columbia Law Review Sidebar* 113 (2013): 102.

715 Shawn Marie Boyne, *The German Prosecution Service: Guardians of the Law?* (Heidelberg: Springer, 2013). David Crawford and Mike Esterl, "Siemans Settlement Sets off Criticism of German Inquiries," *The Wall Street Journal*, October 8, 2007, http://www.wsj.com/articles/SB119179176083751435.

integrity[716] of prosecutors in order to have more legally objective employment of the rule of law.

To that extent, neither the Federal Constitution, nor the Constitutions of the *Länder* denote exactly where the prosecution offices fit within the State's constitutional structures. Nevertheless, Article 92 of the German Constitution (*Grundgesetz*) gives full decision-making independence to the judicial branch. It is characteristic that German legal practitioners deem that "the Prosecution Services are criminal justice authorities within the executive whose individual agents exercise their power in non-political fashion.[717]" Besides, even though many of the battles over prosecutors' decision-making independence occur away from the public eye, German prosecutors strive to weigh up their loyalty to the state with their normative directive to find the objective "truth."

Like the United States, Germany is a federal system which means that there is both a federal prosecution service located in Karlsruhe on top of independent prosecution services organized at the level of the sixteen *Länder*. However, Germany's federal prosecutors concentrate their practice on crimes against the state and crimes against humanity representing the State in cases before the Federal Court of Appeals[718].

In contradiction of the American adversarial system, where prosecutors act as a party to the criminal proceeding, in the German system, most prosecutors are not devoted in "winning a case." German prosecutors do not bear the burden of proof at trial but they are free to give their own sentencing recommendations examining the evidence through an objective lens. Moreover, German prosecutors' role is to find the truth which means a pledge to objectivity and to the law itself is embedded in the German conception of the State. The German ideal is rooted in the civil law tradition which it not only embodies the perception that the authority of the state is confined by law, but more notably, it means that the state acts in a lawful (*rechtlich*) way. To that extent, any action undertaken by the state has to be based on law which means that every citizen has the right to contest the constitutionality of a government action before the Federal Constitutional Court adding to the demand for acting according to the rule of law. Thus, the law is the medium through which the State governs compelling state action to avert arbitrariness and to ensure

[716] John Worrall, M. Elaine Nugent-Borakove (eds.), *The Changing Role of the American Prosecutor* (Albany: SUNY Press, 2014), 94-97.

[717] Ekaternia Trendafilova and Werner Róth, "Report on the public prosecution service in Germany," in *Promoting Prosecutorial Accountability, Independence and Effectiveness. Comparative Research.* Ed. Open Society Institute (Sofia: Open Society Institute, 2008), 237, citing German Code of Criminal Procedure (StGB) Sect. 160, https://www.opensocietyfoundations.org/sites/default/files/promoting_20090217.pdf.

[718] Gwladys Gilliéron, *Public Prosecutors in the United States and Europe: A Comparative Analysis with Special Focus on Switzerland, France, and Germany* (Switzerland: Springer 2014), 243, citing GVG Sect. 142 (1).

certainty and predictability[719]. In addition, as an organized entity, the state is restricted not only by law, but also by the primary principles of legality[720].

It is worth mentioning that the state is not a political entity engaging in policies that abolish the law which means that prosecutors, as agents of the state, regard their function in less-instrumental terms than American prosecutors. To that extent, the German prosecutor is a "guardian of the law" and, by implication, a pillar of the *Rechtsstaat* which means that the rule of law is above everything. Does the rule of law is above everything in implementing justice in the national and international fora? Is the rule of law under threat? The threats against the rule of law are founded on many factors such as the need to combat physical terrorism and cyber-attacks, the need to fulfill public concern about crime, IT-based intrusion into individual privacy, government cut-backs on the legal system, escalating inequality and globalization, and repressive regimes in some countries.

For the reason that prosecutors materialize their own opinion about the evidence displayed at trial and even move for an acquittal, their pledge to objectivity on top of their professional outlook overlaps the executive and judicial functions. Above all, prosecutors assess their performance, not by their conviction rate or the length of the defendant's sentence, but by whether they employed the law accurately in a specific case which means that the application of the rule of law is the only basis for prosecutors' exercise of law rejecting any political influence. German prosecutors are compelled by law to investigate the facts both for and against the defendant.

Which is the location of the law in reference to the state? It has to be taken into consideration that in a rule of law state, the law stands above the state and limits the sovereign's discretionary authority which means that the judiciary functions as its key guardian based on an objective implementation of the law rather than interpreting the law in a way of promoting the demands of a political interests of any group. In contrast, in the German *Rechtsstaat*, the law originates with the legislature law is not above the state but rather part of the state's composition as well as its product which means that the state does not ignore the law rather than the state implements accurately the law as being its product not influenced by any political interests.

It could be said that the legislature, courts, and prosecutors function as the guardians of the law in the German system. The birth of the Federal Constitutional Court in the post-war era and the postwar Constitution's hold of human dignity have not only enhanced control over state authority but have also implanted a pledge to social welfare in the make-up of the State.

---

[719] Martin Krygier, Rule of Law (and Rechtsstaat), *University of New South Wales Faculty of Law Research Series* No. 53 (October 2013): 6, http://law.bepress.com/cgi/viewcontent.cgi?article=1052&context=unswwps-flrps13.

[720] T.R.S. Allan (1998). Rule of law (Rechtsstaat). In *Routledge Encyclopedia of Philosophy* (1998). London: Routledge, DOI: 10.4324/9780415249126-T022-1, https://www.rep.routledge.com/articles/rule-of-law-rechtsstaat/v-1/.

Civil law systems count on two devices for warranting that prosecutors are responsible such as a penal code restraining prosecutors' decision-making choices and the principle of mandatory prosecution[721]. As initially planned, the German Code of Criminal Procedure sought to eliminate arbitrary political intrusion in the criminal justice system. However, prosecutors retained some flexibility in their investigation and charging decision-making and so authorizing prosecutors and judges to guarantee that the system is fair, it also invites the delivery of arbitrary justice. Besides, the Land-level Ministries of Justice sometimes attempt to quash prosecutions for political reasons and so drawing political consideration encompassing the investigation of politicians, campaign contributors, or well-known entrepreneurs.

Prosecutors receive political pressure delivered in the form of phone calls and informal oral suggestions in order to work behind the curtains indicating that there is no action against the rule of law. It has to be taken into account that the Minister of Justice may reassign a case to another prosecutor[722]. It is characteristic that the threat to prosecutors' fidelity to the law exists in those states where prosecutors turn around between positions in the judiciary, the Ministry, and the prosecution service at standard periods. Even though prosecutors have life-time tenure, the Ministry or a prosecutor's superiors exploit the likelihood of a future rotation to remunerate or penalize prosecutors who stick to or reject the Ministry's desires by progress up the ranks or get side-tracked due to lack of "social competence" accordingly.

It is characteristic the case of Helmut Kohl for political retaliation where the prosecutor who filed the opening charges found himself "promoted" to a position of family court judge in a small German town[723] proving the interference of politics over the rule of law. Even though the first prosecutor filed felony-level bribery charges against the former Chancellor, the case eventually was dismissed under Sect. 153a which permits prosecutors to discharge minor cases that are not in the public's interest to prosecute indicating how in a legal way politics interfere in the application of the rule of law in order to avoid a direct and open intervention negating the rule of law[724]. To that extent, members of the opposition parties on the Federal and state levels may operate as a prospective safeguard on arbitrary interfering by the Ministry of Justice in a particular

---

[721] Emilio S. Binavince, The Structure and Theory of the German Penal Code, *American Journal of Comparative Law* 24 (1976): 601. Horacio Spector, The Future of Legal Science in Civil Law Systems, *Louisiana Law* Review 65 (2004): 261. Markus Dirk Dubber, The Promise of German Criminal Law: A Science of Crime and Punishment, *German Law Journal* 6 (2005): 1051, http://www.germanlawjournal.com/pdfsNolO6NoO7fPDF_-Vol_-06_-No_-07_-1049-1073_Articles Dubber.pdf.

[722] Trendafilova and Roth, Report on the public prosecution service in Germany, 221 (citing Werner Beulke), *Strafprozessrecht* (2006) at marginal no. 85.

[723] David Crawford & Mike Esteral, Germany: Siemens Settlement Sets off Criticism of German Inquiries, *Wall Street Journal,* October 8, 2007, http://www.wsj.com/articles/SB119179176083751435. Senior Prosecutor Interview, [8HL], May 22, 2006. Stefan Mayr, Brisante Aktenvermerke im Fall Schottdorf, *Süddeutsche Zeitung,* January 26, 2015, http://www.sueddeutsche.de/bayern/laboraffaere-brisante-aktenvermerke-im-fall-schottdorf-1.2319780.Senior Prosecutor Interview [16PP], April 30, 2008.

[724] Germany's Party Finance Scandal "Ends" With Kohl's Plea Bargain and Too Many Unanswered Questions, *German Law Journal* 2 (2001), http://www.germanlawjournal.com/index.php?pageID=11&artID=60.

case for the reason that the Ministry of Justice is politically liable to the Parliament, members of Parliament may instigate investigations into specific cases and present written questions to the Ministry. Nonetheless, while legislative hearings draw media coverage, the range of the parliamentary investigation is reduced to whether or not the law was followed having little to do with whether the prosecutor applied the law rightly[725]. Anyway, the level of political interfering in prosecutorial decision-making diverges from Land to Land[726].

Also the nation's top prosecutor position is exceptional under German law as the Federal Prosecutor is a "political civil servant" who, by law, may be sent into temporary retirement at whatever time. In line with the Act Defining the Scope of Civil Servants' Rights and Duties (*Beamtenrechtsrahmengesetz*-BRRG), "political civil servants" has to coincide with the government's political beliefs and policy goals[727]. Where is the rule of law? Is the rule of law a cover-up for political manipulations of a society?

Germany's domestic intelligence agency is accountable for protecting the country's internal security[728]. It is characteristic that Christoph Frank, the head of the Federation of German Judges and State Prosecutors (*Richterbund*) called the firing a "significant threat" to the rule of law and charged that political impact on prosecutorial decision-making damages the public's confidence in the criminal justice system.[729] Moreover, Thomas Heilmann, assessed the Justice Minister affirming that: "I can't accept the behavior of Minister Maas," . . . "[e]ither he understands himself as the supervising authority over the state prosecutors, in which case he should have already intervened two months ago, or he is, like me, of the opinion that politicians can't decide on political criminal investigations, in which case he shouldn't have been allowed to intervene[730]."

---

725 Gilliéron, *Public Prosecutors in the United States and Europe*, 282.

726 Stefan Mayr, Justiz im Zwielicht, *Süddeutsche Zeitung*, October 20, 2015, http://www.sueddeutsche.de/bayern/affaere-schottdorf-justiz-im-zwielicht-1.2700023.

727 Beamtenrechtsrahmengesetz, Sect. 31 I (BRRG). [Act Defining the Scope of Civil Servants' Rights and Duties].

728 German Prosecutors investigate Internet Journalists for Treason, *Deutsche Welle*, July 30, 2015, http://www.dw.com/en/german-prosecutors-investigate-internet-journalists-for-treason/a-18619254. Klaus Brinkbäumer, Berlin's NSA Fears: Treason Investigation Reveals Anxiety at the Top, *Der Spiegel*, August 10, 2015, http://www.spiegel.de/international/germany/german-treasoninvestigation-reveals-anxiety-among-leaders-a1047256.html. *Pew Research Center's 2014 Global attitudes Survey*, http://www.pewglobal.org/2014/07/14/nsaopinion/country/germany/ Thousands March in Berlin over Journalist 'Treason' Claims, *Deutsche Welle*, August 1, 2015, http://www.dw.com/en/thousands-march-in-berlin-over-journalist-treason-claims/a-18621978. Melissa Eddy, Germany Drops Inquiry into Claims U.S. Tapped Angela Merkel's Phone, *New York Times*, June 12, 2015, http://www.nytimes.com/2015/06/13/world/europe/germany-dropsinquiry-us-tapped-angela-merkel-phone.html?_r=0. Ben Knight, Outrage as Range Turns Netzpolitik Treason Storm into Constitutional Row, *Deutsche Welle*, August 4, 2014, http://www.dw.com/en/outrage-as-range-turns-netzpolitiktreason-storm-into-constitutional-row/a-18626420. Ben Knight, How the World Misunderstood Germany's Netzpolitik Affair, *Deutsche Welle*, August 5, 2015, http://www.dw.com/en/how-the-world-misunderstood-germanys-netzpolitik-affair/a- 18630649.

729 Plugging Leaks: Merkel's War on Germany's Press and Parliament, *Der Spiegel*, August 7, 2015, http://www.spiegel.de/international/germany/berlin-goes-after-journalists-to-protect-statesecrets-a-1047265.html . Deutscher Richterbund, Richterbund kritisiert Eingreifen des Bundesjustizministers, *Press Release*, August 4, 2015, http://www.drb.de/cms/index.php?id=917&L=0.

730 Critics Hunt Fresh Scalps in Treason Scandal, *The Local.De*, August 6, 2015, http://www.thelocal.de/20150806/critics-hunt-fresh-scalps-in-treason-scandal. Naomi Conrad, In Berlin, Probe into

Furthermore, Range was the first Federal Prosecutor in history to blame the Minister of Justice of intervening in a case for political reasons[731]. Is the law the instrument for political imposition accordingly? Have all political goals achieved via law and the rule of law? To that extent, in the *Schottdorf* case the political intrusion damage the investigation's scope which means that political authority acted to weaken the justice system's pledge to the principle of mandatory prosecution to go forward the interests of Mr. Schottdorf and his political allies.

While the United States was founded on the objective that authority should flow from the people rather than from a King, the representative democracy has not always assured that prosecutorial decision-making has been responsive to public values and so according to the rule of law. To that extent, even when that decision making has respected public values, the events mirrored by those values have not always guaranteed that the system's results are both fair and just. Even though elections tie prosecutors to some type of democratic control, they have also encouraged the unrestrained augmentation of prosecutorial authority and have sometimes damaged prosecutors' duty to do justice which means that the rule of law is not the sole basis of decision making but politics imposes in a way the duty. It is worth mentioning that Darryl Brown has written that: "prosecutorial authority has grown and judicial authority contracted because, in various ways, U.S. criminal process trusts political decision-making over legal regulation.[732]" In other words, the election of top prosecutors has led to a system that is "administered less by rules grounded in public values and principles and more by private interests, partisan motivations, and political preferences[733]."

It is argued that the German system trusts fidelity to the principle of mandatory prosecution and the civil legal code over political decision-making. On the other hand, the underling link of the prosecution service within the Ministry of Justice is both a source of political answerability in addition to a prospective source of political influence which means that when political figures seek to affect prosecutorial decision-making, it damages the German principle of legality[734].

Netzpolitik Inquiry Drags on, *Deutsche Welle,* August 19, 2015, http://www.dw.com/en/in-berlin-probe-into-netzpolitik-inquirydrags-on/a-18658583.

[731] John Blau, Prosecutor Fired after Targeting Journalists, *Handlesblatt*, August 5, 2015, https://global.handelsblatt.com/edition/234/ressort/politics/article/prosecutor-fired-for-targeting-journalists.

[732] Darryl K. Brown, *Free Market Criminal Justice: How Democracy and Laissez Faire Undermine the Rule of Law* (New York: Oxford University Press, 2016), 4. Andrew Chongseh Kim, Underestimating the Trial Penalty: An Empirical Analysis of the Federal Trial Penalty and Critique of the Abrams Study (June 23, 2015). *Mississippi Law Journal*, Vol. 84, No. 5, 2015, http://ssrn.com/abstract=2635657.

[733] Darryl K. Brown, *Free Market Criminal Justice: How Democracy and Laissez Faire Undermine the Rule of Law*, 2. Amita Kelly, Does it Matter that Ninety Five Percent of Elected Prosecutors are White? *National Public Radio*, July 8, 2015, http://www.npr.org/sections/itsallpolitics/2015/07/08/420913118/does-itmatter-that-95-of-elected-prosecutors-are-white.

[734] 84 Recommendations for More Integrity: Transparency Germany Presents its National Integrity Assessment for Germany, *Transparency International Press Release*, January 19, 2012, http://www.transparency.org/news/pressrelease/20120119_germany_nis. Ministry Interview [9RR], June 2, 2006. Shawn Marie Boyne, Prosecutorial Accountability in the Rechtsstaat: The Tension between Law, Politics, and the Public Interest, Robert H. McKinney School of Law, Legal Studies Research Paper No. 2016 – 29.

There are calls to augment prosecutors' political independence resonate with the recommendations of the Council of Europe's Committee of Ministers ordering members of the government accountable for oversight of the prosecution office to "exercise their powers in a transparent way" and so stating that "such instructions must carry with them adequate guarantees that transparency and equity are respected[735]."

Does China lack a modern set of constraints in the form of a rule of law or democratic accountability? Is there a different understanding of legal politics in China? How political and legal orders advance over time there and in other contexts? Chinese civil dispute resolution has been categorized as a rule by law regime since the mid-1980s[736]. China's civil law system is a kind of rule by law regime, while the criminal law system is neo-traditional. China's substantial reforms and moves toward judicialized dispute resolution in a wide variety of areas indicate a system abiding by the rule of law. A modern state must be balanced both by binding rules that limit its authority and democratic responsibility to a populace that eventually has the power to reconstitute the state's leadership. The rule of law and democratic accountability are meaningful in the absence of strong and reliable structures of state authority. A powerless state cannot enforce any laws. On the one hand, the concept of rule of law is highly problematic in its basic theoretical underpinnings. On the other hand, legal orders come in many varieties. The politics of legal systems are multipart and multidimensional. To that extent, China's explicit legal order is not monolithic and, in fact, departs in different areas of the law, with one set of arrangements prevailing in the civil arena and a very different one in criminal law.

States and legal systems are seldom straight or unidirectional which means that there is no single scale of bad-to-good or primitive-to modern that any state can pursue, and so no precisely differentiable "modern" or "pre-modern" legal order. Moreover, the idea of an articulate state, a rule of law, and democratic accountability as strategic machinery of modern governance seems uncontroversial, maybe even obvious or commonplace.

China's hybrid blend of a rule by law regime in the civil arena and a neo-traditional regime in criminal law is among the more common and stable admixtures of possible types[737]. It seems that based on an authoritarian polity, the Chinese state is effective despite lacking control or accountability. Chinese state advances the legitimacy of the political system control exercised through the criminal justice system upholding their rule. Thus, politics influence the application of criminal law to the advantage of specific

[735] *Council of Europe Committee of Ministers, Recommendation Rec (2000) 19 of the Committee of Ministers to member states on the role of public prosecution in the criminal justice system.* Adopted October 6, 2000. Rec 13(b), https://wcd.coe.int/ViewDoc.jsp?id=376859.

[736] Rachel E. Stern, From Dispute to Decision: Suing Polluters in China *The China Quarterly* 206, pp.294-312 (June 2011).

[737] William Hurst & Jessica Teets, Compliance, Resistance, Innovation, and Involution–Assessing the Politics of Experimentation and Diffusion in Jessica C. Teets & William Hurst eds. *Local Governance Innovation in China: Experimentation, Diffusion, and Defiance* London: Rotuleddge, 2015– pp.174-179. William Hurst *Local Governance Innovation in China: Experimentation, Diffusion, and Defiance* (Routledge 2015).

economic elite and against the right application of the rule of law. It has to be taken into account that the rule of law has to apply in both civil and criminal areas within a jurisdiction in order to say that the legal system functions in line with the rule of law. It seems that in both legal systems of Germany and China there is an impact of politics upon the rule of law particularly concerning the implementation of criminal law.

CONCLUSION

The above analysis shows the impact of politics on the law making and the appliance of the rule of law. There is an obvious interference of politics above the rule of law leading to the emergence of the politics of law. Especially, the impact of politics above the law and the rule of law are higher in criminal law cases. It could be said that politics overrule the rule of law not only in international criminal law cases but also on national criminal law cases having an impact upon national and global political affairs.

The rule of law means equality and stability instead of the political approach to implement and interpret the law according to the needs of the prevailing group against the interests of a democratic society. It could be argued that there is a prevalence/ dominance of the Justinian approach concerning the rule of law and politics.

It is worth mentioning that, on March 24, 2016, the ICTY issued its judgment in which the Chamber concluded that there was not enough evidence to find Milosevic guilty of the war crimes and crimes against humanity in which he had allegedly been complicit[738]. The proven innocence of Milosevic is a big blow to the international justice system establishing that politics overrules the rule of law in cases where it counts the application of the rule of law. Finally, it has to be mentioned that judges have shown courage/ bravery in applying the rule of law and objectively the law by acquitting Slobodan Milosevic which means that there is hope for a better application of the rule of law in the future liberated from the chains of politics.

It is worth mentioning here that the judiciary must be independent from other State authorities, but at the same time has to take part in the State monopoly of power. The judiciary is a highly political institution, which simultaneously has to be committed to the law and not to policy. It is part of the entire system of separation of powers in a State and has to control this system all at once. Arbitration is complement State judiciary but not replace it which does not mean that cannot be a co-equal to courts in dealing with civil cases and nor criminal ones. When citizens and companies within a State preferably apply to the courts of arbitration with the purpose of obtaining a decision on their disputes, it cannot be seen as a symptom of the lack of confidence of the society in the

---

[738] G Zekos, *The United States of Europe in place of the European Union*, 2017 Nova Science Publications New York USA. www.novapublishers.com.

quality, impartiality and/or the honesty of their courts but an established independent arbitration[739] and co-equal to courts will strengthen the value of courts by allowing an antagonism for a better justice via a dual co-equal dispute mechanisms which parties by choice can utilize in a single jurisdiction. Besides, as enforcement certainly originates from the State monopoly of power, it requires the participation of a State institution. Arbitration awards by no means will be enforced by a private mechanism but arbitration awards as co-equal to court's judgments can be enforced by the same state enforcement mechanism. Under the conditions of democracy in globalization, state courts cannot be considered to be the single guarantors for the protection of the socially weaker parties. It is worth mentioning here that the parties' choice to solve their dispute via arbitration cannot end up into a joint decision of the arbitration and courts rather than the award of an independent arbitration.

[739] G Zekos, *The Independence of Arbitration*, 2016 Nova Science Publications New York USA. www.novapublishers.com.

Chapter 5

INVESTMENT ARBITRATION

1. INTRODUCTION

The right for commercial arbitration and so for the competence to define *lex mercatoria* as a source of law is also bounded by States, due to the fact that this power originates in the State's own[740] endorsement of an agreement of the disputing parties to withdraw a specific dispute or legal relationship from the primary jurisdiction of the courts and subject it instead to arbitration. To that extent, arbitration is defined or endorsed by the State as .private based on the State's decision to recognize the autonomous decisions of non-State actors to displace the courts competence with a mutually constructed alternative[741]. Moreover, States have established an international adjudicative system, based on investment treaties, that gives to arbitrators a comprehensive jurisdiction over what are in actual fact regulatory disputes.

Investment treaty arbitration is the system of international dispute settlement embedded in a majority of IIAs dealing with prevention against expropriation without sufficient compensation, full protection and security, fair and reasonable treatment, national treatment, most-favoured nation treatment and free transfer of capital and so offering protections to eligible foreign investors for investments made in a host state party to the same IIA. Moreover, Investment treaty arbitration permits private parties to bring direct claims against states, avoiding prior rations of diplomatic espousal under international law[742]. It is worth mentioning that in a typical investment treaty, the nationality of a company is defined by either (a) the place of incorporation or seat of the

---

[740] F Snyder, Governing Economic Globalisation: Global Legal Pluralism and European Law (1999) 5 *Eur L. J.* 334, 341.

[741] A Redfern and M Hunter, *Law and Practice of International Commercial Arbitration* (4th ed., Sweet & Maxwell, London, 2004) 138–9 and 256.

[742] Jan Paulsson, 'Arbitration Without Privity' (1995) 10 *ICSID Review* 232. UNCTAD IIA http://investment policyhub.unctad.org/IIA.

legal entity, or (b) the country of ownership or control of the legal person.' While an investment contract that incorporates an arbitration clause can be assigned to a nonsignatory, the assignment cannot be used to create jurisdiction under the ICSID Convention or investment treaties that would not otherwise exist[743]. Furthermore, Investment treaty arbitrations take place when a foreign investor claims that a state hosting their investment has desecrated one or more of the substantive provisions in an IIA. A BIT is often conceptualized not as an agreement with an investor but as an "offer" by the state, "accepted" by the investor upon filing a claim[744]. Arbitration provisions in BITs "typically refer to investments as defined in the treaty" and the consequence of such a definition may be "that an investment . . . not in compliance with host State law is not covered by the definition of 'investment' and will not benefit from" treaty protection[745]. To that extent, failure to comply with host State law has the effect that there is no valid consent to arbitration under the treaty.

It could be said that ISDS provisions in IIAs predominantly enable foreign investors to opt to bring an investment-related claim to international arbitration or to initiate a proceeding in a domestic court[746]. IIAs specify for investor–state arbitration under ICSID rules or, instead of, under *ad hoc* arbitration governed by the rules of the United Nations Commission on International Trade Law (UNCITRAL)[747].

Furthermore, arbitrations conducted pursuant to investment treaties are distinct from international commercial arbitration, where the latter engages disputes between the State and a private individual for the reason that States are simulated in the commercial context to be acting in a private capacity. Undeniably, it is not always likely obvious to separate sovereign from private acts of the State concerning international arbitration. Nevertheless, to the extent that international commercial arbitration touches regulatory

---

743 Stephen Jagusch & Anthony Sinclair, The Impact of Third Parties on International Arbitration—Issues of Assignment, in *Pervasive Problems in International Arbitration* 291, 298 (Loukas A. Mistelis & Julian D.M. Lew eds. 2006); at 296 ('In the event of an assignment from an investor having the nationality of an ICSID Contracting State to a third person who does not have the nationality of a Contracting State, an ICSID tribunal would lack jurisdiction, although the arbitration may proceed under the ICSID Additional Facility Rules.').

744 *Garanti Koza LLP v. Turkm.*, ICSID Case No. ARB/11/20, Dissenting Opinion of Laurence Boisson de Chazournes, 26 ("[A] mutual agreement is needed for ICSID arbitration to be initiated by the foreign investor," and absent such agreement "*only*" an ad hoc arbitration under UNCITRAL Rules "can be used by the foreign investor."). *Muhammet Çap & Sehil Inşaat Endustri ve Ticaret Ltd. v. Turkm.*, ICSID No. ARB/12/6, Decision on Objection to Jurisdiction, 6.2.1 (Feb. 13, 2015) ("It is a fundamental principle that an agreement is formed by offer and acceptance," and "there must be acceptance of the offer *as made*."); compare W. Laurence Craig, The Arbitrator's Mission and the Application of Law, 21 *Am. Rev. Int'l Arb.* 243, 257 (2010) ("The beneficiary of an arbitration clause in a bilateral investment treaty may be likened to the assignee of a contractual right to arbitrate.").

745 Christoph Schreuer, Jurisdiction and Applicable Law in Investment Treaty Arbitration, 1 *Mcgill J. Disp. Resol.* 1, 4–5 (2014).

746 Joachim Pohl, Kekeletso Mashigo & Alexis Nohen, Dispute Settlement Provisions In International Investment Agreements: A Large Sample Survey 11 (*OECD Working Papers on Int'l Inv.*, 2012/02, 2012), https://www.oecd.org/daf/inv/investment-policy/WP-2012_2.pdf.

747 Ryan McCarl, ICSID Jurisdiction over International Mass InvestmentArbitrations: Due Process and Default Rules, 51 *Stan. J Int'l L.* 173, 174–75 (2015).Felipe Suescun de Roa, Investor-State Arbitration in Sovereign Debt Restructuring: The Role of Holdouts, 30 *J. Int'l Arb.* 131, 142 (2013)(explaining the variance in national laws regarding execution of arbitration awards).

concerns, its category is nevertheless limited to disputes arising from a certain legal relationship between individual and State. Besides, investment treaty arbitration involves all State's regulatory relations with .foreign investors, who are subject to the State's authority[748]. Consequently, investment treaty arbitration is a much clearer example of the State's retreat from adjudication for the reason that it replaces courts with a private model of adjudication in matters of public law.

Investor-State arbitrations can arise out of treaties (commonly although not exclusively Bilateral Investment Treaties (BITs)), national investor protection legislation, and contracts. The parties to investor-State arbitration are the host State and a foreign investor[749]. Peter Turner[750] says that: 'Even though treaties are concluded between states, a characteristic feature of investment treaties is that they confer the right on legal and natural persons (who are not traditionally thought of as subjects of international law) with the nationality one of the contracting states to benefit from the treaty and issue proceedings against the other state.' It is worth mentioning that states offer their consent to submit future investment disputes to arbitration through bilateral investment treaties (BITs), multilateral treaties, or the state's own domestic legislation. Moreover, manifestation of consent by a state is inadequate to confer jurisdiction on a tribunal: the investor has to make some reciprocal act to perfect the consent. Moreover, BITS have their own, analogous jurisdictional requirements[751]. Dispute resolution clauses in investment treaties include numerous conditions prior to the institution of arbitration (conditions precedent), which activates the question of whether they pertain to the tribunal's jurisdiction or admissibility of the claim, in addition to whether they can be somehow avoided[752].

Does investment arbitration depoliticize investment disputes by moving them from a "power-based" to a "rules-based" form of adjudication? Disputes involving claims between foreign investors and host states continue to achieve wide attention. Investment treaties contain numerous provisions activated by poor governance such as inadequately managed expropriations, arbitrary and discriminatory treatment, or failure to offer physical security[753]. In investment treaty arbitrations, Investment tribunals exercise a de

---

[748] Gus Van Harten, The public-private distinction in the international arbitration of individual claims against the state. *ICLQ* vol 56, April 2007 pp 371.394.

[749]Restatement of the U.S. Law of International Commercial Arbitration, Introductory Note to Ch. 5, at 27-29 (30 Mar. 2017) (Tent. Draft no. 5) (distinguishing among 'treaty-based', 'contract-based', and 'statute-based' investorState arbitrations).

[750] Peter J. Turner, Issues of Scope: Parties, Ownership and Control, in *International Arbitration* 2006: Back to Basics? 444, 444 (Albert Jan van den Berg ed. 2007) (ICCA Congress series no. 13).

[751] Robert Wisner & Nick Gallus, Nationality Requirements in Investor-State Arbitration, 5 *J. World Inv. & Trade* 927, 927 (2004) ('A fundamental requirement of all [investor-State] arbitration is that the investor, whether an individual or a corporation, be a national of a specific foreign country.').

[752] Zachary Douglas, *The International Law Of Investment Claims* 151-60 (2009).

[753] Franck, Susan. 2014. Conflating Politics and Development: Examining Investment Treaty Outcomes, *Virginia Journal of International Law*, 55: 1-71. Franck, Susan, and Linsey Wylie. 2015. Predicting Outcomes in Investment Treaty Arbitration, *Duke Law Journal*, 65: 459.

facto lawmaking role, filling the normative gaps left open by the treaty drafters. Harten[754] argues that there is systematic bias on the part of arbitrators in that 'arbitrators tended to favor claimants in general and claimants from major Western capital-exporting states in particular' which means that if it is true, arbitration is losing its credibility as a dispute mechanism and so parties will decide to solve their dispute via courts.

Since the early 2010s, the growing use of ISDS to tackle international disputes comprises intellectual property investments[755]. It has to be taken into account that ISDS arbitrations encompassing intellectual property disputes denote not only a new edge in investment arbitration, but also unknown territory in the more and more multifaceted and challenged landscape of international intellectual property obligations which means that investment law has entered the intellectual property area. Should Intellectual property be excluded from investor-state arbitration? Regardless that Intellectual property arbitration works as part of commercial arbitration, Intellectual property should not be excluded from investor-state arbitration for the reason that providing enhanced protection of IP does fulfill traditional justifications for investment arbitrations because the protection of IPRs[756] adds to the entering of FDI in an economy as an investment.

It is worth mentioning here that there is absence of effective ways to pursue compensation under international law beyond espousal, when a national government prosecutes a claim on behalf of its national, set a special problem for foreign investors, as national governments classically do not permit a private party, not mentioning much less a foreign private party, to sue them for their discretionary decisions and investors' own governments were often unwilling to sue another nation[757]. In 2006, the ICSID amended its rules to include provisions related to "transparency[758]" and UNCITRAL promulgated the United Nations Convention on Transparency in Treaty-based Investor-State Arbitration[759].

There is growth of international adjudication *fora* and the international system of investment dispute resolution has taken centre stage formulating international investment

---

[754] Gus Van Harten, Arbitrator Behaviour in Asymmetrical Adjudication: An Empirical Study of Investment Treaty Arbitration, 50 *Osg. Hall Law J.* 211-68 (2012).

[755] *Philip Morris Asia Ltd. v. Commonwealth of Austl.*, PCA Case No. 2012–12, Notice of Claim (June 22, 2011); *Philip Morris Brands Sàrl v. Oriental Republic of Uru.*, ICSID Case No. ARB/10/7, Request for Arbitration (Feb. 19, 2010). *Eli Lilly & Co. v. Gov't of Can.*, ICSID Case No. UNCT/14/2, Notice of Arbitration, 4 (Sept. 12, 2013). Ruth L. Okediji, Is Intellectual Property "Investment"? *Eli Lilly v. Canada* and the International Intellectual Property System, 35 *U. PA J. Int'l L.* 1121, 1122 (2014).

[756] G Zekos, IPRs' impact upon FDI, 2013 PhD Thesis, Economics Department University of Peloponnese. G Zekos, *IPRs' influence on FDI inflows & FDI outflows in EU*, 2017 Lambert Academic Publishing www.lap-publishing.com www.morebooks.de Germany, G Zekos, *Law and Economics of IPRs*, 2016 Nova Science Publications New York USA. www.novapublishers.com, G Zekos, *IPRs protection and their impact upon FDI, GDP Growth & Trade*, 2013 Scholar's Press, www.scholars-press.com www.morebooks.de Germany.

[757] Matthew Coleman et al., Choosing an Arbitral Forum for Investor-State Arbitration, *STEPTOE* (Jan. 27, 2015), http://www.steptoe.com/publications-10156.html.

[758] Ignacio Torterola, The Transparency Requirement in the New UNCITRAL Arbitration Rules: A Premonitory View, *Inv. Treaty News* (Sep. 23, 2010), www.iisd.org/itn/2010/09/23/the-transparency-requirement-in-the-new-uncitral-arbitrationrules-a-premonitory-view/.

[759] Status: United Nations Convention on Transparency in Treaty-based Investor-State Arbitration, *UNCITRAL*, http://www.uncitral.org/uncitral/en/uncitral_texts/arbitration/2014 Transparency_Convention_status.html.

law[760]. The influence of the arbitrator in investment rule-setting is vital via arbitral interpretation as a "jurisgenerative" process *per se* having an impact on future treaty making[761]. Investment treaties are often concise instruments leaving gaps that tribunals are called to fill in including the *quasi*-totality of bilateral investment treaties (BITs) concluded by EU Member States[762]. Moreover, in general the BITs handle investment in both directions on an equal footing treating investments made by EU investors in third states and third state investors in the respective Member State of the European Union. As to the conduct of arbitration proceedings, the BITs usually refer to the ICSID Convention, to the ICSID Additional Facility or to the UNCITRAL Arbitration Rules. Arbitrators' 'jurisgenerative' powers span over various aspects of an investment treaty and beyond, from provisions respecting jurisdictional and substantive standards to the interpretation of rules of customary international law and the advance of new treaty models[763]. Would arbitration panels acting under a BIT and in accordance with the arbitration rules mentioned above be entitled to request a preliminary ruling from the Court of Justice of the European Union? It could be said that the six factors which the Court of Justice has listed so as to identify a "court or tribunal of a Member State" for the purposes of Article 267 TFEU indicate the answer. In *Miles v European Schools*[764] the Court of Justice held a referral by the Complaints Board of European Schools to be inadmissible for the reason that the Board "does not have any links with the judicial system of the Member States."

Arbitral interpretation sometimes discloses treaty provisions in a light different than the contracting parties had visualized influencing future treaty negotiations. The model BIT revisions is partly led by arbitral interpretations. It is characteristic that under the NAFTA in the 1990s disclosed a host of obligations undertaken under the US BIT programme which had been understood by the US Administration in a different manner than in the claims brought against it in international arbitration[765].

---

760 UNCTAD (2012). Latest Developments in Investor-State Dispute Settlement. *IIA Issues Note, No.1 April 2012*. www.unctad.org/diae, p. 1 Nikos Lavranos (2010), Bilateral Investment Treaties (BITs) and EU Law. *ESIL Conference 2010*, available from: http://ssrn.com/abstract=1683348, p. 2. Jan Paulsson, Lucy Reed and Nigel Blackaby, *Guide to ICSID Arbitration* (Kluwer Law International, 2010).

761 Christoph Schreuer and Matthew Weiniger (2008), A Doctrine of Precedent? In P. Muchlinski, F. Ortino, C. Schreuer (eds.), *The Oxford Handbook of International Investment Law*. Oxford University Press.

762 Catharine Titi (2013), EU investment agreements and the search for a new balance: A paradigm shift from laissez-faire liberalism toward embedded liberalism? *Columbia FDI Perspectives* No. 86, 3 January 2013, www.vcc.columbia.edu.

763 European Commission (2012). *EU Canada Comprehensive Economic and Trade Agreement – Landing zones. DS 1744/12. Brussels*, 6 November 2012 http://www.s2bnetwork.org/fileadmin/dateien/downloads/CETA_-_EU_leaked_investments_protection.pdf CETA Investment Rules Consolidated 7 February 2013, Investment Chapter http://tradejustice.ca/pdfs/CETA_Investment_Rules_%20February7_2013.pdf.

764 CJEU 14 June 2011, Case C-196/09 (*Miles v. European Schools*), [2011] ECR 2011-I, 5105, 41.

765 Kenneth J. Vandevelde (2009). A Comparison of the 2004 and 1994 U.S. Model BITs: Rebalancing Investor and Host Country Interests. In K. P. Sauvant ed. *Yearbook on International Investment Law & Policy 2008-2009*. New York: Oxford University Press, p. 290-292. Walter, A. von (2011). Balancing Investors' and Host States'Rights – What Alternatives for Treaty-makers? In M. Bungenberg, J. Griebel and S. Hindelang eds, *European Yearbook of International Economic Law 2011, Special Issue: International Investment Law and EU Law*. Heidelberg: Springer, p. 141; European Parliament (2011). European Parliament Resolution of 6

As a result of public elements, investment arbitration has transformed into a hybrid procedure in which dispute resolution and the articulation of public interests walk together. Investment treaty arbitration is not a substitute for local institutions; rather, it provides a complement to domestic institutional reform[766]. Endorsing the use of arbitration augments contract enforceability. A larger question is whether investment treaty arbitration advances the rule of law and supplies enticements to further fair and legitimate decision making in national institutions.

Investment arbitration is an influential example of arbitration's ability. Consequently, Investment arbitration and the related use of the WTO dispute settlement system[767] point out that arbitral adjudication has shortened the absolutism of sovereignty in trans-border commercial activity. Thus, States are open to accepting the power of arbitrators and arbitration in exchange for a prize in the profitable business of global commerce[768]. Waibel and Wu[769] argue that arbitrator decisions are influenced by policy preferences, among which home country development status matters greatly. On the other hand, Weijia Rao[770] says *that* "no evidence suggests that arbitrators vote in biased ways to increase reappointment by shaping reputations over time or to cater to entities responsible for a greater number of past appointments." It has to be taken into account that parties confront an arbitrator for disqualification due to evidence indicating "manifest lack of the qualities" required to serve as an arbitrator, which would take in previous decisions or appointments indicative of bias which means that reputation for bias weakens an arbitrator's credibility within a tribunal and erodes their career prospects long term[771].

April 2011 on the future European international investment policy (2010/2203(INI)), P7_TA(2011)0141, recital H.

766 Susan D. Franck, Foreign Direct Investment, Investment Treaty Arbitration, and the Rule of Law *2007 Global Business & Development Law Journal* 337 / *Vol. 19* p 367. Jeswald Salacuse, *The Law of Investment Treaties* 37 et seq. (Oxford 2010).

767 G. Zekos, The case for giving to private parties access to the WTO dispute settlement system, 2007 *Journal of World Investment & Trade* 441. www.wernerpubl.com.

768 Ivar Alvik, Contracting With Sovereignty: State Contracts and International Arbitration (2010); David Schneiderman, Investing in Democracy? Political Process and International Investment Law, 60 U. *Toronto L. J.* 909 (2010); Thomas E. Carbonneau, Arguments in Favor of the Triumph of Arbitration, 10 *Cardozo J. Conflict Resol.* 395, 398 (2009) (Believing the term "mandatory arbitration" is a misnomer. When disagreements involve parties of disparate levels of sophistication and arise from adhesive contracts, arbitration is 'mandatory' only in the sense that it is imposed by the stronger party as a precondition to transacting with the weaker party. It is, therefore, both more accurate and user-friendly to name this form of arbitration 'adhesionary' or 'disparateparty' arbitration.").

769 Michael Waibel and Yanhui Wu, *Are Arbitrators Political? Evidence from International Investment Arbitration* (2017), http://www-bcf.usc.edu/~yanhuiwu/arbitrator.pdf.

770 Weijia Rao, *Are Arbitrators Biased in ICSID Arbitration? A Dynamic Perspective*, https://ssrn.com/abstract=3203019 p23.

771 *Blue Bank International & Trust (Barbados) Ltd. v. Bolivarian Republic of Venezuela*, Decision on the Parties' Proposal to Disqualify a Majority of the Tribunal, ICSID Case No. ARB/12/20, 12 November 2013, at 10 – 13; *Caratube International Oil Company LLP & Mr. Devincci Salah Hourani v. Republic of Kazakhstan*, Decision on the Proposal for Disqualification of Mr. Bruno Boesch, ICSID Case No. ARB/13/13, 20 March 2014, at 15 – 35.

2. Courts in Investment Arbitration

The accessibility of treaty arbitration assists investment by providing adjudicative independence and/or a model for national courts to follow the rule of law. Investment arbitration has the aptitude to fuel domestic support for the rule of law instilling a belief in the capability of institutions to administer justice impartially. National courts are an imperative counterpart to the resolution of investment disputes. Domestic courts of general jurisdiction have little stimulus to compete with specialist arbitral tribunals for the resolution disputes correlated to international law. Investors select between court litigation and arbitration.

National courts provide critical support to the investment arbitration procedure. While a court's role tends to be limited in ICSID arbitration proceedings, national courts have a role to play in enforcing ICSID arbitration awards. The tribunal in *Ping An v. Belgium* upheld 'Belgium's objection to the jurisdiction *ratione temporis*' indicating caution against reading into an IIA by implication consent to arbitration over particular disputes, and particularly pre-existing disputes[772]. Moreover, the jurisdictional decision in *Ambiente Ufficio v. Argentina*[773] stipulates an example of implied jurisdiction or implied consent that is more difficult to patch up with the plain words of the relevant BIT. Furthermore, the tribunal in *Roussalis v. Romania*[774] asserts a straightforward interpretation of the terms of the BIT based on their ordinary meaning and in the context of the ICSID proceedings.

In the context of an ad hoc UNCITRAL arbitration, national courts are playing a greater role[775]. The adjudicative fairness and neutrality of treaty arbitration offers a helpful model for national decision makers and conveniently upgrade adherence to the rule of law. Martin Malin[776] argues that the courts' involvement in an arbitration procedure makes this arbitration a system of public law and otherwise arbitration will be

---

[772] Ping An v. Belgium (2015).Alemanni v. Argentina (2014) *Giovanni Alemanni v. Argentina*, ICSID Case No. ARB/07/8, Decision on Jurisdiction and Admissibility (17 November 2014).

[773] *Ambiente Ufficio v. Argentina* (2013) Ambiente Ufficio S.P.A. (Case formerly known as *Giordano Alpi and Others) v. Argentina* ('*Ambiente Ufficio v. Argentina*'), ICSID Case No. ARB/08/9, Decision on Jurisdiction (8 February 2013).

[774] *Roussalis v. Romania (2011) Spyridon Roussalis v. Romania*, ICSID Case No.ARB/06/1, Award (7 December 2011).

[775] United Nations Commission on International Trade Law ("UNCITRAL") Model Law on International Commercial Arbitration, June 21, 1985, *Annex* 1, art. 13, U.N. Doc. A/40/17, 24 I.L.M. 1302 (1985), http://www.uncitral.org/pdf/english/texts/arbitration/ml-arb/ml-arb-e.pdf(permitting courts to hear challenges to arbitrators).

[776] Martin H. Malin, Privatizing Justice—But by How Much? Questions Gilmer Did Not Answer, 16 *Ohio St. J. on Disp. Resol.* 589, 627 (2001) (positing that "[i]f courts do not review employment arbitration awards for errors of law, we risk transforming a system of public law into a system of private justice"); ("De novo judicial review of arbitral interpretations of law is necessary to . . . ensure that arbitration does not result in contracting out of statutory compliance.").

transformed into a private justice system. It is argued that investment arbitration is an alternate for dysfunctional domestic courts in states with a weak rule of law tradition[777].

The question that has to be answered is if a domestic court system following the rule of law provides a valuable backing to the integrity of the investment treaty arbitration process. An autonomous[778] arbitration dealing exclusively with the dispute resolution without the need to have courts to intervene causing confusion, cost rise and time consuming further enhances investor confidence in the resolution of investment-related disputes by arbitration.

Angualia Daniel[779] argues that "While it is argued that arbitration must be free from courts, in order to be effective, it is also accepted that arbitration needs the support of national courts to be effective." How effective a dispute system could be if it is controlled by another dispute system? What is the use to have an incomplete dispute system such as arbitration as long as it is possible to merely improve courts and eradicate arbitration as it is currently functioning by not be able to deal alone with not even a stage of its whole process? Why is considered that only courts protect the public interest? What is the use of a non-independent dispute system such as arbitration as long as it is not considered to be able to protect the public interests?

A dispute system can be effective only if it is autonomous, complete and independent from commence of its process till the award. Is it time to have arbitration totally independent and complete dispute system co-equal to courts unchained totally from courts' control? Is there a reason for arbitration not be considered co-equal to courts as another independent dispute system in a jurisdiction? Can be suggested that there is a behind the curtain controlling of a single dispute system and so making difficult to allow a totally independent arbitration?

International commercial arbitration is a method by which disputes arising out of international trade and commerce are determined pursuant to the parties' voluntary agreement, through a procedure other than a court of competent jurisdiction. One of the distinguished features of international arbitration is the virtual absence of review on the

---

777 Thomas Schultz, Cédric Dupont, Investment Arbitration: Promoting the Rule of Law or Over-Empowering Investors? A Quantitative Empirical Study. *King's College London Dickson Poon School of Law Legal Studies Research Paper Series*, paper no. 2014-16.

778 Thomas E. Carbonneau, *Cases And Materials On Arbitration Law And Practice* 794 (5th ed. 2009) at 191 ("[T]he view that arbitration is an autonomous and fully-functional adjudicatory process and that the contract of arbitration is the law between the parties ... allows for the possibility that the earlier arbitral award constitutes a final and binding determination of the question, precluding the court from ruling ... on the basis of *resjudicata.")*. Thomas Carbonneau, The Revolution in Law Through Arbitration, 56 *Clev. St. L. Rev*. 233, 266 (2008) ("Individual parties gained access to a viable form of adjudication that provided workable remedies and basic fairness. Arbitral adjudication also had an extensive track record of adaptability to new circumstances ... [aldaptability, expertise, and eventual finality are the principal characteristics of arbitration."); Thomas E. Carbonneau, At the Crossroads of Legitimacy and Arbitral Autonomy, 16 *Am. Rev. Int'l Arb*. 213, 258 (2005) ("The functionality and adaptability of arbitration became attractive in all areas of civil litigation.").

779 Angualia Daniel, *The Role of Domestic Courts in International Commercial Arbitration* September 2010 http://ssrn.com/abstract=1674760 p 9.

merits and so the finality of arbitral awards is a characteristic quality of arbitration and a natural result of the long-recognized principles of *pacta sunt servanda* and res judicata[780].

The rise of international arbitration in the resolution of individual claims against States does not change the fact that adjudication goes to the core of juridical sovereignty. Moreover, the upsurge of international *commercial* arbitration marks a retreat of the State from its classical role in relation to adjudication but it should not be exaggerated because in fact the state shows a retreat without losing the final say on arbitration' award since courts have the final say by keeping the intervention in all stages of arbitral process.

It is worth mentioning that investment arbitration has been portrayed by an approach seen in international commercial arbitration being that of a need for a quick and inexpensive decision to resolve the dispute which means[781] that investors continue to favor finality and so there is no appeal to force the adoption of an Appeals Facility. Besides, Zekos regards that an appellate mechanism re-examining only the legal basis of the award and not encompassing the repeat of the whole process will add to the legality of arbitration with no influence upon time and cost of arbitration. It could be said that the foremost disadvantages of the making of the ICSID Appeals Body embrace jeopardy of the principle of finality, which has always been considered among the key advantages of arbitration over judicial settlement but an appellate step, as zekos proposes, will add to the compatibility among courts and arbitration concerning their legality which lead to the acceptance of an independent arbitration. On the one hand, *ad hoc* investor-State arbitration is presently not perceived as 'doing justice' by a significant part of the public but on the other hand, any ad hoc arbitration with a swift appellate step will do justice in parallel / in competition to courts gaining its independence. Conversely, the advantage of arbitration lies in the punctuality of the proceedings which has not to be undercut for the sake of having an appellate system.

Decolonization and socialism placed emphasis on sovereign control over natural resources, which often conflicted with existing foreign ownership rights[782]. It is worth mentioning that the establishment of an international arbitration mechanism that would depoliticize foreign investment relations by permitting private investors to bring their claims directly against host states before international arbitration tribunals[783]. In line the WTO rules governing amicable settlements are an example of this bidirectional

---

[780] Gary Born, International Arbitration: Law and Practice 8 (*Kluwer Law Int'l* 2012). Doak Bishop & Silvia Marchili, *Annulment under the ICSID Convention* 17 (Oxford 2012). Samuel A. Haubold, Opting Out of the US Legal System:The Case for International Arbitration, 10 *Int'l L. Practicum* 43, 44 (1997) (affirming that "most parties who elect to arbitrate rather than litigate do so because they want finality").

[781] Thomas W. Walsh, Note, Substantive Review of ICSID Awards: Is the Desire for Accuracy Sufficient to Compromise Finality? 24 *Berkeley J. Int'l L.* 444, 446 (2006).

[782] Jonathan Gimblett & O. Thomas Johnson, Jr., From Gunboats to BITs: The Evolution of Modern International Investment Law, in *Yearbook on International Investment Law & Policy* 2010-2011, at 650 (Karl P. Sauvant ed., 2011).

[783] ANTONIO R. PARRA, THE HISTORY OF ICSID (2012). Gus Van Harten, A Case for an International Investment Court (*Soc. of Int'l Econ. L., Inaugural Conference*, 2008), http://digitalcommons.osgoode.yorku.ca/ all_papers/259.

interaction of law and politics. It has to be taken into account that the idea of "arbitration without privity" which today permits an investor to perfect an arbitration agreement with the host state by merely accepting an offer of consent unilaterally given by the host state in the investment treaty is a legal innovation[784].

Furthermore, where the courts' endorsement of arbitration is restrained to commercial disputes between private parties instead of allowing arbitrability to all types of disputes as long as there is parties' agreement, even if one party happens to be a State entity, the State all the same preserves its control over the recognition of party autonomy and of the right of individuals to give up the courts in favor of arbitration, the State holds noteworthy control over the entrustment of this public law. It has to be taken into account that investment treaty arbitration is a kind of public law adjudication, both because it is formed by a sovereign act of the State and because it is used to resolve regulatory disputes. Thus, the rulings of arbitrators pursuant to investment treaties are distinct conventional awards issued in the arbitration of disputes between juridical equals implicating governmental choices that are analogous to the judicial determination of individual property and economic rights in domestic public law. Taking into account that investment treaty arbitration is a category of international commercial arbitration, there is a need to devalue its transformative influence owing to courts' involvement. Moreover, an arbitrator may interpret a stabilization clause in a contract broadly so as to constitute arbitration as a method of government[785].

While investment arbitration incorporates applicable public elements, international commercial arbitration in general is more concerned with determining disputes between two or more parties of different jurisdiction. International commercial and investor-state arbitration involve resolution of international disputes[786]. While commercial arbitration relates to private parties and their interests, investment arbitration has more in common with public international law and so awards of arbitral tribunals in investment arbitrations have the prospective to directly or indirectly alter acts of states[787] and, as a result, the rights and obligations of their nationals. Due to the need for transparency and greater public participation there is increasing number of amicus curiae submissions in NAFTA and ICSID arbitrations[788]. Moreover, arbitrations implicating the State or State entity

---

[784] Jan Paulsson, Arbitration Without Privity, 10 *ICSID Rev.* 232 (1995).

[785] *Texaco Overseas Petroleum Co & California Asiatic Oil Co v. Government of the Libyan Arab Republic (Merits)* (19 Jan 1977), 17 ILM 4.

[786] Zachary Douglas, The Hybrid Foundations of Investment Treaty Arbitration, 74(1) *Brit.Y.B. Int'l L.* 151,151–55 (2003). Hans van Houtte & Maurizio Brunetti, Investment Arbitration: Ten Areas of Caution for Commercial Arbitrators, 29(4) *Arb. Int'l* 553 (2013).

[787] In *Occidental Petroleum Corp. v. Ecuador*, ICSID Case No.ARB/06/11,Award, Oct. 5, 2012, the tribunal found that Ecuador had breached the United States-Ecuador Bilateral Investment Treaty (BIT), and awarded damages in the noteworthy amount of USD 1.77 billion. In*Yukos Universal Ltd. (Isle of Man) v. Russia*, UNCITRAL, PCA Case No.AA 227, Award, Jul. 18, 2014, damages exceeded the amount of USD 50 billion.

[788] Dugan-Wallace Jr.-Rubins-Sabahi, *Investor-State Arbitration* 707-8 (Oxford 2011). Joaquim Delaney & Danili Barstow, Procedural Transparency, in *The Oxford Handbook of International Investment Law* 777 (Muchlinsk, Ortino & Schreuer ed.) (Oxford 2008).

entail openness and transparency due to the public interest created by the conditions[789]. Besides, commercial arbitrations have a public interest aspect, as well[790].

It is worth mentioning that domestic adjudication regularly tenders parties the option to have a judgment of a first instance court reviewed by a court of appeal, and conceivably even to challenge the appeal decision before a supreme court. Besides, in international dispute settlement, judicial review long formed the exception: arbitral awards, such as those of the Permanent Court of Arbitration (PCA) or the Iran-US Claims Tribunal, like judgments of the International Court of Justice (ICJ), are final – no appeal is conceivable, even though there is limited provision for revision. Nonetheless lately established forms of international adjudication permit for appeal such as the proceedings before the World Trade Organization (WTO), the International Criminal Court or the Court of Justice of the EU dealing with public/private disputes. In reality, the piling of mechanisms unreasonably one to control the other it makes the system very slow and even ineffective which means that arbitration in order to keep its features as being an alternative to courts must not follow the same pattern of courts and so the establishment of an appellate step has to be focused only into the investigation of the interpretation of the legal basis in order to avoid any major illegality.

It has to be taken into account that there are problems relating to the existing ISDS mechanism categorized as process-related, interpretation-related, and outcome-related which means that there are substantive and procedural flaws. It is necessary to have a more consistent and predictable arbitration system regardless of what subject matter the investor-state disputes cover. To that extent, in ISDS cases, the absence of consistency and predictability is generally attributed to three reasons. The first reason is that ISDS lacks binding precedents. It could be argued that regardless of the absence of a formal doctrine of binding precedent, investment tribunals[791] depend on earlier awards to reinforce their legal reasoning, often treating them as formative or commanding statements of applicable rules or principles of law which indicates that arbitration is based on law creating res judicata[792] and precedent analogous to courts. It has to be taken into consideration that although it cannot be said that the rule of legal precedent (*stare decisis*) applies in international arbitration in general, investment arbitration[793] has certified an evolution in reported jurisprudence. In an analogous way litigation parties

---

[789] Anthea Roberts, Clash of Paradigms: Actors and Analogies Shaping the Investment Treaty System. 7 *Am. J.Int'l L.* 45, 45-6 (2013).

[790] Gabrielle Kaufmann-Kohler, In Search of Transparency and Consistency: ICSID Reform Proposal, 2 *Transnat'l Disp. Mgmt.* at 1 et seq. (2005). Joaquim Delaney & Danili Barstow, Procedural Transparency, in *The Oxford handbook of international investment law* 721 (Muchlinsk, Ortino & Schreuer eds.) (Oxford 2008).

[791] Marc Bungenberg & Catharine Titi, Precedents in International Investment Law, in *International Investment Law: A Handbook* 1505, 1508 (Marc Bungenberg et al. eds., 2015).

[792] Res judicata does not merely prevent future judgments from contradicting earlier ones, but also prevents litigants from multiplying judgments, and confusion.

[793] Loretta Malintoppi, Independence, Impartiality, and Duty of Disclosure of Arbitrators, in *Oxford Handbook of International Investment Law* 1188, 1196 (Peter Muchlinski et al. eds., 2008), at 789, 792. Christoph Schreuer & Matthew Weiniger, A Doctrine of Precedent? in *The Oxford Handbook of International Investment Law* 1188, 1196 (Peter Muchlinski et al. eds., 2008).

depend on this jurisprudence to reinforce their legal arguments and so tribunals apply these precedents as grounds for their findings which add another argument towards the independence of arbitration.

Even though arbitrators in investment treaty arbitration are not formally bound by precedent in the same manner as common-law judges, there is an unofficial, but influential, system of precedent that compels arbitrators to account for prior published awards and to stabilize international investment law[794] which means that, like judges, arbitrators follow precedent augmenting the rule of law in arbitration. There is unpredictability and incoherence in investor-state dispute settlement in a considerable degree which means the existence of inconsistent decisions in investment treaty arbitrations and so inconsistency of arbitral awards is a common criticism of investment arbitration[795]. On the other hand, arbitration is not litigation which means that it has to keep its characteristics such as a kind of informality. Moreover, ISDS lacks an appellate mechanism and the existing ISDS mechanism does not offer much transparency. It is worth mentioning that even though ISDS cases resolve questions marking noteworthy matters of public policy, the public does not have entrée to the documents, the proceedings are conducted behind closed doors, and the submission of amicus curiae briefs is restricted.

It could be said that the second limitation relates to the lack of finality at the panel stage and many investors, having the ability to swiftly and efficiently resolve a dispute with a sovereign state is one of the main values of ISDS. Thus, it is argued that the introduction of an appellate mechanism undercuts this crucial value of ISDS. It is worth mentioning that the more phases there are in a procedure such as appellate the longer it will take for a dispute to be finally resolved. So far, arbitral rules have fluctuated noticeably, with some jurisdictions permitting arbitral awards to be appealed to local courts. Section 69(1) of the Arbitration Act 1996 specifies, "Unless otherwise agreed by the parties, a party to arbitral proceedings may (upon notice to the other parties and to the tribunal) appeal to the court on a question of law arising out of an award made in the proceedings." Similarly, Section 49(1) of the Singapore Arbitration Act stipulates, "A party to arbitral proceedings may (upon notice to the other parties and to the arbitral tribunal) appeal to the Court on a question of law arising out of an award made in the proceedings." Provided the high stakes involved in ISDS arbitrations and the interconnected controversy and opposition, having an appellate mechanism built into ISDS to make certain grander fairness and legitimacy will alter the good practical

---

794 Cheng Tai-Heng, Precedent and Control in Investment Treaty Arbitration, 30 *Fordham Int'l L.J.* 1014, 1016 (2007) Charles N. Brower & Stephan W. Schill, Is Arbitration a Threat or a Boon to the Legitimacy of International Investment Law? 9 *Chi. J. Int'l L.* 471, 473 (2009).

795 Susan D. Franck, The Legitimacy Crisis in Investment Treaty Arbitration: Privatizing Public International Law Through Inconsistent Decisions, 73 *Fordham L. Rev.* 1521, 1558–82 (2005); Stephan W. Schill, The European Commission's Proposal of an "Investment Court System" for TTIP: Stepping Stone or Stumbling Block for Multilateralizing International Investment Law?, *ASIL INSIGHTS* (Apr. 22, 2016), https://www.asil.org/insights/volume/20/issue/9/european-commissions-proposal-investment-court-system-ttipstepping.

perception which means that any upgrading upsurges its use in new areas, like intellectual property.

In the lack of a doctrine of binding precedent/*stare decisis*, arbitral interpretation did not establish rules that reach beyond the dispute at hand[796]. In line with the International Centre for Settlement of Investment Disputes (ICSID) Convention an award is binding 'on the parties'. While awards rendered by prior tribunals are admittedly 'not a primary source of rules', investment tribunals gradually more depend on them to hold up their legal reasoning by generating standards and expectations about the understanding of often vague or incomplete provisions[797]. To that extent, tribunals cite antecedent awards leading to arbitral precedent. Tribunals refer to earlier awards as common law courts do and so relying on prior awards[798] creating the law by way of interpretation.

Arbitral tribunal interpretive lawmaking relies mainly on filling in treaty lacunae. To that extent, an arbitral competence explicitly provided for in relevant legal texts such as the ICSID Convention, states that in the absence of agreement by the parties on the applicable law, the tribunal employs 'such rules of international law as may be applicable', while if questions of procedure arise not covered by the arbitration rules or any rules agreed by the parties, 'the Tribunal shall decide the question'[799]. Tribunals affect the law through a course of creative interpretation aiding their own policy interests bearing typically pejorative connotations of an adjudicatory institution exceeding its judicial functions and taking up a quasi-legislative role[800]. Within international investment law, awards are favourable to investor interests, since they are generally extending the point and scope of investment protections beyond the purported intentions of the contracting parties[801]. In the *Maffezini* case, the MFN clause was endorsed a broad

[796] Article 53 ICSID Convention. *Cf.* Article 59 of the Statute of the International Court of Justice ('*The decision of the Court has no binding force except between the parties and in respect of that particular case.*'). Christoph Schreuer and Matthew Weiniger, *Conversations Across Cases – Is There a Doctrine of Precedent in Investment Arbitration*, 5 January 2007, p. 2. *Cf.* August Reinisch (2008), The Role of Precedent in ICSID Arbitration, *Austrian Arbitration Yearbook,* 2008.

[797] Enron Corporation and Ponderosa Assets, L.P. v. Argentina, ICSID Case No. ARB/01/3, Decision on Jurisdiction, 14 January 2004, para. 40. Continental Casualty Company v. Argentina, ICSID Case No. ARB/03/9, Annulment Proceeding, 16 September 2011, para. 84, where the Annulment Committee explicitly positioned itself in favour of the materialization of a *jurisprudence constante*. F. Ortino (2012). Legal Reasoning of International Investment Tribunals: A Typology of Egregious Failures. *Journal of International Dispute Settlement* 3 (1), p. 39.

[798] Jeffery P. Commission (2007), Precedent in Investment Treaty Arbitration: The Empirical Backing, *Transnational Dispute Management,* 4 (5), p. 5-6. Christoph Schreuer, *Diversity and Harmonization of Treaty Interpretation in Investment Arbitration*, 7 February 2006, p. 11; Christoph Schreuer and Matthew Weiniger, *Conversations Across Cases – Is There a Doctrine of Precedent in Investment Arbitration*, 5 January 2007, p. 1. (Sempra Energy *International v. Argentina*, ICSID Case No. ARB/02/16, Award, 28 September 2007).

[799] Article 42(1) Article 42(2) Article 44 ICSID Convention.

[800] S. A. Lindquist and F. B. Cross (2009). *Measuring Judicial Activism*. NY: Oxford University Press; T. Tridimas (1996), The Court of Justice and judicial activism. *European Law Review*, 21(3).

[801] UNCTAD (2012). *World Investment Report 2012: Towards a New Generation of Investment Policies.* New York and Geneva: UN; M. Sornarajah (2010), Toward Normlessness: The Ravage and Retreat of Neo-Liberalism in International Investment Law. In K. P. Sauvant ed. *Yearbook on International Investment Law & Policy 2009-2010.* New York: Oxford University Press, p. 618 et seq.; Wei Shen (2011), The Good, the Bad or the Ugly? A Critique of the Decision on Jurisdiction and Competence in *Tza Yap Shum v. The Republic of Peru, Chinese Journal of International Law,* 10 (1) p. 74.

meaning so as to evade a limited local remedies clause – a prerequisite to resort to local courts for eighteen months prior to initiation of arbitration[802]. It has to be taken into account that the *Maffezini* Award caused debate around the applicability of the most-favoured-nation treatment to a treaty's dispute settlement provisions, lately reignited by arbitral awards introducing ambiguity over the issue and postpone its final resolution[803]. There are cases where the arbitrators have produced the law governing investment at the jurisdictional stage involving determination of the range of covered investment by enlarging the definition of covered investment in an attempt to embrace ventures that may not *prima facie* qualify as such. To that extent, tribunals have accepted that comprise investment a contract for the construction of a fertilizer plant, promissory notes, minority shareholdings, loans, accessing an internal market and the procurement of security entitlements in government bonds[804]. The *Salini v. Morocco* Tribunal, in determining the definition of covered investment within the meaning of Article 25 of the ICSID Convention, adopted the *Salini* test which means that the existence of covered investment necessitates 'contributions, a certain duration of performance of the contract', 'participation in the risks of the transaction' and 'the contribution to the economic development of the host State'[805]. The rations set in the *Salini* Award were expanded

[802] F. O. Vicuña (2012), Reports of [Maffezini's] demise have been greatly exaggerated. *Journal of International Dispute Settlement* 3 (2); UNCTAD (2010). Most-Favoured-Nation Treatment. *UNCTAD Series on Issues in International Investment Agreements II*. UNCTAD/DIAE/IA/2010/1. New York and Geneva: UN, p. 66-84.

[803] *Emilio Agustín Maffezini v. Spain*, ICSID Case No. ARB/97/7, Decision on Jurisdiction, 25 January 2000. Marc Bungenberg and Catharine Titi (2013). Developments in International Investment Law. In C. Herrmann, M. Krajewski and J. P. Terchechte eds, *European Yearbook of International Economic Law 2013*. Berlin Heidelberg: Springer, p. 458 et seq. Z. Douglas (2011), The MFN Clause in Investment Arbitration: Treaty Interpretation Off the Rails. *Journal of International Dispute Settlement,* 2(1); S. W. Schill (2011), Allocating Adjudicatory Authority: Most-Favoured-Nation Clauses as a Basis of Jurisdiction – A Reply to Zachary Douglas. *Journal of International Dispute Settlement* 2(2).

[804] *Klöckner v. Cameroon*, ICSID Case No. ARB/81/2, Award, 21 October 1983, *Československá Obchodní Banka (CSOB) v. Slovak Republic*, ICSID Case No. ARB/97/4, Decision on Objections to Jurisdiction, 24 May 1999, para. 283. *Fedax v. Venezuela,* ICSID Case No. ARB/96/3, Decision on Jurisdiction, 11 July 1997, para. 29. *Lanco International, Inc. v. Argentina*, ICSID Case No. ARB/97/6, Preliminary Decision on Jurisdiction, 8 December 1998, 40 *ILM* 457 (2001), para. 10; *Continental Casualty Co. v. Argentina*, ICSID Case No. ARB/03/9, Decision on Jurisdiction, 22 February 2006, paras 77, 86. *Pope & Talbot v. Canada*, NAFTA arbitration, Interim Award, 26 June 2000, para. 96. *Abaclat and Others v. Argentina*, ICSID Case No. ARB/07/5, Decision on Jurisdiction and Admissibility, 4 August 2011, para. 387.

[805] *Salini v. Morocco* Decision on Jurisdiction (*Salini Costruttori S.p.A. and Italstrade S.p.A. v. Morocco,* ICSID Case No. ARB/00/4, Decision on Jurisdiction, 23 July 2001). *Jan de Nul N.V. and Dredging International N.V. v. Egypt*, ICSID Case No. ARB/04/13, Decision on Jurisdiction, 16 June 2006, para. 91; *Joy Mining Machinery Limited v. Egypt*, ICSID Case No. ARB/03/11, Award on Jurisdiction, 6 August 2004, para. 53, (requiring for the existence of investment 'a certain duration, a regularity of profit and return, an element of risk, a substantial commitment and that it should constitute a significant contribution to the host State's development'); *Malaysian Historical Salvors, SDN, BHD v. Malaysia*, ICSID Case No. ARB/05/10, Award on Jurisdiction, 17 May 2007, para. 74; *Helnan International Hotels A/S v. Egypt*, ICSID Case No. ARB/05/19, Decision on Objection to Jurisdiction, October 17, 2006, para. 77. *Fedax and Consortium R.F.C.C. Tribunals* (see *Fedax N.V. v. Venezuela*, ICSID Case No. ARB/96/3, Decision on Objections to Jurisdiction, 11 July 1997, para. 43 and *Consortium R.F.C.C. v. Morroco*, ICSID Case No. ARB/00/6, Décision sur la compétence, 16 July 2001, para. 60. *Biwater Gauff (Tanzania) Ltd. v. Tanzania*, ICSID Case No. ARB/05/22, Award, 24 July 2008, para. 312 et seq. *Electrabel S.A. v. Hungary,* ICSID Case No. ARB/07/19, Decision on Jurisdiction, Applicable Law and Liability, 30 November 2012, *Deutsche Bank AG v. Sri Lanka*, ICSID Case No. ARB/09/02, Award, 31 October 2012, para. 295. *Quiborax S.A. and others v. Bolivia*, ICSID Case No. ARB/06/2, Decision on Jurisdiction, 27 September 2012, para. 219. *Abaclat and Others v. Argentina*, ICSID

raising higher the jurisdictional threshold and the *Phoenix* Award added two new criteria, namely the legality and *bona fide* nature of the investment[806]. However, these requirements have been clearly rejected by the *Saba Fakes* Tribunal concerning the *Salini* condition for investment contribution to the economic development of the host state[807]. The *Tza Yap Shum* Tribunal decided that jurisdiction to decide the amount of expropriation could not but extends to jurisdiction to determine whether there had been an expropriation in the first place, in that way directly enlarging Chinese BITs scope of jurisdiction[808]. In *Abaclat the* tribunal determined that the mass aspect of the proceedings 'relates to the modalities and implementation of the ICSID proceedings and not to the question whether Respondent consented to ICSID arbitration[809]. The Tribunal has the power under Article 44 ICSID Convention to fill any gap and so setting the 'law' permitting future mass claims to be brought into investment dispute settlement.

It is worth mentioning that there is no consistency in the jurisprudence of arbitral tribunals established under different arbitration institutions and rules[810]. To that extent, in investor-State arbitration, litigants have three options to challenge an award that has been delivered in an investor-State dispute settlement (ISDS) process: they can have the award set aside by the courts of the seat of the arbitration; they can resist any enforcement action, expecting that the courts of third States will decline to enforce the award; or, against awards under the Convention on the Settlement of Investment Disputes between States and Nationals of other States (ICSID Convention),they can apply for annulment. Besides, these 'status quo' mechanisms are inadequate for the reason that they do not permit for any substantial review. Moreover, grounds for intervention are limited and do not extend to the merits of awards.

Case No. ARB/07/5, Decision on Jurisdiction and Admissibility, 4 August 2011, paras 362 et seq. Cf. *Toto Costruzioni Generali S.p.A. v. Lebanon,* ICSID Case No. ARB/07/12, Decision on Jurisdiction, 11 September 2009.

806 *Phoenix Action Ltd v. Czech Republic*, ICSID Case No. ARB/06/5, Award, 15 April 2009, para. 114. *Malicorp Limited v. Egypt*, ICSID Case No. ARB/08/18, Award, 7 February 2011, para 109. *Salini Costruttori S.p.A. and Italstrade S.p.A. v. Morocco,* ICSID Case No. ARB/00/4, Decision on Jurisdiction, 23 July 2001, para. 52. ICSID Case No. ARB/00/4, Décision sur la competence, 23 July 2011.

807 *Mr. Saba Fakes v. Turkey*, ICSID Case No. ARB/07/20, Award, 14 July 2010, paras. 110 *et seq*.

808 Article 8(3) *China-Peru BIT. Sr. Tza Yap Shum v. Peru*, ICSID Case No. ARB/07/6, Decision on Jurisdiction and Competence, 19 June 2009, para. 188. Wei Shen (2011), The Good, the Bad or the Ugly? A Critique of the Decision on Jurisdiction and Competence in *Tza Yap Shum v. The Republic of Peru*, *Chinese Journal of International Law* 10 (1). Marc Bungenberg and Catharine Titi (2013). The Evolution and Future of EU-China Investment Relations. In Shan, W. ed. *Collected Courses on International Investment law and Arbitration –* Silk Road Collected Courses in International Economic Law. Brill; E. Dulac (2010), The Emerging Third Generation of Chinese Investment Treaties, *Transnational Dispute Management* 7 (4); Cf. W. Shan and S. Zhang (2013), The Potential EU-China BIT: Issues and Implications. In M. Bungenberg, A. Reinisch and C. Tietje eds, *EU and Investment Agreements: Open Questions and Remaining Challenges*. Baden Baden: Nomos/Hart, p. 90 et seq. Valentina Vadi (2013), Converging Divergences: The Rise of Chinese Outward Foreign Investment and Its Implications for International (Investment) Law, in Karl P. Sauvant (ed.) *Yearbook on International Investment Law & Policy 2011-2012*, New York: Oxford University Press, p. 719.

809 *Abaclat and Others v. Argentina*, ICSID Case No. ARB/07/5, Decision on Jurisdiction and Admissibility, 4 August 2011, *Ambiente Ufficio S.p.A. and others (Case formerly known as Giordano Alpi and others) v. Argentina*, ICSID Case No. ARB/08/9, Decision on Jurisdiction and Admissibility, 8 February 2013.

810 UNCTAD, Reform of Investor-State Dispute Settlement: In Search of a Roadmap, *IIA Issues Note* 2, June 2013, http://unctad.org/en/PublicationsLibrary/webdiaepcb2013d4_en.pdf.

Standards of review are a critical matter in the investment treaty system for the reason that investor-state awards are not presently subject to a full-blown appellate review mechanism[811]. As an alternative, awards issued under the Convention on the Settlement of Investment Disputes between States and Nationals of Other States are subject to annulment on certain bases, which include that the tribunal "manifestly exceeded its powers[812]." To that extent, contracting states recognize awards as binding and to enforce them as if they were final judgments of their own courts[813]. Besides, non-ICSID Convention awards are open to judicial review by domestic courts either seeking to set aside the award in the seat of arbitration under the laws of that state or resisting recognition and enforcement on certain precise grounds of NYC on the Recognition and Enforcement of Foreign Arbitral Awards such as that the award deals with a dispute or matters outside the scope of the submission to arbitration[814].

It is worth mentioning that within investment arbitration, the term 'standard of review' is commonly understood to refer to the intensity of the scrutiny applied by an international arbitral tribunal to prior determinations of fact and/or law made by a host state[815]. Moreover, investment treaties (Investments, Bilateral Treaties [EPIL]) do not clearly express the relevant standard of review for international arbitral tribunals to apply when scrutinizing prior determinations made by host states[816]. Furthermore, in investment arbitration the standard of review is determined by arbitrators exercising their *integral powers* to regulate their own procedures.

It has to be taken into account that investment arbitrators execute a limited role of determining the host state's compliance with investment treaties and awarding compensation in cases of breach but this role is much more confined than the role of domestic public law adjudicators in deciding the legitimacy of governmental conduct and possibly invalidating the conduct of other branches of government[817]. In addition,

---

811 Anthea Roberts, Clash of Paradigms: Actors and Analogies Shaping the Investment Treaty System, 107 *AJIL* 45 (2013).

812 Convention on the Settlement of Investment Disputes between States and Nationals of Other States, Art. 52(1)(b), Mar. 18, 1965, 17 UST 1270, 575 UNTS 159.

813 ICSID Art. 54(1).

814 Convention on the Recognition and Enforcement of Foreign Arbitral Awards, Arts. III, V, June 10, 1958, 21 UST 2517, 330 UNTS 3 .UNCITRAL Model Law on International Commercial Arbitration (June 21, 1 1985), *as amended* July 7, 2006, Arts. 34, 36, *in* UN GAOR, 40th Sess., Supp. No. 17, at 81, UN Doc. A/40/17 (1985),&UN GAOR, 61st Sess., Supp. No. 17, at 56, UN Doc. A/61/17, UN Sales No. E.08.V.4 (2008) .Art. 34(2)(a)(iii); New York Convention, *supra* note 4, Art. V(1)(c).

815 W Werner and L Gruszczynski, Introduction in L Gruszczynski and W Werner (eds) *Deference in International Courts and Tribunals: Standard of Review and Margin of Appreciation* (OUP 2014) 2-16. C Henckels, *Proportionality and Deference in Investor-State Arbitration: Balancing Investment Protection and Regulatory Autonomy* (CUP Cambridge 2015).

816 See the WTO Anti-Dumping Agreement, Art 17.6.

817 Fahner, From Dispute Settlement to Judicial Review? The Deference Debate in International Investment Law in M Duchateau, S Fikkers, L Lane and E van Schagen (eds.) *Evolution in Dispute Resolution. From Adjudication to ADR?* (Eleven International Publishing 2016) 61-85.

investment arbitrators' role is only to determine compliance with international obligations, and they do not 'sit in judgment' over the policies of a host state[818].

It is worth mentioning that the *Pope & Talbot* Tribunal issued an interim award on the merits determining that the NAFTA requirement to offer fair and equitable treatment under Article 1105(1) was independent of the customary international law minimum standard of treatment of aliens[819].To that extent, the NAFTA Free Trade Commission (FTC) delivered some clarifications concerning Chapter Eleven of the NAFTA, including one relating to the treatment under discussion in the *Pope & Talbot* case[820]. In particular, the FTC's clarifications provided that Article 1105(1) NAFTA stipulates the minimum standard under international law. Moreover, the FTC also clarified that the full protection and security standard, equally anchored in Article 1105(1) NAFTA.

Nothing in the Convention's *travaux préparatoires* indicates that investment tribunals should apply the doctrine of *stare decisis*[821]. Judicial decisions are explicitly mentioned in Article 38 of the Statute of the International Court of Justice (ICJ) as 'as subsidiary means for the determination of rules of law'. While customary law, treaties and general principles, also set out in Article 38 of the Statute of the ICJ, are considered as the key or formal sources of international law, doctrine and judicial decisions are classified as subsidiary or material sources.

International law has no doctrine of binding precedent or *stare decisis*. The wording of Article 38 of the ICJ Statute means that judicial decisions are not a means for the *creation* of rules of law. Notwithstanding the lack of any rule on binding precedent in international and in international investment law, many investment tribunals very often refer to preceding investment law cases in their decisions[822]. Investment tribunals refer to decisions of courts and tribunals when coping with issues other than international investment law[823].

Significant is the influence of arbitral decisions on subsequent treaty practice upon the US and Canadian Model BITs of 2004, leading to a new generation of – more balanced – investment treaties that take into consideration the host states' right to regulate, as expressed in particular through the more frequent use of exceptions for policy space[824]. It has to be observed that this paradigm shift has taken place in North America,

---

[818] ICSID, *Enron Corporation and Ponderosa Assets LP v. Argentina*, 2004, paras 29-30; ICSID, *Continental Casualty Company v. Argentina*, 2008, para 199.

[819] *Pope & Talbot Inc v. Canada, (NAFTA) Award on the Merits of Phase* 2, 10 April 2001, paras 105 et seq.

[820] *NAFTA Free Trade Commission Clarifications Related to NAFTA Chapter 11*, 31 July 2001 http://www.worldtradelaw.net/nafta/chap11interp.pdf.

[821] Michael Waibel, Coordinating Adjudication Processes, Paper No. 6/2014 January 2014 *Law Legal Studies Research Paper Series* http://www.law.cam.ac.uk/ssrn/.

[822] Mohamed Shahabuddeen, *Precedent in the World Court* (Cambridge: Cambridge University Press, 1996), 1.

[823] Gilbert Guillaume, The Use of Precedent by International Judges and Arbitrator, 2 *Journal of International Dispute Settlement* (2011): 5-23.

[824] Peter Muchlinski (2009), Trends in International Investment Agreements: Balancing Investor Rights and the Right to Regulate. The Issue of National Security. In K. P. Sauvant ed. *Yearbook on International Investment Law & Policy 2008-2009*. New York: Oxford University Press; Catharine Titi (2013), EU investment

while European treaty practice has stayed unchanged[825]. Arbitral interpretation has led to a revision of the wording employed in North American treaty practice.

European Model BITs have not followed the route of their North American counterparts because the bulk of their investment treaties have concluded with developing countries[826]. Moreover, EU Member States have had only minor exposure to arbitration, so their bilateral investment treaties have been predominantly protective of their own multinational enterprises in their ventures in the developing world[827]. To that extent, the surfacing of the South as a source of investment and the new trend of concluding treaties between developed countries is expected to augment arbitration activity concerning EU Member States and consequently the power of the arbitrator in the system[828]. It is worth mentioning that the European Union's proposal for the investment chapter ("EU Proposal") calls for the establishment of a new investment court system[829]. Thus, the solution proposed by the European Commission is to include an Investment Court System (ICS)[830] in the investment chapters of pending EU Free Trade Agreements (FTAs), such as the Transatlantic Trade and Investment Partnership (TTIP), the EU–Vietnam FTA and the Comprehensive Economic Trade Agreement (CETA) with Canada. The CJEU has accepted that the jurisdiction of international courts or tribunals to assert on the legality of EU measures, considering that even a remote option of such a ruling will be in conflict with the EU legal order[831].

Even in the absence of a doctrine of binding precedent, extensive citations of earlier awards and arbitral influence on future treaty making are to some extent foreseeable.

agreements and the search for a new balance: A paradigm shift from laissez-faire liberalism toward embedded liberalism? *Columbia FDI Perspectives* No. 86, 3 January 2013, www.vcc.columbia.edu.

825 Catharine Titi (2013), EU investment agreements and the search for a new balance: A paradigm shift from laissez-faire liberalism toward embedded liberalism? *Columbia FDI Perspectives* No. 86, 3 January 2013, www.vcc.columbia.edu.

826 UNCTAD's Country-specific Lists of Bilateral Investment Treaties http://unctad.org/en/Pages/DIAE/International%20Investent%20Agreements%20%28IIA%29/Country-specific-Lists-ofBITs.aspx.

827 UNCTAD (2013), Recent Developments in Investor-State Dispute Settlement (ISDS), *IIA Issues Note* No. 1 (Revised) May 2013, www.unctad.org/diae, p. 29-30.

828 UNCTAD (2009). The Protection of National Security in IIAs. *UNCTAD Series on International Investment Policies for Development*. UNCTAD/DIAE/IA/2008/5. New York and Geneva: UN, p. 17; P. Economou and K. P. Sauvant (2013). FDI Trends in 2010-2011 and the Challenge of Investment Policies for Outward Foreign Direct Investment. In K. P. Sauvant ed. *Yearbook on International Investment Law & Policy 2011-2012*. New York: Oxford University Press, p. 13. Cf. A. Joubin-Bret, M.-E. Rey and J. Weber (2011), International Investment Law and Development. In M.-C. Cordonier Segger, M. W. Gehring, and A. Newcombe eds, *Sustainable Development in World Investment Law*. Alphen aan den Rijn: Kluwer Law International, p. 19, 21-22.

829 European Comm'n, *European Union's Proposal for Investment Protection and Resolution of Investment Disputes (2015)*, http://trade.ec.europa.eu/doclib/docs/2015/november/tradoc_153955.pdf.

830 European Commission, *Report - Online public consultation on investment protection and investor-to-state dispute settlement (ISDS) in the Transatlantic Trade and Investment Partnership Agreement (TTIP)*, SWD (2015) 3 final, 13 January 2015 TTIP: Agreed text as of November 2015, http://trade.ec.europa.eu/doclib/docs/2015/november/tradoc_153955.pdf; EU-Vietnam FTA: Agreed text as of January 2016, http://trade.ec.europa.eu/doclib/docs/2016/february/tradoc_154210.pdf; CETA: Agreed text as of February 2016, http://trade.ec.europa.eu/doclib/docs/2016/february/tradoc_154329.pdf.

831 Opinion 2/13 on the Accession of the European Union to the European Convention for the Protection of Human Rights and Fundamental Freedoms; Opinion 1/09 on the establishment of a European Patent Court (8 March 2011, ECR 2011 I-01137).

Treaty texts explained in greater detail, clarifications and interpretive statements, as well as subsequent authoritative interpretations, and treaty renegotiations are some methods available to countries to offset the quasi-legislative power of the arbitrator and make certain that arbitral interpretation better echoes the choice of the negotiating parties.

BG Group v. Argentina examined whether it is the arbitral tribunal that has the exclusive say on its own competence or whether national courts have a role in making certain that arbitral tribunals cannot depart from the consent of the parties[832]. Moreover, the Supreme Court, in *BG Group PLC v. Republic of Argentina*, ruled that the standard of review U.S. courts should apply when examining investment treaty awards to verify whether an arbitral tribunal exceeded its powers[833]. The Supreme Court agreed to review the case and ultimately reversed the Court of Appeals and ordered that the award be reinstated[834]. It is argued that national courts has to engage the Vienna Convention and accord international investment treaty awards deference consistent with the "ordinary meaning" of the relevant investment treaty diminishing the likelihood of subjecting investment treaty awards to changeable standards of review protecting the sovereign desire of the state parties to the treaty.

It is characteristic that in *Republic of Ecuador v. Occidental Exploration & Production Co* held that to decide whether the arbitral tribunal had "*substantive*

---

[832] Michael Waibel, *Investment Arbitration: Jurisdiction and Admissibility* 24 (Univ. of Cambridge Legal Studies Research Paper Series, No. 9/2014, 2014), http://www.academia.edu/8680141/Investment_Arbitration_Jurisdiction_and_Admissibility. José Alvarez & Gustavo Topalian, The Paradoxical Argentina Cases, 6 *World Arb. & Mediation Rev.* 491, 510 (2012) ("recurrent jurisdictional issues in Argentine cases"). Michael Waibel & Yanhui Wu, *Are Arbitrators Political?* 36 (2011) (cited with author permission) (empirical study of ICSID arbitrations provides support for hypothesis that "arbitrators in full time private practice are more likely to affirm jurisdiction," a result "significant for the jurisdictional stage alone"). Anthea Roberts & Christina Trahanas, Judicial Review of Investment Treaty Awards: *BG Group v. Argentina*, 108 *Am. J. Int'l L.* 750, 754 (2014) (criticizing the Supreme Court for using interpretive tools from contract and commercial arbitration contexts in evaluating a case about investor-state arbitration under the Argentina-UK investment treaty).

[833] Jarrod Wong, *BG Group v. Republic of Argentina:* A Supreme Misunderstanding of Investment Treaty Arbitration, 43 *Pepp. L. Rev.* 541 (2016) at 547 ("[T]he U.S. courts should have viewed the arbitration agreement between BG Group and Argentina through the prism of the U.K.-Argentina BIT and its provisions on investor-state dispute settlement and interpreted the BIT under international law in reviewing the *BG Group* award instead of relying exclusively on FAA case law."). W. Laurence Craig, The Arbitrator's Mission and the Application of Law, 21 *Am. Rev. Int'l Arb.* 243, 257 (2010) ("The beneficiary of an arbitration clause in a bilateral investment treaty may be likened to the assignee of a contractual right to arbitrate.").

[834] BG Grp, *PLC v. Republic of Argentina*, 134 S. Ct. 1198, 1213 (2014). *Republic of Argentina v. BG Group, PLC*, 764 F. Supp. 2d 21, 35 (D.D.C. 2011) (To create duties to a third-party beneficiary, "the parties' intent to benefit a third-party [must] be shown on the face of the contract."), rev'd, 665 F.3d 1363 (D.C. Cir. 2012), overruled by 134 S. Ct. 1198 (2014); *Spears, Leeds & Kellogg v. Cent. Life Assurance Co.*, 85 F.3d 21, 26, 27 (2d Cir. 1996) ("No agreement is required between the parties to the arbitration before a non-member may invoke [the Exchange Rules]"; "[the claimants'] lack of direct contact with [the broker] does not prevent them from asserting their rights as third party beneficiaries"; and "a beneficiary need not be identified prior to seeking enforcement of its rights under a contract."). *BG Grp., PLC v. Republic of Argentina*, 134 S. Ct. 1198, 1206, 1208 (2014) ("we shall initially treat the document before us as if it were an ordinary contract between private parties"; "relax[ing] our ordinary contract assumption" changes nothing since "a treaty is a contract"). John James Barceló III, Substantive and Procedural Arbitrability in Ad Hoc Investor- State Arbitration—*BG Group v. Argentina*, in *Contemporary Issues In International And Mediation: The Fordham Papers* 355, 360, 362 (Arthur W. Rovine ed., 2015) ("All these and similar preconditions represent 'claims selecting rules' not preconditions to the formation or validity or scope of the arbitration agreement[;] . . . [t]hese issues thus have a 'procedural' cast."). See *BG Grp., PLC v. Republic of Argentina*, 134 S. Ct. 1198, 1223 (2014) (Roberts, C.J., dissenting) ("A court can assess compliance with the requirement at least as well as an arbitrator can.").

jurisdiction[835]," the relevant question was "whether, on the true construction of the [treaty]...the Tribunal has jurisdiction to determine the dispute.[836]" Thus, the prospect of having an award set aside or not enforced provides an inducement for arbitrators to scrutinize their approach to jurisdiction and not overreach which means that arbitrators do apply law and arbitration is not lawless[837].

In the end, Investment Treaty Arbitration offers equal opportunities to favor both States and foreign investors but the problem does not arise only when it is realized that there are more awards or arbitrators appearing biased in favor of one or the other side because the problem is that investment treaty arbitration offers such opportunities in the first place[838].

Although there is no formal rule of precedent in investment law, parties and tribunals plentifully refer to prior arbitral interpretations in subsequent cases, comprising but not limited to disputes including the same treaty and so this practice has given rise to a sort of "investment common law" and so a body of investment case law that is used to reveal the meaning of core IIA provisions across treaties[839].

Aside prospective disadvantages in terms of extra cost and length of proceedings, it is clear that an appellate mechanism, reviewing only the legal basis of the award and not reopening the whole process from the beginning, augment the coherence, consistency, and, ultimately, the public reading of the legitimacy of international awards[840].

The existence of a parallel judge-made rulemaking process influences how states as principal lawmakers construct their treaties and so where they disagree with arbitral interpretations, states utilize their normative powers to contract unambiguously out of arbitral case law. On the other hand, states can also plainly approve an arbitral interpretation. To that extent, where arbitrators resolve a difficult/new issue not predicted by the drafters, their interpretation may operate as a template in future treaty-making. It could be said that arbitration is contributing to law making which means getting acceptance in the official public law making and in a way e-quality in producing precedent. Thus, it is the first step in awarding equality to arbitration as a dispute system which means the need for eliminating the courts' intervention in arbitration process.

---

[835] Arbitration Act 1996, c. 23, § 30 (Eng.) ("arbitral tribunal may rule on its own substantive jurisdiction, that is, as to . . . what matters have been submitted to arbitration in accordance with the arbitration agreement"—subject to "challenge" "in accordance with the provision of this Part").

[836] *Republic of Ecuador v. Occidental Exploration & Prod. Co.*, [2006] EWHC 345, [79] (Comm), [2006] 1 Lloyd's Rep. 773 (High Ct.), *aff'd*, [2007] EWCA Civ 656 (Ct. App.).

[837] Gus Van Harten, Sovereign Choices and Sovereign Constraints: Judicial Restraint in Investmen Treaty arbitration 45–46 (2013); GusVanHarten, Arbitrator Behaviour in Asymmetrical Adjudication: An Empirical Study of Investment Treaty Arbitration, 50 *Osgoodehall L.J.* 211, 214–16, 237–40, 252 (2012).

[838] Relja Radovic, Inherently Unneutral Investment Treaty Arbitration: The Formation of Decisive Arguments in Jurisdictional Determinations, 2018 *J. Disp. Resol.* (2018).

[839] Florian Grisel, The Sources of Foreign Investment Law, in The Foundations Of International Investment Law: Bringing Theory Into Practice 213, 223-33 (Zachary Douglas et al. eds., 2014); Anthea Roberts, Power and Persuasion in Investment Treaty Interpretation, 104 *Am. J. Int'l L.* 179 (2010).

[840] *Reuters Report*, 29 Oct. 2015, http://www.reuters.com/article/2015/10/29/us-trade-ttip-idUSKCN0SN2 LH20151029; *Borderlex PRO, Daily EU trade briefing*, 14 Apr. 2016, http://www.borderlex.eu/pro-daily-news-todays-headlines/.

Finally, Soft law generates "*legalitis*" that diminish the appeal of arbitration as an adaptable system of dispute resolution. Moreover, Soft law enhances the flexibility or adaptability of the law introducing greater uncertainty, as undermining the rule of law. Thus, soft law utilized ex post by arbitrators to fill legal gaps in IIAs can fuel fears of "elitist" global actors bypassing legitimate national legislatures. It could be said that forms of soft law are perceived as *lex mercatoria* chosen by MNEs, or "the market" which means that its aid can propagate understandings that the investment regime and ISDS favors an ideologically prejudiced application of international law.

Chapter 6

WTO Arbitration Mechanism

1. Introduction

The WTO is the institutionalized umbrella of the multilateral trading system (MTS) succeeding the earlier diplomacy based General Agreement on Tariffs and Trade (GATT). Moreover, it is a semi-autonomous regime that promulgated its own administrative, legislative and judicial procedures and so illustrates a certain degree of self-sufficiency. Arbitration is often preferred to traditional court proceedings because it can offer the prospect of reaching a relatively economical final solution by specialist arbitrators through a quick and often less formal procedure. The discrete character of arbitral proceedings can add to its attractiveness, particularly when trade secrets are involved. Furthermore, arbitral awards are quite easily enforced both in the country of origin and abroad. It can be said that the two basic principles underlying arbitration are that of party autonomy and that of limited judicial review of arbitral awards. The principle of party autonomy is reflected in the consensual nature of the parties' choice to have their claims arising out of their contractual relationship submitted to arbitration; in the selection of the arbitral tribunal; and the applicable law and the autonomy afforded to the parties in structuring the proceedings. The control by courts of arbitral awards takes the form of a review of final awards on limited grounds. The arbitration will be subject to the law chosen by the parties, unless the arbitrators have been authorized by the parties to decide the dispute *ex aequo et bono*.

Additionally, an important feature of arbitration is the *res judicata*, the binding effect of arbitral decisions that lead to a total or partial settlement of a dispute. The moment when, and the circumstances under which, an award assumes its *res judicata* effect are determined by national arbitration law. Finally, the procedure for setting aside an award is an exception to the general rule of the finality of arbitral awards.

Arbitration also has a number of advantages for international litigants. It allows the use of rules of procedure which are less formal and more flexible. This leads to a process that is less time-consuming and expensive and which can be tailored to handle the specific characteristics of each dispute. Furthermore, in arbitration proceedings none of the litigants enjoy a home court advantage, thus increasing the international acceptability of the resulting awards. In the field of international trade, by allowing individuals or entities direct access to resolving a dispute to settle claims against a state, arbitration reduces the potential politicization of this kind of litigation. Let us now investigate if these principles or advantages of arbitration are applicable in the case of arbitration under the General Agreement on Tariffs and Trade (GATT) and the World Trade Organization (WTO).

2. From GATT to WTO

GATT still exists as an internal part of the WTO Treaty as included in GATT 1994, which includes the text of the original GATT agreement—called GATT 1947—together with amendments. GATT was originally an agreement containing the results of multilateral tariff negotiations undertaken at the initiative of the U.S. and the U.K. after World War II. GATT contained commercial disciplines, the purpose of which was to ensure that governments would effectively respect multilateral tariff reductions and maintain the overall economic balance of tariff concessions.

The purpose of the initially limited GATT dispute settlement rules was to maintain the balance of reciprocal rights and obligations relating to tariffs and non-tariff measures. The ultimate sanction for involuntary compliance with a panel recommendation was a unilateral readjustment of concessions.

WTO, like GATT, is about market-access guarantees. It can be said that the main principles of GATT law are still applicable to the WTO agreement. The purpose of the dispute settlement mechanism of WTO is to guarantee WTO members full access to their expected commercial and competitive opportunities. However, it seems that the only remedy that can be recommended by a WTO panel is to bring the measure into conformity with the WTO agreement. If the losing member does not bring its measure into conformity with the WTO agreement, the panel, and the appellate body recommendations, then compensation may be agreed upon. Enforcement is difficult because a WTO member not directly affected by the dispute may not be interested in initiating the dispute settlement mechanism. A member state may not have the legal standing to do so. The retaliation possibilities under the WTO may appear to be inadequate, taking into account that smaller countries are not economically able to retaliate effectively against stronger economies. This handicap of the GATT dispute settlement mechanism has not been completely overcome.

The WTO, as did GATT, contains a set of binding rules, but noncompliance by a party leads only to the re-establishment of the balance of economic concessions between the parties. Under the WTO agreement—as it was under GATT—the losing party does not risk any fine or any sanction affecting its membership status in the case of noncompliance with a panel recommendation. The WTO agreement has established an integrated system for the settlement of all WTO disputes whereby WTO members can base their claims on any multilateral trade agreement contained in Annexes 1, 2, and 3 of the WTO. This seems to remedy the fragmentation of the old GATT and the forum shopping possibilities. The WTO agreement seems to have a single understanding for which there is one single dispute settlement mechanism. The GATT/WTO dispute settlement process is open exclusively to WTO members.

Disputes are decided by *ad hoc* tribunals to which independent experts are appointed. Panel decisions can be appealed to the newly created Standing Appellate Body, composed of international lawyers. The WTO Dispute Settlement Body (DSB) is bound to approve the decisions of panels, unless it decides not to do so by consensus. WTO dispute settlement is short, when compared to most domestic litigation. The DSB consensus would have to be reached within thirty days after the decision has been circulated. If the losing party does not implement the decision within a reasonable time (usually fifteen months) the winning party can retaliate.

3. Characteristics of the WTO Dispute System

The WTO is not a "soft law" scheme subject matter to independent freedom of choice and negotiated modifications in case of non-compliance by Members. Expert dispute settlement bodies such as panels, the newly established Appellate Body and arbitration have to make their awards based on legal principles. On the other hand, law has to be interpreted by means of the "customary rules of interpretation of international law" and applying the principles of interpretation, provided for in the Vienna Convention on the Law of Treaties of 1969.[841]

It has to be taken into account that there is growing workload of the World Trade Organization (WTO) Appellate Body. Moreover, dispute settlement activity has amplified over the years, both in terms of the number of appealed cases and the length of submissions, but also concerning the difficulty of matters extended and the number of participants[842].

General international law is the basis for the resolution of disputes within which the DSU and its rules function. So, DSU functions inside of the international legal order.[843] *Ad hoc* panels have been retained but an appellate review has been introduced, conducted

[841] Article 3.2 of the DSU. Giorgio Sacerdoti, The Dispute Settlement System of the W.T.O.: Structure and Function in the Perspective of the First 10 Years, Research Paper No. 07-03, IDC-Bocconi University., Rachel Brewster, "Rule- Based Dispute Resolution in International Law," 72 *Va. L. Rev*. (2006) 251.

[842] Claus-Dieter Ehlermann, The Workload of the WTO Appellate Body: Problems and Remedies, 20 *J. Int'l Econ. L.* 705, 706. (2017).

[843] *US–Gasoline*, p. 17, *DSR* 1996:1, p.3 at 16.

by a permanent body endowed with most of the characteristics representative of an international tribunal. Appellate review characterizes most of interstate litigation submitted to dispute resolution bodies.

Moreover, an appellate review of arbitral awards is a progress ousting national courts involvement in judicial review of awards regardless that in general appellate review is not established yet in *ad hoc* justice relying on an arbitral agreement between the parties to a dispute. On the other hand, the award of the dispute settlement bodies does not result in *per se* binding judgments' (awards) but they are instead recommendations addressed to the parties in dispute all the way through the Dispute Settlement Body. The lack of officially obligatory results of the awards issued by the panels and of the Appellate Body is a weakness of the new system. By contrast, Sacerdoti[844] thinks that "what is generally deemed by legal observers to be a weakness, namely the lack of formally binding effects of the findings the panels and of the Appellate Body establishing whether there has been a breach of a WTO obligation, should be viewed rather as an advantage of the new system."

Formally awards deriving from the Dispute Settlement Body (DSB) are considered to be mere recommendations. Hence, the WTO political body becomes the source of the award and takes that decision by adopting a panel or Appellate Body report. Moreover, it is the political body calling for performance from the Member concerned and eventually authorizes retaliation as a sanction, if the dispute has not been resolved in accordance with the rules, principally by on time compliance.[845] Putting the influence of the entire WTO after any decision resolving a dispute persuades performance by making the political consequences of non-implementation unbearable for any party that has to face the whole WTO, and not just its antagonist in the dispute. The system intends at avoiding the defeat of certainty in the organizations' reputation that would otherwise follow. At the enforcement point, the DSU takes into consideration the economic and political responsibility faced by States when they have to embark on legislative or administrative changes in order to comply with the supposed award.[846] A State has a rational period of time to comply, a time that can last up to 15 months, and even beyond, from the date of adoption of an award.[847] On the other hand, according to the general principle of international law a State has to remedy a violation of a legal obligation *ex tunc* and not only *ex nunc*.

The DSU echoes the objective to limit and define the suitable function of the dispute settlement mechanism regardless that disputes are decided by autonomous and unbiased institutions through application of the WTO rules, these institute have not been defined as

---

[844] Giorgio Sacerdoti, The Dispute Settlement System of the W.T.O.: Structure and Function in the Perspective of the First 10 Years, Research Paper No. 07-03, IDC-Bocconi University. p5.

[845] Article 21.1 of the DSU.

[846] John H. Jackson, 'International Law Status of WTO Settlement Reports: Obligation to Comply or Option to "Buy Out"'? 2004 *American Journal of International Law* 98, 109–123, p. 109.

[847] Article 21.3 of the DSU.

judicial institutions spelling out that awards by either the DSB, panels or the Appellate Body cannot enhance or lessen the rights and obligations presented in the covered agreements.[848] The function of panels, according to Article 11 of the DSU (reflecting the GATT), is to help out the DSB in fulfilling its tasks under the DSU.

Recommendations and decisions are intended at accomplishing an acceptable settlement of the matter in accordance with the rights and duties under the DSU and the covered agreements.[849] On the other hand, the award of a dispute mechanism should be enforced as such and not to be acceptable. Furthermore, the DSB adopts, instead of awards being directly enforced, reports by panels and the Appellate Body within the time limit of 60 or 30 days after their issue, except if "the DSB decides by consensus not to adopt the report."[850] The DSB does not decide according to its own rules, but just approves the suggestion contained in the report and the parties fulfill the suggestion of the report.[851]

The Appellate Body has been developed according to the pattern of other international tribunals composed by people with experience in law, international trade and the subject matter of the covered agreements, appointed on a personal basis appointed for a 4-year term. On the other hand, there is a need member of the panels and the appellate body to be appointed an individual any time only for a specific case. Presently, a certain number of people are appointed to WTO based not only on knowledge but also on a lobbying mechanism as well. Independence, impartiality and competence should be ensured with attention to avoid any conflict of interest is required like in any judicial body. Appellate Body' set-up increases the role of individual members in sharing the accountability for every decision because an exchange of views among all members takes part before the decision in any appeal. Panels and the Appellate Body do not refer an issue to intergovernmental political bodies.[852] At least functional independence from the WTO is ensured at the appellatc level.[853]

The role delegated to is, without any hesitation, that of judging. The task of panels and the Appellate Body should be to settle a dispute between WTO Members by estimating the conventionality of the measures or the behavior of the defendant assumed by the claimant to be in violation of a legal requirement owed to it under a treaty and so they should function as judicial bodies rather as semi judicial and semi political bodies trying to balance their theoretically judicial duty with politically balanced interpretation of rules and customs. There is a need for an objective assessment of the facts based only

---

[848] Article 3.2 and 19.2 of the DSU.

[849] Article 3.4 of the DSU.

[850] Articles 16.4 and 17.4 of the DSU.

[851] Appellate Body Report, *EC – Export Subsidies on Sugar*, para. 334; upon adoption the recommendation of a panel "will become a recommendation or ruling of the DSB."

[852] Article 17.12 of the DSU.

[853] Steve Charnovitz, 'Judicial independence in the WTO', in Laurence Boisson, Cesare. Romano, Ruth Mackenzie (eds.) *International Organizations and International Dispute Settlement: Trends and Prospects* (Transnational Publishers, New York 2002), 219–240 at p. 219.

on international law. The bodies deal with issues of international legality and do not seek at assessing and awarding damages. The dispute is resolved through the issuance of what is in fact a declarative judgment deciding which party is right and which one is wrong with reference to customary international law rules of interpretations.[854]

The Appellate Body has paid attention to the terms of the treaty provisions with a systematic and precise recourse to the interpretative criteria laid down in Articles 31 and 32 of the Vienna Convention.[855] There is highlighting on the ordinary meaning of the terms of the treaty rather to the purpose of the parties of the treaty in order to avoid giving too much weight on the political balance of interests of the WTO. The Appellate Body has to be engaged in judicial law making as a real judicial body.[856]Moreover, in the WTO, even though the dispute panels and the Appellate Body are not entailed to follow any precedent, they have used previous cases for explanation and support. As the Appellate Body reasoned in *Japan—Taxes on Alcoholic Beverages*, the use of earlier relevant cases generates legitimate expectations among WTO Members[857].

All WTO Members, in respect of all the WTO agreements, are bound by the DSU and subject to WTO dispute settlement proceedings. Jurisdiction is exclusive and so members cannot apply to other *forum* or they can consider violations by other members.[858] The dispute settlement institutions interpret scientifically a complete and significant collection of agreements. On the other hand, the DSU does not ascribe the effect of binding precedents to prior appellate decisions in the same matter.[859] Panels and the Appellate Body cannot directly influence the legal position of third parties to the dispute.[860]

Actually, by introducing a permanent Appellate Body in charge of reviewing the awards in law of the first instance panels, the findings of this institution should serve as guidance in future cases. Moreover, Article 3.2 of the DSU illustrates the general role and function of the dispute settlement mechanism as "providing security and predictability to the multilateral trading system" and "preserve the rights and obligations of Members under the covered agreements" by assisting WTO Members in the implementation of their WTO obligations, and in their dealings within the WTO which that it is not a precisely judicial dispute mechanism. Panels rely on and conform to the jurisprudence of the Appellate Body and so one third of panel reports have not been appealed. It is vital that panels and the Appellate Body cannot be officially defined as "tribunals" because of the lack of authority to resolve disputes with binding effect on the parties on the basis of

---

[854] Article 3.2 of the DSU.

[855] WTO Appellate Body Repertory of Reports and Awards 1995-2004, www.wto.org.

[856] José Alvarez, *International Organisations as Law-Makers* (Oxford 2005). Gregory Shaffer, *Defending Interests. Public-Private Parnership in WTO Litigation*, (Washington, D.C., Brookings Institution Press, 2003).

[857] Appellate Body Report, *Japan—Taxes on Alcoholic Beverages*, WTO Docs. WT/DS8/AB/R, WT/DS10/AB/R, WT/DS11/AB/R (adopted Oct. 4, 1996).

[858] Articles 23 of the DSU.

[859] Raj Bhala, *Modern GATT Law* (Sweet & Maxwell, London 2005).

[860] Article 19.2 of the DSU.

adjudication alone, that is, the lack of *res iudicata* effect of panel or Appellate Body awards. However, the transformation of reports into judgments builds up to it all the way through the approval of the reports by the DSB, since acceptance takes place mechanically on the basis of the "negative consensus" rule.[861] The DSB has no authority to alter reports, even though it is entitled to not adopt them.

The binding *res judicata* power of adjudicatory institutions derives from the agreement of the parties to assign the binding resolution of their dispute to a specific dispute settlement system (*ad hoc* or permanent tribunal). Adjudication generates obligations for the parties explicitly those contained in the decision, and, so, establishes new legal standards between them. On the other hand, WTO adjudication influences all the members all the way through their participation in the monitoring of execution and bilateral adjudication should be subject to multilateral inspection or recognition before being enforceable *erga omnes*. Thus, known the inevitable adoption of any report, the undisputed will of all members would be required in order to set such report aside, not detracting from the legal character of the adjudication. In the WTO, the annulment of a report once issued would entail not only the assent of the parties to the litigation, but, in addition, the consent of the total WTO.[862]

The DSB is not a judicial body with regard to which panels and the Appellate Body would exercise only an advisory or simply preparatory function. The DSB is a political body and its role is just that of granting, without any judgment regarding the merits of the case, official binding force on the decisions of the particular disputes, issued by panels and the Appellate Body, which act in reality as the judicial bodies of the WTO.[863] In fact, they do not issue judgments or awards, but only make advisory reports containing recommendations to the Members. The DSB is assigned with approving the awards of the adjudicatory institutions, rather than with powers of independent decision.[864] Arbitration is a faster option than the normal panel process but international arbitrations can be quite costly as well taking into consideration the fact that arbitration procedure has adopted many formalities occurring in litigation. Even though arbitration is within WTO law, it is not administered by the DSU nor is subject to acceptance by the DSB.[865] States often

[861] Article 16.4 and 17.14 of the DSU.

[862] WT/DS184/19 of 8 July 2005 and WT/DS176/16 of 1° July 2005.

[863] Horn, H., Mavroidis, P. and Nordström, H. (1999). Is the Use of the WTO Dispute Settlement System Biased? Center for Economic Policy Research Discussion Paper 2340. Shaffer, G. (2003). How to make the WTO Dispute Settlement System Work for Developing Countries: Some Proactive Developing Country Strategies in Towards A Development-Supportive Dispute Settlement System in the WTOS, ICTSD resource paper no. 5: 5–65.

[864] EC – ACP/EC Partnership Agreement, Recourse to Arbitration Pursuant to the Decision of 14 November 2001, Award of the Arbitrator, 1 August 2005 (WT/L/616).

[865] Article 25 Arbitration 1. Expeditious arbitration within the WTO as an alternative means of dispute settlement can facilitate the solution of certain disputes that concern issues that are clearly defined by both parties. 2. Except as otherwise provided in this Understanding, resort to arbitration shall be subject to mutual agreement of the parties which shall agree on the procedures to be followed. Agreements to resort to arbitration shall be notified to all Members sufficiently in advance of the actual commencement of the arbitration process. 3. Other Members may become party to an arbitration proceeding only upon the agreement of the parties which have agreed to have recourse to arbitration. The parties to the proceeding shall agree to abide by the arbitration

resort to arbitration or to the judiciary only as an extreme choice when negotiations are unsuccessful to resolve a dispute.[866]

The TRIPS Agreement entails WTO members to promulgate enforcement procedures, institute fair and equitable enforcement procedures, decide cases on the merits, and permit for appellate review of trial court decision. Individuals without an interest in the dispute comprise the panel producing a report containing a binding decision. After the panel produces the report, the participants may review it, and present comments to the panel which the panel has to consider implementing them. After review, the panel may either amend its previous report, or ignore the proposed comments. At the conclusion of this process, the dispute settlement board adopts the panel's report. Adoption of the report is involuntary upon finally approval by the dispute settlement board. However, there is an appeals process nations may participate in should they be discontented with any portion of the panel's report. Article 17 provides the procedures and rules governing the appeal process. Thus, for instance, the object of the DSU proceedings is to effectuate compliance with the TRIPS Agreement[867].

Is the DSU effective? DSU, the WTO's enforcement system, is at least somewhat unproductive[868]. In fact, key states of the WTO have decided the destiny of the DSU by implicitly declaring it a setback[869].

The DSU relies entirely on members to complain about other member's unfulfilled obligations because time passes before a member discovers, for instance, noncompliant copyright. Effectuating the DSU procedure takes too long. The DSU permits only members to ask for consultation which means that the efficacy of the DSU depends on nations to claim non-compliance ousting companies needing urgent action. Dependence on members diminishes the possibility of determining whether a nation, for instance, complies with the TRIPS Agreement.

The WTO provisions protect private rights only in indirect ways by entailing WTO members to protect private rights to trade, intellectual property rights protected by the TRIPS Agreement, private rights of due process in administrative proceedings, private rights of access to national courts or, especially to international arbitration. WTO dispute settlement mechanism over private intellectual property rights, the permissibility of

---

award. Arbitration awards shall be notified to the DSB and the Council or Committee of any relevant agreement where any Member may raise any point relating thereto. 4. Articles 21 and 22 of this Understanding shall apply mutatis mutandis to arbitration awards.

866 EC – ACP / EC Partnership Agreement, Recourse to Arbitration Pursuant to the Decision of 14 November 2001, Award of the Arbitrator, 1 August 2005 (WT/L/616).

867 Yuka Fukunaga, Securing Compliance through the WTO Dispute Settlement System: Implementation of DSB Recommendations, 9 *J. Int'l Econ. L.* 383, 386 (2006) (discussing the implementation of DSB recommendations). Wilfred J. Ethier, Intellectual Property Rights and Dispute Settlements the World Trade Organization, 7 *J. Int'L Econ. L.* 449, 455 (2004).

868 In Bad Company, *The Washington Times*, Oct. 11, 2006, at A14 (stating the U.S. refuses to assent to Russia's accession to the WTO until Russia complies with the TRIPS Agreement).

869 Anna Smolchenko, Music Web Site Blocking WTO Bid, *Moscow Times* (Ru.), Oct. 6, 2006 ("'I have a hard time imagining Russia being a member of the WTO with [AllofMP.com] operating,' [U.S. Trade Representative Susan] Schwab told reporters.").

amicus curiae submissions and WTO politics continue to be hesitant to declare that the purpose of WTO provisions should protect private transactions, other private interests and legitimate expectations of private rights holders. The guidelines for the participation of non-state actors all the way through *amicus curiae* submissions by increasing the "accountability" of the dispute settlement mechanism seem not to have any further developments. Additionally, other proposals designed to increase party control over the dispute settlement procedure. Since judicialized dispute settlement requires politically intricate constraints on key countries of the WTO and does not materially advance their economic interests, then there is modest basis to expect continued support which is against the principle of the existence and function of a dispute mechanism which is supposed to be the achievement of justice and an equally fair treatment of all parties.

It has to be taken into consideration that the WTO Appellate Body[870] offers a good example of an often-used international appellate mechanism and as it is the central model on which the European Commission has chosen to base its ICS Appellate Tribunal proposal. Moreover, it is argued that the formation of a standing Appellate Body for investment matters is visualized by the European Commission[871] as a course making certain consistency and augmenting the legitimacy of the system by subjecting awards to review.

4. Arbitration under WTO

During the Uruguay round of multilateral negotiations, contracting parties agreed to further strengthen the dispute settlement system.[872] There are numerous layers to the WTO's dispute resolution body.[873] Unlike the classic civil justice system, in which the winning party is able to force the losing side to comply with the court's judgment forthwith, in the WTO construct a decision by the panel or appellate body is often just the preliminary point for a lengthy arbitration process which eventually results in a settlement that the parties jointly agree to be bound by. Surprisingly, this means that the parties themselves may amend a judicial order to the extent required to make it acceptable to all parties.

Taking into consideration that arbitration has a long history and has been applied to extensively varying types of disputes among States, an elastic concept, arbitration spans from informal to formal procedures, which may result in nonbinding advisory opinions or

---

870 https://www.wto.org/english/tratop_e/dispu_e/stats_e.htm.

871 *European Commission Fact sheet: Investment Protection and Investor-to State Dispute Settlement in EU agreements*, Nov. 2013, at p. 9, http://trade.ec.europa.eu/doclib/docs/2013/november/tradoc_151916.pdf.

872 BISD, 365/61FF.

873 Understanding the WTO: Settling Disputes, *The World Trade Organization*, available at http://www.wto.org/english/thewto_e/whatis_e/ tif_e/disp1_e.htm.

binding awards, and so involving *ad hoc* proceedings along with adjudication before what are permanent 'courts of arbitration'[874].

In fact, WTO arbitration is provided for in articles 21.3c[875], 22.6, and 25 of the DSU, Article 8.5 of the Agreement on Subsidies and Countervailing Measures, and Articles XXI:3 and XXII:3 of the General Agreement on Trade in Services. While these sections are all named arbitration, there are differences in jurisdiction. Arbitration under Article 21.3(c) decides the periods in which the respondent must abide by the rulings of the DSB. Arbitration under Article 22.6 settles on the suspension level of concession that the respondent objects to in the proposal of the complaining party. It should be distinguished that the DSU has no rigorous rule on the connection between Articles 21.5 and 22.6. If a respondent did not employ rightly, then there is a problem whether the complaining party must first use Article 21.5, then Article 22, or if it can straightforwardly invoke Article 22. According to Joost Pauwelyn,[876] arbitration does not have an optimistic future and does not match under WTO's Dispute Settlement Mechanism.

It is worth mentioning that the possibility of resorting to arbitration within the WTO as an alternative means of dispute settlement is stipulated in Article 25 DSU[877]. Moreover, arbitration under Article 25 is different from other types of arbitration because it is actually alternative dispute resolution. Even though the arbitration alternative has very infrequently been utilized, it has to be utilized predominantly if quick and successful legal remedy cannot be attained through ordinary panel and Appellate Body proceedings.

Moreover, article 25 DSU allows WTO Members the freedom to devise their own adjudicatory dispute settlement mechanisms, to define the scope of their jurisdiction and to design their procedural architecture which means that this freedom is subject to the predominant duty of consistency with the covered agreements not resulting in the nullification or diminishing of benefits accruing to other Members under those agreements, nor in hindering the accomplishment of any point of those agreements.

In addition, article 25 invoked in U.S. Section 110(5) of the Copyright Act.[878] It is obvious from Paragraph 4 of Article 25 that Arbitration is an alternative dispute resolution for the Panel Process. Moreover, paragraph 4 of Article 25 states: "Article 21 and 22 of this Understanding shall apply *mutatis mutandis* to arbitration award" and arbitrators in that case recognized this. Article 25.2 DSU sets forth the prerequisite that

[874] Jackson H. Ralston, *International Arbitration from Athens to Locarno* 153 (1929).

[875] Arbitration under Article 21.3 (c) of the Understanding of the Rules and Procedures Governing the Settlement of Disputes, United States – Anti-Dumping and Countervailing Measures on Large Residential Washers from Korea, circulated on 13 April 2017, WT/DS464/RT.

[876] Joost Pauwelyn, The Limits of Litigation: "Americanization" and Negotiation in the Settlement of WTO Disputes, 19 *Ohio St. J. on Disp. Resol.* 121 (2003) at 138.

[877] Scott Anderson et al., *Using Arbitration Under Article 25 of the DSU to Ensure the Availability of Appeals* (Graduate Institute Geneva, Working Paper No. CTEI-2017-17, 2017). T. Payosova, G. Clyde Hufbauer and J. Schott, *The Dispute Settlement Crisis in the World Trade Organization: Causes and Cures* (Peterson Institute for International Economics, Policy Brief No. 18-5,2018).

[878] United States—Section 110(5) of the U.S. Copyright Act Recourse to Arbitration under Article 25 of the DSU, para. 2.4, WT/DS160/ARB25/1 (Nov. 9, 2001) (using arbitration as an alternative to negotiation).

disputing parties wanting to recourse to arbitration enter into a mutual agreement to arbitrate, '[e]xcept as otherwise provided in the DSU'. Nevertheless, arbitrators justified recourse to arbitration under Article 25 on the grounds that "Article 22.2 refers to 'negotiations […] with a view to developing mutually acceptable compensation.' There is no language in that provision which would make it impossible to consider arbitration as a means of reaching a mutually acceptable compensation." Nevertheless, any other arbitration is not alternative dispute resolution but somewhat the only procedure the parties have if they refer their disputes to third parties. The need to use arbitration as an alternative means to resolve disputes had been decided. Thus, there should be notification of recourse to arbitration and the parties should be notified and agree to abide by the arbitration award.

It could be said that arbitration exists *within* the WTO dispute settlement system being subject to the exclusive jurisdiction of that system which is an integral part of, and not a *self-governing alternative to*, the WTO dispute settlement system. Somewhat, it is an alternative to panel and Appellate Body proceedings within the broader dispute settlement system.

As mentioned above, the Dispute Settlement Body (DSB) has the authority to establish panels, adopt reports, maintain surveillance of implementation of rulings and recommendations, and authorize suspension of concessions and other obligations under the various agreements that are incorporated in the final WTO act. All WTO members participate in the DSB.

Arbitration under WTO largely confirms principles already agreed upon in the GATT decision. In GATT practice, bilateral arbitration has rarely been employed in resolving disputes. There is a lack of detailed provisions regulating the procedures to be followed, and parties have to agree upon the procedures to be used in their arbitral process. The arbitration agreement links to an already existing dispute (submission agreement) or to disputes arising in the future (general arbitration agreement). Moreover, in the latter case, the agreement has to stipulate for compulsory arbitral jurisdiction, Consequently, the arbitration agreement has to lay down the arbitration procedures, which would involve the number of arbitrators and the method of their selection, but also the applicable basis of the arbitral award indicating the applicable law or empowering the arbitrators to provide a ruling on equitable grounds (*ex aequo et bono*). The parties have the autonomy to define the issues of a dispute to be brought into arbitration. However, there are also limitations on the autonomy of parties in arbitration, and the resort to arbitration is integrated into the multilateral WTO dispute settlement system. The agreement to arbitrate has to be disseminated to all members of the WTO, in contrast with the established principles of arbitration where there is a need only for the parties' agreement to arbitrate a specific issue. So, third parties can become parties to the arbitration.

Which are the essential elements of an article 25 arbitration[879] agreement? The following are the contents of an arbitration agreement: commencement of proceedings, parallel and subsequent proceedings[880], appointment of arbitrators and secretarial support, arbitration terms of reference, procedural rules, third party participation and interpretation, correction, revision, annulment and appeal. In line, the arbitration agreement has to specify that, if the importance or span of an award is unclear or if there is a clerical error in the award, the arbitral tribunal interprets it or corrects it upon a party's demand. In addition, the agreement provides for a right to request revision of an arbitral award, such as upon discovery of new facts or evidence, reducing the risk of a disputant by declaring its own determination of nullity, addressing the likelihood of annulment of an award. Moreover, the arbitration agreement extends for full appellate review of awards by a separate arbitral body identified in the agreement, predominantly with the aim of replicating the aids of panel and Appellate Body proceedings.

The arbitration award is sent to the DSB where any member may raise any point relating thereto, and hence the award becomes a subject of consideration by all the members of the WTO, rather than the parties taking part in the arbitration. The discrete character of arbitration is abolished by this demand. Arbitration has been transformed into an open-to-the-public litigation hearing rather than an arbitration procedure. The award will be legally binding on the parties to the proceedings and may be enforced pursuant to Articles 21 and 22 of the DSU. The arbitral tribunal cannot enforce its award, but the DSB is responsible for its application, although not in the sense that national courts enforce international arbitral awards.

Moreover, aside from an appellate process to re-examine disputed legal interpretations, the main change lies in the fact that the scale of trade sanctions is now subject matter to central oversight through an arbitration process under DSU Article 22.[881] The consequence of this arbitral process has been to decrease the magnitude of the trade (or other) sanctions that the complaining state(s) may enforce. It could be taken into consideration that panel and appellate proceedings can make use of electronic arbitration. Also arbitration as provided for in article 21.3(c), 22.6, and 25 DSU could be run by means of electronic arbitration model. As mentioned above, the DSU provided that the member must maintain its objective to put into practice within 30 days of the DSB's adoption of the Panel/Appellate Body report. If the complainant is not pleased by the respondent's proposal, the parties then may consult on a reasonable period of time for implementation.[882] If there is disagreement, this matter may be referred to arbitration for an implementation timeframe. A guideline for arbitrators set out in the DSU states that the period should not exceed 15 months and so disputed issues usually pertain to the

---

879 *Appellate Body Report*, Mexico – Taxes on Soft Drinks (2006), at 53.

880 Mexico – Taxes on Soft Drinks (2006).

881 WTO, United States – Continuing Dumping and Subsidy Offset Act of 2000, Recourse to Arbitration by the United States under Article 22.6 of the DSU.

882 Art. 21.3 DSU art. 19.1.

length of a reasonable period of time and the ambiguous language of the DSU led to several early WTO decisions embracing the 15-month standard. In all cases the responding party raised arguments concerning domestic legislative procedures. Moreover, the ambiguous language of 21.3c has led to confusing decisions and has revealed unresolved technical issues.[883] Domestic legislative procedure is the most frequent factor addresses in the arbitration's decisions (awards). Article 21.3 arbitrations are important mechanisms for balancing the respondent's need for an indefinite compliance period and the petitioner's desire for immediate compliance. Thirty-nine cases resulted in findings against the respondent state but resulted in further arbitration or panel discussion. Even in cases where there have been judicial decisions, there were many occasions in which these cases were remanded for additional arbitration and panel discussion, which as a rule led to a commonly agreed result between the parties rather than the implementation of a judicial decision in its total.

For instance, the controversy between the United States and the Republic of Korea (Korea) regarded the obligation of definitive anti-dumping and countervailing duties by the United States Department of Commerce (USDOC) on imports on Large Residential Washers from Korea[884]. Both the Panel and the Appellate Body found the anti-dumping measures enacted by the USDOC to infringe provisions of the Agreement on Implementation of Article VI of the Anti-Dumping Agreement, the SCM Agreement, and the GATT.

As a result of the failure of the resulting consultation between Korea and the United States, Korea requested the passable period of time to be determined through binding arbitration under Article 21.3 (c) of the DSU. Consequently, on 12 January 2017, Claudia Orozco selected as Arbitrator under Article 21.3 (c) of the DSU so as to decide the time period within which the United States needed to comply with the recommendations and rulings of the DSB. The Arbitrator's award was issued by April 2017. Moreover, article 21.3 (c) DSU is to be interpreted in common with other provisions of the DSU providing context to it which means that account must be taken of Article 21.1 DSU, establishing that "prompt compliance" with the DSB's recommendations and rulings is essential "to ensure effective resolution of disputes" and also of the introductory clause of Article 21.3 DSU calling for a rational period of time for implementation in the case it is "impracticable to comply immediately." To that extent, the rational period of time has to be settled on the footing of the means of implementation available to the Member concerned which means that the concerned Member's municipal law has to be taken into account. In line, the choice of the available means of implementation is submitted to the

---

[883] US-Gambling WT/DS285/13 (2005), EC-Sugar Subsidies WT/DS 283/14(2005), US-Offset Act WT/DS217/14-WT/DS234/22 (2003), US-Copyright WT/DS160/12 (2001), EC-Tariff Preferences WT/DS246/14 (2004), Argentina-Bovine Hides WT/DS155/10 (2001).

[884] Panel Report, *United States – Anti-dumping and Countervailing Measures on Large Residential Washers From Korea*, adopted on 26 September 2016, WT/DS646/R; Appellate Body Report, *United States – Anti-dumping and Countervailing Measures on Large Residential Washers From Korea*, adopted on 26 September 2016, WT/DS464/AB/R.

Member State's discretion, given that the means are suitable in form, nature and content to bring the Member into compliance with its WTO obligations[885].

As a result, the Arbitrator detected that the period rationally required for the implementation of the DSB's recommendations and rulings concerning the Washers countervailing duty investigation are shaped by a partial sequencing of the proceedings for implementing the DSB's recommendations and rulings vis-à-vis the anti-dumping measures which means that the realistic period of time in this dispute should have been longer than the time necessitated for the Section 129 countervailing duty proceeding. Moreover, the Arbitrator underlined the significance of the principle of prompt compliance under Article 21.1 DSU.

It has to be taken into account that the arbitration procedure under Article 21.3(c) DSU is a consolidated means for constraining the implementation of the DSB's recommendations and rulings into the frame of a reasonable period of time, in the case immediate compliance is unfeasible to accomplish. It is a way for balancing two opposite interests, on the one hand the respondent's interest in an indefinite compliance period and on the other the petitioner's one of immediate compliance. Thus, the Arbitrator in this dispute has indicated, the theoretical foundation of the procedure lies in the principle of prompt compliance under Article 21.1 DSU, of which Article 21.3 DSU[886] is the direct procedural expression which means that the provision at stake guarantees that the parties involved in a dispute comply with the issued recommendations and rulings within a specific deadline. Eventual reason of the procedure is the successful resolution of the dispute for the benefit of all WTO Members and for the establishment of the WTO rule of law.

Article 3.5 DSU specifies that arbitration awards 'shall be in line with the covered agreements and shall not nullify or prejudice profits accruing to any Member under those agreements, nor hinder the attainment of any objective of those agreements'. Thus, the arbitration award is final and binding on the disputing parties (Article 25.3 DSU) and does not rest on the Dispute Settlement Body (DSB) approving the award or taking any other action. Furthermore, while there is no prerequisite that arbitration awards be published, absence of publication inhibits the award from serving to make clear WTO law and wielding precedential influence beyond the parties in dispute and any intervening third participants.

Nevertheless, Article 25.3 DSU does stipulate that arbitration awards shall be notified to the DSB and the Council or Committee of any relevant agreement, which in practice makes certain that the award will come into the public domain. In that context, In

---

[885] *Colombia – Textiles*, circulated 15 November 2016, WT/DS461/13, para. 3.4; *US – Countervailing Measures (China)*, circulated on 9 October 2015, WT/DS437/16, para. 3.3; *China – GOES*, circulated on 3 May 2013, WT/DS414/12, para. 3.2; and *Colombia – Ports of Entry*, circulated on 2 October 2009, WT/DS366/13, para. 64.

[886] Shin-yi Peng, How Much Time Is Reasonable - The Arbitral Decisions under Article 21.3(c) of the DSU, *Berkeley Journal of International Law* 26, no. 1 (2008): 325.

addition, article 25.3 also specifies that 'any WTO Member may raise any point' regarding the arbitration award, which means that the award has to be fully dis-closed to the entire WTO membership and so in reality, it is difficult to preclude an award from being made public[887].

Furthermore, it is worth mentioning that Article 21.3 of the DSU indicates that a Member found to be in violation of its WTO obligations has to cope with the rulings and recommendations of the Dispute Settlement Body right away. When immediate compliance is unworkable, nonetheless, the Member shall have a "reasonable period of time" to implement the DSB's rulings and recommendations. The "reasonable period of time" may be "the period of time proposed by the Member concerned, provided that such period is approved by the DSB" or "a period of time mutually agreed by the parties to the dispute." If neither of these two alternatives is achievable, Article 21.3(c) provides that the "reasonable period of time" shall be "a period of time determined through binding arbitration." Arbitrators are selected by the parties to the arbitration or, if they cannot agree on an arbitrator, the Director-General appoints the arbitrator. Consequently, under Article 21.3(c) arbitration has been conducted by Appellate Body Member acting in his individual capability.

It is worth mentioning that an arbitration award made under Article 25 DSU is subject to the same implementation surveillance and enforcement regime as panel reports and Appellate Body reports. Moreover, article 25.4 DSU offers that Articles 21 and 22 DSU shall apply *mutatis mutandis* to arbitration awards which mean that such awards have the same status as recommendations or rulings of the DSB, as revealed in panel reports or Appellate Body reports, when applying Articles 21 and 22 DSU. In other words, an arbitral award comprises a final settlement of a dispute once it has been reported to the parties and entered into effect. Furthermore, an award is not become applicable where it is developed by irregularities so severe that it institutes a nullity, such as if the award is not based on a valid arbitration agreement, a party has been denied justice, or the arbitral proceedings have nit observed due process or other fundamental procedural requirements. On the other hand, even though Articles 21 and 22 DSU make certain that—once an arbitral award has been handed down—the award is recognized and enforceable, these articles do not stipulate a procedure whereby a declaration of nullity could be reviewed, confirmed, formalized and publicized. Moreover, the DSU does stipulate any other procedure whereby an arbitral award is annulled or set aside or refused recognition or enforcement or otherwise declared ineffective. To that extent, a respondent declaring a nullity declines to abide by the award and as an alternative start new dispute settlement proceedings directed against the complainant's measures to enforce the award which means subjecting the award to *indirect* panel and Appellate Body review. Correspondingly, a *complainant* claiming that an arbitration award is a nullity would be

---

[887] *Appellate Body Report*, US – Stainless Steel (Mexico) (2008), at 160.

persuaded to start following panel proceedings on the basis of its original claim being a clear case of *res judicata*.

As discussed earlier, the procedure for arbitration is not provided in the DSU or any other WTO agreement. The only procedure for arbitration is for disputes under Article 8.5 as presented by the SCM committee[888] being a documents-only arbitration. Article 19 of the procedure states: "Arbitration proceedings shall be conducted on the basis written submissions and documents." However, Article 20 states: "The arbitration body also may hold meetings with the Parties and shall hold one such meeting if any Party so requests at an appropriate stage of the proceedings." It has to be taken into account that this procedure is not binding in any other form of arbitration and the parties to the disputes must choose the procedure to be followed. Consequently, the parties may agree to conduct electronic arbitration without any impediment. Additionally, disputes arising from retaliation measures may be referred to arbitration. The following conditions must be fulfilled: the losing party objects to the level of suspension proposed, or the party claims that the principles and procedures have not been followed where a complaining party has requested authorization to cross-retaliate.

This arbitration can be carried out by the original panel but there is a possibility that the director general will appoint another arbitrator who can be an individual or a group. Thus, the new dispute system is an integrated system in the sense that disputes related to instruments annexed to the WTO agreement can be treated by the same panel. This is rather different from cases where, upon the parties' agreement to arbitrate a specific claim, an arbitral tribunal is established in order to solve the dispute. There is a time limit of sixty days in which the arbitration should be completed. The arbitrator does not examine the nature of the concessions or other obligations to be suspended, but determines whether the level of the suspension is equivalent to the level of nullification or impairment. The allowance of the proposed retaliation under the covered agreement is investigated by the arbitrator.

The arbitrator's decision shall be accepted by the parties as final, which means that there is no recourse to an appellate body and therefore a court's review of the award. Hence, slight modifications of the suspension of concessions could result from the intervention of the arbitrator, who may influence the mode of cross-retaliation and the level of suspension of concessions, and whose recommendations must be followed by the DSB, barring negative consensus. The creation of the appeals body and the possibility of a review of panel reports strictly for legal mistakes will contribute to the judicialization of the dispute settlement procedure. It could therefore be said that the principles of litigation rather than that of arbitration have influenced the whole understanding of the structure of the dispute settlement mechanism.

---

[888] *Committee on Subsidies and Countervailing Measures*, *Procedures for Arbitration under Article 8.5 of the Agreement on Subsidies and Countervailing Measures*, arts. 19-20, G/SCM/19 (June 2, 1998), available at http://www.wto.org/english/ news_e/news98_e/scm19.htm.

During the 2014 there was neither any awards circulated dealing with the determination of reasonable periods of time for implementation of DSB recommendations under Article 21.3 of the DSU, nor any arbitration on the level of nullification or impairment pursuant to Article 22.6 of the DSU[889].

CONCLUSION

It could be said that GATT arbitration procedure, originating from the simple language in article XXIII, developed into a comprehensive system. GATT arbitral practice was promoted as an answer to expanding pressures for a comprehensive system for coping with international trade disputes. The main disadvantage is that the initiation of proceeding depends on the discretion of other states. It seems that in practice, arbitration will play a minimal role in disputes under the WTO, as has happened under GATT. In fact, all claims brought in the WTO context have to be espoused by a member state and need to be lodged against another member country and not an enterprise or an entity. The dispute settlement procedures still engender a great deal of political attention, which seems disproportionate, rather than being arbitral proceedings enveloped with the advantages of international arbitration. Hence, procedures under both GATT and WTO reflect the political negotiation from which they arose.

The enforcement of arbitral awards under WTO depends upon the economic strength of the losing country rather than the application of legal rules of enforcement of international commercial arbitrations. The applicable law is defined by the treaty rather than by the parties' agreement, although the arbitrator decides the arbitral procedure. The discrete character of arbitration is not retained under WTO arbitration. National courts have little role to play in arbitrations where the arbitral award is referred to states.

The character of the WTO itself is intergovernmental regardless that disputes often relate to particular industries or even single companies and that they are carried out by States in their interest, if not officially on their behalf. Private parties lack *locus standi* at the WTO, but its dispute settlement proceedings are meant to serve their interest. The general acceptance of the legitimacy and binding effects of the WTO dispute settlement proceedings is a significant accomplishment and precedent. On the other hand, there is a need for a reform to admit claims by private parties and granting to the judicial organs the power to award damages.

Currently the use of decidedly legalized mechanisms to resolve trade disputes turns more on practical and appropriate calculations than on an abstract commitment to judicial dispute resolution. It is worth mentioning here that the dispute settlement system under GATT/WTO has undergone a process of legalization, judicialization and adjudication but

---

[889] *WTO Case Law in 2014*, http://ssrn.com/abstract=2587648.

the arbitral decisions under articles 21.3c of the DSU cause a number of legal questions that may threaten the certainty and predictability of the WTO regime. The WTO dispute System has to be transformed into a purely judicial system rather than it currently works as a semi judicial and semi political mechanism. It has to be taken into account the direct settlement of international economic disputes arising between States and foreign private parties by resorting to international arbitrations or tribunals. For instance, not only private parties are admitted before the E.C.J. or the European Court of Human Rights, but this is the situation also for investment arbitration before the ICSID or under Chapter 11 of NAFTA.[890]

Private parties cannot rely on WTO legislation before national courts.[891] For instance, private parties also prevented from challenging the validity and applicability of EC legal rules that are in violation of WTO obligations.[892] Thus, the transformation of the WTO dispute System into a clearly judicial system with more strict procedural rules and time of compliance should be accompanied with an acceptance of all WTO rulings as precedents applicable directly to other judicial forum as well.

The WTO should have stated that the parties could submit their disputes directly to arbitration rather than having to go through all the stages of dispute settlement currently specified within the conventions. Exhausting other kinds of dispute settlement mechanisms before going to arbitration prolongs the dispute resolution process and only serves to mire the parties in the compulsory elements of the present system. The utilization of arbitration with the introduction of an appellate arbitration tribunal in order arbitration to become a self-contained method, independent and co-equal to national courts as a dispute mechanism will add into the effectiveness of the WTO dispute system[893].

It is worth mentioning that the Appellate Body issued five reports and so eleven panel reports were issued in 2017, two of which in compliance proceedings under Article 21.5 DSU, six of which were not appealed. One arbitration award was issued under Article 21.3(c) DSU for the determination of the "reasonable period of time" to comply[894].

---

890 G. Zekos, The case for giving to private parties access to the WTO dispute settlement system, 2007 *Journal of World Investment & Trade* 441. www.wernerpubl.com.

891 The European Court of Justice Biret C-93/02 of 30 September 2003 and Van Parys C-377/02 of 1 March 2005, notwithstanding the contrary conclusions by the Advocates General.

892 Antonio Tancredi, EC Practice in the WTO: How Wide is the "scope of Manoeuvre"? in *European J. of International Law*, 15 (2004), p. 933–961, at p. 934.

893 G Zekos, *International Commercial and Marine Arbitration*, 2008 Routledge-Cavendish Publishers London www.routledge.com.

894 Arbitration On The Reasonable Period Of Time, United States – Anti-Dumping And Countervailing Measures On Large Residential Washers From Korea (DS464)243.

Chapter 7

ELECTRONIC ARBITRATION

1. INTRODUCTION

As discussed earlier, the ADR mechanisms are rising in the international level to diminish the burden of the ordinary courts of law. The ADR mechanisms are expanding to settle the disputes particularly in the commercial field which means that ADR is viewed as litigant friendly system in any kind of economic setup[895].

Traditional arbitrations form by three parties (plaintiff, defendant, and arbitrators) and face to face discussion is an essential factor in them. By emergence of technology as a fourth party in the online arbitrations and elimination of face to face discussion, noteworthy alterations have transpired in these arbitrations[896].

Online arbitration is fully admissible and operational under the current legal framework of many states, as long as certified requirements are met. Nevertheless, electronic commerce does not alter the fundamental reason of business transactions, which is to gain profits; the difference lies in the new mode of communication[897]. Arbitration has the power of electing arbitrators and governing law, and binding awards which can enforce easily in many states, give a specific meaning to this method in electronic disputes as well. Electronic arbitration has specific communication tools such as: email and online conferences[898]. Another issue which is appeared in the setting of

---

[895] Georgios Zekos, The Role of Courts and ADR in the Rule of Law, *ICFAI University Journal of Alternative Dispute Resolution*, Vol. VII, No. 3, 2008, pp. 11 - 36 at p. 11.

[896] Pablo Cortes, *The potential of online dispute resolution as a consumer redress mechanism*, 2007, p 13, available at: http://ssrn.com/abstract=998865.

[897] Sacha Wunsch-vincent, *The WTO, The Internet And Trade In Digital Product, USA,* Oxford and Portland, Oregon, 2006. Yun Zhao, *Dispute Resolution In Electronic Commerce*, volume 9, Boston, Martinus Nijhoff publisher, 2005, p 25. Rafal Morek, *Online Arbitration: Admissibility within the current legal framework*, p 18, www.odr.info/Re%20greetings.doc.

[898] Julia Hornle, *Cross-Border Internet Dispute Resolution*, USA, Cambridge University Press, 2009, p 75. .Armagan Ebru Bozkurt Yuksel, Online International Arbitration, *Ankara Law Review*, Vol.1, No.1, 2007, p 84. Richard Hill, *On-line Arbitration: Issues and Solutions*, p 202-203 available at: http://www.umass.edu/

electronic arbitration contract is consent of parties in arbitration clause and security of these kinds of contracts. Moreover, nowadays electronic signature which is adopted in many states is a sign for parties' consent in arbitration contract or arbitration clause. When a person adds electronic signature into an email, his consent is apparent and it's not different mostly by the time that he sings a deed by his hand[899].

When a contract is concluded in commercial web sites, clicking "I agree with contract" button when software is bought in the internet is like accepting arbitration when the contract is contained that clause[900]. Moreover, arbitration agreements are produced by sending email, selecting "I agree" button or by referring to a document containing an arbitration clause. The common approach in these kinds of contracts is selecting the applicable law by one party and adoption of another. Nowadays, dependence of the law of arbitration agreement or an arbitration clause on the consensus of the parties is a certain and noncontroversial issue. On the other hand, article 5 (1) (a) of New York Convention implied that arbitration agreement depends on the law which parties have specified it, otherwise, it is depend on the law of the country where award was made. Accordingly, lots of national courts, in their decisions, prefer law of the country where the award was made.

Confidentiality and security are important issues to online dispute resolution. Private and confidential ODR encourages openness and honesty between the parties and the third-party neutral. One of the biggest advantages of ADR over traditional litigation is the participant's choice of a neutral third-party. Most ODR sites assure users that the third-party neutral will reveal no information to the opposing party unless the revealing party grants permission. Moreover, ODR sites are open twenty-four hours a day[901], seven days a week solving many of the scheduling problems that arise with traditional litigation and traditional ADR. Parties participate in ODR from their computers at home or work eliminating the necessary travel expenses for both the participants and the neutral third parties. The use of online dispute resolution decreases the chances of unnecessary confrontation. The expansion of online dispute resolution will increase people's awareness of alternative dispute resolution and help to decrease the overwhelming caseload in national courts. The use of online dispute resolution may help to level the

---

dispute/hill.htm. Jana Herboczkova, certain aspects of online arbitration, *Journal of American Arbitration*, Vol. 1, No. 1, 2001, p 5.

[899] . Article 6(1), UNCITRAL Model Law on Electronic Signatures, 2001.

[900] Rafal Morek, *Online Arbitration: Admissibility within the current legal framework*, p 18, available at: www.odr.info/Re%20greetings.doc.

[901] Cybersettle.com is available to users 24 hours a day, 7 days a week and enables users to negotiate settlements within short periods of time. It is available at http://www.cybersettle.com/. iCourthouse provides real jurors and binding verdicts for those who choose to use its services at http://www.i-courthouse.com/. ClickNSEttle.com is available to users 24 hours a day, 7 days a week and offers negotiation services and available at http://clicknsettle.com/. CompuJustice offers mediation and binding arbitration services as an alternative to litigation at http://www.compujustice.com/. Resolution Forum, Inc. is yet another alternative dispute resolution service that provides arbitration, mediation, and neutral case evaluation by alternative dispute resolution professionals. It is a non-profit educational organization created in conjunction with the South Texas College of Law. Its services include on-line conferencing at http://www.resolutionforum.org/.

playing field. For instance, a small consumer is more likely to accept ODR to resolve a dispute because there are no travel expenses and potentially inferior overall expenses[902]. The ability to choose an expert to be a neutral also results in decisions that are more accurate.

Parties can compromise out of cyberspace and settle their disputes in written form in the cyberspace. The arbitration agreement is concluded in three forms in the cyberspace: 1. opposite parties announce their consent by referring their dispute to arbitration by email. 2. The second approach is that websites which sell goods and services put an arbitration clause in the "terms and conditions" section of their web sites. In this part consumers affirm their consent by clicking "I agree" or "I accept" button in a pop-up box on computer screen. 3. The third approach is what is cited in the UNCITRAL Modal Law, in which parties in the cyberspace, refer their dispute to a document containing an arbitration clause. Concerning the validity of arbitration contract, in many arbitration codes declare "in written form" as a necessary issue[903].

The nations of the world need to develop a system to determine applicable law for on-line disputes. Online dispute resolution may have problems with large disputes involving numerous participants. For instance, arbitration online with more than ten parties will be difficult to control and focus. So, keeping the number of parties involved to a minimum is best for ODR at this time. An arbitrator must read all of the messages sent by participants and a large number of parties may make this a discouraging task. A high number of parties will make it very difficult for an arbitrator to keep the conversation focused on the related issues. Given the asynchronous character of e-mail, parties can all send messages concurrently, which will make it nearly impossible for an arbitrator to keep a discussion focused.

In the online arbitration about the law applicable to substantive issues it seems that traditional rules which are intensive and slow cannot keep track with new and fast developments, especially in the online segment. Party autonomy has to be encouraged in the case of electronic commerce because of these two key factors: the possibility of doing business on cyberspace without knowing the other party's physical location; and the instantaneous presentation of information on cyberspace to all jurisdictions.

Language may also be an issue in online dispute resolution. If a dispute arises over a domain name, and one party lives in Greece and the other party lives in Spain, there will likely be a language barrier between the two parties. Individuals with little education may find it more difficult to type out their side of the story rather than orally explaining the

---

[902] Frank A. Cona, Application of Online Systems in Alternative Dispute Resolution, 45 *Buff. L. Rev.* 975 (1997); Peter H. Ney, The Internet Offers Alternative Dispute Resolution Options, 29-May *Colo. Law.* 75 (2000). Benjamin G. Davis, Franklin G. Synder, Kay Elkins Elliott, Peter B. Manzo, Alan Gaitenby, And David Allen Larson, The First International Competition for Online Dispute Resolution: Is this Big, Different and New? *Journal of International Arbitration* 19(4): 379–392, 2002.

[903] Article. 178 of the Swiss Act on Private International Law, Article 1443 of French Code of Civil Procedure, and also Article 1449; Article 1677 of the Belgian Judicial Code, Section2 of the US Federal Arbitration Act; and Article 16 of the Arbitrations Law of the People's Republic of China 1995.

incident. The third-party neutrals need to be aware of the potential for power imbalance in online dispute resolution. In cyberspace setting, a power balance may result if one party is very comfortable using online resources and another party is unfamiliar with the practice.

2. Developments on E-Arbitration

ODR procedures should comply with standards of due process, two conclusions from an examination of consumer ODR are clear. Firstly, it can be concluded that ODR schemes forming part of the guarantees given by a trust-mark or ODR schemes forming part of the services of a marketplace are more effective. Secondly low value e-commerce consumer disputes cannot be solved by expensive dispute resolution procedures and certainly for disputes up to a value of £100 or $100 a highly automated procedure and one more akin to customer complaints services should be used. However in the higher value consumer sector, ODR should incorporate certain procedural requirements to guarantee due process as described above. The more difficult and yet unresolved question is who should formulate and enforce these standards. It is probably less difficult than it might appear at first to reach broad international consensus on minimum due process requirements. A precedent for such a consensus has been achieved in the related area of consumer protection in the OECD Consumer Guidelines[904] and such consensus can be found at an international level as well.

Under some schemes, online arbitration is used as the last resort layer of a scaled approach to ODR. In such schemes the parties start with negotiation and if this fails they move on to mediation and only if this fails will they resort to arbitration. Online arbitration is a rapidly growing method of resolving cyberspace related disputes. In addition to Virtual Magistrate[905] (VMGA), other online arbitration[906] services include WIPO and CyberTribunal[907]. WIPO's current services are more tailored to resolving domain name disputes. The primary advantages of online arbitration over court litigation are threefold: (1) it keeps courts from restricting cyberspace, (2) it allows cyberspace to regulate itself, and (3) it promotes freedom, prosperity, and utilization of cyberspace to its fullest extent. Electronic commerce demands prompt and effective resolution of its

---

[904] www.oecd.org.

[905] *Virtual Magistrate*, at http://www.vmag.org/. see www.interarb.com http://www.microsoft.com/info/cpyrtInfrg.htm.

[906] V. Heiskanen, Dispute Resolution in International Electronic Commerce 1999 *J. Int'l Arb*. 29. R Alford The virtual world and the arbitration world 2001 *Journal of International Arbitration* 450, S Donahey, A proposal for an appellate panel for the uniform domain name dispute resolution policy 2001 *Journal of International Arbitration* 131.Stacy B. Sterling, New Age Bandits in Cyberspace: Domain Names Held Hostage on the Internet, 17 *Loy. L.A. Ent. L.J.* 733, 742 (1997).Tricia A. Hoefling, Note & Comment: The (Draft) WIPO Arbitration Rules for Administrative Challenge Panel Procedures Concerning Internet Domain Names, 8 *Am. Rev. Int'l Arb.* 173 (1997).

[907] *CyberTribunal*, at http://www.cybertribunal.org/.

disputes,[908] and online arbitration satisfies the swiftly changing needs of cyberspace as it allows for the rapid resolution of disputes. Arbitration resolves disputes effectively because it allows parties to bypass the overcrowded dockets at the courthouse and to schedule hearings at each party's convenience. To speed the process, the individual parties may select a judge who possesses expert knowledge of the subject matter of the dispute enabling parties to avoid spending time and money. Especially, cyberspace copyright infringements, which often incur high costs for the reason that they involve fact-intensive research, requiring numerous experts and costly surveys. Will the question of what law to apply increasingly become irrelevant than the location of the parties when they log onto the net is no more relevant from the point of view of the arbitrator than the 'law' which obtains in their respective geographical jurisdiction? It could be said that cyberspace exists outside of geographic boundaries, and no state or nation will succeed in utilizing its laws to completely restrict the use of cyberspace. States can no more exist outside cyberspace than they can exist outside of the worldwide banking and finance networks[909].

In addition, online dispute resolution (ODR) has been generally addressed as presenting a chance for the fair and effective resolution of consumer disputes. While the key attraction of ODR mechanisms is that they offer a low cost and speedy route for consumer dispute resolution, they are also seen as actually offering parties a more user-friendly and informal formula than either litigation or arbitration, and especially one that is not hampered by the formalities, costs, and delays that characterise both of these processes[910].

The American Bar Association's Task Force on Electronic Commerce and Alternative Dispute Resolution Task Force[911] have provided the description of "online dispute resolution": "Online Dispute Resolution can be done entirely on the Internet, or 'online', through email, videoconferencing, or both. The parties can also meet in person, or 'offline'. Sometimes, combinations of 'online' and 'off-line' methods are used in Online Dispute Resolution."

Moreover, "online arbitration" can be understood to refer to a significant series of activities, from arbitration procedures in which all aspects of the proceedings are conducted online. Certainly, as law-related technology advances, the role of technology, via blockchain, smart contracts and software platforms, in particular arbitrations will be so great that it will effectually supersede the role of the arbitrator, so substantially changing the entire dynamics of the dispute resolution process[912].

---

[908] Alejandro E. Almaguer & Roland W. Baggott III, Shaping New Legal Frontiers: Dispute Resolution for the Internet, 13 *Ohio St. J. on Disp. Resol.* 711, 715 (1998).

[909] Dan O'Hanlon and Jerry Blair, Mediation on the Net: A Unique Jurisdiction with Unique Possibilities, 1 *W. VA J. L. & Tech.* 1.2 (1997).

[910] C. Drahozal and S. Zyontz, Private Regulation of Consumer Arbitration (2012) 79 *Tennessee Law Review* 289.

[911] *What is Online Dispute Resolution? A Guide for Consumers* (March 2012). http://www.americanbar.org/content/dam/aba/migrated/2011_build/dispute_resolution/consumerodr.authcheckdam.pdf.

[912] E. Katsh and J. Rifkin, *Online Dispute Resolution* (Jossey-Bass, 2001) pp. 93-116.

It could be said that the consequence of cyberspace to contemporary life and business guarantees that almost every arbitration will implicate some online activity. Besides, in "online arbitration," the "online" element has to be central to the procedure as a whole, rather than simply peripheral.

It is worth mentioning that enforcement of an arbitral award under the New York Convention necessitates that the party seeking enforcement provide "[t]he duly authenticated original award or a duly certified copy thereof." However, where an award has been provided in an online procedure, such as by being emailed to the parties or by being read on a website, the "original" of the award can be proved by the electronic signature of the arbitrator[913].

It is argued that online arbitration is *sui generis* due to the "asynchronous" nature of many online arbitration proceedings. Besides, it could be said that an "asynchronous" pilling of electronic documentation without any on line interaction cannot be seen as arbitration rather than an investigation of an expert based on submitted data. An online arbitration has to accumulate the characteristics of a conventional arbitration and the only difference should be the utilization of cyberspace for the whole process.

Offline arbitration is referred to as a "synchronous" proceeding, in that interactions between the parties entail synchronized and often concurrent actions which mean that hearings call for the parties and the arbitrator(s) to arrange a mutually appropriate time and place for a hearing to be held. Correspondingly, even activities not demanding physical presence such as the exchange of documents during the disclosure process entail matching of schedules for the controlled handover of physical materials.

It is argued that an online arbitration can function as an "asynchronous" procedure, in the sense that by and large all three actors (the arbitrator and the two parties) need not take part in the steps of the arbitration such as hearings and discovery concurrently or in a coordinated way. Documents can be uploaded on to a website unilaterally, to be examined by the other party when convenient. Correspondingly, hearings can be operated successively, through unilateral uploading of presentations, rather than calling for the simultaneous engagement of all three actors. Nevertheless, while the potentially asynchronous character of online arbitration generates noteworthy benefits, and be desirable for that reason, it is significant also to acknowledge its influence on the character of the arbitral process.

Arbitration has advanced as an alternative to traditional court-based dispute resolution mechanisms, and so as a forum in which disputing parties meets one another before a neutral adjudicator and receives a binding resolution of their dispute. Moreover, the procedural freedom of arbitration leads to face-to-face engagement between the

[913] J. Betancourt and E. Zlatanska, Online Dispute Resolution (ODR): What Is It, and Is It the Way Forward? (2013) 79 *Arbitration* 262 C. Liyanage, Online Arbitration Compares to Offline Arbitration and the Reception of Online Consumer Arbitration: An Overview of the Literature (2010) 22 *Sri Lanka Journal of International Law* 175.

parties guiding both formal and informal regulation of arbitration around the world. Certainly, the concept of "party autonomy," which is so vital to arbitration, is built on directly engaged parties who are mutually engaged in the arbitral process.

It has to be taken into consideration that a totally asynchronous online arbitration disengages the parties from the dispute resolution process in which they are involved, as it denies them of the many chances for direct interaction with both the arbitrator(s) and the other party that describe traditional arbitration. Such interactions offer the basis for party engagement with the arbitral process and the capacity of parties to feel that the arbitral process is one that they control. Consequently, while online arbitrations continue officially party controlled, in practice they lack the inputs of party engagement that give practical meaning to the concept of "party autonomy" that has so notably characterized the regulation of arbitration. It is worth mentioning that regulation of arbitration has centered on the picture of arbitration as a less formal option of court litigation, with an independent decision-maker participating directly with the substance of the dispute to deliver a fair and just decision. Moreover, the rising sophistication of computer software advances the possibility that computers will be able to act as either a substitute for, or at least a complement to, human arbitrators, generating a dispute resolution process drastically different from the conventional model on which the present regulation of arbitration is based.

Certainly online arbitration processes already exist in which disputing parties simply upload documents onto a website, have an arbitral procedure that implicates merely typing responses to questions from the arbitrator, and then receive a decision from an arbitrator they have never me[914]t which means that this process has nothing to do with arbitration but it is merely an experts opinion on a problem. Thus, online arbitration has to engage parties in the arbitration process alike the conventional arbitration and the only difference should be the utilization of cyberspace in contacting the whole process in order to avoid the inconveniences of traveling in the place of arbitration. In case that computers will undertake arbitrations, even though the arbitrator has still made the final decision, that decision is no longer the decision of the arbitrator alone, but is instead more correctly described as a decision produced by a combination of the mind of the arbitrator and that of the software programme the arbitrator was using.

By way of a contract with the ISP, a party submits a dispute to online arbitration. Consequently, arbitration should be the preferred method of resolving copyright disputes on cyberspace. Arbitrations can be scheduled to minimize problems caused by conflicting time zones[915]. In on-line arbitration the arbitrator cannot observe the parties' body language, mood, and facial expressions, which may be important factors in rendering a

---

[914] C. Schoenberger, *Computers' Reasoning Skills to Equal Humans by 2029* (26 June 2012). Available at http://www.wsj.com/articles/SB10001424052702303640804577490681107864926.

[915] Trevor Cox, Information and the Internet: Understanding the Emerging Legal Framework for Contract and Copyright Law and Problems with International Enforcement, 11 *Transnational Law* 23, at 74 (1998).

just and fair decision. In the case of copyright disputes, applying local, formal law to cyberspace is difficult, if not impossible, because of the global nature of cyberspace disputes.[916] Some difficulties that have been identified are: (1) cyberspace crosses local and international geographical and jurisdictional boundaries, making application of local law troublesome, and (2) cyberspace evolves rapidly that applying and developing formal laws may result in poorly tailored and ineffective solutions. Arbitrators are not bound to follow particular laws of a certain jurisdiction unless the parties contract to assert a particular jurisdiction's law. Also important, particularly for foreign parties, is that on-line arbitration decreases the extensive and expensive travel to a court of competent jurisdiction in a country to resolve the dispute[917].

By designating the use of arbitration to resolve conflicts arising out of electronic commerce business of its member states, cost and time will be saved and privacy will be protected and European competitiveness will be secured in the present global market. In Europe, governments and most notably the European Commission have strongly advocated the use of ODR systems for consumer disputes.[918]Litigating and enforcing disputes about e-commerce through the courts can be disproportionately expensive for smaller and medium claims due to added costs e-commerce transactions undertaken by consumers are often very small value, covering items such as books, music, software and other consumer goods, albeit this may change in the future if consumers feel confident to buy higher value goods such as cars or financial services over cyberspace. Thus, at least for the time being, for most consumer e-commerce disputes the cost of legal redress by litigation is not proportionate to the value of the claim. Consumer disputes different from other disputes because of the unequal bargaining power of consumers when compared to the seller of products and services. Can we secure the agreement[919] of the other party, usually the business, to binding arbitration after the dispute has arisen? The e-commerce provider subscribes to online arbitration in advance and markets this fact to its customers in order to enhance trust and branding. For such e-commerce providers ODR is part of the customer services they offer to the consumer. The European Union should guarantee that consumers have plain and efficient access to justice and encourage and facilitate the settling of consumer disputes at an earlier stage[920]. The e-Europe Action Plan, agreed by the Feira European Council on 19 and 20 June 2000[921], acknowledged that for e-

[916] Paul D. Carrington, Virtual Arbitration, 15 *Ohio St. J. Disp. Res.* 669 (2000).

[917] *The Internet Corporation for Assigned Names and Numbers*, at http://www.icann.org/.

[918] See Article 17 of the E-commerce Directive (2000/31/EC) of 8th June 2000; the European Commission has funded a consumer mediation project called ECODIR, European Commission's E-confidence Forum.

[919] See Katsh/Rifkin, *Online Dispute Resolution* (Jossey-Bass 2001), p.56.

[920] Article 17 of Directive 2000/31/EC of the European Parliament and of the Council of 8 June 2000 on certain legal aspects of information society services, in particular electronic commerce in the internet market stipulates that Member States should make sure their legislation does not hinder the use of out-of-court schemes existing under national law, for dispute settlement.

[921] The Recommendation on the Principles Applicable to the Bodies Responsible for Out-of-Court Settlement of Consumer Disputes (98/257/EC) applies to binding arbitration procedures and the Recommendation on the Principles for Out-of-Court Bodies Involved in the Consensual Resolution of Consumer Disputes

commerce to reach its full potential consumer confidence must be improved, in partnership with consumer groups, industry and Member States, by promoting access to alternative dispute resolution systems.

Electronic commerce facilitates cross-border transactions between business and consumers and because such transactions are normally of low value the resolution of any dispute needs to be simple, quick and inexpensive. Hence, new technology can contribute to the development of electronic dispute settlement systems, providing a mechanism to effectively settle disputes across different jurisdictions without the need for face-to-face contact[922]. The impartiality of these dispute resolution procedures must be guaranteed to ensure that all parties have confidence in its fairness, both parties should have access to the information they need, and the transparency of the procedure must be guaranteed. While such an obligation can be imposed against the subscribing supplier, it may not be binding on the consumer. In European jurisdictions, an arbitration clause incorporated in standard contract terms, which binds the consumer to present a dispute to an arbitral tribunal expected to consider it as unfair[923]. So, a standard arbitration clause cannot be enforced against a consumer which means that the arbitration clause would only be binding on the business, but not obligatory for the consumer. The right to a fair hearing means that each party must be given an opportunity to state their case and to hear and respond to the other party's submissions. Online Dispute Resolution schemes usually rely on written (web-based or email) submissions by the parties. The parties should also be given a fair time in which to respond. To the extent that the 'hearing' is conducted in writing only, signs of non-verbal communication will be lost. The inexperienced or inarticulate claimant may be disadvantaged against the professionally presented case of the respondent. This may have an impact on the fairness of the evidence and fact-finding process and is a factor the arbitrator has to take into account in consumer disputes.

However, while strongly protective of consumers, and inclined to overrule arbitration agreements when needed in the interests of consumer protection, the EU has passed legislation that supports the use of high quality consumer ADR/ODR schemes. In line with the ADR Directive, all Member States have to make certain the availability within their jurisdiction of ADR entities that adhere to legal standards when resolving disputes

---

(2001/310/EC) is applicable to consensual, non-binding forms of consumer dispute resolution. 98/257/EC: Commission Recommendation of 30 March 1998 on the principles applicable to the bodies responsible for out-of-court settlement of consumer disputes *Official Journal L* 115, 17/04/1998 P. 0031 – 0034.

922 Commission Recommendation of 4 April 2001 on the principles for out-of-court bodies involved in the consensual resolution of consumer disputes (notified under document number C(2001) 1016) Official Journal L 109, 19/04/2001 P. 0056 – 0061. Council Resolution of 25 May 2000 on a Community-wide network of national bodies for the extra-judicial settlement of consumer disputes (*Official Journal C* 155, 06/06/2000 p. 0001 – 0002) encourages the activities of bodies for the out-of-court settlement of consumer disputes, also as regards transborder transactions, and where appropriate, the setting-up of such bodies, on the basis of Recommendation 98/257/EC.

923 Hornle, J, Online Dispute Resolution in Business to Consumer E-commerce Transactions, *The Journal of Information, Law and Technology (JILT)* 2002 (2) http://elj.warwick.ac.uk/jilt/02-2/hornle.html.

between traders and consumers[924] which means that certified ADR entities, including arbitration providers, must be able to process consumer complaints online. However, the ADR Directive includes two principles with which certified arbitration bodies have to comply that are the principles of "liberty" and "legality," which were originally encompassed in the 1998 European Commission Recommendations[925]. Consumers cannot be forced to agree on a legally binding dispute resolution process before the dispute has materialized and an arbitral procedure has to abide by the requirements set in the Unfair Terms Directive without providing an advantage to the trader[926]. The ADR Directive demands consumers to be informed about the binding nature of arbitration and to accept this specifically[927]. In line with the principle of "legality," arbitral awards are not allowed to result in the consumer receiving a lower level of protection than the mandatory law of the Member State in which they reside. In cross-border disputes, the Rome I Regulation will apply, under which the applicable law will often be the law of the consumers' residence, specifically where the trader has actively targeted the consumer's jurisdiction by offering goods online in the language and currency of the consumer[928].

The ODR Regulation complements the ADR Directive and compels the European Commission to establish and uphold a pan-European ODR Platform to function as a single point of entry for resolving consumer complaints[929] but the platform does not itself resolve consumer disputes, on the other hand links parties in a dispute to nationally certified ADR entities, empowering the online resolution of national and cross-border disputes that result from e-commerce. In contrast to the U.S., the EU has combined legislative and case law-based restrictions meant to prevent unfair consumer arbitration processes while concurrently boosting and facilitating the use of certified high quality arbitral procedures. Moreover, consumer arbitration has not caused the same hostility in the EU that it has generated in the U.S.

Online consumer arbitration needs specific attention beyond the traditional regulation of arbitration since it combines two features, namely online technology and the involvement of consumers, each of which deeply alters arbitration. Therefore, while online consumer arbitration is eventually a form of arbitration, it has to be the subject of particularly directed legislation if it is to function fairly and successfully.

---

[924] Directive 2013/11/EU on Alternative Dispute Resolution for Consumer Disputes OJ L165/63.

[925] Commission Recommendation 98/257/EC of 30 March 1998 on the Principles Applicable to the Bodies Responsible for Out-of-Court Settlement of Consumer Disputes O.J. 1998, L 115.

[926] Art. 10. Annex I[q] of the Unfair Terms Directive 93/13/EEC of 5 April 1993 OJ L 95/29. M. Piers 'Is Europe Skipping a Step? Exploring the Harmonisation of ADR Agreements' (2013) 20(4) *Maastricht Journal of European and Comparative Law* 506, 520.

[927] Art. 10(2).

[928] Art. 11. Art. 6(2) of the Rome I Regulation (O.J. 2008, L 177/6) and Peter Pammer (C 585/08).

[929] Regulation 524/2013 on Online Dispute Resolution for Consumer Disputes OJ L165/1.

The American Arbitration Association ("AAA") has led the way in developing procedures for fair and effective consumer arbitrations, as exemplified by the AAA Consumer Arbitration Rules and the Consumer Arbitration Due Process Protocol[930].

Lord Justice Briggs[931] argues for the creation of an "Online Solutions Court," separate from the ordinary court of first instance and with mandatory jurisdiction within its scope which indicates the tendency of litigation to want to replace arbitration in the resolution of disputes eliminating arbitration as a dispute resolution instead of allowing the development of the voluntary arbitration as an independent dispute resolution mechanism.

Online dispute resolution has great potential. It should be taken into consideration that in the consumer context, there are public policy concerns involved. For example, in cases of widespread business malpractice on the mass consumer e-commerce market, the public should have a right to know. It could be argued that if e-arbitration becomes the dominant form of dispute resolution in e-commerce disputes, e-arbitration decisions should form a body of law as there will be few court decisions and otherwise the rights and obligations of parties in e-commerce will be uncertain. This contradicts the advantage of arbitration not to publish the proceedings and the award. Will the law governing e-commerce develop further and be not transparent, unless decisions are published? Obviously this argument only applies to binding online arbitration, as online mediation does not produce authoritative rulings. Under the UDRP all decisions rendered by the arbitration panels are published on the ICANN website. As a consequence, a body of case law has been developed and panels regularly quote the decisions of their sister panels for authority, albeit there is no system of precedent. Also, unless there is sufficient transparency through publication of results it is impossible to check the quality and impartiality of dispute resolution. For the purposes of transparency, e-arbitration should also make clear the type of rules, standards or law (such as legal provisions, equity, codes of conduct) serving as the basis for the settlement or decision. Who is going to review e-awards of e-arbitration? Will courts intervene to solve disputes regarding the arbitration agreement, arbitrability, arbitrators' selection and review of awards? National law becomes a factor during the enforcement of an arbitral award. Arbitral awards and e-awards should stand outside of the forum state. Should national courts ensure the integrity of awards or e-awards rendered within national borders? A state's possibility to nullify an award frustrates the objectives of autonomous arbitration. Since arbitration and e-arbitration are considered to be alternative dispute resolution mechanisms the state should not assume control of the arbitral process to ensure that national policies and

---

930 *AAA Consumer Arbitration Rules 2014.* Available at http://tinyurl.com/hqj2b7h and *Consumer Due Process Protocol.* Available at http://tinyurl.com/h3qgtfp.

931 Lord Justice Briggs, Final Report, *Civil Courts Structure Review* (July 2016). Lord Justice Briggs, Interim Report, *Civil Courts Structure Review* (December 2015) and Civil Justice Council Online Dispute Resolution Advisory Group, 'Online Dispute Resolution for Low Value Claims' (February 2015). https://www.judiciary.gov.uk/publications/civil-courts-structure-review-final-report/.

concepts of justice are the foundation for arbitral proceedings. The author considers that only for purposes of public policy there is a need for a common perception of the substance of the term public policy between independent arbitral tribunals and courts in order not to have a divergence in the fundamental principles of a state as they are expressed in the constitution. Moreover, the author supports the creation of second degree of arbitral tribunals and e-arbitral tribunals to deal not only with review of awards but also with any dispute regarding the arbitral process rather than the national courts[932]. The EU should consider and treat arbitral tribunals equal to national courts regarding the application of EU law.

It is worth mentioning that nowadays enforcing of foreign arbitration awards is easier than enforcing of foreign court sentences. National and international arbitration codes do not have any consensus about required points in an award. Nevertheless, necessity of arbitrators' signature and necessity of being in written are the only issues which are cited in many arbitration codes and may instigate problems in the online arbitration awards[933]. On the other hand, some codes show more flexibility and believe that digital signature or record of an award will be satisfactory[934].

At present, the enforcement of e-awards considering disputes on domain names can be done by ICANN and the national authorities responsible for allocation of domain names. E-awards concerning matters of electronic transactions regarding on line products and services can be enforced by the relevant providers. Besides, the authority enforcing court judgments can enforce matters regarding compensation. The provider and national authorities under the New York Convention can enforce international e-awards.

It is worth mentioning that in the Netherlands, ADR is to a large extent self-regulated and arbitration is used as a mechanism to enforce claims against consumers as well[935] and to that extent, the establishment of 'e-Court' a private foundation is launched. Moreover, E-Court is an online platform that presents itself as an easier, faster and cheaper alternative to the judicial system, with lower fees and a completely digital procedure[936]. In the Netherlands, online arbitration in consumer cases has given rise to a debate about the lack of judicial control over commercial 'adjudication'.

Using of arbitration in the cyberspace has become noticeable as a consequence of its acceleration and decreasing expenses. It is time that the use of independent online arbitration and co-equal to courts to become more widespread.

---

932 G Zekos The Role of Courts in Maritime versus Labor Arbitration in USA law 2000 *ADRLJ* 174.

933 Article 31 (1) of Canadian Commercial Arbitration Act, Article 1057 (2) of Dutch Code of Civil Procedure, or Article 1473 of French New Civil Procedure Code; also Article 32(2) of the UNCITRAL Arbitration Rules states that "*the award shall be made in writing.*"

934 According to English Arbitration Act 1996 "*the parties are free to agree on the form of the award*" & Section 52 (1). In the United States, the Revised Uniform Arbitration Act of 2000 provides for the use of electronic signatures by arbitrators. According to its Article 19, "*an arbitrator shall make a record of an award.*"

935 http://ec.europa.eu/newsroom/just/document.cfm?action=display&doc_id=49503 Pablo Cortés, The Impact of EU Law in the ADR Landscape in Italy, Spain and the UK: Time for Change or Missed Opportunity? (2015) 16 *ERA Forum* 125, 133ff.

936 www.e-court.nl.

Blockchain technology has made the guarantee of uniqueness feasible in a decentralised system. Transactions take place peer-to-peer on an open platform where no prior subscription to membership is required and so this openness makes certain global reach of the participants. Integration through the blockchain technology can achieve an unsettling transformation in digital supply chains and networks[937]. Besides, intermediates such as EDI operators including banks such as SWIFT operators have been operating and collaborating in this area, but services still lack some fundamental functionality such as standards, monitoring and tracking of information flows and secure end-to-end delivery of information. Thus, the open source blockchain technology presents functionalities beyond those of present legacy technologies; furthermore, this technology presents data security and cost-effective transmission of transactions in peer-to-peer networks with no central system which means that blockchain technology makes simpler integration.

It has to be taken into account that Blockchain technology security and smart contract platforms, on top of software connectors[938], tender tools to develop a cost-effective and adaptable DSC network to be utilized by electronic arbitration. Moreover, DSC transactions sporadically necessitate financing services that must be integrated to the DSC network. It could be said that Blockchain technology is a good fit for such integration because data-encrypting private and public keys make possible secure data transfer and digital signatures for smart contracting. On the other hand, DSC integration entails standards for system interoperability, which blockchain technology itself does not offer.

Furthermore, Blockchain' and distributed ledger technology (DLT) allow the independent verification of the integrity of the shared database without having to count on a trusted third party is one of the main value propositions of using a blockchain. The main differences between open and closed blockchains relate to their security and threat model. Blockchain technology empowers the formation of decentralized currencies, self-executing digital contracts (smart contracts) and intelligent assets that can be operated over cyberspace (smart property). Thus, cyberspace has inaugurated a new phase of decentralization[939]. The blockchain decentralizes the manner we store data and manage information, possibly leading to a diminished role for one of the most imperative regulatory actors in society which are the middlemen. Moreover, the blockchain

[937] Kosba, A., Miller, A., Shi, E., Wen, Z. & Papamanthou, C. (2015) Hawk: The Blockchain Model of Cryptography and Privacy-Preserving Smart Contracts. *IACR working paper*, http://eprint.iacr.org/2015/675 Mainelli, M. &Smith, M. (2015). Sharing ledgers for sharing economies: an exploration of mutual distributed ledgers (aka blockchain technology). *The Journal of Financial Perspectives* 3 (3), 1-44.

[938] K. Korpela, U. Kuusiholma, O. Taipale and J. Hallikas, "A framework for exploring digital business ecosystems," in *System Sciences (HICSS)*, 2013 46th Hawaii International Conference on, 2013, pp. 3838-3847. Xu, X., Pautassso, C., Zhu, L., Gramoli, V., Ponomarev, A., Tran, A.B. & Chen, S. (2016). The Blockchain as a Software Connector. Proceedings of the 13th Working IEEE/IFIP Conference on Software Architecture (WICSA), April 2016.

[939] Yochai Benkler, The Wealth Of Networks 62 (2006) G Zekos, *Monetary Policy and Risk Management in Financial Globalization*, 2015 Nova Science Publications New York USA. www.novapublishers.com Chapter 2.

facilitates the development of new governance systems with more democratic or participatory decision-making, and decentralized (autonomous) organizations functioning over a network of computers without any human involvement which means that these applications have directed many to parallel the blockchain to cyberspace, with supplementary prognostications that this technology will move the balance of power away from centralized authorities in the field of communications, business, and even politics or law. It is worth mentioning that the switch towards more decentralization may not only influence the implementation or application of laws, but also how we administer trade organizations and society. In addition, Blockchain-based applications portray new types of scalable innovations in governance and institutional design. In a world of decentralized autonomous consensus, collective decision-making undertakes more prominence, resulting in the quick reformulation of corporate structures and the more effective distribution of corporate resources. Further than corporate governance, the blockchain aid instigate new decentralized models of commons-based management which means that commons based communities are institutionalized around centralized or federated structures[940], which produce a sequence of trade-offs in terms of democratic governance, flexibility, and capacity to advance. Moreover, these institutions make possible the synchronization of disparate groups.

It has to be taken into account that there is a mishandling of government authority and so depressing the economic profits that blockchain technology offers which means that there is a retreat from current reinforce of the free exchange of information, ideas, and commerce on cyberspace raising noteworthy constitutional issues[941]. By levying obligations on software developers, the government instructs the code that software developers can write[942]. Correspondingly, laws demanding the development of broken hardware to preclude encryption infringe fundamental human rights by forcing citizens to communicate in a manner that restricts their capability to protect their own privacy.

---

[940] Greg R. Vetter, "Infectious" Open Source Software: Spreading Incentives or Promoting Resistance? 36 *Rutgers L. J.* 53, 80 (2004) ("Most large open source software projects, including Apache and GNU/Linux, operate using this collaborative development model. A core development group generates a substantial portion of the software. Other non-core developers and users operate and debug the software. The leaders of the project make design decisions and filter software submittals for inclusion in the product.").

[941] Henry Corrigan-Gibbs, Keeping Secrets, *Stanford Alumni Magazine* (Nov. 2014), https:// alumni.stanford.edu/ get/page/magazine/article/?article_id=74801. ("At the time, knowledge of how to encrypt and decrypt information was the domain of government; the NSA feared that making the secrets of cryptography public would severely hamper intelligence operations. But as the researchers saw it, society's growing dependence on computers meant that the private sector would also need effective measures to safeguard information. Both sides' concerns proved prescient; their conflict foreshadowed what would become a universal tug-of-war between privacy-conscious technologists and security-conscious government officials.").

[942] *Bernstein v. U.S. Dep't of State*, 922 F. Supp. 1426, 1436 (N.D. Cal. 1996) (mathematician sought declaratory and injunctive relief against enforcement of the Arms Export Control Act and the International Traffic in Arms Regulations on the grounds that they were unconstitutional on their face and as applied to mathematician's cryptographic computer source code. The District Court held that cryptographic computer source code is "speech" protected by First Amendment, and colorable constitutional challenges to statute and regulations were justiciable).

To that extent, Software developers have started to use blockchain technology to create digital currencies[943], self-executing *smart contracts*[944], along with cryptographic tokens representing property or ownership interest in emerging services. Moreover, blockchain technology is being used to create: censorship-resistant communications and file sharing systems; decentralized domain name management systems (DNS); and fraud-resistant digital voting platforms[945]. For the reason that the blockchain support machine-to-machine communications that will soon materialize from cyberspace enabled devices that constitute the Internet of Things which means that by joining digital currencies, smart contracts, and distributed data storage, the blockchain further is leading in totally new decentralized organizations that employ source code to define an organization's governance structure. Moreover, Blockchains are not just operating digital currencies but they are also permitting the creation smart contracts, one of the first troublemaking technological developments to the practice of law since the invention of the printing press because by utilizing a distributed database, like the blockchain, parties can approve that an event or condition has in fact happened without the need for a third party[946]. Furthermore, using decentralized, encrypted[947] communication protocols and a blockchain, parties store and recover messages/ letters without the risk of government involvement.

Nevertheless, smart contracts in the DLT[948] context hold the promise that they can be used as an instrument to automate a large number of business processes across different entities. The execution of smart contracts is guaranteed by system rules and the outcome is verifiable and auditable by all network participants. Moreover, smart contracts have been seen as applications that are wider than just contractual language and so they are stated as "cryptographic 'boxes' that contain value and only unlock it if certain circumstances are met[949]. It is worth mentioning here that software developers consider that smart contracts are used to smooth machine-to-machine communications and the making of decentralized organizations. In other words by the utilization of progressively

---

[943] *Litecoin*, https://litecoin.org/; *Darkcoin*, https://www.darkcoin.io/ G Zekos, *Monetary Policy and Risk Management in Financial Globalization*, 2015 Nova Science Publications New York USA. www.novapublishers.com Chapter 2.

[944] Nick Szabo, *The Idea of Smart Contracts* (1997), http://szabo.best.vwh.net/smart_contracts_idea.html.

[945] See Scott Rosenberg, How Bitcoin's Blockchain Could Power an Alternate Internet, *Medium* (Jan. 13, 2015), https://medium.com/backchannel/how-bitcoins-blockchain-couldpower-an-alternate-internet-bb501855af67 (distributed finance, distributed data, distributed identity, and others).

[946] Susan Athey, 5 Ways Digital Currency Will Change the World, *World Economic Forum Agenda* (Jan. 22, 2015), https://agenda.weforum.org/2015/01/5-ways-digitalcurrencies-will-change-the-world.

[947] *Bitcrypt*, https://github.com/barisser/bitcrypt (explaining that the BitCrypt software package allows users to "[w]rite encrypted messages in the language of Bitcoin" and "[s]end encrypted messages to Bitcoin addresses"). Joshua Fairfield, *BitProperty*, http://papers.ssrn.com/sol3/papers.cfm?abstract_id=2504710 (outlining how blockchain technology could be used to create a digital property registry).

[948] In re *Dole Food Co., Inc.*, No. CV 8703-VCL, 2017 WL 624843 (Del. Ch. Feb. 15, 2017), at *5 (noting that the only feasible solution to stock ledger discrepancies caused by the current system's inadequacies disproportionately benefits large holders).

[949] Vitalik Buterin, A Next Generation Smart Contract & Decentralized Application Platform, *GITHUB* (last edited Jan. 5, 2015), https://github.com/ethereum/wiki/wiki/White-Paper.

byzantine systems of smart contracts and decentralized organizations, the technology inaugurates rules and structures for organizations, formal bodies, and possibly even governmental associations. It could be argued that if planned to seize human input, the technology reveals community values and social norms, mechanically enforced through self-executing code. Moreover, smart contracts re-write or evade some of the most basic principles of property law, actually turning property or even constitutional rights into a subsection of contract law.

CONCLUSION

Arbitration operates as a globally dispersed set of private, decentralized, and very competitive institutions, administered or *ad hoc* organized proceedings, international and domestic framework regulations, procedural rules, on top of professional traditions and practices. Moreover, Arbitration as an adjudicatory, binding method of dispute resolution is founded on application of applicable rules of law to the merits of the dispute. Owing to international character of the disputes, as well different legal systems interested in the outcomes of the case arbitrators are faced with the demands of decision-making in legally, linguistically and culturally expanded surroundings[950].

It is worth mentioning that arbitration served as a tool for parties to voluntarily agree about how to resolve future disputes without going to court[951]. On the other hand, it could be said that parties would negotiate and select arbitration forums and procedures that offered a superior alternative to judicial resolution and that is why congress enacted the FAA to protect these contracts from sceptical courts.

Parties can only submit to arbitration to the extent expressly allowed by the law. Arbitrators exercise a public function to the extent that law allows them. The judicial model of decision-making has been worked out in detail over centuries; and deep in our culture is a habit of obeying it. To that extent, courts' confirmation is needed to enforce arbitral decisions[952]. Justice emanates from sovereignty and imposes itself upon obedience and arbitration has its source in liberty[953].

---

950 Joanna Jemielniak, *Legal Interpretation in International Commercial Arbitration* (Ashgate. 2014). Emmanuel Gaillard, *Legal theory of international arbitration* (Martinus Nijhoff Publishers. 2010).

951 Jean R. Sternlight, Hurrah for the Consumer Financial Protection Bureau: Consumer Arbitration as a Poster Child for Regulation, 48 *St. Mary's L.J.* 343, 346 (2016) ("Once upon a time, arbitration was a dispute resolution process that was adopted knowingly and voluntarily by two or more businesses that preferred to resolve disputes outside of court.").

952 "Common Law" is the legal system of England, the Commonwealth countries and the United States. Beginning in England in the 11th century, the Common Law developed through a long accumulation of judicial decisions, bound together by a flexible requirement of following earlier decisions on the topic. "Civil Law" legal systems rely on detailed statutory codes as the main source of law, and judicial decisions matter much less. As an illustration of how dependent upon the authority of the Common Law the arbitration tradition has become, one leading article on reinsurance arbitration cites court decisions 132 times, custom & practice once,

It is characteristic that historically[954] trade associations have included in their contract arbitration clauses for the resolution of disputes among their members and any disobedience meant expulsion from the association which means that arbitration had been accepted as an alternative to courts offering justice regardless of the courts' view concerning arbitration clauses.

Law provides justice but justice is a concept with a broader and deeper meaning than law and law can be one of the instruments that can be used in order to achieve justice. On the other hand, Informality[955] can make the created norms, soft or formal law more accessible and applicable to disputes[956]. Formal law strictly interpreted can destabilize norms that are already operating effectively and successfully[957]. The rule of law has itself been recognized as a principle behind a legal system as a whole. Judicial independence is required to uphold the rule of law and courts have the capacity to review the implementation of the law[958]. Taking into consideration that arbitrators are experienced scholars/lawyers or judges, arbitration has the capacity to review the implementation as well. Arbitration is not the rejection of law but it depends on law[959].

---

and arbitral decisions not at all. Paul M. Hummer, Reinsurance Arbitrations from Start to Finish: A Practitioner's Guide, 63 *Def. Counsel J.* 228 (1996).

953 *Sutcliffe v. Thackrah* [1974] AC 727 HL.

954 Samuel Williams Cooper, The Law's Delay, 19 *The American*, 499, 394 (1890) ("The rules of the various trade associations throughout the country contain provisions that differences between members shall be settled by arbitration before an appropriate committee, and the fact that any member appeals to the court for his rights made the ground for his expulsion from the society,"); *Farmer v. Bd. of Trade of Kans. City*, 78 *Mo. App.* 557, 566-67 (1899) ("It is well known that parties can not by agreement to arbitrate future differences, oust the courts of jurisdiction. But that principle of law does not affect our statement that the association may have a rule requiring all differences between members to be settled by arbitration and to impose expulsion as a penalty for disobedience of such rule."); Don Antonio De Alcedo, New York, Iii The Geographical And Historical Dictionary Of America And The West Indies 408 (stating that refusal of a member of a New York trade organization to submit a dispute to arbitration would result in the member's expulsion from the organization) (G.A. Thompson trans., 1812).

955 Carrie Menkel-Meadow, Exporting and Importing ADR: "I've Looked at Life from Both Sides Now," *Disp. Resol. Mag.*, Spring 2006, at 5. (explaining that ADR's legitimacy can be established by values other than the rule of law, such as treaties, consent, and economic and trade values).

956 Frank K. Upham, Who Will Find the Defendant if He Stays with His Sheep? Justice in Rural China, 114 *Yale L.J.* 1675, 1714 (2005) (reviewing Zhu Suli, Sending Law To The Countryside: Research On China's Basic-Level Judicial System (2000), describing justice in rural China and urging that "[t]he solution [to the tension], therefore, may be to institutionalize the dialectic that Zhu describes between formal and informal, modern and customary, center and periphery in a manner designed to make the norms created more accessible to the public while also being respectful of local practices"). Lan Cao, Introduction to Symposium, The "Rule of Law" in China, 11 *Wm. & Mary Bill Rts. J.* 539, 542 (2003) (noting that the Chinese may have a very different attitude toward the rule of law than Americans do, and that "rule of law" translates into Chinese as "rule *by* law," which implies a more authoritarian approach); Pat K. Chew, The Rule of Law: China's Skepticism and the Rule of People, 20 *Ohio St. J. On Disp. Resol.* 43, 48–54 (2005) (discussing China's ongoing tension between the Western rule of law approach and the traditional Chinese preference for rule of people);

957 Richard H. Pildes, The Destruction of Social Capital Through Law, 144 *U. PA L. Rev.* 2055, 2057 (1996). Haini Guo & Bradley Klein, Bargaining in the Shadow of the Community: Neighborly Dispute Resolution in Beijing Hutongs, 20 *Ohio St. J. On Disp. Resol.* 825, 885–86 (2005) (stating that in China, formal law is "muddy" and more unpredictable than social norms).

958 Joseph Raz, 'The Rule of Law and its Virtue' (1977) 93 *Law Quarterly Review* 195.

959 Aaron-Andrew P. Bruhl, The Unconscionability Game: Strategic Judging and the Evolution of the Federal Arbitration Act, 83 *NYU L. Rev.* 1420, 1435 (2008) (Supreme Court"s talk "of combating hostility to arbitration is today largely anachronistic in that it has come unmoored from the conditions that provided it"). David Horton, The Shadow Terms: Contract Procedure and Unilateral Amendments, 57 *UCLA L. Rev.* 605,

An independent arbitration can be used to achieve justice in a deeper and more socially acceptable way than formal law[960]. Levin presents[961] that in recent years the private sector has begun to use binding arbitration as the favourite method of dispute resolution and the payback appears to be that arbitration is a "quicker, less expensive and more private alternative to litigation." Besides Jean sternlight[962] argues that it is unsuitable for a society to establish completely private dispute resolution processes. Kyron Huigens[963] argues that Aristotle maintains the rule of law on the position that only governance by reason can be impartial and equitable which reflects the way that arbitration deals with the disputes nowadays.

Arbitration arising out of contract supposed to be an entrepreneurial, private-sector innovation producing what disputing parties want: quick, inexpensive, common-sense adjudication of disputes. Economic barriers avert many, if not most, parties in the United States from achieving meaningful access to courts justifying the employment of ADR[964]. Procedural party autonomy endows the parties with the power to choose in advance the forum that suits them best, instead of having their disputes resolved by the default forum, which in many cases it is hard to predict. Litigation in the public-sector court system is slow and archaic, full of legalistic technicalities and formalities that produce a lot more work for lawyers without producing a corresponding enhance in justice for the disputing parties who have to pay the lawyers.

The FAA incorporates a "liberal federal policy favoring arbitration[965]." In 1925, Congress enacted FAA in response to widespread judicial hostility toward arbitration and this resistance stemmed from American courts adopting the practice of English courts to protect their jurisdiction against perceived competitors which means that hostility has not

665-66 (2010) (showing how assertions that unilateral amendments to arbitration clauses are valid under Court"s federal arbitration jurisprudence are invalid under basic contract law).

[960] Jean R. Sternlight, ADR Is Here: Preliminary Reflections on Where It Fits in a System of Justice, 3 *Nev. L.J.* 289 (2002–2003) (urging that a proper system of justice should resolve societal as well as individual interests, seek societal harmony, and that both litigation and ADR can serve such goals); Jean R. Sternlight, In Search of the Best Procedure for Enforcing Employment Discrimination Laws: A Comparative Analysis, 78 *Tul. L. Rev.* 1401 (2004) (examining tensions between using formal and informal systems to resolve employment discrimination complaints in the United States, Great Britain, and Australia).

[961] Murray S. Levin, The Role of Substantive Law in Business Arbitration and the Importance of Volition, 35 *Am. Bus. L.J.* 105 (1997), at 106.

[962] Jean sternlight, Creeping Mandatory Arbitration: Is it Just? *Stanford Law Review*, Vol. 57, p. 1631, 2005.

[963] Kyron Huigens, The Dead End of Deterrence, and Beyond, 41 *Wm. & Mary L. Rev.* 943, 1033 (2000) ("Aristotle insists on the rule of law, not of men, on the ground that only governance by reason can be impartial and even-handed."). Aristotle, *The Politics* 219–24, 226 (T.A. Sinclair trans., rev. ed. 1981) ("Therefore he who asks law to rule is asking God and intelligence and no others to rule; while he who asks for the rule of a human being is importing a wild beast too; for desire is like a wild beast, and anger perverts rulers and the very best of men. Hence law is intelligence without appetit[e].").

[964] Robert Rubinson, A Theory of Access to Justice, 29 *J. Legal Prof.* 89, 100–02 (2005) (specifying that, for the most part, the only persons or groups able to obtain access to the U.S. litigation system are commercial organizations, affluent individuals, and persons engaged in "values conflicts" of significant interest to attract pro bono or reduced-fee representation).

[965] *AT&T Mobility LLC v. Concepcion*, 563 U.S. 333, 339 (2011). *Perry v. Thomas*, 482 U.S. 483, 489 (1987).

derived from matters of rightfully applying the law but merely derived from the economic interests of a group of people[966].

Arbitration's adjudicatory features respond well to the sui generis dispute resolution needs of international commercial contracts by generating a more realistic and effective framework that supplants the fundamentally parochial alternative offered by national legal systems. On the one hand, an arbitration agreement means that the parties gain the right to arbitrate their disputes and so the parties lose the right to resort to national courts. On the other hand, in fact the courts play supervise arbitrations seated within their jurisdiction undertaking particular functions to support the arbitral process, as set out in the relevant arbitration legislation which means that in fact the parties do not have the right for the entire solution of their dispute by arbitration[967]. In other words, parties' right for arbitration is annulled by courts' involvement within the whole arbitral course. The uniformly favorable stance of many advanced Western legal systems toward arbitration by the amplification of customary legal norms for private international law has in actual fact formed a situation of *de legeferenda* which has to be advanced in an entire liberation from courts' supervision.

Investors' consistent selection of arbitration as the dispute resolution mechanism of choice reflects an appreciation of the shortcomings of the legal system. Arbitral adjudication efficiently intermediates between the need for functional trial procedures and the imperative of safeguarding legal rights. According to Chief Justice Warren E. Burger, "ADR devices are often superior to litigation 'in terms of cost, time, and human wear and tear[968].'" Moreover, Robin J. Effron[969] argues that "Arbitration and other private dispute resolution forums provide a complete exit from the procedure and personnel of the public courts. But even parties that remain in the federal or state courts have access to an increasingly sophisticated set of contractual tools that allow them to shape, change, and even opt out of many of the courts' rules of practice and procedure." It is worth mentioning here that extralegal, custom-based regimes of dispute resolution do not implicate a delegation of state power which is another example that can be taken into account for the independence of arbitration[970].

---

[966] *Allied-Bruce Terminix Cos. v. Dobson*, 513 U.S. 265, 270 (1995).

[967] Art. 5 Model Law for international arbitration, and in the *Commercial Arbitration Act 2011* (Vic) s 5 for domestic arbitration. Art. 8(1) Model Law; Commercial Arbitration Act 2011 (Vic) s 8(1). Gary Born, *International Commercial Arbitration* (Kluwer, 2nd ed., 2014).

[968] *AMF Inc., v. Brunswick Corp.*, 621 F. Supp. 456, 462 (E.D.N.Y. 1985) (citing remarks of Warren E. Burger, Chief Justice of the United States, at the Twin Cities Advisory Council of the American Arbitration Association, St. Paul, Minn., August 21, 1985).

[969] Robin J. Effron, Ousted: The New Dynamics of Privatized Procedure and Judicial Discretion, 2018 *Boston University Law Review* [Vol. 98:127 p128 (cataloging the various ways in which the Federal Rules defer to party "preference" or "agreement").

[970] Robert C. Ellickson, *Order Without Law: How Neighbors Settle Disputes* (1994) (using disputes between cattle ranchers in Shasta County, California, to demonstrate how neighbors often rely on social norms, rather than the formal legal system, to resolve disputes); Lisa Bernstein, Opting Out of the Legal System: Extralegal Contractual Relations in the Diamond Industry, 21 *J. Legal Stud.* 115 (1992) (explaining how the diamond industry has established its own dispute-resolution system independent of any state-run legal system).

Arbitration has to guarantee legal certainty, predictability, and settlement being costless. The emergence of many non-independent arbitral tribunals creates a Gordian knot by merely adding more work for courts in order to deal with so many requests for intervention in arbitrations. As illustrated above arbitration is ineffective and costly demanding either co-equality of arbitration to courts or courts have to be the sole dispute resolution system for civil cases eliminating the existence of such an ineffective and costly arbitration. It is obvious that any method for dispute resolution has to be autonomous and independent in order to be regarded as an ADR. So, it could be said that arbitration cannot be named as ADR as being not real ADR for the reason that arbitration is not autonomous system[971] not be able to issue directly enforceable award without the courts' authorization. It seems that courts' involvement in the international arbitration process remains indispensable to its effectiveness[972].

It is argued that the consistency between the pro-arbitration and anti-litigation litigation makes sense for the reason that "arbitration" and "litigation" are usually understood to be opposites[973]. As the Supreme Court[974] has stated, the "essence" of arbitration includes "its speed and simplicity and inexpensiveness" being all characteristics that differentiate arbitration from litigation. Taking into account that the FAA must preserve these "virtues," the Court recently proclaimed, for the reason that if not "arbitration would wind up looking like the litigation it was meant to displace." Therefore, the Court distinguishes that party autonomy eventually governs arbitration clauses and "parties remain free to alter arbitration procedures to suit their tastes".

It could be said that arbitration, in national and international level, has to become a system that independently accounts for the source of the juridicity of national and international arbitration a system having its own sources advancing a sound and consistent body of principles, independent of any specific national system, which exists or would find mutual acceptance among all those involved with arbitration across the world. Moreover, there is an international and a national arbitral order owing to the effect given to arbitration by the actors involved and by states. It has to be taken into account that Party autonomy and consent definitely have both a recognized value and recognized outcomes – but these do not amount to, and can exist quite independently of, the law which means that law allows the party autonomy and the employment of arbitration is legalized by law and so arbitration complies with the rule of law. On the other hand, the award's dependence upon recognition by at least one national legal system shows the

[971] W. Michael Reisman & Heide Iravani, *The Changing Relation of National Courts and International Commercial Arbitration*, 21 *Am. Rev. Int'l Arb.* 5, 16 (2010) ("But arbitration is not an autonomous system . . . its functioning is inextricably linked to national courts.").

[972] William W. Park, *Arbitration Of International Business Disputes: Studies In Law And Practice* 181 (2d ed. 2012) ("[S]ome measure of judicial scrutiny over arbitral jurisdiction remains a vital safeguard to the integrity of the process, and constitutes an essential corollary to enforcement of legitimate awards.").

[973] Michael A. Helfand, Arbitration's Counter-Narrative: The Religious Arbitration Paradigm, 124 *Yale L.J.* 2994 (2015); Imre S. Szalai, Reconciling Fault Lines in Arbitration and Redefining Arbitration Through the Broader Lines of Procedure, 18 *Nev. L.J.* 511 (2018);

[974] *Epic Systems v. Lewis*, 138 S. Ct. 1612 (2018)

dependence of arbitration. It is characteristic that when the Brussels Regulation was recently recast[975], France and the United Kingdom joined to resist any further incursion of EU law into the world of arbitration.

Concerning e-ADR and e-arbitration, in the Netherlands, ADR is to a large extent self-regulated and arbitration is used as a mechanism to enforce claims against consumers as well[976] and to that extent, the establishment of 'e-Court' a private foundation is launched. Thus, it is worth mentioning here that the adoption of blockchain technology in the field of arbitration would have a flowing force, making simpler the arbitral process and dropping the burden on arbitration[977].

It is worth mentioning that in international arbitration, there is the "applicable substantive law," which may or may not have been designated by the parties. On the other hand, national legal systems often have a specific provision or commonly accepted rules requiring State-appointed judges to render judgments according to the applicable substantive law, whether the parties have provided evidence on the content of such law or not[978], but very few national legal systems have a specific provision setting forth an equivalent obligation upon arbitrators. Swiss Courts apply the provisions of the Code of Civil Procedure referring to the powers of judges also to arbitrators[979]. To that extent it does not mean that arbitrators do not apply the same rules like judges for the same type of disputes in order the award not to be reviewed. It has to be taken into account that while US courts generally take a pro-arbitration approach, parties still can and do make court applications in an effort to delay arbitral proceedings. Moreover, the application of mandatory rules in arbitration is "inspired by considerations related to the efficiency of the arbitral process to ensure a valid and enforceable award" which does not mean that the *iura novit curia* principle does not apply in arbitration because arbitration deals more with disputes on practical commercial matters. Arbitrators must behave like judges in their concern for the public interest.

---

[975] Council Regulation (EU) No 1215/2012.

[976] http://ec.europa.eu/newsroom/just/document.cfm?action=display&doc_id=49503 Pablo Cortés, *The Impact of EU Law in the ADR Landscape in Italy, Spain and the UK: Time for Change or Missed Opportunity?* (2015) 16 ERA Forum 125, 133ff.

[977] Hegadekatti, Kartik (2017) *Legal Systems and Blockchain Interactions. Working paper.* Available at SSRN: https://ssrn.com/abstract=2893128.

[978] In Italy, Article 113 of the Italian code of civil procedure ("c.p.c."); in Switzerland, Article 57 of the Swiss code of civil procedure ("ZPO"): "The court applies the law of its own motion," confirmed in the judgment of BGE 139 III 126; in Germany, *iura novit curia* is perceived as the unwritten principle of German civil procedure.

[979] G. Kaufmann-Kohler and A. Rigozzi, *International Arbitration: Law and Practice in Switzerland,* Oxford University Press, 2015, at. para. 7.87; Article 1044 of the Dutch Code of Civil Procedure, Section 27(2) of the Danish Arbitration Act and Article 34(1)(2)(g) of the English Arbitration Act 1996.

REFERENCES

Anderson, Scott, et al., *Using Arbitration Under Article 25 of the DSU to Ensure the Availability of Appeal*s (Graduate Institute Geneva, Working Paper No. CTEI-2017-17, 2017).

Andrias, Kate, The New Labor Law, 126 *Yale L.J.* 2, 13-46 (2016).

Barber, Sotirios A., *The Constitution of Judicial Power* 50 (1993).

Bermann, George, & Alan Scott Rau, Gateway-Schmateway: An Exchange between George Bermann and Alan Rau, 43 *Pepp. L. Rev*. 469, 475 (2016).

Brunet, Edward, Arbitration and Constitutional Rights, 71 *N.C.L. Rev.* 81, 102 (1992).

Burger, Warren E., Isn't There A Better Way? 68 *A.B.A. J.* 274, 275 (1982).

Burger, Warren E., The State of Justice, 70 *A.B.A. J.* 62, 66 (1984).

Burton, Steven J., The New Judicial Hostility to Arbitration: Federal Preemption, Contract Unconscionability, and Agreements to Arbitrate, 2006 *J. Disp. Resol.* 469.

Carbonneau, T., Arbitral Justice: The Demise of Due Process in American law, 70 *Tulane L Rev.* 1945 (1996).

Chew, Pat K., Arbitral and Judicial Proceedings: Indistinguishable Justice or Justice Denied? 46 *Wake Forest L. Rev.* 185, 200 (2011).

Cohen, Julius Henry, and Kenneth Dayton, The New Federal Arbitration Law, 12 *Va. L. Rev.* 265, 281 (1926).

Cohen, Julius Henry, *Commercial Arbitration and the Law*, 25 (1918).

Cole, Sarah Rudolph, Arbitration and State Action, 2005 *BYU L. Rev.* 1.

Colvin, Alexander J. S., An Empirical Study of Employment Arbitration: Case Outcomes and Processes, 8 *J. Empirical Legal Stud.* 1, 2 (2011).

Daniel, Angualia, *The Role of Domestic Courts in International Commercial Arbitration* September 2010 http://ssrn.com/abstract=1674760.

Dezalay, Y., and B.G. Garth, 'The role of lawyers in South and East Asia' in C. Antons (ed.), *Routledge Handbook of Asian Law* (London: Routledge, 2017).

di Brozolo, Luca G. *Radicati, Res Judicata and International Arbitral Awards*, ASA Special Series 2011.

di Brozolo, Luca G. Radicati, The Relation between Courts and Arbitration: Support or Hostility, *Op. J.*, Vol. 1/2012, Paper n. 7, pp. 1 - 12, http://lider-lab.sssup.it/opinio.

Drahozal, Christopher R., New Experiences of International Arbitration in the United States, 54 *Am. J. Comp. L.* 233, 251–53 (2006).

Drahozal, Christopher R., Why Arbitrate? Substantive Versus Procedural Theories of Private Judging, 22 *Am. Rev. Int'l Arb.* 163, 165 (2011).

Edwards, Harry T., Alternative Dispute Resolution: Panacea or Anathema? 99 *Harv. L. Rev.* 668, 669 (1986).

Endicott, Timothy A. O., Arbitrariness, 27 *Can. J. L. & Jurisprudence* 49 (2014).

Fallon, Jr., Richard H., "The Rule of Law" as a Concept in Constitutional Discourse, 97 *Colum. L. Rev.* 1 (1997).

Feinman, Jay M., Un-Making Law: The Classical Revival in the Common Law, 28 *Seattle Univ. L. R.* 1 (2004).

Feyissa, Hailegabriel G., The Role of Ethiopian Courts in Commercial Arbitration, *Mizan Law Review* Vol. 4 No.2, Autumn 2010, 298.

Fiss, Owen, Against Settlement, 93 *Yale L. J.* 1073 (1985).

Fiss, Owen, Law Is Everywhere, 117 *Yale L. J.* 256, 259 (2007).

Friedman, Lawrence M., *A History of American Law* 45 (2d ed. 1985).

Friedman, Stephen, Arbitration Provisions: Little Darlings and Little Monsters, 79 *Fordham L. Rev.* 2035, 2067 (2011).

Fuller, Lon, The Forms and Limits of Adjudication, 92 *Harv. L. Rev.* 353, 357 (1978).

Galanter, Marc, Case Congregations and Their Careers, 24 *Law & Soc'y Rev.* 371, 371 (1990).

Galanter, Marc, In The Hundred Year Decline of Trials and the Thirty Years War, 57 *Stan. L. Rev.* 1255, 1264, 1270 (2005).

Gerbay, Rémy, *The Functions of Arbitral Institutions* 45 (2016).

Glover, J. Maria, Disappearing Claims and the Erosion of Substantive Law, 124 *Yale L.J.* 3052, 3066 (2015).

Gross, Jill I., Justice Scalia's Hat Trick and the Supreme Court's Flawed Understanding of Twenty-First Century Arbitration, 81 *Brooklyn L. Rev.* 160, 2015.

Guthrie, Chris, Misjudging, 7 *Nev. L.J.* 420 (2007).

Hart, H. L. A., *The Concept of Law* 97-107 (1972).

Holdsworth, William, *xiv A History of English law* 187 (A.L. Goodhart and H.G. Hanbury eds. 1964).

Horton, David, Federal Arbitration Act Preemption, Purposivism, and State Public Policy, 101 *Geo. L. J.* 1217, 1223 (2013).

Horwitz, Henry, and James Oldham, John Locke, Lord Mansfield and Arbitration during the Eighteenth Century, 36 *The Historical J.* 137, 138 (1993).

Hurwitz, Andrew D., When Judges Err: Is Confession Good For The Soul? 56 *Ariz. L. Rev.* 343, 344 (2014).

Isaacs, Nathan, Two Views of Commercial Arbitration, 40 *Harv. L. Rev.* 929, 930-37 (1927).

Jones, William Catron, Three Centuries of Commercial Arbitration in New York: A Brief Survey, 1956 *Wash. U. L.Q.* 193, 207 (1930).

Karton, Joshua, The Arbitral Role in Contractual Interpretation, 6 *J. Int'l Disp. Settlement* 4, 30-31 (2015).

Karton, Joshua, *The Culture of International Arbitration and the Evolution of Contract Law* 95-96 (2013).

Kim, Anne S., Rent-A-Judge and the Cost of Selling Justice, 44 *Duke L. J.* 166 (1994).

King, D. Brian, & Rahim Moloo, International Arbitrators as Lawmakers, 46 *NYU J. Int'l L. & Politics* 875, 877 (2014).

Klonoff, Robert H., *The Decline of Class Actions*, Lewis and Clark Law School Legal Research Paper Series Paper No. 2012-6.

Lande, John, Judging Judges and Dispute Resolution Processes, 2007 *Nevada Law Journal* 457.

Lempert, Richard, More Tales of Two Courts: Exploring Changes in the "Dispute Settlement Function" of Trial Courts, 13 *L. & Soc'y Rev.* 91, 99-100 (1978).

Liyanage, C., "Online Arbitration Compares to Offline Arbitration and the Reception of Online Consumer Arbitration: An Overview of the Literature" (2010) 22 *Sri Lanka Journal of International Law* 175.

Lorang, Karen A., Mitigating Arbitration's Externalities: A Call for Tailored Judicial Review 59 *UCLA L. Rev.* 218 (2011).

MacCormick, Neil, *Institutions of Law: An Essay in Legal Theory* (Oxford: Oxford University Press, 2007) 255-61.

Mann, Bruce H., The Formalization of Informal Law: Arbitration before the American Revolution, 59 *N.Y.U. L. Rev.* 443, 468-81 (1984).

Monaghan, Henry P., Stare Decisis and Constitutional Adjudication, 88 Colum. *L. Rev.* 723, 748 (1988).

Moses, Margaret L., *Principles and Practice of International Commercial Arbitration*, Cambridge University Press, 2008.

Murray, John E., Jr., The Judicial Vision of Contract: The Constructed Circle of Assent and Unconscionability, 52 *Duq. L. Rev.* 263, 265 (2014).

Oppetit, Bruno, Philosophie de l'arbitrage commercial international, *J. De Droit Int'l* 819 (1993).

Paulsson, Jan, Why Good Arbitration Cannot Compensate for Bad Courts, 30 *J. Int'l Arb.* 345 (2013).

Pauwelyn, Joost, The Limits of Litigation: "Americanization" and Negotiation in the Settlement of WTO Disputes, 19 *Ohio St. J. on Disp. Resol.* 121 (2003).

Payosova, T., G. Clyde Hufbauer and J. Schott, *The Dispute Settlement Crisis in the World Trade Organization: Causes and Cures* (Peterson Institute for International Economics, Policy Brief No. 18-5, 2018).

Poor, Wharton, Arbitration under the Federal Statute, 36 *Yale L.J.* 667, 676-78 (1927).

Puig, Sergio, Social Capital in the Arbitration Market, 25 *Eur. J. Int'l L.* 387 (2014).

Radicati di Brozolo, L. G., *Party Autonomy and the Rules Applicable to the Merits in International Arbitration, in Limits To Party Autonomy In International Commercial Arbitration* (F. Ferrari ed., 2016), 331-362.

Radin, Margaret Jane, *Boilerplate: The Fine Print, Vanishing Rights, and the Rule of Law* 16–17 (2013).

Resnik, Judith, Diffusing Disputes: The Public in the Private of Arbitration, the Private in Courts, and the Erasure of Rights, 2015 *Yale Law Journal* 124:2804.

Reuben, Richard C., Democracy And Dispute Resolution: The Problem Of Arbitration, Winter/Spring 2004 *Law And Contemporary Problems* Vol. 67:279.

Reuben, Richard C., Public justice: toward a state action theory of alternative dispute resolution, 85 *Cal. L. Rev.* 577.

Roebuck, Derek, *Ancient Greek Arbitration* (2001).

Rogers, Catherine A., Transparency in International Commercial Arbitration, 54 *Kan. L. Rev.* 1301, 1314–17, 1319–20 (2006).

Rudolph, Sarah E., Blackstone's Vision of Alternative Dispute Resolution, 22 *Memphis State L. Rev.* 279 (1992).

Rutledge, Peter B., Arbitration and constitution *Advocate 2011* www.law.uga.edu.

Schultz, Thomas, *Transnational Legality: Stateless Law and International Arbitration* 122 (2014).

Shilston, L., The evolution of Modern Commercial Arbitration, 1987 *J Int'l Arb* 45.

Stipanowich, Thomas J., The Third Arbitration Trilogy: Stolt-Nielsen, Rent-A-Center, Concepcion and the Future of American Arbitration, 22 AM. *Rev. Int'l Arb*. 323, 422 (2011).

Stipanowich, Thomas, Of "Procedural Arbitrability": The Effect of Noncompliance with Contract Claims Procedures, 40 *S.C. L. Rev.* 847, 861–64 (1989).

Stone, Katherine V. W., *Private Justice, The Law of Alternative Dispute Resolution* 305 (Foundation Press) (2003).

Szalai, Imre Stephen, Exploring the Federal Arbitration Act through the Lens of History, 2016 *J. Disp. Resol.* 115, 118 (2016).

Szalai, Imre Stephen, More than Class Action Killers: the Impact of Concepcion and American Express on Employment Arbitration, 35 *Berkeley J. Emp. & Lab. L.* (2015).

Szalai, Imre Stephen, *Outsourcing Justice: The Rise of Modern Arbitration Laws in America* (2013).

Troum, Neal, Drawing a Line after AT&T Mobility: How Far Does The FAA Reach into State Contract Regulation? 29 *Alternatives* 129, 133 (July-Aug. 2011).

Vetter, Greg R., "Infectious" Open Source Software: Spreading Incentives or Promoting Resistance? 36 *Rutgers L.J.* 53, 80 (2004).

Viscasillas, Pilar Perales, The Role of Arbitral Institutions under the 2010 UNCITRAL Arbitration Rules, 6 *Lima Arb*. 26, 31 (2014).

Ware, Stephen J., The Politics of Arbitration Law and Centrist Proposals for Reform, 53 *Harv. J. On Legis.* 711, 734 (2016).

Weidemaier, W. Mark C., Judging-Lite: How Arbitrators Use and Create Precedent, 90 *N.C. L. Rev.* 1091, 1092 (2012).

Young, Ernest A., Supranational Rulings as Judgments and Precedents, 18 *Duke J. Comp. & Int'l L.* 477, 491-96 (2008).

Zekos, G., Cyberspace and IPRs Stimulus on Foreign Direct Investment in the European Union, 2016 *Journal of Internet Law*, Volume 20 Number 6, December 2016 3-29 Wolters Kluwer. www.wrightsmedia.com.

Zekos, G., *Constitution, Arbitration and Courts* www.novapublishers.com.

Zekos, G., Internet or Electronic Technology: A Threat to State Sovereignty 1999 *JILT,* http://www.law.warwick.ac.uk/jilt/99-3/zekos.html.

Zekos, G., *Συμβάσεις Μεταφοράς, Ευθύνη των Μεταφορέων & Διαδίκτυο-* [*Contracts of Transportation, Carrier's Liability and Cyberspace*] 2017 Εκδόσεις Π. Σάκκουλα https://www.sakkoulas-online.gr/profiles/georgios-i-zekos/.

Zekos, G., *An investigation of WTO Arbitration Mechanism, ICDR Handbook on Arbitration & ADR*, 3rd Edition, JurisNet LLC 2017 www.arbitrationlaw.com.

Zekos, G., Arbitrability and Regulation (EU) No 1215/2012, *Dispute Resolution Journal* Vol. 70 No. 4 JurisNet, LLC 2015 www.arbitrationlaw.com.

Zekos, G., *Constitution, Arbitration and Courts*, 2013 Nova Science Publications New York USA. www.novapublishers.com.

Zekos, G., Constitutionality of Commercial/Maritime Arbitration, 2014 *Journal of Maritime Law and Commerce* Vol. 24 Issue N.1 www.jmlc.com.

Zekos, G., Copyrights and Trademarks in Cyberspace: A Legal and Economic Analysis, 15 Chi. -*Kent J. Intell. Prop.* 313 (2016). Available at: http://scholarship.kentlaw.iit.edu/ckjip/vol15/iss1/10.

Zekos, G., Cyber Versus Conventional Personal Jurisdiction, 2015 *Journal of Internet Law,* Volume 18 Number 10, April 2015 3-35 Wolters Kluwer. www.wrightsmedia.com.

Zekos, G., Cyber-Territory and Jurisdiction of Nations, 2012 *Journal of Internet Law,* Number 12/3 Aspen Publications.

Zekos, G., Demolishing State's sole power over Sovereignty & Territory via Electronic Technology & Cyberspace, 2013 *Journal of Internet Law,* Volume 17 Number 5 November 2013 27-41 Aspen Publications.

Zekos, G., *Developments on applicable Law, Jurisdiction and E-Bills of Lading*, 2016 Annuaire de Droit Maritime et Océanique, Centre de Droit Maritime et Océanique, Université de Nantes. p 115, http://www.cdmo.univ-nantes.fr/32672322/0/fiche___pagelibre/&RH=1380012194211&RF=1380012521640.

Zekos, G., Economics and Law on Competition in 21st Century Globalization 2014 Nova Science Publications New York USA. www.novapublishers.com.

Zekos, G., *Economics, Finance and Law on MNEs*, 2007 Nova Publishers, New York www.novapublishers.com.

Zekos, G., EDI: *Electronic techniques of EDI, legal problems and EU law*, 1999, webjcli.ncl. ac.uk/1999/issue2/zekos2.html.

Zekos, G., ePen Technology and Electronic Signatures, 2003 *IP&ITL* Issue 6, pp2-7 www.emispp.com.

Zekos, G., EU Law and IPRs Concerning FDI Inwards and FDI Outwards, *The IUP Journal of Knowledge Management* Vol. XV No 2 2017, 43.

Zekos, G., Expansion of IPRs and FDI, *Current Politics and Economics of Russia, Eastern and Central Europe*, Volume 31 Issue 3-4.

Zekos, G., *International Commercial and Marine Arbitration*, 2008 Routledge-Cavendish Publishers London www.routledge.com.

Zekos, G., *IPRs protection and their impact upon FDI, GDP growth & trade*, 2013 Scholar's Press, www.scholars-press.com www.morebooks.de Germany/PhD Thesis Economics Department, University of Peloponnese.

Zekos, G., Issues of Intellectual Property in Cyberspace, 2002 *Journal of World Intellectual Property* 233.

Zekos, G., *Judicial analysis of the contractual role of bills of lading as it stands in Greek, United States and English law*, PHD Thesis, Law School, University of Hull https://hydra. hull.ac.uk/resources/hull:8290.

Zekos, G., *Law and Economics of Corporate Governance and Insider Trading*, 2016 Nova Science Publications New York USA. www.novapublishers.com.

Zekos, G., *Law and Economics of IPRs*, 2016 Nova Science Publications New York USA. www.novapublishers.com.

Zekos, G., Maritime Arbitration and the Rule of Law, 39 *J. Mar. L. & Com.* 523, 524 (2008).

Zekos, G., *MNE's in 21st Century*, 2016 Nova Science Publications New York USA. www.novapublishers.com.

Zekos, G., *Monetary Policy and Risk Management in Financial Globalization*, 2015 Nova Science Publications New York USA. www.novapublishers.com.

Zekos, G., *Risk Management, Corporate Governance in 21st Century Digital Economy*, 2014 Nova Science Publications New York USA. www.novapublishers.com.

Zekos, G., State Cyberspace Jurisdiction and Personal Cyberspace Jurisdiction, *Int J Law Info Tech* 2007 15: 1-37; doi:10.1093/ijlit/eai029 www.ijlit.oxfordjournals.org.

Zekos, G., The case for giving to private parties access to the WTO dispute settlement system, 2007 *Journal of World Investment & Trade* 441.

Zekos, G., *The Independence of Arbitration*, 2016 Nova Science Publications New York USA. www.novapublishers.com.

Zekos, G., *The Law of Air, Road & Sea Transportation*, 2016 Nova Science Publications New York USA. www.novapublishers.com.

Zekos, G., *The United States of Europe in Place of the European Union*, 2017 Nova Science Publications New York USA. www.novapublishers.com.

Zekos, G., The use of electronic technology in maritime transport, 1998 *Web Journal of current legal issues,* http:// webjcli.ncl.ac.uk/1998/issue3/zekos3.html.

Zekos, G., *Διαδίκτυο, H/Y & Τηλεπικοινωνίες στο Ελληνικό Δίκαιο –[Cyberspace, H/Y and Telecommunications],* 2017 Εκδόσεις Π. Σάκκουλα https://www.sakkoulas-online.gr/profiles/georgios-i-zekos/.

About the Author

Georgios I Zekos, BSc (Econ) Aristotle University, JD Democritus University, LLM University of Hull, PhD (Law) University of Hull, PhD (Econ) University of Peloponnese. Attorney at Law 1989-2008, ΟΓΑ Tripoli 2008-2012, Asylum Office of Thessaloniki 2012- 2016, TEI of Central Macedonia 2016- presently,Serres- Hellas.

Email zekosg@teicm.gr, zekosg@uop.gr, zekosg@yahoo.com

INDEX

A

B

C

D

E

F

G

H

I

T

U

V

W

Constitution, Arbitration and Courts

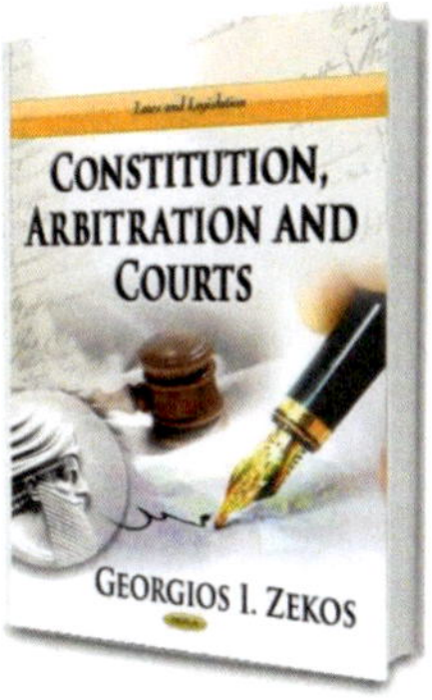

Author: Georgios I. Zekos

Series: Laws and Legislation

Book Description: In "Constitution, Arbitration and Courts", arbitration is examined as it began, as an extrajudicial mechanism for resolving disputes. Private arbitration predates the public court system.

Hardcover ISBN: 978-1-62417-941-9
Retail Price: $320

The Independence of Arbitration

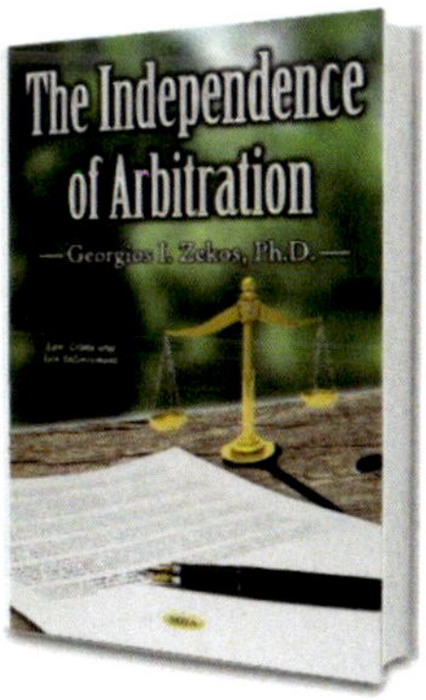

Author: Georgios I. Zekos, PhD

Series: Law, Crime and Law Enforcement

Book Description: Arbitration is the process by which a difference among parties as to their mutual legal rights is referred and determined with a binding effect by the application of law through an arbitral tribunal instead of a court.

Hardcover ISBN: 978-1-53610-170-6
Retail Price: $230